RACE TO INJUSTICE

RACE TO INJUSTICE

LESSONS LEARNED FROM THE DUKE LACROSSE RAPE CASE

Edited by
Michael L. Seigel

CAROLINA ACADEMIC PRESS
Durham, North Carolina

Library of Congress Cataloging-in-Publication Data

Race to injustice : lessons learned from the Duke lacrosse rape case / Michael L. Seigel.
    p. cm.
  Includes bibliographical references and index.
  ISBN 978-1-59460-514-7 (alk. paper)
  1. Malicious prosecution--North Carolina--Durham--History. 2. Criminal investigation--North Carolina--Durham--History. 3. Rape--North Carolina--Durham--History. 4. Nifong, Michael Byron. 5. Criminal investigation--North Carolina--Durham. 6. Discrimination in criminal justice administration--United States. 7. Campus violence--United States. 8. College students--United States--Alcohol use. I. Seigel, Michael L. II. Title.

  KFN7977.R33 2008
  364.15'32092--dc22

                                2008043688

CAROLINA ACADEMIC PRESS
700 Kent Street
Durham, North Carolina 27701
Telephone (919) 489-7486
Fax (919) 493-5668
www.cap-press.com

Printed in the United States of America

Contents

Preface   xiii

Acknowledgments   xix

Part One
Introduction

Chapter One · The Facts and Only the Facts
      Robert J. Luck & Michael L. Seigel   3

Durham and Duke Before the Storm   3

March 13, 2006, and the Morning After   4

The Investigation and Indictment   9

The Prosecutor and the Press   13

The Response of Duke's Administration and Faculty   17

About the Truth   22

Epilogue   26

Part Two
Lessons Learned about College Campuses

Chapter Two · Faculty Reactions, Contentious Debate, and
      Academic Freedom
      Robert M. O'Neil   31

Duke in Context: A Singular Institution   31

Early Faculty Reactions—and Responses   35

Possible Academic-Freedom Issues   38

The Administration Responds—Overreaction?   41

Dissonant (and Uncollegial) Voices within Duke's Faculty   44

Grading: How Strong a Faculty Prerogative?   46

Is There a Faculty-Student Privilege?   48

An Embattled Faculty: Did They Deserve Better?   50

Lessons Learned—and Shared   53

Chapter Three · The Town-Gown Relationship
        Sharon Rush   55
    Town-Gown Relations   57
        Generally: The Role of Social Dignity   57
        Durham and Duke: The Role of Class and Race   58
        Class, Race, and Assumptions about "Intelligence"   61
        Inherent Dignity   62
    The Role of Dignity   63
        Prior to That Evening   63
            The Players   63
            Crystal Mangum   66
        That Evening   68
        What's Race Got to Do with It?   69
        After That Evening: Enter Mike Nifong   72
    Summary   77

Chapter Four · Alcohol Consumption on College Campuses
        George W. Dowdall   79
    The Lacrosse Rape Case   79
    Alcohol and Duke Lacrosse   81
    The Duke Alcohol Scene   84
    National Patterns of College Drinking   88
    Health and Behavioral Consequences of College Drinking   91
    Intoxicated Rape   94
    The Culture of College Drinking   96
    Lessons Learned from the Lacrosse Rape Case   99

Chapter Five · Invisible Criminality: Male Peer-Support Groups,
              Alcohol, and the Risk of Aggressive Sexual Behavior
        Michelle S. Jacobs   103
    Introduction   103
    Athletes, Fraternities, and Sexual Assault   104
        Masculinities and Male Peer Support   104
        Support of the Rape-Myth Risk Factor   107
        The Role of Alcohol as a Risk Factor   109
    Exotic Dancers and the Danger of Violence in the Workplace 114
    False Rape Reports   119
    Conclusion   123

Part Three
Lessons Learned about Race

Chapter Six · Black Venus Hottentot Revisited: Gratuitous Use
of Women of Color's Bodies and the Role of Race
and Gender in Campus and Academic Reactions
Michèle Alexandre   127
Introduction   127
Perception of Women of Color's Bodies, Both Historically and
in the Era of *Flavor of Love* and *I Love New York*   130
Sexual Profiling and the Erotic-Labor Force   133
Class-, Race-, and Gender-Based Dynamics in Events and
Narratives Relating to the Rape Allegations   137
The Accountability and Ethical Responsibilities of University
Administrators   142
Possible Equitable or Contractual Claims for Added Protections
for Erotic Workers   146
Conclusion   151

Chapter Seven · Racial Politics and Discretion in Criminal Law
Janine Young Kim   155
Case Background   155
Historical and Legal Context   159
Some Lessons from the Case   166

Part Four
Lessons Learned about the Criminal-Justice System

Chapter Eight · The Duke Lacrosse Players and the Media: Why the Fair
Trial-Free Press Paradigm Doesn't Cut It Anymore
Andrew E. Taslitz   175
Introduction   175
Part II: Undervaluing Reputational Injury   178
Part III: Media Coverage in High-Profile Cases   182
Is Media Coverage Antidefendant?   182
Press Dependency on Law Enforcement   183
Cultivating Deviancy   185
The Impact of Media Coverage   186
The Pessimistic View   186
The Optimistic View   189
Implications for the Duke Rape Case   191

Part IV: Pretrial Publicity and Reputational Harms
    in the Duke Rape Case   191
    The Antidefendant Content of the Press Coverage   191
    Tainting the Team: The Publicity's Negative Effects   193
Part V: Fair Trial-Free Press   197
    The Tension   197
    The Elected Nature of Most Prosecutors:
        A First Amendment Wrinkle?   204
Conclusion   209

Chapter Nine · When Prosecutorial Discretion Meets
                Disaster Capitalism
                Lenese Herbert   211
Prosecutorial Discretion   213
Disaster Capitalism   216
When Discretion Meets Disaster   220
    Crisis   221
    Shock   224
    Disaster Capitalism   226
Shockproof?   227
    The Central Park Jogger Case: Mission Accomplished   227
    The Duke Lacrosse Case: Disaster Capitalism, Demurred?   232
Conclusion   235

Chapter Ten · The Duke Defendants Reaped the Benefits of a Zealous
             Defense—But Do Only the Rich Get Real Lawyers?
             Rodney Uphoff   237
Introduction   237
The Defense Lawyers: The Early Stages   241
Trying to Stop a Train Wreck   244
The Players Are Indicted and the Defense Does Not Rest   247
The Pivotal Role of Defense Experts and Investigators   253
The Struggle for Justice for Those without Money   255
Conclusion   260

Chapter Eleven · An Examination of the District Attorney's
                Alleged Unethical Conduct
                Kenneth Williams   261
Introduction   261

The Ethical and Legal Obligations of Prosecutors 262
The Unethical and Illegal Conduct of Mike Nifong 264
  Clear Violations 265
    Failure to Disclose 265
    False Statements to the Court 266
    Prejudicing the Proceeding and Disparaging the Accused 267
  Possible Violations 270
    Pursuing Charges Not Supported by Probable Cause 270
    Intimidating Players Who Remained Silent 271
    Pursuing Cases for Political Gain 272
    Employing an Unconstitutional Lineup 273
  No Violations 274
    Failure to Speak to the Accuser 274
    Failure to Present Exculpatory Evidence to the Grand Jury 274
Prosecutorial Misconduct in the United States 275
Why Prosecutorial Misconduct Occurs and
  What Can Be Done about It 279
Conclusion 281

Chapter Twelve · The Moment of Truth: The Decision
               to Institute Charges in a Rape Case
               Michael L. Seigel 283
Introduction 283
North Carolina Grand Jury Procedure 286
Does It Really Matter? 290
Basic Grand Jury Procedures 291
Select Grand Jury Reforms 293
  Permitting Counsel in the Grand Jury Room 294
  Requiring Prosecutors to Present Exculpatory Evidence 294
  Prohibiting Prosecutors from Knowingly Presenting
    Constitutionally Inadmissible Evidence 295
  Providing Targets or Subjects with an Opportunity to Be Heard 295
  Prohibiting Hearsay in the Grand Jury 296
  Requiring Prosecutors to Instruct the Jurors on the Law 296
Application of These Reforms to the Duke Case 297
The Preliminary Hearing as an Alternative? 299
Whither the Balance? 301
Is the Duke Case Special? 302
Proposal 303

Part Five
Lessons Learned about Criminal Evidence

Chapter Thirteen · The Duke Lacrosse Rape Investigation: How Not
                   to Do Eyewitness-Identification Procedures
                   Gary L. Wells, Brian L. Cutler, & Lisa E. Hasel   307
  Introduction   307
  The Logic and Science of Eyewitness Identification   309
  Primary Features of Good Eyewitness-Identification Procedures   313
  The Duke Lacrosse Rape Investigation   314
  Analysis of the Identification Procedures in the Duke Case   318
  Final Remarks   319

Chapter Fourteen · DNA Profiling
                   Paul C. Giannelli   323
  Introduction   323
  DNA Exonerations   325
  DNA Databases   326
    Problems   327
  DNA Profiling   328
    Short Tandem Repeats (STR) Testing   329
    Y-Chromosome (Y-STR) Testing   331
  The Duke Lacrosse Case   331
    Gathering the Forensic Evidence   331
    The DNA Analysis   332
    The DSI Laboratory Report   334
    More Discovery Requests   336
    The Underlying Data   336
    The December 15 Hearing   338
    The Aftermath   340
    An Explanation?   341
  Lessons Learned   342
    Pretrial Disclosure   342
    Defense Experts   344
    Nontestimonial Identification Orders   344
  Conclusion   346

Chapter Fifteen · Presuming Guilt or Protecting Victims?: Analyzing
                       the Special Treatment of Those Accused of Rape
                       Aviva Orenstein   351
   Introduction   351
   Competing Narratives   353
       Frat Boys Gone Wild   354
       The Lying Ho   354
   Special Accommodations for Victims in Rape Trials, Special Burdens
       for the Accused   357
       Naming Names   357
       Rape Shield   359
       Character Evidence about the Accused   362
       Hearsay Issues   365
       Rape Trauma Syndrome and Expert Testimony   368
   Postconviction Experiences in Prison and Beyond   370
       Rape in Prison   370
       Postconviction Limits on Liberty   372
   Concluding Observations   374

Authors' Biographies   379

Index   387

Preface

The American criminal-justice system, though undoubtedly one of the best in the history of the world, is far from perfect. We all know this—yet most of the time we pay little or no attention to its obvious flaws. Every once in a while, however, a notorious case comes along and shatters our self-protective complacency by revealing the uglier side of the system—for instance, its differential treatment of whites and people of color. Cases of this kind often garner huge amounts of national media attention and capture the sustained interest of a normally restless American public. Whatever their outcome, these cases provide academics with exceptional opportunities to study, learn, and teach about the system. They also offer the chance to study related matters, such as the conduct of particular law-enforcement and other officials, as well as the underlying causes of the crime and the public's reaction to it.

The Duke lacrosse players' rape prosecution is one such case. The basic facts are well known. One evening in March 2006, members of the lacrosse team held an off-campus party during which alcohol was served and two exotic dancers performed. A disagreement broke out between the dancers and the players and, later, one of the former, Crystal Mangum, alleged that three players had raped her. Mangum was black and relatively poor; she was attending North Carolina Central University and was stripping to help pay her bills. The defendants were white Duke students from comparatively privileged backgrounds. Up for re-election in a jurisdiction with many African American voters, District Attorney Mike Nifong pursued the case very aggressively. He used questionable identification procedures and was very vocal in numerous local and national media appearances. Even after DNA evidence indicated that the defendants had not engaged in sexual activity with the victim, he declined to drop the charges.

The case split the Duke campus into sharply divided factions. Eighty-eight faculty members signed a petition that focused on the campus' history of racial problems and, to many readers, obliquely criticized the boys. Later, other professors made public statements welcoming the lacrosse players into their classes.

Desperately trying to preserve its hard-won reputation as an upper-echelon school, the university quickly cancelled the lacrosse season, suspended the three indicted players, and commenced a series of internal investigations.

After nine months of dramatic revelations and much discussion in the press and elsewhere, Nifong dismissed the rape allegations because Mangum belatedly claimed that she could not be sure that she had been penetrated. Despite this equivocation, Nifong refused to drop the pending sexual-assault and kidnapping charges. Soon after, however, the North Carolina Bar Association charged Nifong with violating several ethics provisions based on his handling of the prosecution. This was the first time that the Bar had ever filed ethical charges prior to the disposal of the underlying case. Within days of being charged, Nifong passed the case along to the North Carolina Attorney General who, after reviewing the proof, dismissed all remaining charges against the lacrosse players and publicly declared their innocence. After a thirteen-month ordeal, the case was finally over. Eventually, the disgraced Nifong was disbarred.

As this brief rendition of the facts makes clear, the Duke lacrosse rape case presents the opportunity to consider a wide range of issues, including alcohol consumption on college campuses; the impact of race, gender, and class on the criminal-justice system and perceptions thereof; the use of DNA evidence and eyewitness-identification procedures in criminal cases; prosecutorial ethics; and even academic freedom. This book aims to capitalize on this unique academic opportunity.

Chapter One, by Robert J. Luck and Michael L. Seigel, sets the stage by telling the story of the Duke rape case in an essentially chronological fashion. Its goal is to set out the facts gleaned from other sources in a succinct and accurate manner. It strives for as neutral a presentation as possible, leaving it to the authors of other chapters to draw inferences from, and argue positions based on, the raw facts.

Robert M. O'Neil, in Chapter Two, takes up the issue of academic freedom. Although university professors are predictably contentious on many issues, the intensity and occasional acerbity of debate within the Duke faculty following the rape charges were exceptional if not unprecedented. That debate opened, or reopened, many wounds close to the core of faculty concerns, including the treatment of student-athletes and even the proper role of intercollegiate sports in a university of the highest academic standing. It eventually exposed the inherent tension between basic values that a faculty must reconcile, however uncomfortably, at an institution like Duke. A faculty's capacity to address that tension, and the consequences for academic freedom as well as academic values, has never been so severely tested as at Duke during 2006 and 2007.

In Chapter Three, Sharon Rush explores the peculiar dynamics that often exist between residents of a college town and its university's students. She demonstrates that, although class and race generally characterize the divide between these two groups, the tension goes much deeper and touches on many human emotions. For example, some people associate having a lot of money with being intelligent (and lacking money with being "not so smart"), which can be quite upsetting to the permanent residents who have no way of defending themselves against accusations that they are "inferior." Some university students believe that they are the "real mission" of the town and that the residents, who often work at the university, are only there to serve them. To them, the townspeople have no independent identity or worth. As Rush reveals, the incident at Duke offers a perfect illustration of the tensions inherent in the town-gown paradigm: the prosecution premised its entire investigation on underlying and often unstated assumptions about credibility and "worth" that derive from it. Rhetorically, how could an "uneducated" (that is, non-Duke) resident of Durham hope to successfully impugn the integrity of a Duke student? Was Mangum's accusation doomed from the start—regardless of the "truth?" Did the outcome actually exacerbate the tensions inherent in the town-gown paradigm? Rush answers these questions, and more.

The fourth chapter, by George W. Dowdall, examines the role alcohol abuse plays in the darker side of college life. Internal Duke investigations after Crystal Mangum's rape allegations indicated that members of the school's lacrosse team had a history of committing minor infractions on and off campus. Many of these were direct violations of alcohol regulations and ordinances, such as underage drinking and drinking in dorm rooms. Others were alcohol-related, including noise violations, property damage, and physical altercations. In addition, the literature is rife with of studies linking more serious crimes, such as sexual assault and rape, to alcohol abuse. This chapter makes clear that, despite the innocence of the defendants on the rape charges, there is still much taking place on college campuses that ought to concern administrators, faculty, and parents alike.

In Chapter Five, Michelle S. Jacobs tackles the link between sports, violence, and male privilege on college campuses. She argues that the Duke case is one of an increasing number in which athletes or members of campus fraternities have become involved in off-campus incidents allegedly involving sexual misconduct. Despite two decades of legal reforms, the problem of rape and other unwanted sexual conduct continues to plague college environments. Jacobs explores this complex topic.

In Chapter Six, Michèle Alexandre analyzes the race and gender implications of the Duke and Durham communities' reactions to the rape allegations. In particular, Alexandre explores issues involving the historical and ongoing objectification and subjugation of black women in Western society. She also examines existing legal protections for women working in the sex industry and makes proposals for reform.

Janine Young Kim takes the opportunity in Chapter Seven to analyze the Duke rape prosecution as a case study in racial politics, which shape both the substance and enforcement of criminal law in America. She explores the varied racial dimensions of the case within the context of Duke and Durham as well as the history of white-on-black rape in the South. This chapter links the Duke case to more general themes of race and the law, including problems of over- and underenforcement and the role of criminal law in effecting racial (in)justice.

In Chapter Eight, Andrew Taslitz considers the impact that high-profile media coverage, such as that given to the Duke rape case, has on the possibility of providing criminal defendants a fair trial. His major focus is on the tension between the First Amendment right of the press to report the news and the fair-trial rights of defendants. The Duke case, however, raised an unusual, although by no means unique, twist: later coverage was more harmful to the state than to the defendants, thus raising the risk that the prosecution would have been unfairly handicapped had the case gone to trial. This risk arguably involved tainting the victim's credibility in the public's mind before trial ever began. The chapter thus fuses social-science research on the impact of media attention on jury pools and sitting jurors with case law on the tension between free speech and trial fairness. The combination yields broader lessons about the state of the law in this area and the best way, as a policy matter, to balance the interests of all concerned.

Lenese Herbert, in Chapter Nine, identifies the Duke case as a moment when prosecutorial discretion met "disaster capitalism." The latter is an economic theory explaining how capitalists take advantage of catastrophic events, which leave large portions of the public in shock, to impose their private will upon consumers; Herbert applies the concept to political actors and motivations. She first details the vast power that the American legal system grants prosecutors by giving them sole discretion to decide whether to charge a case and, if so, which charges to bring. She then discusses disaster capitalism. Herbert makes the case that, by bringing Durham's latent racial tension to the surface, Mangum's rape allegations against the Duke lacrosse players amounted to a public disaster with potential catastrophic results. Nifong attempted to capitalize on this disaster by publicly playing the "race card" to win re-election. He failed, but the consequences were still very harmful. Worse, opportunities for other disaster capitalists to wreak havoc will undoubtedly arise in the future.

Rodney Uphoff focuses in the tenth chapter on the sad fact that only a minority of defendants in America could have received the benefit of the zealous representation afforded those in the Duke case. As he sets out, the Duke situation highlighted the enormous difference that competent counsel can make in the outcome of a serious felony case. Sadly, many defendants are doomed to a plea bargain because they are represented by lawyers without the time, ability, or expert assistance needed to mount a successful defense. Ultimately, he concludes, uneven access to counsel in America means unequal justice for many.

Prosecutors are key players in the criminal-justice system. They decide whether to charge a person with a crime and, if there is a prosecution, which charges to bring against the accused; their decisions are effectively unreviewable. Along with this enormous decision-making authority, however, come critical ethical duties. In Chapter Eleven, Kenneth Williams explores the parameters of prosecutors' ethical responsibilities and discusses how, in the Duke case, Mike Nifong egregiously violated them. He further argues, however, that Nifong was not the aberration that many saw him to be. Williams makes the case that prosecutorial misconduct is a systemic problem, and suggests some tentative solutions.

In Chapter Twelve, I take a hard look at a critical but undervalued step in the criminal-justice system: the moment when a grand jury is asked to return a true bill. Although our Founding Fathers intended the grand jury to be a bulwark against unwarranted prosecutorial power, it no longer serves this function in most jurisdictions. In North Carolina, in fact, it operates as an unreviewable indictment mill that actually hampers a defendant's ability to mount a pretrial challenge to the charges against him. I argue that the present grand jury system should be abandoned and replaced by one of two charging methods. For run-of-the-mill cases, the ideal procedure would consists of prosecutor-instituted charges followed by a preliminary hearing; for cases involving reputation-ruining accusations, such as rape and child molestation, a grand jury inquiry with significantly beefed-up protections for the accused would be best.

In Chapter Thirteen, Gary Wells, Brian L. Cutler, and Lisa E. Hasel review the basic principles of proper lineup procedure and demonstrate the many flaws in the lineups conducted by Nifong and the Durham police. Indeed, they demonstrate how the procedures in the Duke case violated almost every important standard of how lineups should be conducted, including the failure to use known-innocent fillers. Their conclusion is that, as conducted, the

Duke lineups offered no real opportunity to assess the credibility of Mangum's identifications.

Chapter Fourteen, authored by Paul Giannelli, examines the DNA evidence in the Duke case. It starts out as a primer on DNA evidence in general, setting out its scientific basis and discussing the powerful effect it had on the criminal-justice system immediately upon its introduction in criminal cases in the late 1980s. Next, Giannelli delineates the DNA evidence gathered in the Duke case and analyzes its significance. He reaches the frightening conclusion that the only thing that may have prevented the wrongful conviction of the Duke defendants was the DNA evidence.

The final chapter, contributed by Aviva Orenstein, explores how American law and society treat those accused of sex crimes differently from other criminal defendants in both favorable and (mostly) unfavorable ways. For example, evidence law provides special shields excluding victims' sexual history but admits character evidence of the accused's prior sexual misconduct. Additionally, in prison, inmates tend to single out sex offenders, particularly pedophiles, for especially harsh treatment, including rape. Even after completing their sentences, sex offenders may face preventive detention if a court deems them dangerous, and must comply with laws limiting their privacy and, sometimes, their mobility. Orenstein establishes, however, that the public's heightened awareness of these issues and its increased concern about false rape accusations has complicated this situation in recent years, particularly when the accused is rich, white, or famous. The backlash against perceived false allegations and the cultural suspicion of alleged rape victims, particularly those who are seen as promiscuous, incautious, inebriated, crazy, or vindictive, make the legal and social status of sex offenders more nuanced and ambiguous than would initially appear.

I expect that the reader will agree with some of the chapters in this volume and disagree—perhaps vehemently—with others. That, at least, is my intention, because that is the nature of the academic enterprise.

Michael L. Seigel
Tampa, Florida
October 29, 2008

Acknowledgments

I would like to thank, first and foremost, the thirteen contributors to this book. Each of these scholars embraced this project from the outset and signed on to it even before it had a publisher. Without their enthusiastic support, and their hard earned reputations as experts in their respective fields, this endeavor never would have been launched. In addition, of course, without their hard work and dedication, the book would not have been completed.

Second, I would like to extend a special thanks to Assistant United States Attorney Robert J. Luck, my co-author on Chapter One and behind-the-scenes assistant in virtually every phase of the book's production. Of the thousands of students I have taught over the years, he ranks as one of the best and brightest, and I know he has a very promising career in front of him.

I would also be remiss if I were to fail to give David Saltzman, Esquire, a special "shout-out." Several years ago, as a member of the Wisconsin Law Review, David edited an article of mine that the review had accepted for publication. His work so improved that piece that I knew he would do the same for this book. Although he was officially a "proof-reader," in characteristic fashion David went above and beyond the call of duty to edit the book in a careful and comprehensive way. It was at times a painful process, but we both learned from it, and the final product benefitted immensely.

Next, I say thank you to the many research assistants who worked with me on this project. First mention goes to Tiffany Cummins, now law clerk to the Honorable Mary Scrivens, United States District Court, Middle District of Florida, who headed up a team of students assigned to the task of bringing me up to speed on the details of the case. The other students in this group were Lisa Blum, Ryan Maxey, and Ryan Nelson. After Tiffany graduated, Elizabeth Manno filled her shoes spectacularly, spending countless hours assisting me in editing drafts, tracking down sources, and checking footnotes for proper citation form.

Finally, I am grateful to Keith Sipe, publisher of Carolina Academic Press, for immediately believing in the value of this project and my ability to get it done. I am also grateful to my wife Sharon and my daughters Nicole and Jessica for giving me the mental space to complete an undertaking of this magnitude, and for their unfailing support.

Michael L. Seigel
Tampa, Florida
October 29, 2008

PART ONE

INTRODUCTION

CHAPTER ONE

The Facts and Only the Facts

Robert J. Luck & Michael L. Seigel

Durham and Duke Before the Storm[1]

Duke University is located in Durham, North Carolina, one of the three point cities in the state's famed "triangle" of research-based and high-tech companies. Durham, however, is the poor, redheaded stepchild compared to its nearby sister cities, Raleigh and Chapel Hill. Unlike those two, Durham's poverty and crime rates are "alarming." The median per-capita income of Durham residents is only $23,000, a little more than half the annual tuition at Duke; the city has an acknowledged crime problem—the mayor made crime the focus of his 2006 State of the City speech—and beat out much-larger cities like Charlotte for the "dubious distinction of being North Carolina's murder capital."[2]

Durham was once in the thriving center of the tobacco and, later, the textile industries, but by 2006, most of these jobs were gone. Duke University is now Durham's largest employer: 15 percent of Durham's workforce (19,000 residents) draw their paycheck from Duke, mostly from low- or unskilled jobs.

---

1. This factual summary is just that, a summary. It is by no means intended as a comprehensive account of a months-long and factually complicated case. For a full account of the Duke lacrosse rape case, we recommend that the reader look to STUART TAYLOR & KC JOHNSON, UNTIL PROVEN INNOCENT: POLITICAL CORRECTNESS AND THE SHAMEFUL INJUSTICES OF THE DUKE LACROSSE RAPE CASE (2007), and DON YAEGER, IT'S NOT ABOUT THE TRUTH: THE UNTOLD STORY OF THE DUKE LACROSSE CASE AND THE LIVES IT SHATTERED (2007). We relied heavily on these books ourselves.

2. TAYLOR & JOHNSON, *supra* note 1, at 17–18; YAEGER, *supra* note 1, at 27, 31–32; William Yardley, *Duke's Struggling Cousin Rises From Its Shadow*, N.Y. TIMES, May 1, 2006, at A1; Ted Vaden, *Durham Sees Red Over Crime*, NEWS & OBSERVER (Raleigh, N.C.), Jan. 22, 2006, at A27.

Duke's workforce reflects the demographics of its Durham home: 44 percent of Durham residents are African-American, and a sizable portion of them are Duke employees. Over the years, many of them have referred to Duke as "the plantation."[3]

As Durham's fortunes have sagged with the departure of the tobacco farms and textile mills, Duke's have flourished. Academically, in 2006, Duke for the first time was ranked as one of the top five universities in the country; if it wanted to, it could fill every seat in every one of its undergraduate classes with high-school valedictorians. Athletically, Duke was again a contender for the Sears Cup, given to the best all-around athletic program in the country. The Blue Devils men's basketball team, coached by Mike Krzyzewski, earned its annual bid to the NCAA tournament. The men's lacrosse team was coming off a one-goal loss in the national championship game the year before, and was favored to win it all in 2006.[4]

Duke was also known as a party school; its unofficial motto was "work hard, play hard." For this reason, Duke served as the model for Tom Wolfe's fictional, academically elite, party- and sex-obsessed, "Dupont University" in his 2005 novel, *I Am Charlotte Simmons*. Duke's football-game day "Tailgate" celebrations were famous for their all-day drinking and partying; most of the student body didn't bother showing up at the game, opting for the kegs in the parking lot outside the stadium instead. Eventually, in an effort to change its image, the university imposed strict prohibitions on alcohol use on campus. The students, however, reacted by moving most of their partying and drinking to off-campus fraternities, sororities, and student-rented houses, much to the frustration of their full-time resident neighbors.[5]

March 13, 2006, and the Morning After

On March 13, 2006, Duke students were on their annual spring-break vacation. Most of them headed home or went to spring-break hot spots like Myr-

---

3. TAYLOR & JOHNSON, *supra* note 1, at 18, 131; YAEGER, *supra* note 1, at 27–28; Rick Lyman, *New Strain on Duke's Ties with Durham*, N.Y. TIMES, Mar. 31, 2006, at A10; Yardley, *supra* note 2, at A1.

4. TAYLOR & JOHNSON, *supra* note 1, at 2, 5, 7, 18, 63; YAEGER, *supra* note 1, at 30–31, 39–40; Duff Wilson & Viv Bernstein, *Duke Cancels Season and Begins Inquiries*, N.Y. TIMES, Apr. 6, 2006, at D1.

5. TAYLOR & JOHNSON, *supra* note 1, at 2–5, 74–75; YAEGER, *supra* note 1, at 41–42; Lyman, *supra* note 3, at A10.

tle Beach, Panama City, and Cancun. Lacrosse players, however, had no vacation. They were required to stay in Durham to practice for their upcoming games against Cornell, North Carolina, and Georgetown.[6]

Traditionally, during the spring break week when the lacrosse players were stuck in town, the team had a "bonding party" at a local strip club. But the previous year, the club they selected began cracking down on fake identification and excluded the underage team members. To avoid this problem, some of the seniors decided to hire strippers to come to their off-campus house so that everyone could participate in the fun.[7]

Dan Flannery, a senior cocaptain of the Duke lacrosse team, found the phone number for Allure Escort Service on the internet. Flannery called, and when the woman on the other end of the line asked, "What do you want," he said that he was hosting a party at his house for twenty to thirty guys and he needed two white women to strip. The woman from Allure said this wouldn't be a problem; she had two women, one Hispanic and one with brown hair and blond highlights, who would be available at 11:00 p.m. that night. Flannery agreed; he gave the woman from Allure his credit-card information and the address of the off-campus house he shared with cocaptains Dave Evans and Matt Zash.[8]

Lacrosse players began showing up at the cocaptains' house at 2:00 p.m. that afternoon. They passed the time playing "beer pong" and watching television, waiting for the strippers to show up.[9] At about 11:15 p.m., Kim Roberts, a thirty-one year old African-American mother, arrived. While the partygoers and Kim waited for the other woman to come, Kim had a drink, smoked a cigarette, and chatted with Flannery.[10] Crystal Mangum, the second dancer, arrived at 11:40 p.m. Mangum, also an African-American woman, was a single mother of two, and lived with her parents in Durham. Mangum was taking courses at North Carolina Central University, and working as an exotic dancer at a local strip club.[11]

---

6. TAYLOR & JOHNSON, *supra* note 1 at 4, 16–17; YAEGER, *supra* note 1, at 4; Duff Wilson & Jonathan D. Glater, *Files from Duke Rape Case Give Details But No Answers*, N.Y. TIMES, Aug. 25, 2006, at A1.

7. TAYLOR & JOHNSON, *supra* note 1, at 16–17; YAEGER, *supra* note 1, at 4–5; Wilson & Glater, *supra* note 6.

8. TAYLOR & JOHNSON, *supra* note 1, at 11, 16–17; YAEGER, *supra* note 1, at 5–7; Duff Wilson & Juliet Macur, *Call to Escort Service Began Night of Trouble at Duke*, N.Y. TIMES, Apr. 23, 2006, at 122.

9. TAYLOR & JOHNSON, *supra* note 1, at 21.

10. *Id.* at 23; YAEGER, *supra* note 1, at 8.

11. TAYLOR & JOHNSON, *supra* note 1, at 19–20, 23; Juliet Macur, *Duke Players' Accuser Moves Out to Avoid News Media*, N.Y. TIMES, Apr. 3, 2006, at D8; Wilson & Macur, *supra* note 8.

Roberts and Mangum had never worked together before. When the two women finally met, they went into the bathroom shared by cocaptains Dave Evans and Matt Zash. Roberts changed into her outfit—Mangum had shown up in hers—and they discussed their plan for the performance.[12]

At midnight, Roberts and Mangum left the bathroom and went to the living room, where the lacrosse players were waiting for the show to begin. The women began dancing and taking off their clothes, but this didn't last long. Mangum was intoxicated and had taken a powerful muscle relaxant; she could barely stand up. She "repeatedly tripped and stumbled over" Roberts, and at one point "tumbled to the floor."[13] While Mangum was on the floor, Roberts got on top of her and began to simulate oral sex. Roberts then asked the lacrosse players if any of them wanted to take off their pants so the women could "play with it." None of the players took her up on the offer, but one of them asked, "Do you have any toys?" Roberts indicated that she didn't, responding: "I'd use your dick, but it's too small." The same player picked up a broom and said, "Why don't you use this?"[14]

That ended the performance, at 12:05 a.m. Some of the guests at the party left, including sophomore lacrosse team member Reade Seligmann. Roberts yelled at the player who made the broom comment and stormed out of the living room and into the bathroom. Mangum followed her, "tripping, stumbling, and banging into walls" along the way.[15]

At 12:20 a.m., the women came out of the bathroom, left the house, and made their way to Roberts's car parked outside. One of the players went up to the window of Roberts's car and apologized for what had happened. He asked the two women to come back into the house to get Mangum's purse, which she had left in the bathroom, and her shoe, which she had left in the living room.[16]

Mangum returned to the house to retrieve her purse and shoe. After exiting the house a second time, she stood on the stairs of the front porch. At

---

12. Taylor & Johnson, *supra* note 1, at 23–24; Yaeger, *supra* note 1, at 9–10; Wilson & Macur, *supra* note 8, at 122.

13. Taylor & Johnson, *supra* note 1, at 23–25; Yaeger, *supra* note 1, at 9–10; Wilson & Macur, *supra* note 8, at 122; Wilson & Glater, *supra* note 6.

14. Taylor & Johnson, *supra* note 1, at 25; Yaeger, *supra* note 1, at 10; Wilson & Bernstein, *supra* note 4; Wilson & Macur, *supra* note 8, at 122; Wilson & Glater, *supra* note 6, at A1.

15. Taylor & Johnson, *supra* note 1, at 25; Yaeger, *supra* note 1, at 10; Duff Wilson & Juliet Macur, *2 Duke Athletes Charged With Rape and Kidnapping*, N.Y. Times, Apr. 19, 2006, at A14; Wilson & Macur, *supra* note 8, at 122; Peter Applebome, *As Duke Accusation Festers, Disbelief Grows*, N.Y. Times, Jul. 16, 2006, at 123.

16. Taylor & Johnson, *supra* note 1, at 26–27; Yaeger, *supra* note 1, at 11–12.

12:26 a.m., she called another escort service with which she worked, Center-fold Escorts. Mangum then tripped, fell down the stairs, and passed out in the driveway.[17] Roberts told Flannery that if he carried Mangum to her car, Roberts would take Mangum away with her. At 12:41 a.m., Flannery carried Mangum into Roberts's car.[18]

Roberts then went into the backyard to retrieve Mangum's things. While there, some of the lacrosse players complained to her about paying $800 for what amounted to a five-minute show. Roberts yelled back at one of them that he was "a little dick white boy, who probably couldn't get it on his own and had to pay for it." He responded by calling Roberts the N-word.[19]

Roberts went back to her car, and as she began to drive off she yelled out to the lacrosse players milling outside the house, "F___ Duke. I'm calling the cops. That's a hate crime." One of the lacrosse players hollered back, "Hey, b___, thank your grandpa for my nice cotton shirt." Roberts then called 911 and told them that some guys at the cocaptains' house had yelled racial slurs at her. It was 12:53 a.m.[20]

Mangum had passed out in Roberts's car, and Roberts couldn't get her out. She drove two miles to a Kroger grocery store and asked the security guard there to help her. The security guard called the Durham police at 1:22 a.m.[21] Sergeant John C. Shelton and two other officers responded to the call. When Shelton arrived, Mangum was still unconscious and he had trouble putting her into another officer's patrol car. He could not rouse her. Shelton decided that Mangum met the criteria for involuntary confinement—that she was a danger to herself and others—and told one of the other officers to take her to Durham Access Center, the local facility for patients with mental illness or drug addiction.[22]

Mangum arrived at Durham Access at 1:55 a.m. She said that she didn't want to go to jail, and that Roberts had stolen her cell phone, identification,

---

17. YAEGER, *supra* note 1, at 11–12; Wilson & Macur, *supra* note 8, at 122.

18. TAYLOR & JOHNSON, *supra* note 1, at 28; YAEGER, *supra* note 1, at 12; Wilson & Macur, *supra* note 8, at 122.

19. TAYLOR & JOHNSON, *supra* note 1, at 29; YAEGER, *supra* note 1, at 12.

20. TAYLOR & JOHNSON, *supra* note 1, at 29; YAEGER, *supra* note 1, at 12–13; *911 Call Lead the Police to Duke's Lacrosse Team*, N.Y. TIMES, Mar. 30, 2006, at D6 [hereinafter "*911 Call*"]; Wilson & Macur, *supra* note 8, at 122; Wilson & Glater, *supra* note 6, at A1.

21. YAEGER, *supra* note 1, at 30; *911 Call*, *supra* note 20, at D6; Joe Drape, *Lawyers for Lacrosse Players Dispute Accusations*, N.Y. TIMES, Mar. 31, 2006, at D5; Wilson & Macur, *supra* note 8, at 122; Wilson & Glater, *supra* note 6, at A1.

22. YAEGER, *supra* note 1, at 30–31; *Officer Describes Woman in Duke Case as Drunk*, N.Y. TIMES, Apr. 14, 2006, at D7; Wilson & Macur, *supra* note 8, at 122; Wilson & Glater, *supra* note 6, at A1.

and $2,000. A nurse asked Mangum if she'd been raped, to which Mangum nodded yes. This was Mangum's first statement to anyone that she had been raped; her story would change a number of times that night.[23]

At 2:40 a.m., the Durham police took Mangum to the Duke University Medical Center for treatment and a sexual-assault workup. There, Officer Gwendolen Sutton interviewed her. Mangum told Sutton that five men at the cocaptains' house, including one named Brett, had taken her into a bathroom and forced her to have intercourse and perform sex acts on them. Mangum also said that Roberts had stolen her money and cell phone.[24] Later, Shelton conducted a follow-up interview, in which Mangum told him that some of the guys from the party pulled her from Roberts's car and groped her, but that she was not forced to have sex with them.[25] Later still, another Durham police officer, B.S. Jones, interviewed Mangum, who told him that "Brett knew the deal" but "the guys weren't with it." Mangum said nothing to Jones about being raped.[26]

Doctors at the Duke hospital then examined Mangum. She told them that she had been raped vaginally, but not orally or anally, and denied any physical attack. Mangum said that she had "great pain," rating it a 10 on a scale of 1 to 10. The doctors found fluid that they thought was semen. (It was later tested for DNA.) Other than "three small nonbleeding cuts" on her knee and heel, however, the doctors found "no physical evidence of the attack described by [Mangum].… No bruises. No bleeding. No vaginal or anal tearing. No grimacing, sweating, changes in vital signs, or other symptoms ordinarily associated with the serious pain of which she complained."[27]

Finally, a sexual-assault-nurse trainee, Tara Levicy, examined and interviewed Mangum. Mangum told Levicy that Roberts had helped three men at the party, Adam, Brett, and Matt, drag her from the car into the house. The three men, Mangum claimed, undressed her and held her down. Matt, who said he was getting married the next day, raped her vaginally without a condom. Adam raped her vaginally and anally. Brett raped her orally. Once they

---

23. TAYLOR & JOHNSON, *supra* note 1, at 31; Nicholas D. Kristof, *Jocks and Prejudice*, N.Y. TIMES, June 11, 2006, §4, at 13.

24. TAYLOR & JOHNSON, *supra* note 1, at 31; *Defense Criticizes Duke Case Accuser*, N.Y. TIMES, Jun. 23, 2006, at A22; Wilson & Glater, *supra* note 6.

25. TAYLOR & JOHNSON, *supra* note 1, at 30–31; Kristof, *supra* note 23, §4, at 13; Wilson & Glater, *supra* note 6, at A1.

26. TAYLOR & JOHNSON, *supra* note 1, at 32.

27. *Id.* at 32–33; Duff Wilson, *New Filing in Duke Case Aims to Refute Accusations*, N.Y. TIMES, Jun. 9, 2006, at A18; Wilson & Glater, *supra* note 6.

were done, Mangum said, Roberts cleaned her up and they took her back to the car.[28]

Levicy, too, found no evidence of a physical assault. Mangum's head, back, neck, chest, breasts, nose, throat, mouth, abdomen, and extremities were all normal, with no sign of rectal penetration or trauma. All that Levicy found was "diffuse edema of the vaginal walls," which could be evidence of rape, but is also consistent with smoking, consensual sex within twenty-four hours of the exam, frequent sex, or a reaction to antidepressant medication.[29]

The Investigation and Indictment

Sergeant Mark Gottlieb of the Durham police department was assigned Mangum's case hours after she reported the rape at the hospital. Gottlieb had a reputation of singling out Duke students for prosecution. During a ten-month period from 2005 to 2006, Gottlieb arrested 28 people. Twenty of them were Duke students, and of those 20, 15 were immediately taken to jail for minor crimes such as violating Durham's noise ordinance or its open-container law. In contrast, during the same period, three other sergeants working in the Duke University police district arrested a total of only two students.[30]

Gottlieb first interviewed Mangum on March 16, two days after she had been treated at the hospital. Mangum told Gottlieb that three men at the party—Matt, Brett, and Adam—had raped her. Roberts, Mangum continued, had tried to help her. After the three men were done, Adam carried her to Roberts's car. Mangum described Adam as "short" with "red cheeks," a "chubby face," and brown "fluffy hair"; she described Matt as "heavy set," with a "short haircut," weighing "260–270"; the only detail she gave about Brett was that he was "chubby." No lacrosse players matched Mangum's description of Matt or Brett.[31]

At the March 16 interview, and again on March 21, Gottlieb showed Mangum pictures, taken from the Duke University website, of the lacrosse team. Mangum identified four players with 100 percent certainty—none were among the three players later indicted. She identified a fifth lacrosse team member, Reade Seligmann, with 70 percent certainty. Defense attorneys were not told about these identifications until May 17, a month after the first set of indictments. Gottlieb

---

28. TAYLOR & JOHNSON, *supra* note 1, at 33–34.
29. *Id.* at 33–34; Wilson, *supra* note 27.
30. TAYLOR & JOHNSON, *supra* note 1, at 36; YAEGER, *supra* note 1, at 56–58.
31. TAYLOR & JOHNSON, *supra* note 1, at 38; Wilson & Glater, *supra* note 6.

typed up notes from these interviews, from memory, four months after they took place.[32]

Based on Mangum's March 16 statement, Gottlieb obtained a warrant to search the cocaptains' house. During the search, Evans, Flannery, and Zash fully cooperated with Gottlieb. The cocaptains showed Gottlieb where they had stored the items Mangum had left behind; answered all of Gottlieb's questions; went down to the station house; gave written, signed statements; volunteered DNA samples; gave Gottlieb the passwords to their e-mail and instant-messenger accounts; and volunteered to take a lie detector test. Gottlieb never took them up on that last offer.[33]

The Durham police department's first conversation with Roberts took place on March 20, six days after the party. Gottlieb's chief investigator, Detective Benjamin Himan, spoke with her by phone. Roberts told Himan that Mangum's claim that she had been sexually assaulted was a "crock." Roberts said that she and Mangum had been together at the party for all but five minutes, not enough time for the triple rape that Mangum had described to occur.[34] Two days later, Himan met with Roberts in person. In a seven-page handwritten statement, Roberts wrote that no one at the lacrosse party had touched either woman, that the two women lingered without fear in and around the house for forty-five minutes after the dancing had stopped, and Mangum said nothing to her in the half hour they were together after they left the cocaptains' house about being raped.[35]

The next day, March 23, Gottlieb and some attorneys in the Durham DA's office applied for, and received, a nontestimonial identification order to obtain DNA samples from all forty-six white lacrosse players. They supported the application with Mangum's March 16 and March 21 statements to Gottlieb, the crude comment made by one of the lacrosse players at the party asking the women if they wanted to use a broom stick as a sex toy, and medical evidence that "the victim had signs, symptoms, and injuries consistent with being raped and sexually assaulted vaginally and anally." The application stated that "[t]he DNA evidence requested will immediately rule out any innocent

---

32. TAYLOR & JOHNSON, *supra* note 1, at 39–39, 41; YAEGER, *supra* note 1, at 60–61; Wilson & Glater, *supra* note 6; Byron Calame, *Revisiting the Times's Coverage of the Duke Rape Case*, N.Y. TIMES, Apr, 22, 2007, §4, at 12.

33. TAYLOR & JOHNSON, *supra* note 1, at 42–44; *911 Call*, *supra* note 20, at D6; Shaila Dewan, *3rd Duke Lacrosse Player Is Indicted in Rape Case*, N.Y. TIMES, May 16, 2006, at A16.

34. TAYLOR & JOHNSON, *supra* note 1, at 46; Wilson, *supra* note 27, at A18.

35. TAYLOR & JOHNSON, *supra* note 1, at 57; Wilson, *supra* note 27, at A18.

persons, and show conclusive evidence as to who the suspect(s) are in the alleged violent attack upon this victim." It did not say anything about Mangum's inconsistent accounts of the party and the rape allegations, Roberts's statements to Himan that the allegations were a "crock" and that the women had been apart for no more than five minutes, the cocaptains' cooperation with the police, or the lack of medical evidence indicating any sign of a physical assault on Mangum.[36]

Later that day, the team collectively went to the police station to have DNA swabs taken pursuant to the court's order. The police had tipped off the media, who were waiting for the players as they arrived at the station; the next day, the front page of Raleigh's *News & Observer* featured a picture of the lacrosse players covering their faces so they would not be identified.[37]

From this point on, Durham District Attorney Mike Nifong took exclusive control of the investigation. On March 24, Captain Jeff Lamb of the Durham police department ordered "all Durham police 'to go through Mr. Nifong for any directions as to how to conduct matters in this case.'" This action was contrary to the normal chain of command within the Durham police department: it completely bypassed the district commander and the chief of police.[38]

On March 28, Nifong learned the results of the North Carolina State Bureau of Investigation's DNA test on Mangum's rape kit. The state investigators reported that "there had been no semen, blood, or saliva anywhere on or in" Mangum. The results of the DNA test seriously called into question Mangum's claim that three men had penetrated her vagina, anus, and mouth without condoms, and had ejaculated.[39] Nifong took two steps in response to this information. First, he had the police conduct a third photo lineup with Mangum at the station and ordered that they take her sworn, written statement. Mangum had not given an official statement in the three weeks since the lacrosse party. Second, Nifong hired a private firm, DNA Security, Inc., to perform more sensitive DNA tests on the rape kit, hoping that they would isolate male DNA.[40]

---

36. TAYLOR & JOHNSON, *supra* note 1, at 57–59; *911 Call, supra* note 20, at D6; Duff Wilson, *Lawyer Says Two Duke Lacrosse Players Are Indicted in Rape Case*, N.Y. TIMES, Apr. 18, 2006, at A23.

37. TAYLOR & JOHNSON, *supra* note 1, at 59–61; YAEGER, *supra* note 1, at 75–76; Samiha Khanna & Anne Blythe, *DNA Tests Ordered for Duke Athletes*, NEWS & OBSERVER (Raleigh, N.C.), Mar. 24, 2006, at A1.

38. TAYLOR & JOHNSON, *supra* note 1, at 63.

39. *Id.* at 96; Duff Wilson & Juliet Macur, *Lawyers for Duke Players Say DNA Evidence Clears the Team*, N.Y. TIMES, Apr. 11, 2006, at D1.

40. TAYLOR & JOHNSON, *supra* note 1, at 154, 158–59; Juliet Macur & Duff Wilson, *Duke Inquiry to Continue, and So Will Campaign*, N.Y. TIMES, Apr. 12, 2006, at A1.

The police scheduled the third photo lineup for April 4. Departmental procedures for eyewitness identification required that: (1) an officer uninvolved with the investigation should conduct the lineup, (2) the officer should instruct the witness that the lineup may or may not contain any suspects, and (3) the officer should use five filler photos of nonsuspects per lineup. The April 4 lineup violated all three guidelines. Gottlieb, the chief police investigator on Mangum's case, conducted the lineup; he told Mangum that all the pictures were of people that the police suspected were at the party; and the only photos that Mangum was shown were of the forty-six white Duke lacrosse players—no fillers were used. Mangum identified three lacrosse players as her attackers: Collin Finnerty, Reade Seligmann, and Dave Evans. None of them matched her earlier descriptions of her attackers.[41]

Mangum made a written statement two days later, on April 6. In it, she related that three guys from the party took her to the bathroom, while three other partygoers took Roberts to the master bedroom. In the bathroom, three men raped her: Matt raped her vaginally and orally and hit her in the face; Adam raped her orally and ejaculated in her mouth; Brett raped her vaginally and orally. Adam, Mangum said, was the one who was getting married the next day.[42]

On April 10, Nifong received word from Dr. Brian Meehan at DNA Security concerning the results of the new tests: the lab had found no DNA matching any of the lacrosse players on any of the evidence. Meehan's people had found, however, the DNA of four unidentified men on the rectal swabs and undergarment taken from Mangum at the hospital on March 14. Nifong and Meehan agreed that Meehan would exclude this latter fact from his final report.[43]

At this point, Nifong stopped investigating. He never personally interviewed Mangum about the rape allegations, and refused to meet with counsel for the lacrosse players who offered to show him exculpatory evidence. Instead, he focused on campaigning for the Democratic nomination for Durham district attorney.[44]

---

41. Taylor & Johnson, *supra* note 1, at 155–58; Juliet Macur, *Lawyers for Lacrosse Players at Duke Say They Expect Indictment in Rape Case*, N.Y. Times, Apr. 13, 2006, at A18; Wilson & Macur, *supra* note 8, at 122; Duff Wilson & Jonathan D. Glater, *Prosecutor's Silence on Duke Rape Case Leaves Public with Plenty of Questions*, N.Y. Times, Jun. 12, 2006, at A13; Wilson & Glater, *supra* note 6, at A1.

42. Taylor & Johnson, *supra* note 1, at 159–60.

43. *Id.* at 163; *New Duke DNA Tests Are Reportedly Inconclusive*, N.Y. Times, May 13, 2006, at A14; David Barstow & Duff Wilson, *DNA Witness Jolted Dynamic of Duke Case*, N.Y. Times, Dec. 24, 2006, at 11.

44. Taylor & Johnson, *supra* note 1, at 86, 160–61, 175; Wilson & Glater, *supra* note 6, at A1; David Barstow & Duff Wilson, *Charges of Rape Against 3 at Duke Are Abandoned*,

A Durham grand jury indicted Finnerty and Seligmann on April 17 for rape, sexual assault, and kidnapping; it indicted Evans on May 15.[45]

The Prosecutor and the Press

North Carolina Governor Mike Easley appointed Nifong to be Durham's interim district attorney in April 2005. Nifong had worked as a prosecutor in the district attorney's office for twenty-six years, trying many complex and serious felony cases, but—following a corruption scandal—had spent the previous four years as the district attorney's point man for negotiating pleas in traffic court.[46] One of his first acts as Durham's district attorney was to fire Freda Black, "a longtime rival in the office." Black, well known in Durham for successfully prosecuting novelist and former mayoral candidate Michael Peterson a few years earlier, decided to run against Nifong in the Democratic mayoral primary on May 2, 2006. If Black had won the nomination and then the general election (there were no Republicans running in overwhelmingly Democratic Durham), she would "surely" have fired Nifong.[47]

When accepting the interim DA position, Nifong had promised Easley that he would not run for the open district-attorney position the following year, which made Easley's decision a nonpolitical one. But Nifong had three-and-a-half years of service left before he would max out on his pension. With the threat of the popular Black winning the election and firing him, cutting his annual pension by $15,000, Nifong decided to go back on his promise and run against her.[48]

By March 2006, however, Nifong's campaign had stalled. He was running out of money; Black had raised four times more than Nifong in the first few months of 2006; Nifong had to lend himself $30,000 to compete. A poll that Black's campaign conducted on March 27 showed her with a seventeen-point lead over Nifong. At the same time, African-American leaders in Durham had recruited a third candidate, Keith Bishop, to run for district attorney. It was

---

N.Y. Times, Dec. 23, 2006, at A1; Duff Wilson, *"Credibility Issues" Undid Duke Case, Report Says*, N.Y. Times, Apr. 28, 2007, at A14.

45. Taylor & Johnson, *supra* note 1, at 173–78; Yaeger, *supra* note 1, at 309–10; Duff Wilson & Juliet Macur, *2 Duke Athletes Charged with Rape and Kidnapping*, N.Y. Times, Apr. 19, 2006, at A14; Dewan, *supra* note 33, at A16.

46. Taylor & Johnson, *supra* note 1, at 78–81; Yaeger, *supra* note 1, at 90–92; Macur & Wilson, *supra* note 40, at A14.

47. Taylor & Johnson, *supra* note 1, at 82, 84; Macur & Wilson, *supra* note 40, at A14.

48. Taylor & Johnson, *supra* note 1, at 81–82.

widely assumed that Bishop would get the endorsement of the politically in-
fluential Durham Committee on the Affairs of Black People.[49]

Then along came Mangum's claim that she had been raped. Nifong decided
to make this "the campaign's main event." As the authors of one book about
the Duke lacrosse case put it:

> The black community was understandably outraged at the lurid, ini-
> tially uncontested story of a local women being brutally gang-raped by
> white Duke lacrosse players "barking racial slurs," as the *News & Ob-
> server* described them on March 25. So suddenly the black vote was in
> play. Nifong's best hope was to make the rape case the campaign's
> main event. At the least, he could garner publicity and match Freda
> Black's name recognition. At best, he could use the case to inflame
> the black community and win over minority voters who would oth-
> erwise support Bishop.

And that's exactly what Nifong did.[50]

Between March 24, the day he took control of Mangum's case as chief investigator, and April 11, when he received the DNA results from Meehan at
the private testing firm, Nifong gave about seventy interviews; newspapers,
television programs, and radio broadcasts all carried his comments.[51] Nifong
stated unequivocally that Mangum had been raped and, despite the contrary
evidence, that the lacrosse players were responsible. Even a small sampling of
his many remarks reveals the breadth of his publicity campaign and the venom
in his comments:

Durham's *NBC 17 News*:

> The information that I have does lead me to conclude that a rape did
> occur.... I'm making a statement to the Durham community and, as
> a citizen of Durham, I am making a statement for the Durham com-
> munity.... This is not the kind of activity we condone, and it must
> be dealt with quickly and harshly.... The circumstances of the rape
> indicated deep racial motivation for some of the things that were
> done.... It makes a crime that is by its nature one of the most offen-
> sive and invasive even more so.

---

49. *Id.* at 82–84; Macur & Wilson, *supra* note 40, at A14; William Yardley, *Prosecutor in
Duke Case Is Winner in Election*, N.Y. TIMES, May 3, 2006, at A16; Kristof, *supra* note 23.

50. TAYLOR & JOHNSON, *supra* note 1, at 84–85.

51. *Id.*; YAEGER, *supra* note 1, at 99–101; Kristof, *supra* note 23; Wilson & Glater, *supra*
note 41, at A13; Samiha Khanna & Anne Blythe, *Dancer Gives Details of Ordeal*, NEWS &
OBSERVER (Raleigh, N.C.), Mar. 25, 2006, at A1.

Raleigh's *News & Observer*:

> I would like to think that somebody who was not in the bathroom has the human decency to call up and say, "What am I doing covering up for a bunch of hooligans?" I'd like to be able to think that there were some people in that house that were not involved in this and were as horrified by it as the rest of us are.

USA Today:

> There's been a feeling there in the past that Duke students are treated differently by the court system.... There was a feeling that Duke students' daddies could buy them expensive lawyers and that they knew the right people. It's discouraging when people feel that way, and we try not to make that the case.

ESPN:

> One would wonder why one needs an attorney if one was not charged and had not done anything wrong.

The *New York Times*:

> There are three people who went into the bathroom with the young lady, and whether the other people there knew what was going on at the time, they do now and have not come forward.... I'm disappointed that no one has been enough of a man to come forward. And if they would have spoken up at the time, this may never have happened.... The thing that most of us found so abhorrent, and the reason I decided to take it over myself, was the combination of gang-like rape activity accompanied by the racial slurs and general racial hostility.

The *CBS Early Show*:

> I still think that the racial slurs that were involved are relevant to show the mind-set, I guess, that was involved in this particular attack, and obviously, to make what is already an extremely reprehensible attack even more reprehensible.[52]

---

52. YAEGER, *supra* note 1, at 100–03; Viv Bernstein & Joe Draper, *Rape Allegation Against Athletes Is Roiling Duke*, N.Y. TIMES, Mar. 29, 2006, at A1; Anne Blythe & Jane Stancill, *Duke Puts Lacrosse Games on Hold*, NEWS & OBSERVER (Raleigh, N.C.), Mar. 29, 2006, at A1; Sal Ruibal, *Assault Scandal Highlights Divide for Durham*, USA TODAY, Mar. 31, 2006, at 9C.

To *Newsweek*, Nifong "hinted" that a "date rape drug may have been used in the alleged gang rape of the woman by three Duke lacrosse players at a March party." He told the *CBS Early Show* that there was "no doubt" Mangum had been sexually assaulted. And, in perhaps his most famous media appearance, Nifong demonstrated for the audience of MSNBC's *The Abrams Show* how Mangum had been grabbed from behind, choked, and struggled to breathe.[53]

Not that some members of the media needed much goading. *USA Today* columnist Christine Brennan wrote that the Duke lacrosse players were "giving us all a new definition of the word teamwork.... Perhaps if no one is found guilty of any criminal activity in this unseemly affair, the collective silence of the Blue Devils will be seen as admirable. For now, though, the sports world's vaunted concept of team is reaching a frightening extreme." Best-selling author and sportswriter John Feinstein said to the Duke lacrosse team members: "We know you had this party. We know it got out of hand. None of you is man enough to come forward and say what happened. You were witnesses to a crime. We're shutting down the program and you're all gone." *New York Times* columnist Selena Roberts wrote of the lacrosse team that

> a group of privileged players of fine pedigree entangled in a night that threatens to belie their social standing as human beings.... At the intersection of entitlement and enablement, there is Duke University, virtuous on the outside, debauched on the inside.... Does [Duke] President Brodhead dare to confront the culture behind the lacrosse team's code of silence or would he fear being ridiculed as a snitch?

And CNN's Nancy Grace said on her March 31 program,

> There's really no good reason why, if you're innocent, you won't go forward and go, "Hey, you want my DNA? Take it. I insist." ... [Y]ou've got these probably rich kids, lacrosse players, claiming consent or I didn't do it.... If there had been evidence, I'm sure it was flushed down the commode or gotten rid of, innocently or not.... The Blue Devils! It may not be just a nickname at Duke University.[54]

---

53. TAYLOR & JOHNSON, *supra* note 1, at 97; YAEGER, *supra* note 1, at 104; Wilson & Glater, *supra* note 41, at A13; Susannah Meadows & Evan Thomas, *What Happened at Duke?*, NEWSWEEK, May 1, 2006, at 40.

54. TAYLOR & JOHNSON, *supra* note 1, at 118–24; Selena Roberts, *When Peer Pressure, Not a Conscience, Is Your Guide*, N.Y. TIMES, Mar. 31, 2006, at D1; Christine Brennan, *Wrong Time for Team Unity in Duke Probe*, USA TODAY, Mar. 30, 2006, at 6C.

Nifong also made Mangum's rape allegations the central focus of the election-candidate forums. At one, he said that "I'm not going to allow Durham's view in the minds of the world to be a bunch of lacrosse players at Duke raping a black girl from Durham." At another, explaining why the tests had revealed no DNA from the players on Mangum, he said that "[i]n 75 percent to 80 percent of sexual assault cases, there is no DNA evidence.... It doesn't mean nothing happened, it just means nothing was left behind."[55]

Nifong's media offensive stopped on April 11, the day after he received the results of the tests from DNA Security, but by then the die was cast. He edged out Black to win the Democratic Party nomination by 883 votes; he received 45 percent of the votes, Black 42 percent, and Bishop 13 percent. Nifong went on to win the general election against two write-in candidates.[56]

The Response of Duke's Administration and Faculty

Dean of Students Sue Wasiolek was the first Duke administrator to respond to the rape charges. On March 15, Wasiolek contacted lacrosse coach Mike Pressler while he was at a team function. She told him that some team members had hired two women to strip for a party two nights earlier, and one of the dancers claimed that she was gang-raped. Wasiolek also told Pressler that the police did not think the rape claim was credible and that it would "go away." Wasiolek, an attorney, then talked to two of the cocaptains who hosted the party, Dan Flannery and Matt Zash. She told them that she believed that no rape had occurred; that they did not need an attorney; and that they should tell no one, not even their parents or teammates, about the allegations. "[C]ooperate with the police if they contact you," she said, "If you tell them the truth, it will work out."[57]

Two days later, after the cocaptains' house had been searched and they had volunteered DNA samples, Flannery, Evans, and Zash met with Assistant Athletic Director Chris Kennedy. Kennedy told them that they had to tell their

---

55. YAEGER, *supra* note 1, at 99, 101; Wilson & Macur, *supra* note 39, at D1; Macur & Wilson, *supra* note 40, at A14.

56. TAYLOR & JOHNSON, *supra* note 1, at 203–04, 296; YAEGER, *supra* note 1, at 99, 104; Yardley, *supra* note 49, at A16; Wilson & Glater, *supra* note 41, at A13.

57. TAYLOR & JOHNSON, *supra* note 1, at 37; YAEGER, *supra* note 1, at 15, 20–22; Karen W. Arenson, *Duke Failed to See Gravity of Rape Case, Report Says*, N.Y. TIMES, May 9, 2006, at A18.

parents right away, and that they would need lawyers. He passed along Wasi-olek's recommendation of Wes Covington, a former colleague of hers, who was known as a "fixer" and a guy who "knew how to work the system of Durham." When the players later met with Covington, he said that he had spo-ken with Wasiolek and assured them that he would make the problem "go away."[58]

The problem, of course, did not go away. After the March 23 order requiring all the lacrosse players to submit DNA samples, the cocaptains, Pressler, and Kennedy met with Duke Executive Vice President Tallman Trask III and Athletic Director Joe Alleva. Trask and Alleva asked the players to tell them everything that had happened at the party. When they responded that their lawyers had ad-vised them to keep quiet because anyone with whom they spoke could be called as a witness, Trask told them that it was all right to talk to him and Alleva because the "faculty-student privilege" would protect the administrators from ever hav-ing to testify about the discussion in court. The cocaptains relented; they went on to describe exactly what had happened at the party. At the end of the students' presentation, Trask and Alleva said that they believed what the three had said.[59]

As the cocaptains left the meeting, Trask told them that he had experienced a similar ordeal in his youth. "I got through it," he said, "and so will you. Beat Georgetown." After the players were gone, Alleva told Pressler that the ad-ministration would have to punish the team for hiring strippers and permit-ting underage drinking. Pressler agreed, saying that he would suspend the organizers of the party; Trask suggested that they also be made to clean up the Trinity Park neighborhood where they lived.[60]

At a faculty meeting the same day, a number of professors demanded that Duke President Richard Brodhead order all the lacrosse players to talk to the po-lice; some even demanded that he disband the team. The chairman of the Aca-demic Council, law professor Paul Haagen, commented to Raleigh's *News & Observer* that "[t]here's a sense of, 'This is sad, and it's terrible.'" He told the paper "that violence against women is more prevalent among male athletes than among male students in general," particularly those in the "helmet sports," which he called "sports of violence," somberly noting that "[t]his is clearly a concern."[61]

The lacrosse team was scheduled to play Georgetown two days later, on March 25. In anticipation of the match, Duke professor Faulkner Fox distrib-

---

58. TAYLOR & JOHNSON, *supra* note 1, at 42, 69; Arenson, *supra* note 57, at A18.

59. TAYLOR & JOHNSON, *supra* note 1, at 62–63.

60. *Id.* at 63.

61. *Id.* at 63, 65–66; Samiha Khanna & Anne Blythe, *Dancer Gives Details of Ordeal*, NEWS & OBSERVER (Raleigh, N.C.), Mar. 25, 2006, at A1.

uted an e-mail encouraging people to show up at the game with signs bearing slogans like "Don't Be a Fan of Rapists." Concerned that the game would be a media spectacle, Brodhead decided to cancel it and the next game as punishment for hiring strippers and underage drinking.[62]

Brodhead refused to meet with the lacrosse players' parents who had come to see their sons play, but Alleva, Wasiolek, Trask, and Vice President of Student Affairs Larry Moneta were willing to see them. Alleva, Wasiolek, and Trask told the parents that they believed the players were innocent, but that Duke would not be making any more statements that day about the case. Alleva stated to the parents that the March 13 party was "inconsistent with Duke's values"; Trask added that everything would have worked out had their sons not consulted with attorneys and just cooperated with the police. Finally, the administrators pledged that the suspension would only be for those two games.[63]

Despite the assurance to the contrary, Brodhead issued a statement later that night. It began: "Physical coercion and sexual assault are unacceptable in any setting and have no place at Duke.... The criminal allegations against three members of our men's lacrosse team, if verified, will warrant very serious penalties." The statement went on to point out that "there are very different versions of the central events. No charges have been filed, and in our system of law, people are presumed innocent until proven guilty." Brodhead urged the team "to cooperate to the fullest with the police."[64]

Around the same time, John Burness, Duke's vice president of public affairs, sent an e-mail to the board of trustees. Burness wrote that Trask had spoken with the lacrosse players and he was inclined to believe them. Burness continued, however, to note that the situation was complicated by the team's silence and "by the behavior of the lacrosse team over many years which for those predisposed to be angry with them, presumes their guilt."[65]

The cocaptains finally had a chance to meet with Brodhead on March 28. They told him what happened at the party and apologized for their behavior. Brodhead urged them to publicly deny Mangum's allegations, which they did later that day. Brodhead also said that he believed them.[66]

Nevertheless, Brodhead canceled the lacrosse season only hours later. "Sports have their time and place," he said, "but when an issue of this gravity is in question, it is not time to be playing games." Bob Steel, chairman of the board of

---

62. TAYLOR & JOHNSON, *supra* note 1, at 66–67.
63. *Id.* at 67–69, 93–94.
64. *Id.* at 69–70.
65. *Id.* at 71.
66. *Id.* at 92–93; Bernstein & Drape, *supra* note 52, at A1; Drape, *supra* note 21, at D5.

trustees, later acknowledged that the lacrosse season was canceled because "[w]e had to stop those pictures [of the players practicing].... It doesn't mean it's fair, but we had to stop it. It doesn't necessarily mean I think it was right—it just had to be done."[67]

The next day, the tape of Kim Roberts's 911 call, in which she told police that some men had yelled the N-word at her as she drove by the cocaptains' house, was released to the public. Brodhead immediately issued another statement reading, in part: "Racism and its hateful language have no place in this community.... I am sorry the woman and her friend were subjected to such abuse."[68]

That same day, the Academic Council held an emergency meeting. A number of professors spoke out against the lacrosse team. One said that Duke tolerated drinking and rape, and that the incident with the lacrosse team reflected that attitude; another argued that the lacrosse team should be suspended for three years and downgraded to a club sport. English professor Houston Baker said that the lacrosse players had harmed an African-American woman, and that the white, female students in his class were terrified by the administration's failure to respond.[69]

Baker also sent a public letter to the Duke administration on March 29. In it, he demanded that the lacrosse players be expelled and their coach dismissed; he called them "white, violent, drunken men ... veritably given license to rape, maraud, and deploy hate speech." According to Baker, the team's behavior was evidence of "abhorrent sexual assault, verbal racial violence, and drunken white, male privilege loosed amongst us."[70]

Baker was not the only faculty member to attack the lacrosse team. History professor Peter Wood told the *New York Times* on March 31 that the "lacrosse players on campus stood out for their aggression, which he said was in some ways endemic to the violent nature of the game they played." Wood continued: "Too often, there seems to be a surliness about some lacrosse players' individual demeanor. They seem hostile, and there is this group mentality."[71]

Similarly, in a student-newspaper column that same day William Chafe, a history professor and former dean of the faculty, likened the lacrosse team

---

67. TAYLOR & JOHNSON, *supra* note 1, at 93–94; Bernstein & Drape, *supra* note 52, at A1.

68. TAYLOR & JOHNSON, *supra* note 1, at 96.

69. *Id.* at 106, 135.

70. *Id.* at 106; Karen W. Arenson, *Duke Grappling with Impact of Scandal on Its Reputation*, N.Y. TIMES, Apr. 7, 2006, at A16.

71. TAYLOR & JOHNSON, *supra* note 1, at 107–08.

members to "white slave masters [who] were the initial perpetrators of sexual assault on black women.… [and] white men [who] portrayed black women as especially erotic, more driven to sexual pleasure and expressiveness than white women." The team's having "hired a black woman from an escort service to perform an erotic dance," Chafe wrote, "[was the] latest example of the poisonous linkage of race and sex as instruments of power and control."[72]

Some professors offered private support and encouragement to the lacrosse players in their classes, while others targeted the lacrosse students in their classes for harassment and ridicule. Sam Veraldi, a markets and management instructor at Duke, was an example of the former. He had four lacrosse player students in his class. Veraldi would ask them for updates in the case each week and offered them encouragement and even his home as a refuge if they ever needed to get away from the hostility on campus.

Rhonda Sharpe, a visiting economics professor, also lent a sympathetic ear to the six lacrosse players in her class. After Mangum's allegations became public, Sharpe told them that they could come talk to her if things ever got tough on campus.[73]

Other Duke faculty members were less supportive. After Mangum's allegations became public, history professor Reeve Huston, who had five members of the lacrosse team in his labor history class, began a class by saying that he wanted to break the silence. He stated that his research had uncovered a long history of exploitation of African-American women. He claimed that Mangum had been raped at the March 13 party. An "ejaculation had occurred," he said. Professor Sally Deutsch, in her United States-history course, talked about how white men from the South had taken sexual advantage of African-American women throughout history.[74] Instructor Clair Ashton-James gave one lacrosse player a bad grade on an assignment because he had missed a class to meet with his attorney. When the player asked Ashton-James about the grade, she said that the lacrosse team "wasn't right" and that she didn't feel bad for them because "if you guys really were innocent, I would feel sorry for you." Finally, (perpetually) visiting political-science professor Kim Curtis gave lacrosse team member Kyle Dowd a C-minus and an F on his second and third term papers for Curtis' class; the grades were later set aside by Duke administrators.[75]

The faculty's animosity toward the lacrosse players culminated on April 6 with a full-page ad in the student newspaper. The open ad was signed by eighty-

---

72. *Id.* at 108–09.
73. *Id.* at 109.
74. *Id.* at 110–11.
75. *Id.* at 210–11.

eight faculty members, and appeared to be endorsed by five academic departments and thirteen academic programs. The ad asked, "What does a social disaster look like?" Although something "happened to this young woman," "the disaster didn't begin on March 13 and won't end with what the police say or the court decides." It concluded, "To the students speaking individually and to the protesters making collective noise, thank you for not waiting and for making yourselves heard."[76]

A day earlier, on April 5, Brodhead had taken three steps of his own. First, he formed committees to study (1) the problems with the lacrosse team and its use of "racist language and a pattern of alcohol abuse and disorderly behavior," (2) the administration's response to the party and Mangum's allegations, (3) Duke's disciplinary process, and (4) the campus culture. Brodhead appointed Professor Wood, who earlier had told the *New York Times* that the "lacrosse players on campus stood out for their aggression" and "seem hostile," as chairman of the campus-culture committee.[77]

Second, Brodhead sent his own letter to the Duke community. In it, he wrote that this case has

> brought to glaring visibility underlying issues that have been of concern on this campus and in this town for some time ... concerns of women about sexual coercion and assault ... concerns about the culture of certain student groups that regularly abuse alcohol and the attitudes these groups promote ... [and] concerns about the survival of the legacy of racism, the most hateful feature American history has produced.[78]

Finally, he decided to fire Coach Pressler. Alleva, the athletic director, broke the news to Pressler, telling him that "[i]t's not about the truth anymore. It's about the faculty, the special interest groups, the protesters, our reputation, the integrity of the university."[79]

About the Truth

The tide began to turn against Nifong's prosecution in the second half of 2006. On May 1, the Brodhead-appointed faculty committee tasked with re-

---

76. *Id.* at 144–45; Arenson, *supra* note 70, at A16.
77. TAYLOR & JOHNSON, *supra* note 1, at 139–40; Wilson & Bernstein, *supra* note 4, at D1; Arenson, *supra* note 70, at A16.
78. TAYLOR & JOHNSON, *supra* note 1, at 140; Wilson & Bernstein, *supra* note 4, at D1.
79. TAYLOR & JOHNSON, *supra* note 1, at 141–42.

viewing the lacrosse team's conduct at Duke, chaired by law professor James Coleman, issued its report. It found that the team members' "conduct has not been different in character than the conduct of the typical Duke student who abuses alcohol." The Coleman Committee also found no evidence "that the cohesiveness of this group [the lacrosse team] is either sexist or racist." The report recommended that Duke reinstate the lacrosse team the following year.[80]

A critical event took place on October 15, when CBS's *60 Minutes* program ran a thirty-five-minute segment on the case. During the program, Kim Roberts told Ed Bradley that Mangum's allegations—that six lacrosse players had forcibly separated them and dragged her into the bathroom—were untrue. Bradley also interviewed Coleman, who said of Nifong: "He pandered to the community.... What are you to conclude about a prosecutor who says to you, 'I'll do whatever it takes to get this set of defendants'? What does it say about what he's willing to do to get poor, black defendants?"[81]

Following the *60 Minutes* program, Duke chemistry professor Steve Baldwin wrote in the school newspaper that the lacrosse players

> were abandoned by their university. They were denied the presumption of innocence, despite mounting evidence that the case against them is made of smoke and mirrors and is fatally flawed procedurally. They have been pilloried by their faculty and scorned by the administration. They are pariahs.... Their treatment has been shameful.[82]

On October 27, the state trial court ordered Nifong to turn over the 2,000 pages of data generated by Meehan and DNA Security as part of the private testing on Mangum's rape kit. Nifong and the defense lawyers had been sparring for months over the extent of Nifong's mandatory discovery under North Carolina law.[83] Hiding within the mounds of paper turned over by Nifong were the raw DNA test results showing that the DNA of several unknown men had been found on items in the rape kit. Eventually, after dozens of hours of digging and analyzing, one member of the defense team, Brad Bannon, pieced to-

---

80. *Id.* at 207, 209–10; Wilson & Bernstein, *supra* note 4, at D1; William Yardley, *Review by Duke Faculty Sees Both Bad and Good in Lacrosse Team*, N.Y. TIMES, May 2, 2006, at A22; David Brooks, *The Duke Witch Hunt*, N.Y. TIMES, May 28, 2006, §4, at 11; REPORT OF THE LACROSSE AD HOC COMMITTEE TO RICHARD BRODHEAD, PRESIDENT OF DUKE UNIVERSITY 3, 7 (May 1, 2006).

81. TAYLOR & JOHNSON, *supra* note 1, at 282–83; Duff Wilson, *New Account of Party at Duke*, N.Y. TIMES, Oct. 14, 2006, at A14; Duff Wilson, *Rape Accusation Has Ruined Lives, Students Say*, N.Y. TIMES, Oct. 16, 2006, at A14.

82. TAYLOR & JOHNSON, *supra* note 1, at 284.

83. *See, e.g., id.* at 287–89, 301–02.

gether this exculpatory jewel. Defense attorneys disclosed this information to the court in a pretrial motion shortly thereafter and asked for an evidentiary hearing so that they could put Meehan on the stand.[84]

On December 15, the court heard the defense's motion. Nifong began the hearing by representing to the court that the defense motion was "[t]he first that I heard of this particular situation." He then said that Meehan was in the court and was willing to testify about the omission from his report. The defense attorneys jumped at the chance.[85] Under tough cross-examination, Meehan ultimately admitted that his failure to disclose the evidence of non-lacrosse-player DNA in Mangum's rape kit was a violation of state law and his own company's protocols: "By the letter of the law, by the letter of the wording of the standard," Meehan testified, the defense was "absolutely correct" that his public report "might not hold any weight in [the] legal arena."[86]

Meehan explained that his client, "Mr. Nifong, specifically wanted ... to know ... do any of the reference specimens [of the lacrosse players] match any of the evidence? And that's the report we gave him." Meehan's testimony ended this way:

> Attorney: Did your report set forth the results of all of the tests and examinations that you conducted in this case?
>
> Meehan: No. It was limited to only some results.
>
> Attorney: Okay. And that was an intentional limitation arrived at between you and representatives of the State of North Carolina not to report on the results of all examinations and tests that you did in this case?
>
> Meehan: Yes.[87]

The hearing adjourned moments later. Afterwards, Nifong admitted at a press conference that he knew about the other DNA found in the rape kit from the beginning and had failed to disclose it. The case unraveled rapidly from there.[88]

On December 21, less than a week after that hearing, an investigator from Nifong's office interviewed Mangum. For the first time, Mangum said that she

---

84. *Id.* at 303.

85. *Id.* at 305–08.

86. *Id.* at 309–10.

87. *Id.* at 310–11; *Duke Case Accuser Is Pregnant, and Test of Paternity Is Next*, N.Y. TIMES, Dec. 16, 2006, at A13; Barstow & Wilson, *supra* note 43, at 11; Duff Wilson & David Barstow, *Prosecutor Asks to Exit Duke Case*, N.Y. TIMES, Jan. 13, 2007, at A1.

88. TAYLOR & JOHNSON, *supra* note 1, at 311.

was unsure whether the three men had used their penises, or some other object, to rape her, which would explain the lack of DNA. The next day, based on this new story, Nifong dismissed the rape charge against Finnerty, Seligmann, and Evans for lack of evidence. He did not, however, dismiss the sexual-assault or kidnapping charges.[89]

On December 28, the North Carolina State Bar filed ethics charges against Nifong stemming from his March-and-April media bonanza. The Bar's complaint alleged that Nifong's extrajudicial statements prejudiced the administration of justice and in some cases were fraudulent, dishonest, and deceitful. In particular, the complaint focused on Nifong's statement to the media that Mangum's rapists may have used condoms when in fact she had told the police that no condoms had been used.[90]

On January 10, 2007, Nifong hired an attorney to represent him in the Bar proceedings. Two days later, Nifong bowed out of the lacrosse case and asked the attorney general to take over.[91]

Attorney General Roy Cooper appointed two of his senior prosecutors, James Coman and Mary Winstead, to start the investigation anew. Their approach was comprehensive; among other things, the two met with defense attorneys to review the evidence they had collected, talked to seventeen lacrosse players who had attended the party, and reviewed all of the medical evidence. Coman and Winstead also interviewed Mangum; she told them that she had been raped while suspended in midair, and that after the rape ten other lacrosse players assaulted her in the backyard of the cocaptains' house. At a follow-up interview, Mangum showed up impaired on prescription drugs and was incoherent.[92]

Attorney General Cooper announced the findings of Coman and Winstead's investigation on April 11, 2007, noting that "there [was] insufficient evidence to proceed on any of the charges. Today we are filing notices of dismissal for all charges against Reade Seligmann, Collin Finnerty, and David Evans." Cooper concluded:

---

89. *Id.* at 316; YAEGER, *supra* note 1, at 308; Barstow & Wilson, *supra* note 44, at A1; Duff Wilson, *Duke Accuser Contradicts Herself and Say 2, Not 3, Attacked Her*, N.Y. TIMES, Jan. 12, 2007, at A1.

90. TAYLOR & JOHNSON, *supra* note 1, at 321; Rick Lyman & Joe Drape, *Duke Players Practice While Scrutiny Builds*, N.Y. TIMES, Mar. 30, 2006, at D1; Wilson & Glater, *supra* note 41, at A13; David Barstow & Duff Wilson, *Prosecutor in Duke Sexual Assault Case Faces Ethics Complaint from State Bar*, N.Y. TIMES, Dec. 29, 2006, at A22.

91. TAYLOR & JOHNSON, *supra* note 1, at 328; Wilson & Barstow, *supra* note 87, at A1.

92. TAYLOR & JOHNSON, *supra* note 1, at 328, 348–50; Duff Wilson, *Attorney General in North Carolina Agrees to Take Duke Case*, N.Y. TIMES, Jan. 14, 2007, at 120; Wilson, *supra* note 44, at A14.

We believe that these cases were the result of a tragic rush to accuse and a failure to verify serious allegations. Based on the significant inconsistencies between the evidence and the various accounts given by the accusing witness, we believe these three individuals are innocent of these charges.[93]

Epilogue

The Bar later amended its complaint against Nifong to include violations stemming from his agreement with Meehan to intentionally withhold the exculpatory DNA evidence from the defense. The Bar also alleged that Nifong had lied to the court about his conversations with Meehan, and to the Bar in responding to the complaint. After a five-day hearing on the various charges against him, Nifong was disbarred on July 10.[94] He also served one day in jail for contempt of court.

Duke reinstated its lacrosse team in the fall of 2006. In its first season back, Duke reached the NCAA finals.[95] In June 2007, the school reached a financial settlement of undisclosed amounts with each of the accused players and Coach Pressler.

The Duke case has spawned a multitude of lawsuits. In October 2007, Finnerty, Seligmann, and Evans filed a civil action against Nifong, the investigating police officers, the City of Durham, the Durham District Attorney's Office, and the Durham Police Department; they seek damages for Nifong's false prosecution and defamation.[96] That same month, Pressler sued Duke, claiming the university had violated their earlier settlement by publically criticizing him.[97] Finally, in February 2008, 38 members of the 2005 Duke lacrosse team (not including Finnerty, Seligmann, or Evans) filed a lawsuit against Duke, several university

---

93. TAYLOR & JOHNSON, *supra* note 1, at 351–52; Duff Wilson & David Barstow, *Duke Prosecutor Throws Out Case Against Players*, N.Y. TIMES, Apr. 12, 2007, at A1; Wilson, *supra* note 44, at A14.

94. TAYLOR & JOHNSON, *supra* note 1, at 330–31; Duff Wilson, *Duke Prosecutor Denies Ethics Violations*, N.Y. TIMES, Mar. 1, 2007, at A15; Duff Wilson, *Ethics Hearing for Duke Prosecutor*, N.Y. TIMES, Jun. 13, 2007, at A14; *Durham Prosecutor Misses Hearing*, N.Y. TIMES, Jun. 29, 2007, at A20.

95. Pete Thamel, *Duke Ends Comeback Season Just Short of Title*, N.Y. TIMES, May 29, 2007, at D1.

96. *Former Duke Lacrosse Coach Files Lawsuit Against* University, FOXNEWS.COM, Oct. 13, 2007, http://www.foxnews.com/story/0,2933,301539,00.html.

97. *Id.*

officials, and the City of Durham claiming fraud, abuse, and breach of duty.[98]
As of this writing, all of these cases are still pending.

---

98. *Duke Lacrosse Players Seek Damages in Federal Lawsuit*, USAToday.com, Feb. 21, 2008, http://www.usatoday.com/sports/college/lacrosse/2008-02-21-duke-lawsuit_N.htm.

PART TWO

Lessons Learned about College Campuses

CHAPTER TWO

Faculty Reactions, Contentious Debate, and Academic Freedom

Robert M. O'Neil

Although no group emerged unscathed from the Duke lacrosse saga, the university's faculty may well have been the most severely damaged of all campus sectors. The experience left scars and divisions among professors, academic departments, and groups of scholars that will require many years to heal, if healing is even possible. The aftermath of the scandal badly tarnished the national image of Duke's faculty; a detailed report in the CHRONICLE OF HIGHER EDUCATION noted that "as the case has dragged on, the spotlight has shifted from rowdy jocks to outspoken professors," adding that "countless columnists, talk-show hosts and bloggers have used the incident as an opportunity to lambaste professors at the elite university."[1] Although relatively few professors departed, and clearly some of those who did leave had other reasons for moving on from Durham, the scars left by this experience run deep and will be difficult to repair. The goal of this chapter is to appraise the impact on Duke's faculty, in both individual and collective terms, of a uniquely and profoundly unsettling experience.

Duke in Context: A Singular Institution

A bit of background may be helpful. At the time of the lacrosse party, Duke was in the process of developing from what had been, a quarter-century earlier, a respected regional institution with strong Methodist ties to a major research center with international prestige. The decennial review team sent by the

---

1. Thomas Bartlett & Sara Lipka, *One Ad, 88 Professors, and No Apologies*, CHRON. HIGHER EDUC., Feb. 16, 2007.

Southern Association of College and Schools to assure continuing compliance with accrediting standards noted enthusiastically that, in the past decade, no private university in the nation had made more striking academic progress than Duke. Indeed, Duke was the first SACS member institution invited to conduct a focused self-study in preparing for its accreditation; the faculty and administration, collaborating closely in the process, chose interdisciplinary studies as the core of that introspective review. Not surprisingly, continuing accreditation was approved with flying colors. The review team's chairman, invited to meet with the Board of Trustees after filing his report, extolled Duke's achievements and its scholarly potential.[2]

Various factors contributed to such acclaim. Duke's close proximity to and membership in the Research Triangle not only offered unique opportunities for its scientists to collaborate with colleagues from the University of North Carolina-Chapel Hill and North Carolina State University in Raleigh, but also to undertake research projects in industrial laboratories—such as those of Smith Kline-Glaxo Wellcome—that had relocated to central North Carolina to tap the unique academic resources available nearby. Another key element in Duke's rapid rise to academic eminence was its English department. It had attracted an extraordinary group of scholars, most notably those identified as Deconstructionists for their iconoclastic approach to literature. Professor Frank Lentrecchia was internationally renowned for his critiques of conventional analysis, and was joined in Durham by several noted colleagues— among them the highly visible Professor Stanley Fish, who insisted he was the prototype for British novelist David Lodge's transatlantic academic entrepreneur Morris Zapp.

Duke's English department was hardly alone in its remarkable rise in stature; even conservative columnist Charlotte Allen wrote that Duke's aggressive humanities and ethnic-studies programs

> are famous throughout academia as repositories of all that is trendy and hyper-politicized in today's ivy halls—angry feminism, ethnic victimology, dense, jargon-laden analyses of capitalism and "patriarchy," and "new historicism"—a kind of upgraded Marxism that analyzes art and literature in terms of efforts by powerful social elites to brainwash everybody else.[3]

---

2. The author of this chapter chaired the 1988 Duke Southern Association Decennial Reaccrediting Team, and draws upon personal recollection in that regard.

3. Charlotte Allen, *Duke's Tenured Vigilantes: The Scandalous Rush to Judgment in the Lacrosse 'Rape' Case*, WKLY. STANDARD, Jan. 29, 2007.

Nor was such academic prominence confined to the liberal arts; by the 1990s, Duke's professional schools of medicine, law, theology, and business had made their way into almost every top-ten list.

Recruitment of minority scholars had become a special priority during the presidential terms of psychiatrist H. Keith H. Brodie and political scientist Nanerl Keohane. The results were most impressive, coming as they did during a time when most other major universities were seeking to tap the same limited pool of African-American and Hispanic professors. Pulitzer Prize-winning historian John Hope Franklin may have been the most visible of Duke's minority recruits, but he was hardly alone. During the decade from 1994 to 2004, Duke doubled the number of African-Americans on its faculty to a total of eighty, at least 3½ percent of the total roster. Recruitment of minority students had been comparably enhanced; while over 90 percent of the 1984 freshman class was white, two decades later not only were 10 percent of incoming freshmen African-American, but another 7 percent were Latino and 20 percent Asian-American, for a minority share of over one-third.[4]

During these years, Duke also achieved eminence in another area—the athletic field; more precisely, the basketball court. While competing with the Ivy League in scholarship, Duke (along with Stanford and Northwestern) also matched the major state universities when it came to sports, leaving the prestigious New England and New York institutions in the dust. Reflective of this change was then-Senator Bill Bradley's prescient prediction that "the next generation of Bill Bradley's won't go to Princeton [as he had done]—they'll go to Duke and Stanford." The Duke program managed not only to compete effectively in many sports, dominating several (notably both men's and women's basketball, where its meteoric rise and continued success were truly remarkable), but to maintain academic standards that put to shame most of its conference partners and other peers. The nearly unique concurrence of Duke's quest for academic stature and athletic prowess led to a *New Yorker* article's observation that what had emerged in Durham were really two universities, reflecting markedly different missions.[5]

We have now identified all the requisite elements for the "perfect storm" that would soon hit Durham. In December 2005, the university's president, vice presidents, and other senior officers gathered to ponder problem areas that might emerge during the coming year, and to formulate possible responses.

---

4. Karen Arenson, *Duke Grappling With Impact of Scandal on Its Reputation*, N.Y. TIMES, Apr. 7, 2006, at A16.

5. DON YAEGER & MIKE PRESSLER, IT'S NOT ABOUT THE TRUTH: THE UNTOLD STORY OF THE DUKE LACROSSE CASE AND THE LIVES IT SHATTERED 125 (2007).

Executive Vice President Tallman Trask III recalled later that "the thing we were most worried about was that something could happen in athletics." He added that while "we didn't know what or how," the group realized that "Duke athletics are on a pedestal, and the higher you climb, the faster you fall."[6]

So prophetic a sense of Duke's vulnerability would probably not have targeted men's lacrosse—although perfect foresight would have recognized that program could end up in the crosshairs for several reasons more fully developed elsewhere in this volume. An increasingly competitive Blue Devils team, with an aggressive and conscientious coach, had not quite made it to the national championship, but had steadily improved and was well within reach by the late winter of 2006. Senior administrators were acutely aware of a disturbing pattern of lacrosse-team misbehavior, mainly involving alcohol abuse. But because this was lacrosse and not basketball, or football, or even tennis, the sport was virtually unknown to most of Duke's faculty save for a handful of former players and parents of current or former team members at Duke or elsewhere.

Even lacrosse teams can and do become isolated from the rest of the university, as do most intercollegiate teams—though significantly less so at places like Duke than at "football factories" where athletes are routinely assigned to completely separate living, dining, and study areas and thus have little interaction with their nonathlete classmates. Durham, though, was experiencing a growing estrangement between classroom and playing field; as authors Stuart Taylor and KC Johnson later observed, "the emphasis on sports gave many Duke professors a sense of shame about their university."[7] Here, clearly, was a prime ingredient in the perfect storm that was brewing in Durham.

Such ambivalence has been far less evident at the nation's preeminent public institutions. Faculties no less distinguished than Duke's, at state universities like Michigan, Texas, and California (both Berkeley and UCLA), have long been more comfortable as scholars coexisting with competitive and successful sports programs. Several differences, apart from the force of tradition, may help to explain this striking contrast. The sheer size and complexity of the huge top-tier state universities reduce the potential for abrasion or even open warfare over issues such as academics versus athletics. The monetary cost of subsidizing a student-athlete's tuition at Duke or Stanford far exceeds the expense for even the most selective public campus. Most of the academically prestigious state universities offer majors into which scholastically challenged athletes may retreat virtually unnoticed; since Duke offers no such options, an

---

6. *Id.*

7. STUART TAYLOR, JR.,& KC JOHNSON, UNTIL PROVEN INNOCENT: POLITICAL COR-RECTNESS AND THE SHAMEFUL INJUSTICES OF THE DUKE LACROSSE RAPE CASE 5 (2007).

athlete's failure to meet rigorous course requirements is inescapably visible. For these reasons and others, a typical Michigan or Berkeley or Texas professor is readier than his or her Duke colleague to tolerate aberrations in the athletic program. The contrast is especially pronounced with respect to those quintessentially intellectual scholars who had most recently arrived in Durham.

Early Faculty Reactions — and Responses

Within a few days of the initial publicity about the alleged rape and consequent accusations against the men's lacrosse team, faculty reaction erupted in certain quarters. Because the early reports described callous abuse of an African-American woman by white, male athletes, indignation from Duke's minority faculty was both foreseeable and understandable. Less predictable, however, was the intensity and tone of that critique. One of the earliest, and clearly the most widely publicized, responses was that of English and African-American Studies Professor Houston Baker, who sent and publicly released a letter to provost Peter Lange, which demanded the "immediate dismissal" of the lacrosse team and its coach. The letter asked, rhetorically: "How many more people of color must fall victim to violent white, male, athletic privilege?" Baker went on to elaborate the basis for his concerns:

> How is a Duke community citizen to respond to such a national embarrassment from under the cloud of a 'culture of silence' that seeks to protect white, male, athletic, violence? … There can be no confidence in an administration that believes suspending a lacrosse season and removing pictures of Duke lacrosse players from a web page is a dutifully moral response to abhorrent sexual assault, verbal racial violence, and drunken white male privilege loosed among us.[8]

Professor Baker would soon run up the score in a different medium. Invited to appear with CNN's Nancy Grace in early April, he seemed to relish the larger platform. In response to Grace's questions, Baker invoked several of his colleagues who had spoken out at meetings in Durham in the days immediately after the news broke. Lest viewers be in doubt about his take on the charges against the lacrosse players, he declared: "[T]here's testimony to what [happened on the evening in question], albeit eyewitness testimony, but pretty good, since the news has continued to play it and the person who says he heard

---

8. DURHAM HERALD-SUN, Apr. 2, 2006, at A1.

it has stuck by his story." He added, somewhat gratuitously, that "my wife and many, many, many women ... on the campus of Duke University this evening are afraid to walk across the campus." He concluded, though, by conceding that "Duke is no different" from its peers when it came to sexual exploitation: "In tier-one, traditionally all-white universities across this country, administrators know that a culture of violence, a culture of rape, a culture of gay-bashing, a culture of racism and misogyny exist."[9]

Professor Baker's letter would soon be followed by several others, equally strident in tone and import if less widely publicized. History professor and former Dean William Chafe wrote a column for the student newspaper in which he analogized the lacrosse players to "white slave masters [who] were the initial perpetrators of sexual assault on black women," and "white men [who] portrayed black women as especially erotic...." The team's employment of a black woman from an escort service was, for him, "the latest example of the poisonous linkage of race and sex as instruments of power and control."[10] Peter Wood, a white history professor and former Harvard lacrosse player, added his lament that "lacrosse players on campus stood out for their aggression," noting from his experience with team members enrolled in his classes that "there seems to be a surliness about some lacrosse players' individual demeanor ... endemic to the violent nature of the game they played."[11]

By far the most visible faculty reaction came in an advertisement placed in Duke's student newspaper, the CHRONICLE, by eighty-eight professors—mainly those in African-American Studies and several other social-science and humanities departments. The heading declared that "We Are Listening to our Students" and posed the provocative rhetorical question, "What Does a Social Disaster Sound Like?" The ad itself contained a series of excerpts from comments and complaints of Duke students expressed at a campus forum where the faculty group had invited students to convey their concerns, and which the faculty sponsors recorded and now collected in their ad.[12]

Although the ad did not expressly accuse any lacrosse player of having sexually assaulted anyone, the tone and context strongly implied such a suspicion. The focus, however, was more on the general campus and community climate within which the issue had arisen—one which would remain oppressive "regardless of the results of the police investigation." Neither the faculty spon-

---

9. *Nancy Grace Show* (Cable News Network television broadcast Apr. 5, 2006).

10. TAYLOR & JOHNSON, *supra* note 7, at 108.

11. *Id.* at 107–8.

12. CHRONICLE (Duke University), Apr. 6, 2006.

sors nor the quoted students were named in the CHRONICLE, although readers were assured that the signatories' identities were available on request. Although the print text appeared only in a single day's paper, an electronic version remained for some time thereafter on the African-American Studies website.

Controversy over the "Group of 88" ad would have been intense under any conditions. But the level of concern was substantially heightened by the release of a later statement, signed by many of the original 88 and by other Duke professors as well. Given the steady erosion of the premises on which the lacrosse players' guilt had been based at the time of the original ad, many in the Duke community expected any sequel to include, at the very least, a substantial recantation. The second letter did slightly qualify the 88's original position, stating that "we do not endorse every demonstration that took place at the time." It also sought to provide a broader and less passionate context for the Group of 88 ad, insisting that the earlier text had been distorted and misunderstood. Basically, however, the sponsors declined to apologize or retract, and essentially reaffirmed the position they had advanced nine months earlier.[13]

Several serious misgivings about the Group of 88 and their CHRONICLE ad would soon emerge. Perhaps of gravest concern was the absence of any reliable or even credible information about the alleged offense at the time the ad was written and published, leading critics to charge that the authors had "rushed to judgment," seemingly inferring the guilt of some or all of the lacrosse players from rumors that would eventually prove wholly incorrect. The ad's authors and other critics had also made tenuous assumptions about the demography of the team; all but one of the players were indisputably white, and some did indeed come from affluent suburbs, but the intimation that two sons of New York City firemen and others of modest background were "privileged" was at best unfair and at worst inflammatory.[14] Perhaps most serious among the charges against the Group of 88 was a claim that attracted increasing support as the case against the players unraveled: that their early and strident condemnation of the lacrosse team had somehow "enabled" both a runaway prosecutor and scandal-hungry news media.[15] The fact that one could never have established the causal link necessary to validate such a charge did not, however, place this issue wholly beyond consideration.

---

13. Jane Stancill, *Duke Post Seeks to Defuse "88" Ad*, NEWS & OBSERVER (Raleigh, N.C.), Jan. 17, 2007, at A1.

14. *See Special Report/Duke Lacrosse*, SPORTS ILLUSTRATED, June 26, 2006, at 75.

15. Allen, *supra* note 3.

Possible Academic-Freedom Issues

A broader response to these faculty charges now merits closer scrutiny in the context of academic freedom and free expression. There have been serious suggestions, for example, that the Group of 88 and other Duke professors who "rushed to judgment" should be "held accountable," perhaps by being "formally reprimanded." It has even been posited that the Group of 88 should have been charged with violating a provision of Duke's faculty handbook, which declares that, since professors expect their students "to meet high standards of performance and behavior," reciprocity makes it "appropriate … that the faculty adheres to comparably high standards in dealing with students." Given such suggestions, a brief appraisal of possible sanctions seems fitting.

For starters, faculty who teach at a private or independent university like Duke clearly enjoy First Amendment freedoms as citizens when dealing with the government, but may claim no comparable protection against their employer. Thus, even senior scientists working for private companies in Research Triangle laboratories could be disciplined, or even fired, for violating corporate policy on such sensitive matters as publicly faulting a superior or venting grievances against management. Most of Duke's employees could be similarly constrained with relative impunity. But a professor, whether teaching at a state or an independent institution, enjoys the unique protection of academic freedom, and is thus free to make certain statements or engage in expressive activity that elsewhere would be subject to official reprisal. Yet academic freedom has its limitations, three of which might conceivably affect the resolution of any potential charges against the Duke 88 and other early and outspoken critics of the lacrosse team.

The most basic Statement on Academic Freedom and Tenure—issued in 1940 by the American Association of University Professors and later endorsed by every learned society and virtually all reputable colleges and universities— guarantees that university teachers "should be free from institutional censorship or discipline" when they speak or write as citizens. Several caveats follow, however. For one, professors "should make every effort to indicate that they are not speaking for the institution." A later refinement obligates professors to "avoid creating the impression of speaking or acting for their college or university."[16] Therein lies one possible concern about the Group of 88 and their ad. Former Duke lacrosse coach Mike Pressler and his co-author suggest in their poignant account of Pressler's experience that, although the names of the

---

16. Am. Ass'n of Univ. Professors, Policy Documents & Reports 4 (9th ed. 2001).

individual signers were available on request, "the implication in thanking various departments was that the endorsement was a departmentally backed, and, therefore, university-sanctioned action—something that was never the case."[17]

This is not a trivial issue, as one other recent and highly publicized event demonstrates. When Palestinian-born computer-science professor Sami al-Arian appeared soon after the September 11 terrorist attacks on Fox News' *The O'Reilly Factor*, his association with a jihadist organization and his admission of having more than once urged "Death to Israel" brought a torrent of angry protest to the President of the University of South Florida, where he held a tenured position. Soon thereafter al-Arian was suspended and barred from the campus—not for what he had said or for whom he raised money, but for having implied that he was speaking for his university by allowing himself to be listed on the Fox screen as a member of its faculty. That issue was eventually superseded by other and far graver charges: al-Arian was federally indicted on counts of "aiding and abetting terrorist activity." Thus, the "speaking for the institution" issue was never fully addressed. Had there been a careful review of that charge, however, al-Arian would surely have been absolved; a guest being taped from a remote location for later broadcast seldom has the opportunity to influence what viewers will eventually see on the screen, even to correct a blatant misspelling of his or her name.[18]

With that in mind, let's turn back to the Group of 88 and the implications of their CHRONICLE ad. A charge of "purporting to speak for the institution" would seem rather far-fetched in this setting. Nothing in the ad expressly claimed or even strongly implied departmental (much less university) endorsement. Even a casual reading of the text would have belied any such nexus, given the critical tenor of the statements. The sheer number of signers and cosponsors would further undermine any attempt to claim that any of the involved faculty (much less the entire group) were somehow seeking to deceive the CHRONICLE's readers into believing that their academic departments endorsed the ad's critique. So, when scrutinized, the suggestion that the 88 had violated the canon on "speaking for the institution" seems untenable.

Less readily dismissible is a second basic provision of AAUP policy: When professors speak and write as citizens, "they should at all times be accurate, should exercise appropriate restraint, [and] should show respect for the opinions of others."[19] At face value, this canon might seem to pose problems for those

---

17. YAEGER & PRESSLER, *supra* note 101, at 122.

18. *See Academic Freedom and Tenure: The University of South Florida*, ACADEME, May–June 2003, at 59–73.

19. AMERICAN ASSOCIATION OF UNIVERSITY PROFESSORS, *supra* note 19, at 4.

Duke professors who forcefully and visibly spoke out soon after the allegations surfaced. Those critics undoubtedly implied certain conclusions about guilt without the benefit of careful analysis, and thus could fairly be charged with having "rushed to judgment." Could such a sweeping and uncritical inference, without more, sustain a charge of irresponsible or untenable extramural utterance? So it might appear if one consulted only the original text of the policy. But that policy was substantially qualified after the University of California Board of Regents cynically distorted it in the case of UCLA Professor Angela Davis, twisting a seemingly innocuous standard to justify the dismissal of a young scholar whose only sin was outspoken opposition to racism and the Vietnam War.[20]

The current version of this policy (as revised in 1970) declares that "a faculty member's expression of opinion as a citizen cannot constitute grounds for dismissal unless it clearly demonstrates the faculty member's unfitness for his or her position.... Moreover, a final decision should take into account the faculty member's entire record as a teacher and scholar."[21] A conscientious application of this mandate to the Group of 88 and their CHRONICLE ad, or to letters from Professor Baker and other early critics, leads to the conclusion that such statements might be deemed less-than-fully responsible, perhaps not even befitting a Duke professor's stature, but they still fall well short of providing cause for dismissal or any other major sanction. "Rushing to judgment" may depart from the highest expectations of university scholarship, but does not diverge so far as to forfeit membership in the community of scholars.

Before leaving this topic, however, we should probe one issue a bit more deeply. Should the standards that apply to the writings of a physicist be identical to those that govern the extramural speech of a sociologist? Although no AAUP policy speaks directly to this intriguing question, experience offers modest guidance, particularly the case of Northwestern University Engineering Professor Arthur Butz. For over two decades, Butz has publicly insisted that the Holocaust never happened—that six-million European Jews somehow took their own lives or suffered some mysterious malady in the 1930s and early 1940s. That is the central thesis of his widely circulated book "Hoax of the Twentieth Century," and is featured prominently on his university website.

Northwestern steadfastly refuses to curb or silence Butz so long as he continues to fulfill his professorial duties and keeps Holocaust-denial out of his

---

20. The AAUP viewed the Regents' action to be so egregious (and a perversion of the "extramural utterances" policy) that the Davis case remains the one and only censure action voted not against the administration but, uniquely, against the governing board.

21. *See* AMERICAN ASSOCIATION OF UNIVERSITY PROFESSORS, *supra* note 19 at 32.

classes.[22] But suppose his discipline were modern European History. The conventional wisdom is that, rather like a geographer who insists that the earth's surface is flat (a heresy that would be tolerated from teachers in any other field), so clearly erroneous a view within one's own academic discipline would not and need not be tolerated. Thus the persistently Holocaust-denying European historian, like the persistently flat-earth geographer, could be charged (given proper procedures and due process) with a lack of the requisite "fitness" in his or her chosen field—in short, with demonstrated incompetence.

We now return again to Duke's Group of 88. Suppose the signers of the ad had included a professor of criminal justice, identified as such. In that field, as in history or geography, the academy expects substantially greater care and accuracy by an acknowledged expert than it expects from the general run of citizens, academics as much as lay people. Thus, had an expert in the very specialty that was the subject of this extramural statement been a member of the group that "rushed to judgment" under conditions where even a beginning student would know such prejudgment was unacceptable, the situation might have called for closer scrutiny. To be sure, even an expert might be excused a single outburst, while a pattern of persistent heresy need not be tolerated. But the issue seems moot here in any event, since the Group of 88 seems to have included no one with the requisite expertise. Significantly, none of Duke's law faculty signed the statement or made intemperate public remarks. Moreover, we should bear in mind that none of the suspect statements or letters expressly accused anyone of rape or sexual assault, but focused instead on the campus climate within which the issue arose. Therefore, even the "higher expectations" concept as applied to an academic expert turns out to have no direct application to the Duke lacrosse saga, although it does generate a cautionary tale.

The Administration Responds—Overreaction?

We now turn to the other side of the coin: the administrative response to such charges and accusations as those that bedeviled the Duke campus in the days after the news broke. President Richard Brodhead repeatedly declined to decry, or even publicly criticize, his outspoken colleagues. In an interview many months later, he explained: "Faculty members do not, and should not, speak for my approval. I was careful not to make any statements that could make it seem like I was on one person's side rather than another, or to say

---

22. *See* Jodi Cohen, *NU Rips Holocaust Denial; President Calls Prof. an Embarrassment but Plans no Penalty*, Chi. Trib., Feb. 7, 2006, at 1.

'Watch out when you engage in free speech, because the president is watching.' "[23] In a similar vein, Brodhead later confirmed his belief that "the president of the university's role is to protect the space of discourse, not to advance his particular views," adding that "whenever the president speaks, it's read as an exercise of authority."[24]

Finally, in the fall of 2007, Brodhead would offer the University's first apology for his administration's failure to support the accused lacrosse players fully, and in the process he would—also for the first time—slightly temper his hitherto neutral view of his outspoken faculty colleagues. Some Duke professors, he observed, had made public statements that were "ill-judged and divisive." He added that, in retrospect, the University should have taken bolder steps to make clear that those who made such public statements were speaking only for themselves and not for the faculty as a whole, much less for the institution.[25]

Substantially less restrained, however, was Duke's Provost, Professor Peter Lange, who took on at least one of his outspoken colleagues early in the saga. Perhaps in part because Baker's volatile letter was addressed to him (though it was simultaneously released to the campus and the public), Provost Lange responded immediately, using strong language that left little doubt about his views of the critique. Faulting Baker for "prejudgment," Lange wrote

> I cannot tell you how disappointed, saddened and appalled I was to receive this letter from you. A form of prejudice—one felt so often by minorities whether they be African-American, Jewish or other— is the act of prejudgment: to presume that one knows something 'must' have been done by or done to someone because of his or her race, religion, or other characteristic.[26]

In a further implicit rebuke, Lange assured Baker that "we will not rush to judgment nor will we take precipitous actions ... playing to the crowd."[27] Several weeks later, fifteen of Professor Baker's African-American colleagues at

---

23. Rob Copeland, *Duke President Goes on the Record*, CHRONICLE (Duke University), Jan. 22, 2007.

24. TAYLOR & JOHNSON, *supra* note 7, at 117.

25. Jane Stancill & Anne Blythe, *Duke Leader Apologizes in Lacrosse Case*, NEWS & OBSERVER (RALEIGH, N.C.), Sept. 30, 2007.

26. *VU Professor Was Duke Lacrosse Critic*, NASHVILLE TENNESSEAN, Jan. 8, 2007, at 1B.

27. TAYLOR & JOHNSON, *supra* note 7, at 137.

other institutions wrote to Provost Lange, chastising him for "assum[ing] a lofty and condescending position of White authority."[28]

This last counterstatement seems to have terminated the exchange, but hardly mooted the issue. In fact, the question of how far an administrator may go in distancing himself from, or publicly reproving the explosive views of a faculty member, remains a matter of intense interest and conjecture. Each time Professor Arthur Butz publicly reaffirms his denial of the Holocaust, Northwestern's President responds in the strongest possible terms—most recently declaring that "his reprehensible opinions on this issue are an embarrassment to Northwestern." Other presidents and chancellors have used comparably strong language to distance themselves and their institutions from the contentious views of outspoken colleagues. There are, however, two cautions worth noting.

Columbia University President Lee Bollinger (a prominent First Amendment expert) responded to news of a young anthropologist's remark at a teach-in that he "wished for a million Mogadishus" (referencing the tragic events portrayed in the book *Black Hawk Down*) by stating that he was "shocked" and believed "this one had crossed the line [so] I really feel the need to say something." Since the speaker was untenured, some observers felt the presidential condemnation was more than simply a personal statement and went beyond the need to divorce institution and viewpoint. Such a rebuke from the head of the institution, complained one critic, could "intimidate any faculty from speaking with similar positions."[29]

An actual court case suggests further limits to the scope of institutional disclaimers. When Professor Michael Levin, a philosopher at the City College of New York, noted in an obscure foreign journal his endorsement of certain supposed negative correlations between race and intelligence, President Bernard Harleston launched an inquiry into the full range of Levin's writings. At the close of the charge to the inquiry process—almost as an afterthought—Harleston observed that "these views simply have no place here at City College." Although Professor Levin had long been tenured, and thus could not be dismissed without elaborate process and proof of "cause," a federal court ruled that Harleston's statement abridged Levin's academic freedom and right to free speech by posing an implicit threat to the security of his teaching position.[30]

---

28. Paul Bonner, *Six Black Professors Departing from Duke*, Durham Herald-Sun, June 13, 2006, at A1.

29. *See* Robert O'Neil, Academic Freedom in the Wired World 81–83 (2008).

30. Levin v. Harleston, 966 F.2d 85 (2d Cir. 1992).

Obviously nothing in Provost Lange's rebuke to Professor Baker even approached, much less crossed, such lines. The Provost's critical response did not imply any threat to job security, nor could it have been viewed as intimidating. Instead, Lange's reply conveyed one scholar's deep disappointment with the public statements of a valued and respected colleague—perhaps combined with an appeal to other faculty members to reflect carefully before joining the fray. Despite the intensity of Lange's language—not simply "disappointed" and "saddened," but "appalled"—such a harsh and candid critique by a senior administrator would seldom be seen as abridging academic freedom or free speech—especially in the charged atmosphere that prevailed in Durham in the early spring of 2006.

Dissonant (and Uncollegial) Voices within Duke's Faculty

Although relations among Duke professors during this ordeal were generally civil and cordial, a few exchanges might have seemed less than fully collegial. In the fall of 2006, for example, chemistry professor Steven Baldwin sent a letter to the Chronicle in which he denounced some faculty colleagues—particularly the Group of 88—for their "shameful" treatment of the accused lacrosse players who, he lamented, had been "pilloried by their faculty and scorned by the administration." He wrote that his vocal colleagues "who publicly savaged the character and reputations of specific men's lacrosse players ... [should be] tarred and feathered, ridden out of town on a rail, and removed from the academy."[31] In an interview that soon followed, Baldwin specifically charged that the 88 and their supporters had "enabled" District Attorney Nifong, because "he could say, 'Here's a significant portion of the arts-and-sciences faculty who feel this way, so I can go after these kids because these faculty agree with me.' It was a mutual attitude."[32]

Notably, Baldwin's letter was in fact the first dissenting voice heard from anywhere in the arts-and-sciences faculty—a silence that, in Taylor's and Johnson's view, "created the impression that Duke professors en masse condemned the lacrosse players."[33] There would be a few other faculty statements in a similar vein. Engineering professor Michael Gustafson, for example, wrote of the

---

31. Bartlett & Lipka, *supra* note 1.
32. Allen, *supra* note 3.
33. Taylor & Johnson, *supra* note 7, at 105.

Group of 88 and their proclamation that "we have removed any safeguards we've learned against stereotyping, against judging people by the color of their skin or the (perceived) content of their wallet, against acting on hearsay and innuendo and misdirection and falsehoods."[34]

Far subtler than the Baldwin and Gustafson salvos was a letter published in a local newspaper at the start of the 2007 spring semester, signed by nineteen members of Duke's economics department. They began by noting that the ad placed by the Group of 88 appeared to be "the only collective signed statement by faculty members concerning [the lacrosse situation]." Remarking that "the advertisement [had been] cited as prejudicial to the defendants, the economists expressed their "regret that the Duke faculty is now seen as prejudiced against certain of its own students." The letter specifically supported President Brodhead's recent call for an external investigation of law-enforcement actions that were "inimical to students at our university." Then came the clincher: "We welcome all members of the lacrosse team, and all student athletes, as we do all our students as fellow members of the Duke community, to the classes we teach and the activities we sponsor."[35] This closing invitation might have been seen as sending the message that student-athletes who now felt less welcome in certain humanities courses (especially those taught by members of the Group of 88) should know they would be quite welcome studying the "dismal science."

The nineteen economists were certainly not the first Duke professors to reach out to the lacrosse team. Business instructor Sam Veraldi recognized soon after the first accusations became public that four lacrosse players were enrolled in his course. He quietly asked them each week for updates about the case, offered them encouragement, and even volunteered his home as a safe haven from campus tensions should such an escape become necessary. A visiting economics professor reached out to the six lacrosse players in her course, inviting them to meet with her should they ever seek a sympathetic ear.[36] Undoubtedly other faculty members privately conveyed similar support to the embattled student athletes.

The lurking policy question is whether Duke faculty members on either side of the debate could be viewed as having departed from the academy's appropriately high standards of collegiality. Policies of the American Association of University Professors mandate that "professors demonstrate respect for the opinions of others," and particularly that they should "be objective in their professional judgment of colleagues."[37] Indeed, public disparagement of a col-

---

34. *Id.* at 146.
35. NEWS & OBSERVER (Raleigh, N.C.), Jan. 8, 2007.
36. *See* TAYLOR & JOHNSON, *supra* note 7 at 109.
37. AM. ASS'N OF UNIV. PROFESSORS, *supra* note 19.

league's scholarship ranks high among professorial derelictions. But the type of critique that would cross this line differs dramatically from anything that occurred at Duke. Historically, violations of the collegiality standard have arisen from pronouncements by one academic that trivialize or demean the subject matter of a colleague's research program, ridicule the titles of dissertations a colleague has directed, or falsely accuse a fellow scholar of plagiarism. With the possible exception of Professor Baldwin's starkly uncollegial plea that his faculty adversaries should be removed from the academy, what seems remarkable is that such a degree of disrespect was avoided even in the heat of battle. Most Duke professors who undoubtedly held very strong views both on the lacrosse situation and on the fairness or veracity of their colleagues' views either kept such differences to themselves or expressed them beyond reach of the media.

Grading: How Strong a Faculty Prerogative?

In one very different dimension of faculty responsibility—assessment and grading of student academic work—several aberrations merit attention. During the spring semester of 2006, Instructor Clair Ashton-Jones gave one lacrosse player a low grade on an assignment because he missed a class to attend a meeting with his lawyer. When the student inquired about the grade, Ashton-Jones replied that, in her view, the lacrosse team "wasn't right," adding that she had little sympathy for them because "if you guys really were innocent, I would feel sorry for you." Apparently, the student passed the course and this incident received no further attention.

There was, however, another grading issue that would become the subject of both extensive publicity and contentious litigation. Kim Curtis, a perennially "visiting" political science professor (and Group of 88 member) who specialized in political and feminist theory, gave lacrosse player Kyle Dowd a failing grade in her course Politics and Literature. When pressed for an explanation, she attributed the grade to a month of classes Dowd had missed because of meetings with lawyers. Dowd, a senior, sought to appeal the grade, but was initially rebuffed by the administration. Because he was now several hours short of graduation, the registrar eventually agreed to accept credits he had earned at a previous institution from which he had transferred to Duke, and he received his degree with his class.

The Dowd family would not, however, let the matter rest. Several months later they filed suit against Duke University and Curtis, noting that Kyle had been passing the course before the charges went public, and that he and another lacrosse player had received the only failing grades in the class. As the next academic year was ending, Duke and the Dowds announced that they had reached a settlement under which Kyle's transcript would show a "P" for the course. Neither party admitted any liability, and both agreed not to reveal any other terms of the settlement.[38] There appear to have been no other reported grading disputes—nor is there any available account of the disposition of the other lacrosse-related failing grade in Professor Curtis' course.

Grading is obviously an extremely sensitive faculty prerogative, jealously guarded by professors and only very rarely disputed by students or administrators. Suppose, for example, Kyle Dowd had pursued an internal appeal, the administration had changed the grade, and Curtis had then complained that such intervention abridged her academic freedom. Several recent federal decisions have split sharply on precisely this issue. One court of appeals sustained the faculty member's claim, noting that "the freedom of the university professor to assign grades according to his own professional judgment is … central to the professor's teaching method," and thus fully protected by the doctrine of academic freedom.[39] On the other hand, a later ruling of another federal appeals court reached a diametrically different conclusion, recognizing the authority of a public university to compel a professor to alter a grade (or presumably to intervene for that purpose if the professor refused to make the change). In the later court's view, "because grading is pedagogic, the assignment of a grade is subsumed under the university's freedom to determine how a course shall be taught."[40]

Neither a student nor a teacher at a private university like Duke would have much, if any, legal recourse on either side of a grading dispute. In particular, a private university student could pursue only with great difficulty a legal claim against an adverse grade, unless the student could prove that a clear contractual right had been breached, or that the evaluation was not only unfair but defamatory, or that the grade reflected racial or other unlawful bias. Yet Duke's consistent record of respect for academic freedom suggests it would be loath to countermand a professor's judgment with regard to a grade. Policy on this matter is clear: AAUP Statements expressly recognize "the authority of the instructor of record to evaluate the academic performance of students enrolled

38. Sara Hebel, *Duke U. Settles Lawsuit with Former Lacrosse Player Who Alleged Grading Discrimination*, CHRON. HIGHER EDUC., May 14, 2007, http://chronicle.com/daily/2007/05/2007051407n.htm.

39. Parate v. Isibor, 868 F.2d 821 (6th Cir. 1989).

40. Brown v. Armenti, 247 F.3d 69 (3d Cir. 2001). These cases and the grading issue are discussed at length in O'NEIL, *supra* note 29, at 207–8, 219–21.

in a course" as a "direct corollary of the instructor's 'freedom in the classroom'" protected by the Association's basic 1940 Statement on Academic Freedom and Tenure.

The confusion and ambivalence that marked the Dowd-Curtis dispute thus become more understandable. On one hand, failing an otherwise satisfactory student solely for missing classes in order to confer with an attorney might seem problematic, though not a matter of blatant discrimination (like for example, penalizing a student for speaking out publicly for or against the position of the Group of 88). On the other hand, a professor should not only be able to demand faithful attendance and timely completion of assignments save for the most compelling of extenuations (such as disabling illness). The settlement that eventually resolved the Dowd-Curtis litigation thus provided a Solomonic solution to one of the most opaque of academic freedom issues.

Is There a Faculty-Student Privilege?

One other, almost technical, facet of faculty-student relationships merits brief discussion. Very early in the saga, just after all the white lacrosse players had been ordered to submit DNA samples, the team's cocaptains and coach Mike Pressler met with Athletic Director Joe Alleva, Assistant Director Chris Kennedy, and Executive Vice President Tallman Trask III. Trask and Alleva urged the players to report everything that had happened at the party. The cocaptains demurred, insisting that their attorneys had cautioned them to remain silent because anyone with whom they shared such sensitive information might be called as a witness and compelled to reveal everything he had learned. Trask then reassured the cocaptains that they could talk freely in that setting because the "faculty-student privilege" would protect the confidentiality of any such revelations. At this, the cocaptains relented and gave Trask and Alleva a detailed account of what had transpired.[41] Such well-intentioned candor might, under different conditions, have proved disastrous.

The eventual outcome of the criminal charges made moot this issue among many others. But if the charges had gone to trial, and if extensive pretrial discovery by either side had reached Trask, Alleva, or Kennedy—or Pressler, for that matter—a claim of "faculty-student privilege" would have availed little. The recipient of the cocaptains' candid accounts of events at the party would almost certainly have been forced either to breach the promised confidence,

---

41. Taylor & Johnson, *supra* note 7, at 62.

or be jailed for contempt of court if he refused to disclose what he had learned. As appealing as it sounds, "faculty-student privilege" simply does not exist.

Testimonial privileges are almost always statutory; they protect nearly all communications between attorneys and their clients. Typically, though, attorney-client privilege would not protect a confidential disclosure by a law student to a law professor; even the professor's status as an attorney would not, in itself, protect confidentiality. Attorney-client privilege would only apply in the highly unusual case in which a student actually retained his professor. So it is with a few other statutory privileges—universally between doctor and patient, usually between clergy and communicant (or "penitent"), and occasionally in other relationships such as accountant-client or (uniquely in New York State) between clinical psychologist and patient.

In other situations, even the most compelling claim of confidentiality depends on the mercy of the judge before whom the issue comes. So it is that journalists sometimes prevail in their quest to withhold the identity or the statements of a confidential source even where no "shield law" applies; judges sympathetic to the news media are occasionally willing to protect confidentiality on grounds of public policy even where neither statute nor Constitution guarantees it. Even laboratory scientists sometimes succeed in persuading courts that strong public policy should thwart efforts to compel disclosure (and inevitable disruption) of research in progress, particularly when the costs would be substantial and there is no clear proof that less intrusive methods of gathering important information would simply not avail.[42]

Because everyone knows about attorney-client, physician-patient, and priest-penitent privileges, many academics naïvely assume that faculty-student communications enjoy comparable protection. Sometimes that expectation may turn out to be sound, if the case comes before a judge whose sympathies lie with the student, the teacher, or simply with the academic enterprise. But there is little assurance that, in the event of litigation, anything would shield a troubled student's revelations to a sympathetic professor.[43] Thus law professors (who belong to one of the most clearly protected professions) routinely caution students who seem about to utter sensitive revelations that a proffered confidence may prove unshieldable in the face of discovery. Non-lawyer professors would be wise to observe comparable caution.

---

42. *See* O'NEIL, supra note 29 at 109–18.

43. *See* TAYLOR & JOHNSON, *supra* note 7, at 62 ("No such privilege is recognized by the law in North Carolina or anywhere else.").

An Embattled Faculty: Did They Deserve Better?

Within any fair assessment of the Duke faculty's role, substantial credit should be given to the many professors who quietly and willingly agreed to serve on the five committees that President Brodhead appointed within two weeks of the first adverse publicity. There is no public record of any professor refusing to serve in that capacity, even knowing the committees may well reach conclusions uncongenial to widely prevalent faculty views. The earliest group to report did, in fact, express just such dissonant findings. The faculty members serving on the Athletic Council concluded that, although the lacrosse players had abused alcohol and exhibited other "irresponsible behavior" exceeding the norm for Duke's sports program, they could not fairly be charged with a pattern of racist behavior or sexual misconduct of the type the early critics had charged. This committee specifically urged that the team be allowed to resume competition the next academic year, and that the athletics department should develop a code of conduct for all sports.

The other faculty committees continued deliberating throughout the spring and summer, with no apparent dissension. Indeed, the one defection is striking because of its novelty. Soon after President Brodhead announced the reinstatement of two of the three indicted athletes, English Professor Karla Holloway resigned in public protest from the Campus Culture Initiative steering committee. Her role was strategic; she had been instrumental in organizing the Group of 88, and had initially agreed to chair the Culture Initiative's subcommittee on race. But she now declared that she "could no longer work in good faith," viewing the readmission of the suspended players as a "breach of common trust." She elaborated the reasons for her defection: "The decision by the University to readmit the students, especially just before a critical judicial decision on the case, is a clear use of corporate power and a breach, I think, of ethical citizenship."[44] The CCI continued without Professor Holloway, identifying and proposing remedies for a number of weaknesses in campus culture.

One would be naïve to infer from this general pattern of civility and collegiality that the months following the initial charges were easy ones for most of Duke's faculty. Members of the Group of 88 were clearly the most obvious, visible targets of criticism and worse. Political-science professor Rom Coles, one of the ad's sponsors, reported that "all of us who signed that have received hundreds of hate mails and hate calls—it's an unbelievably vitriolic set of rep-

---

44. Sara Lipka, *Embattled Duke Lacrosse Players Abused Alcohol and had Little Oversight*, CHRON. HIGHER EDUC., May 12, 2006, http://chronicle.com/weekly/v52/i36/36a04401.htm.

resentations."[45] Others of the infamous 88 reported receiving demeaning, disparaging, and occasionally even threatening messages, typically in electronic form; Holloway, for example, told a reporter that she "dreads reading her e-mail now but must go through it to make sure there aren't any physical threats."[46] Professor Wahneema Lubiano, another of the group's organizers, reported that she and others of the ad's signers had received "hundreds of e-mail messages, some of which were racist, sexually explicit, or otherwise vile."[47]

Perhaps the most novel disruption of academic life came from a predictable source but in a quite unpredictable fashion. That the signers of the Group of 88 ad would provide ready fodder for Fox News' Bill O'Reilly was hardly surprising. What could not have been anticipated was that, when none of them would agree to appear on *The O'Reilly Factor*, several would be pursued and confronted by a Fox News crew already in Durham for that purpose. Professor Ronen Plesser, greeted by a Fox producer at the door of his home, insisted that "I am not interested in being interviewed on camera"—a demurrer which later that evening appeared on the show. Professor Lee Baker, also confronted at his doorway, proved either less reserved or more forthcoming: "We did not rush to judgment; we presumed they were innocent the whole time. I mean, I did." O'Reilly concluded this segment by reasserting, despite Baker's statement, that "the fact is that none of the eighty-eight teachers who signed the original ad will apologize or even explain themselves, not one." With regard to the recent readmission of the indicted lacrosse players, O'Reilly offered his own solution: "If I were those students, I wouldn't go back."[48]

Such travails invite a further question, even though no member of the Duke faculty seems ever to have raised it: Should the university have gone to greater lengths or taken additional steps to shelter or protect its professors from public obloquy and indignity? The short answer seems quite clearly negative, however one may appraise the merits of the issues that divided faculty from administration. President Brodhead avoided, for a full year and a half, even a hint in his public statements of any displeasure with his outspoken colleagues, even when they criticized university policy and at times harshly criticized his own leadership. Although Provost Lange was not similarly restrained, he spoke out only once—responding to Professor Houston Baker's letter that was ad-

---

45. David Graham, *Reinstatement of Duke Lacrosse Players Sparks Fiery Faculty Response*, CHRONICLE (Duke University), Jan. 11, 2007.

46. Jane Stancill, *Venom Has Aftereffects for Duke*, NEWS & OBSERVER (Raleigh, N.C.), Jan. 12, 2007.

47. Bartlett & Lipka, *supra* note 1.

48. *The O'Reilly Factor* (Fox News television broadcast Jan. 22, 2007).

dressed and sent to him directly. Nor was there any evidence that the provost, in so chastising his colleague, was speaking for the president or the institution; indeed his words had a strikingly personal tone.

As for the university's public-relations effort, similar neutrality seems to have been the hallmark of all official communications, even when a "pro-administration" slant would have been easy to impose. There was not the slightest hint, for example, that Duke's news office colluded with the Fox News crew to facilitate their interviews of elusive or recalcitrant signers. Thus, at the very least it seems clear that the administration did not take sides throughout this very trying experience, even though faculty-bashing probably would have played well with many alumni, parents, community leaders, and even students.

In one specific respect, the administration exceeded any conceivable preexisting obligation to safeguard the interests of its faculty. When the university reached a legal settlement in June 2007 with the three indicted (and exonerated) lacrosse players, the package included immunity for all faculty members, as well as for the institution and its administrators. Incoming Academic Council chair Paula McClain, a prominent political scientist, expressed gratitude for such protection. Though she "[didn't] know if any faculty really felt any liability," she added that "in a very litigious society, anyone can sue for anything." That last comment turned out to be prophetic; although no faculty members were named as defendants, three unindicted Duke lacrosse players did sue the university and a host of administrators in late 2007, alleging a conspiracy to deprive them of various legally protected rights and interests.[49]

Yet the broader question remains: Beyond being neutral or impartial, could the Duke administration have done more to promote or protect academic freedom and the autonomy of its faculty? Here a negative answer emerges in largely practical terms: it is quite unclear what more the administration could have done even had it wished to go an extra mile for its faculty. Had this been a public university, protecting an embattled faculty from governmental attacks would have been appropriate—as had occurred a year or two earlier across town when University of North Carolina President Molly Broad received the AAUP's highest accolade for defending the Chapel Hill faculty's freedom to select a summer reading text for incoming freshmen. But a private university incurs no such risks and its faculty needs no such public defense. In short, in both practical and philosophical terms it seems that the Duke administration did just about all it could have in this regard.

---

49. Newstex Web Blogs, Dec. 20, 2007.

Lessons Learned—and Shared

Finally, what lessons emerge from this searing experience that might assist other institutions facing comparable trauma? Apart from the uniqueness of Duke's travails, and the fervent hope that no other university will ever encounter a challenge of comparable magnitude, a detached perspective might be helpful. At the risk of seeming presumptuous or gratuitous, three specific observations seem appropriate. First, the structural relationship between faculty and athletics may significantly shape how an institution weathers such a crisis. That structure differs sharply between the Atlantic Coast Conference (of which Duke is a charter member) and others assemblies of major research universities, notably the Big Ten. Indeed, the official title of the Big Ten's governing body is the Western Conference of Faculty Representatives, reflecting the fact that it is a group of quite senior professors, including some renowned scholars who happen to care about sports. The faculty body hires and fires the commissioner, sets the standards, and governs the conference. The presidents and chancellors obviously have their say on myriad administrative and fiscal matters, but final authority has always rested and remains with a group of senior professors. One wonders whether events at Duke might have unfolded differently had a similar conference structure prevailed in the ACC.

Second, at the campus level, the relationship between athletics and academics also differs sharply by region and conference. At Indiana University-Bloomington, for example, the chair of the Faculty Council Committee on Athletics—always a different person from IU's Big Ten Faculty Representative—insisted on reporting regularly to the council on various facets of the intercollegiate sports program, even when his or her colleagues showed minimal interest in such briefings. Thus whenever questions arose in the 1970s and 80s about any aspect of Coach Bob Knight's triumphant men's basketball program (and they arose frequently), there was always a campus-wide faculty forum at which those concerns could be candidly aired. (The undoubted absence of comparable concerns in connection with basketball at Duke reflects credit to Coach Mike Krzyzewski rather than to the relationship between Duke's faculty and its athletic program.) Had such a forum existed at Duke for the faculty to explore the mounting uneasiness with the men's lacrosse program, the entire incident might have been avoided.

Finally, a very different dynamic merits closer scrutiny. The faculties of most universities have as little contact as possible with such campus offices as the university attorney, news or public relations, campus police, and student affairs. Yet in the aftermath of the tragic events of September 11, 2001, feelings about such ties seem to have begun a subtle shift. When the AAUP Special Committee was preparing its report on Academic Freedom and National Security in Time of Crisis, an early draft recommended substantially closer links between faculty leaders and such historically remote or even disparaged support services. To the chairman's amazement, not a single voice from the Special Committee or from elsewhere within the organization that safeguards academic freedom urged deletion or even de-emphasis of that recommendation. Thus the final report, released two years to the day after the terrorist attacks, strongly urges faculties to look kindly upon such heretofore alien campus offices.[50] Presumably, the next generation of Duke faculty will also see merit in developing closer ties with the lawyers, security officers, and student personnel administrators whose roles could again become critical at a time of testing and tension such as the traumatic spring of 2006.

---

50. *Academic Freedom and National Security in a Time of Crisis: A Report of the AAUP's Special Committee*, ACADEME, Nov.–Dec. 2003, at 26.

CHAPTER THREE

The Town-Gown Relationship

Sharon Rush

No doubt about it. Dave Evans, Reade Seligmann, Collin Finnerty, and other members of the Duke lacrosse team did not deserve to be falsely accused of raping Crystal Mangum. Nor did they deserve the concomitant maligning of their characters by several media sources, some of their professors, and especially prosecutor Mike Nifong. Evans, Seligmann, and Finnerty were presumed to be rapists, which is abhorrent in and of itself, but the case also is replete with presumptions held by many people that the men also were racially motivated. Assaulting a white person's dignity by the mere suggestion that he or she is racist inflicts its own, and often very deep, damage and hurt.

This next assertion is less clear, although there should be no doubt about this, either: Crystal Mangum did not deserve the maligning of her character by some of the partygoers or by many others who recounted what happened that night in Durham when things went horribly wrong. Among other concerns, she was presumed to be a sex object; that is, a less-worthy human being compared to the lacrosse players. Even though she lied about events that evening, particularly the rape, it is worth exploring the damaging and hurtful assaults made on her dignity in the process of exposing those lies.

Accordingly, this chapter explores the role of dignity in this case. The concept of dignity has many meanings, three of which are the focus of this chapter.[1] First, and least obviously, the idea of dignity includes notions of social status. Specifically, one dictionary's archaic definition of dignity is "a person of high rank or title."[2] *Black's Law Dictionary* defines it as "[t]he state of being

---

1. *See generally* Christopher A. Bracey, *Dignity in Race Jurisprudence*, 7 U. Pa. J. Const. L. 669 (2005). Professor Bracey distinguishes between first- and second-order dignity. First-order dignity focuses on the individual "and is perhaps best understood as a sense of perspective on self-worth." *Id.* at 679. Second-order dignity "operate[s] at the level of community." *Id.* at 680.

2. Random House Dictionary of the English Language 553 (2d ed. 1987).

noble."[3] Ironically, even the title of "Duke" reflected an individual's social dignity. Moreover, the idea of social dignity existed in the Middle Ages, when the concept of town-gown relations came to define the hierarchy between residents of a college town and members of the college community. European university students wore gowns similar to those of the clergy to symbolize their distinct status as students and, correlatively, their status as superior to the working class; that is, the town community.[4] The role that social dignity played in the Duke case cannot be overstated.

From a different perspective, dignity inheres in each individual simply by virtue of being human. An individual cannot choose to abandon his or her "inherent dignity" and neither can the government or anyone else take it away. In fact, the law often is interpreted in particular ways for the purpose of protecting an individual's inherent dignity. For example, in holding that the death penalty as applied to juveniles violates the ban on cruel and unusual punishment, the Supreme Court stated, "By protecting even those convicted of heinous crimes, the Eighth Amendment reaffirms the duty of the government to respect the *dignity* of all persons."[5] Significantly and emphatically, each individual possesses an inherent dignity that transcends all identity characteristics, including class, race, and gender. Issues of inherent dignity also shaped the dynamics of this case.

Finally, and most obviously, each person has a sense of individual dignity with respect to the way he or she chooses to behave. For example, it is common to think of someone acting in a "dignified" or an "undignified" manner. This understanding of dignity gives individuals some control over how others will interpret their behavior. Much of this case is about conduct dignity.

The different understandings of dignity are inextricably intertwined in this case because it took place in an environment that has a long history of strained town-gown relationships. At the time, the Durham income per capita was $23,000—far less than the $41,000 a student paid in annual tuition to attend Duke.[6] Moreover, the relationship between Duke and Durham is as much if not more about race as it is about class. This is especially critical to highlight because issues of race and class are intertwined throughout society[7] and partic-

---

3. Black's Law Dictionary 468 (7th ed. 1990).

4. Town and Gown, Wikipedia, http://www.wikipedia.org/wiki/Town and gown.

5. Roper v. Simmons, 543 U.S. 551, 560 (2005) (emphasis added).

6. Stuart Taylor Jr. and KC Johnson, Until Proven Innocent: Political Correctness and the Shameful Injustices of the Duke Lacrosse Rape Case 17–18 (2007).

7. *See generally* John A. Powell, *The Race and Class Nexus: An Intersectional Perspective*, 25 Law & Ineq. 355 (2007).

ularly in this case. The idea of dignity in the context of racial justice raises complex issues worthy of exploration.

The purpose of this chapter is not to find out what really happened that evening. Rather, its purposes are much more modest. One is to expose and explore how the concept of dignity in its different meanings shaped some of the dynamics of the incident, and concomitantly, some of the responses to it by the wider community. Clearly, many individuals made poor decisions that evening and thereafter. A second purpose of this chapter is to highlight how prosecutor Mike Nifong manipulated the dignity dynamics—particularly as they pertain to race—to secure political and economic gains for himself. In the process, he did immeasurable damage to the lacrosse players, and he virtually reified the racial and economic divides between the Durham and Duke communities that define their town-gown relationship.

Town-Gown Relations

Generally: The Role of Social Dignity

To speak of the town-gown "relationship" is somewhat ironic because it is largely defined by separation and differences. The physical separation of colleges from towns originated with the creation of the first institution of higher education in Western civilization, Plato's Academy, which he located outside the walls of Athens to set it apart from the local community.[8] When universities came into existence in Europe during the Middle Ages, they lacked their own campuses, resulting in much more frequent mixing of college students and local residents. Nevertheless, the students found other ways to separate themselves from nonstudents. Sometimes they carved out special spaces for themselves—the Left Bank in Paris, for example.[9] By far the easiest way for college students to separate themselves from town residents, however, was to don an academic gown. The gown let residents know that students were unavailable to join the work force, because they were busy pursuing knowledge.

The lack of actual campuses created natural tensions between the students and residents, because they competed for the same space and were forced to interact with each other. Day-to-day relationships often were strained because

---

8. Town and Gown, *supra* note 4. His Academy existed for nine centuries before it was closed by Emperor Justinian in 529 CE. "CE" (Common Era) and "BCE" (Before the Common Era) are the secular analogues to the Christian terms "BC" and "AD."

9. *Id.*

of language differences; the students spoke Latin, "the lingua franca of me-
dieval higher education," and the local residents did not.[10] Foreign students
could be especially "threatening" to local residents because of their cultural
differences. Moreover, if local governments did not give the universities favorable treatment, the schools could always leave and settle into friendlier
towns.[11] Understandably, the residents resented the students, who enjoyed
tremendous free time and did not have to work; the students, in turn, felt entitled to their loftier social status. The archaic definition of dignity, tied to social class, aptly describes the primary sentiment behind most town-gown
relationships. Simply put, members of the gown community, especially as it
was historically established, have social dignity and members of the town community do not. This tension-filled dynamic between colleges and residents was
gradually captured by the shortened phrase, "town-gown relations."

Durham and Duke: The Role of Class and Race

In many ways, the development of the town-gown relationship between
Durham residents and Duke students followed the historical pattern. Significantly, however, some prominent business leaders wanted Methodist-affiliated
Trinity College (which became Duke in 1924) to move to Durham because
they believed that it could provide the town with much-needed resources and
generally enhance the town's reputation in the New South.[12] Similarly, John
Crowell, Trinity's president, wanted to relocate the college because it was suffering tremendous financial hardship. He was attracted to Durham because
he believed "[i]t provided the best location to study and develop solutions to
the great challenges facing America's cities."[13] Thus, in 1892, Trinity College relocated from Randolph County to the small town of East Durham.[14]

At the time of Trinity's relocation to Durham, Washington Duke and his
family had already settled into the area.[15] They were by no means a wealthy
family at the time, but eventually the family tobacco business, W. Duke, Sons,
& Co. would become quite prosperous. Duke and his sons, James and Ben-

---

10. *Id.*

11. *Id.*

12. Eric Moyen, *Town-Gown Relations on Trial*, INSIDE HIGHER ED., June 8, 2006,
http://www.insidehighered.com/vews/2006/06/08moyen.

13. *Id.*

14. Kim Koster, *Taking the Initiative*, DUKE MAG., Sept./Oct. 2001.

15. *See* ROBERT F. DURDEN, THE DUKES OF DURHAM, 1865–1929, at 15 (1975) (reporting that the family moved to Durham in 1874).

jamin, were quite philanthropic and donated money to various charities; they were particularly committed to the Methodist Church.[16] Not surprisingly, upon learning of Trinity College's dire financial needs and its desire to relocate to a town, the Dukes offered the financial incentive Trinity College needed to ensure that it would relocate to Durham and not its competitor Raleigh.[17] Over the years, the Duke family would continue to be one of Trinity's primary and most generous donors. In 1924, it established the Duke Endowment with a $40,000,000 donation and promises of more. The trustees voted unanimously to accept this gift and Trinity College officially became Duke University.[18]

At the time, of course, the working class in Durham, and especially blacks, had little to say about the decision regarding the relocation of Trinity (Duke) to Durham. Significantly, the Duke family was generous to the black community: it gave substantial donations to various churches and helped establish Lincoln Hospital to serve the black population.[19] Overall, however, race relations in that area during this time were, quite naturally, characterized by hostility because a large faction of Southern whites continued to believe in the philosophy of White Supremacy. Any mutually positive sentiments between Trinity officials and Durham business leaders did not reflect or factor in the opinion of black residents who consistently comprised approximately 40 percent of the town's inhabitants. Eventually, the black community's characterization of its relationship with Duke University would become well-known. Many who were employed by Duke referred to it as the "plantation, a nickname that seems to have stuck in the minds of many residents."[20]

As the college campus developed separately from the town, Durham also flourished as tobacco hands, textile workers, and other blue-collar laborers continued to settle in the area.[21] In 1915, a granite stone wall was erected around East Campus that dramatically demarcated Duke's boundaries and evidenced the separation between the two communities.[22] Understandably, given the inglorious history of racial injustice in the United States, particularly in that region, racial tensions between the Durham residents and Duke faculty and

---

16. *Id.* at 83.

17. *Id.*

18. *Id.* at 228–32.

19. *Id.* at 104.

20. TAYLOR & JOHNSON, *supra* note 6, at 18.

21. *See generally* DURDEN, *supra* note 15.

22. *See* Olivia Lamberth, *How Attitudes and Perceptions Can Influence Policy Changes*, at 3 (May 4, 2007) (unpublished research paper prepared for Dr. Jean O'Barr, on file with author).

students magnified the huge class divide between them. Indeed, the legal regime during the heyday of Duke's inception and primary growth spurt was the separate-but-equal doctrine, which was constitutionalized in 1896 by the Supreme Court in *Plessy v. Ferguson*,[23] and was not overruled until the Court's 1954 decision in *Brown v. Board of Education*.[24] The wall fit the historical tendency to separate colleges from towns, but, in the case of Duke and Durham, it also symbolized the philosophy of de jure segregation.

Interestingly, the gradual re-establishment of campuses separate from the towns in which they are located, harkening back to Plato's Academy, has not lessened the tensions in most town-gown relationships. Quite the opposite. It has merely entrenched the common understanding that colleges exist to educate an elite group of students who are very different from the local residents. An enduring significant difference between most town-gown communities is socioeconomic class membership. The Durham-Duke relationship fits this general pattern. For example, Duke hires about 15,000 residents of Durham in mostly unskilled jobs.[25]

Moreover, notwithstanding the progress that has been made with respect to achieving racial equality in the United States, significant inequality persists. Consequently, the racial demographics of the Durham and Duke communities are highly relevant. Forty-four percent of Durham's 210,000 residents are African American,[26] approximately 45 percent are white, less than 1 percent identify as Native American, less than 4 percent are Asian, and just under 9 percent are Hispanic.[27] In contrast, Duke's Class of 2009 numbers 1,728 students whose demographics are "53.6 percent white (compared to 57.5 last year), 21 percent Asian (16.8 percent last year), 9.5 percent African American (11.5 percent last year), 6.4 percent Latino (6 percent last year) and 0.6 percent Native American (0.1 percent last year)."[28] The 2006 lacrosse team had only one black member on a team of 47 players. Finally, 86 percent of Duke students come from out of state and, consequently, have little reason to care about the long-

---

23. 169 U.S. 537 (1896).

24. Brown v. Bd. of Educ., 347 U.S. 483 (1954) (overruling *Plessy* in the context of public-school segregation, thus marking the beginning of the end of de jure segregation throughout the United States).

25. TAYLOR & JOHNSON, *supra* note 6, at 18.

26. *Id.*

27. *See* Durham Community Q&A, http://learningtogether.duhs.duke.edu/history (last visited Mar. 7, 2008).

28. *See, e.g.,* Class of 2009 is Duke's Largest, Office of News & Communications, www.dukenews.duke.edu (last visited Feb. 29, 2008). This report indicates that Duke admitted a class of 1,728 students this year, of which 9.5 percent is African American. The numbers Duke reported for the prior year were fairly similar. *Id.*

term development of the town-gown relationship.[29] Not surprisingly, then, the town-gown relationship between Durham and Duke continues to reflect a tension associated not only with economic disparities, but also with racial divisions and memories of longstanding injustices.

Class, Race, and Assumptions about "Intelligence"

At least one other perceived difference commonly attaches to the town-gown relationship and many people also closely relate this perception to class and race. For many, if not most, people, the "real" distinguishing characteristic of the town-gown relationship is the assumed correlation between a person's class and intelligence. Members of the higher socioeconomic classes are presumed to be more intelligent, and conversely, members of the working class are presumed to be less intelligent. Consider the following observation made in a recent study:

> Stereotypes about low-SES people are quite pervasive in American culture. Television shows with "blue collar" humor depict the ways in which poor people are dirty and talk funny. Gag gifts include "trailer trash" dolls that have a cigarette dangling from their lips and multiple babies in tow. Numerous films, commercials and songs portray poor people as stupid yokels who spend all day drinking beer and shooting guns. These stereotypical images are widely held, and accepted; Jeff Foxworthy's "you might be a redneck if ..." stand-up series has been nominated for multiple Grammy awards, and is the largest selling comedy album of all time. Based on such portraits, we can draw the conclusion that the American poor are dirty, violent, inbred, lazy, unkempt, carefree hillbillies. *And, perhaps most damaging, that they are stupid.*[30]

A word of caution. My point here is not to establish whether any of the people involved in this case truly believed in negative stereotypes, including this one, about various groups.[31] Rather, my point is to explore how some per-

---

29. TAYLOR & JOHNSON, *supra* note 6, at 18.

30. Bettina Spencer & Emanuele Castano, *Social Class Is Dead. Long Live Social Class! Stereotype Threat Among Low Socioeconomic Status Individuals*, 20 SOC. JUST. RES. 418, 419 (2007) (emphasis added).

31. This would be an especially frustrating enterprise even if I wanted to accept this challenge, because many people are not aware that they might believe negative stereotypes about other people, *see, e.g.,* Charles Lawrence, *The Id, the Ego, and Equal Protection: Reckoning with Unconscious Racism*, 39 STAN. L. REV. 317 (1987), and others who might privately acknowledge that they do would never publicly admit it. *See generally* LESLIE HOUTS PICCA & JOE R. FEAGIN, TWO-FACED RACISM: WHITES IN THE BACKSTAGE AND FRONTSTAGE (2007).

sistent stereotypes seemed to have influenced this case. Moreover, the significance of this perceived correlation between class and intelligence should not be underestimated. The overlay of race on this general perception merely heightens tensions and resentments. One only needs to remember the controversial scientific assertions in *The Bell Curve*[32] that whites are inherently smarter than blacks to understand the volatility of this particular town-gown relationship. Although other credible scientists have refuted this assertion,[33] it, like most negative stereotypes, lingers.

Inherent Dignity

Notice that social dignity, although seemingly only about social class, also is inextricably tied to a person's perceived intelligence. Closely related, in the United States in particular, ingrained assumptions about inherent differences between whites and blacks (more generally, all people of color) also play critical roles in defining the dynamics of the town-gown relationship.

Specifically, the separate-but-equal doctrine is premised on White Superiority, a philosophy that attracts people who believe that blacks are inherently inferior to whites. Poignantly, the assumed inferiority of blacks during the separate-but-equal days was premised on more than just the belief that blacks were not as intelligent as whites; it was premised on the idea that blacks were not altogether human. It was their presumed lack of humanity, their presumed lack of inherent dignity, that enabled white society to enslave them and treat them like property. Sadly, modern research demonstrates that the perception among many whites that blacks are inherently inferior, partly because of their perceived lower intelligence, continues to be the most pervasive of the negative stereotypes about blacks.[34] Blacks who settled in Durham were about as far removed—both as a physical matter under the separate-but-equal doctrine,

---

32. Richard J. Herrnstein & Charles Murray, The Bell Curve: Intelligence and Class Structure in American Life (1994).

33. *See, e.g.*, Stephan Thernstrom & Abigail Thernstrom, American in Black and White: One Nation, Indivisible 353 (1997) ("The fact that African-American children, on the average, have been performing poorly on [standardized] tests does not suggest that they are deficient in innate intellectual ability. We strongly differ from Herrnstein and Murray on this point.").

34. Alexander M. Czopp & Margo J. Monteith, *Thinking Well of African Americans: Measuring Complimentary Stereotypes and Negative Prejudice*, 28 Basic & Applied Soc. Psych. 233, 236 (2006) ("Beliefs that Blacks are inherently *inferior* to Whites (i.e., they are unintelligent, lazy, and criminal) represent the most commonly recognized negative stereotypes about Blacks....").

and as a matter of white society's perception of their intelligence and basic humanity—from the Duke gown community as one could get.

The Role of Dignity

Prior to That Evening

Even before the players and Mangum met that evening, their lives occupied drastically different positions on the dignity hierarchy. Not surprisingly, the players were much closer to the top of the ladder, and Mangum was closer to the bottom of the ladder. The following exploration offers a possible perspective on how their relative positions may have influenced some of their choices. It is fair to conclude, I think, that their different positions contributed to the unhealthy ways they treated each other. Perceptions governing the dignity hierarchy also influenced the way others reacted to the situation.

The Players

The lacrosse players were profoundly imbued with social dignity. Athletes are highly revered and respected members of society. They are cloaked with immense social dignity because many Americans love sports and annually support the sports industry with billions of dollars. Within the college community, athletes often sit atop the social hierarchy. The more competitive the college's conference, the greater the national reputations of the team and its athletes are likely to be. A young college athlete has an opportunity to be a renown sports hero before he or she even leaves college.

Such are the opportunities for many Duke athletes. As a Division I school, Duke athletes play in the most competitive college division. To be a member of a Duke athletic team sets one apart, not just from the nonathlete Duke students, but also from most other college athletes. Duke athletes are an especially talented group and many of Duke's teams have consistently earned national reputations for being among the best. Lacrosse athletes clearly fall into this category.

Enhancing the Duke athlete's image as a highly respectable individual who is admired for his or her athletic prowess is the reality that Duke athletes also are admired for their academic abilities—their intelligence. Duke's admissions standards are some of the highest in the country and Duke aspires to a reputation equal to or better than the most elite colleges, such as Stanford, MIT, and the Ivies.[35] And while some members of the Duke community express con-

---

35. Taylor & Johnson, *supra* note 6, at 7.

cerns that standards might be lowered for the purpose of admitting star athletes, with respect to lacrosse, the data demonstrate "[t]hat the lacrosse players by and large compiled academic records indistinguishable from a typical group of fifty Duke nonathletes."[36]

In addition to being gifted athletes and scholars, many Duke students also enjoy high socioeconomic status. More than half of the lacrosse players fell into this category.[37] Most of them attended private high schools where lacrosse is a highly valued sport.[38] They essentially had been groomed to attend an elite academic college with an equally elite lacrosse team.

The inherent dignity of Evans, Seligmann, and Finnerty was never seriously subject to question prior to that evening. The inherent humanity of men and whites had always attached to them. In fact, by virtue of being a white person, especially a white man, an individual belongs to the dominant group that generally establishes the prevailing legal and social standards. Sometimes members of dominant groups cannot even see how their race or gender simultaneously privileges them and insulates them from discriminatory laws and negative social stereotypes.

This is not to say that people who enjoy being at the upper end of the dignity hierarchy cannot fall out of legal or social graces. The recent controversy over the use of steroids by many prominent athletes illustrates how vulnerable they can be. Generally, however, it is their own undignified conduct, choosing to use steroids, that impugns their characters. Even then, however, assaults on conduct dignity rarely, if ever, are able to pierce totally through the protective coatings of social and inherent dignity enjoyed by dominant class members. Conversely, it often seems that it is much easier for athletes of color, for example, to topple from the hierarchy. Anecdotally, it is interesting that of all of the athletes (not distributors and trainers) who have been accused of using steroids and lying about it, Marion Jones, a black mother, seems to be only one of a few, if not the only one, who is thus far serving time in prison for her illegal choices.[39]

Focusing on the lacrosse players, prior to that evening none of them, with the possible exception of Finnerty, had engaged in behavior that would seriously call their character into question. Finnerty was involved in a fight while visiting friends in Georgetown that was reported to have occurred due to

---

36. *Id.* at 6.

37. *Id.*

38. *Id.*

39. Jones began serving a six month term on March 8, 2008. She admitted to lying about her use of steroids and her involvement in a check fraud scheme. *See Jones Reports to Prison*, N.Y. Times, Mar. 8, 2008, at D1.

Finnerty's homophobia.[40] Although this claim was ultimately proven false, it would provide fodder for people who wanted to believe the worst of Finnerty following the rape allegations.

Admittedly, many Duke students, including the lacrosse players, were huge party-goers and their rowdy behavior in the neighborhoods where about 20 percent of students lived had become a major problem for Duke and its efforts to establish a healthy relationship with Durham residents. A dramatic measure Duke had undertaken to stop raucous parties and alleviate the tension between boisterous students and residents was to buy neighborhood homes and sell them to quiet families who agree not to rent them to students. Duke also decided to support the local police department's decision to crack down on the students, which meant that the police were extra vigilant in citing students for violations compared to the treatment of residents.[41]

Despite Duke's effort to create a healthier relationship with Durham, some students interpreted Duke's actions as an attempt to keep them from engaging in conduct that they believed they were entitled to engage in *because* they are a part of Duke's community. One student responded to the university's effort to quell the parties by writing in Duke's student newspaper, THE CHRONICLE

> Deans, cops, neighbors, nerds, and the shadow of the Ivy League have gradually and systematically pulled the rug out from underneath the backbone of this school's identity: fun. This is not about [Duke President] Dick Brodhead's master plan to ruin your life. This is about a change in priorities for a university stuck between a rock and a hard place without a clue as to what made my class and I want to come down South instead of going to … Harvard. Who would've wanted to spend four years at a place like this? Duke rained on our parade.[42]

This comes close to suggesting that being a member of the gown community, being someone imbued with social dignity, entitles one to ignore the town's laws. Notice that the student pushed the can-Duke-really-compete-with-Harvard? button, a major goal of Duke's.

In the final analysis, the Duke students' behavior has been judged by many to be, by and large, "normal" college behavior. Many other town-gown relationships also struggle with the "party problem." That the problem is widespread, of course, does not mean it should be excused or justified. Protected

---

40. TAYLOR & JOHNSON, *supra* note 6, at 244–48.

41. *Id.* at 22.

42. *Id.* (attributing the quote to Matt Sullivan, a graduating senior and former managing editor of THE CHRONICLE, in a May 1, 2006, article.)

by their well-established social and inherent dignity, and with their party-goer conduct dignity issues rationalized and excused, the Duke lacrosse players were fortified with all three kinds of dignity before the party ever started.

Crystal Mangum

From a social-dignity standpoint, Crystal Mangum was a member of the Durham town community where she lived with her parents and children.[43] She was far less economically privileged than many of the lacrosse players. She was employed as an exotic dancer at a local club and also performed at private parties.[44] Mangum was also taking classes at North Carolina Central University (NCCU), the local college with a student population of about 8,000, of whom about 6,600 are African American.[45]

Interestingly, however, being a member of the NCCU gown community, which existed even before Duke, did not place Mangum or any of the NCCU students in the "gown" part of the town-gown relationship that defined Durham and Duke. Many reasons might explain why membership in the NCCU community does not separate a student from the town community or, stated alternatively, admit the student into the gown community. For example, it might be due to the fact that NCCU is a local college that serves the local residents. Another reason might be because NCCU is a historically black college, founded in 1909, which went without any financial support from North Carolina until the late 1920s.[46] In other words, NCCU, like other historically black colleges, developed largely as a result of the private efforts of the black community because white society functioned under the presumption that blacks were inherently inferior to whites and should not be educated.

Indeed, NCCU and other historical black colleges were established at a time in history when a nationwide policy made it illegal to provide blacks with a formal education. Then, when the formal education of blacks within white society became legal and acceptable, society still operated under the separate-but-equal doctrine. Even if NCCU students wanted to belong to the gown community with Duke students, which seems unlikely, the line demarcating that community was drawn by *white society* at the perimeter of Duke's campus. Thus, it is not surprising that the town-gown line between Durham and

---

43. *Id.* at 19.

44. *Id.* at 20.

45. North Carolina Central University: General Information, http://www.stateuniversity.com/universities/NC/North_Carolina_Central_University (last visited Feb. 25, 2008).

46. History of North Carolina Central University, www.nccu. edu (last visited Feb. 25, 2008).

Duke is largely co-extensive with racial boundaries. The end result is that many NCCU students are more aligned in identity with the blacks who belong to the Durham town community than with their counterparts at Duke.

Evidence of this loyalty is found in the public response to this case. The NCCU community "adopted" Mangum's cause and it quickly provided a means for some black students to voice their opinions about racial injustice generally and the divide presented by the town-gown relationship in Durham and Duke specifically. One NCCU student was quoted as saying, "This isn't the first incident of racial acts with the lacrosse team, since it's a privilege sport and there's power and all that and Duke, and … the racial comments they've made to other people and things of that nature."[47] Realistically, how could the town's identity not be bound up with Mangum's and the alleged harm inflicted on her by Duke students? As a consequence of their alignment with her and the town, though, they would highlight the divide and the concomitant perception that they do not have the social dignity that attaches to being a member of the Duke community. Their loyalty also would subject them to the negative stereotype held by many individuals that NCCU students are not as intelligent as those at Duke.

The struggle for racial justice for blacks in Durham has been an ongoing battle to establish their dignity as human beings — black human beings. This struggle is one that white town community residents do not share, although they also are excluded from Duke's community from a social dignity viewpoint and also suffer from the negative stereotype about their perceived lower intelligence. Consider, for example, if a white woman had falsely accused the lacrosse players of rape, the idea of her inherent dignity being impugned by the players or by dominant society *on account of her race* would be absurd. Yet, as explored below, Mangum's bad conduct and lack of credibility were closely associated with her blackness by many people.

On the other hand, some individuals might try to impugn any woman's inherent dignity *on account of her sex*, particularly if she were an exotic dancer and stripper. Historically, women have been defined as sex objects and by many other negative stereotypes, including their supposed lower intelligence compared to men. In fact, for most of American history, many colleges would not admit women at all. Integration on the basis of gender did not occur at most elite colleges until the late 1960s and early 1970s. This attitude toward women is illustrated by the more recent example of Virginia's resistance to admitting them to its Military Institute, primarily on the belief that it would "downgrade

---

47. TAYLOR & JOHNSON, *supra* note 6, at 169.

VMI's stature, destroy the adversative system and, with it, even the school."[48] VMI's policy spawned a case before the U.S. Supreme Court. Justice Ginsburg, writing for the majority, rejected VMI's position outright and held that its assertion "is a judgment hardly proved, a prediction hardly different from other 'self-fulfilling prophec[ies]'... once routinely used to deny rights or opportunities."[49] Attending a coed college, of course, does not necessarily mean that female students escape various negative stereotypes. Even today, some Duke women express concern that the age-old double standard regarding sexual behavior still exists; that is, men gain status and women lose status through sexual activity.[50]

Imagine how relatively easy it would be for those atop the dignity hierarchy to conclude that a black woman from Durham is so different—as a matter of socioeconomic status, education, intelligence, race, and gender—from the white Duke lacrosse players that she has no social dignity and, moreover, does not deserve to have her inherent dignity even acknowledged. Given this, Mangum's low conduct dignity prior to that evening merely heightened the divide between her and the lacrosse players. Specifically, she had an arrest record, was known to have a drinking problem, was divorced, and had been discharged from the Navy because she was pregnant.[51] Most telling of all, perhaps, about her lack of conduct dignity, was her choice to be an exotic dancer, a stripper. For many people, Mangum behaved in very undignified ways on numerous occasions and in a variety of contexts. Her bad conduct and poor choices affirmed the perceptions of some observers that she was a black sex object, that is, someone not completely worthy of being called a human being.

That Evening

Understandably, what happened that evening seems to be mostly about bad conduct and poor choices on the part of almost everyone.[52] Certainly, the behavior of many of the players and Mangum was very undignified that evening. Some of the players were drunk, others were drinking illegally because they

---

48. U.S. v. Virginia, 518 U.S. 515, 542–43 (1996) (footnotes omitted).
49. *Id.*
50. TAYLOR & JOHNSON, *supra* note 6 at 3.
51. *Id.* at 19.
52. Some team members declined to participate at all, and others, including Reade Seligmann, dropped out of the activities later on because they became uncomfortable with events in ways that suggest they did have concerns about their conduct dignity, and also might have had concerns about impugning the dignity of Mangum and Roberts. *Id.* at 24–27.

were under-age, and then there was the exotic-dancer decision by the players and by Mangum. The false accusation of rape, of course, was tremendously heinous. Even if one is willing to excuse the drinking behavior as part of "normal" college culture, most reasonable people would agree that hiring a stripper is an undignified choice. They also would agree that being a stripper is an undignified profession, especially for a mother. Accordingly, it is worth exploring how the other types of dignity—social and inherent—provide an overlay to everyone's bad behavior that evening that diminished the seriousness of the players' bad conduct and, simultaneously, magnified the bad conduct of Mangum. Most significantly, in the process of this sleight of hand, so to speak, the tension in the town-gown relationship between Durham and Duke, which is marked by class and especially by race, arguably got more entrenched.

What's Race Got to Do with It?

One negative image of the players lingers even though the rape charges have been dropped. Specifically, the players, and the Duke community more generally, have been accused of being racist. Undoubtedly, some of the reason for this image of the players comes from the exchange of racial slurs between the other dancer, Kim Roberts, and Matt Zash. The exchange occurred after it was clear that the party was over, and Roberts instigated it. She admitted this on *60 Minutes*:

> I called him a little dick white boy, who probably couldn't get it on his own and had to pay for it.... So he was mad, and it ended with him calling me the N word.[53]

Roberts' message to Zash seems like an attempt to assault his dignity on all fronts—social, inherent, and conduct. She seemed to be trying to undermine his identity as a powerful white man by insulting his sexual prowess. Not surprisingly, Zash defended himself by calling her the N-word and thereby trying to demean her to the point of being less than human.

Generally, when a white person uses the N-word to describe a black person, it is interpreted as an indication that the person is racist. But that is not my purpose in pointing out this exchange, because people often say uncharacteristic things in heated moments. The exchange is important, however, as further evidence that race is a pivotal factor in this case and helped shape the dignity dynamics. It is something that everyone had on their minds. More-

---

53. *Id.* at 29.

over, several facts reveal that race dynamics specific to the town-gown relationship that were shaped long before the party started were nevertheless instrumental to setting the stage for the events that were to unfold.

Interestingly, the lacrosse players wanted to hire white strippers.[54] When the women who showed up at the house were not white, the players had to confer with each other before deciding to go ahead and hire them.[55] One can only speculate as to why they were more comfortable with or aroused by a preference for white dancers. It seems ridiculously unlikely that the players preferred white women because they have more respect for women of color and did not want to contribute to their further subordination on account of their race. Yet if the players' partiality toward white women was because they respect white women more, that also would auger in favor of the players hiring women of color because being a stripper is a very undignified job. Many reasonable people believe that a woman who chooses such a profession does so because she is lacking a sense of her own worth as a human being. Generally, men who hire women to do such demeaning jobs—like entertaining them sexually—have little respect for the inherent dignity of women regardless of race. For many of the players at the party, it was acceptable to use women as sex objects.

Some might suggest this is too harsh and the decision to hire the strippers also falls into the category of "normal" college behavior, particularly at Duke. Or, one might take the position that Mangum was fully capable of making an independent choice about her employment and that she might not have thought of her job as undignified or as evidence of her own lack of self-worth. This perspective respects her autonomy as a woman. And then there are other people who suggest that women who allow themselves to be used as sexual objects actually have little choice and suffer from false consciousness; they become strippers or prostitutes, seemingly free choices, but they desperately need the money and, perhaps due to an inadequate education or mental health issues, lack the wherewithal to obtain a dignified job.[56]

Certainly, even if one were inclined to sympathize with Mangum and her choice to be a stripper, for most people any sympathy for her evaporates once her false accusations that the players raped her enter the picture. Her behavior on that score is indefensible. On reflection, though, it also might be understandable. From her perspective on the dignity hierarchy, it might have

---

54. *Id.* at 16.

55. *Id.* at 24.

56. The arguments about whether prostitution liberates or subordinates women are explored in Catharine A. MacKinnon, Sex Equality 1240–84 (2d ed. 2007).

been her one and only way to try to impugn the players' inherent dignity in a manner that increased the odds that she could hold onto her own. It might have been a way for her to challenge the dignity hierarchy, shake things up, whatever she thought of herself.

Again, this is not offered as a way to justify her lies. But notice how even some of the players arguably fell into the same trap, that is, they also exploited the dignity dynamics and tried to hold the hierarchy in place. The most poignant example comes from Ryan McFadyen, a team member, who sent an e-mail out to a few of his friends following the allegations that can only be described as misogynist and racist even if one wants to be generous and attribute the email to his highly emotional response to her lies. The email alluded to his desire to hire more strippers the following evening and skin the "bitches" while masturbating in his Duke-issued spandex.[57] Some accounts of the e-mail suggest that it was nothing more than an oblique reference to a passage from one of the books he had read in one of his courses.[58] Notice, however, the juxtapositions McFadyen makes. He is acting from his social-dignity viewpoint because the scene is acted out in his Duke spandex. The strippers lack inherent dignity because they are likened to animals. The image of skinning the strippers like animals also has racial overtones to it, again, a sign that strippers (especially women of color) have no inherent dignity. Among other things, the content of the e-mail is an attempt to malign Mangum's dignity on all fronts in order to reinforce the dignity hierarchy that puts Mangum at the bottom and he and his teammates at the top.

It is worth emphasizing that at the heart of McFadyen's sentiment is an assumption that being a member of the Duke community, especially as an athlete (which is why his spandex is issued by Duke), entitles the team to "even the score" with Mangum and show her (and all strippers) who has the power to mete out "justice." Significantly, McFadyen's fantasy about how to restore the dignity hierarchy centers around him and his teammates engaging in the same conduct—hiring strippers—that started the whole incident that evening. On some level of consciousness, he seemed to think that his social and inherent dignity not only entitled him to publicly disrespect women and share his fantasy about skinning strippers, but he also seemed to believe that his dignity armor would protect him from the maligning of his character in reaction

---

57. TAYLOR & JOHNSON, *supra* note 6, at 139 ("[T]omorrow night, after tonights [sic] show, I've decided too [sic] have some strippers over to edens 2c. All are welcome. however there will be no nudity. I plan on killing the bitches as soon as the[y] walk in and proceeding to cut their skin off while cumming in my duke issue spandex.").

58. *Id.* at 138–39.

to his bad choices. One must wonder what, if anything, would or could tame this attitude and violent expression of entitlement and dominance?

After That Evening: Enter Mike Nifong

Maybe Prosecutor Mike Nifong thought he could "put the players in their place." As a bonus for trying, he also could win the election for District Attorney. Perhaps without being fully aware of it, by winning the election and winning the case, he also could establish his position atop the dignity hierarchy. After all, he reportedly is not fond of Duke or "Dukies," perhaps because he graduated from the University of North Carolina, although his parents are Duke alumni.[59] In any event, the Duke rape case offered him an opportunity to show everyone that you don't have to be a Duke graduate to be the top "legal beaver" in Durham. It was worth a shot.

To succeed, though, Nifong had to understand and consciously choose to exploit the dignity dynamics of the town-gown relationship. Ostensibly, his strategy seemed to focus on challenging the validity of the dignity hierarchy, which is at the core of that tension-filled dynamic. Accordingly, Nifong did not simply dismiss Mangum's allegations because of who she was and because of all the negative stereotypes that undermined the dignity and credibility of someone in her position: a local black single mother eking out a living as an exotic dancer and stripper. To Nifong's credit, Mangum's position toward the lower end of the dignity hierarchy did not render her inherently unworthy of being believed. Equally interesting, Nifong did not simply dismiss the allegations because of who the accused were and because of all of the positive stereotypes that inflated their dignity: white members of the Duke gown community lacrosse team. Their stereotyped-position toward the upper end of the dignity hierarchy did not render them ipso facto worthy of being believed, either. If anything, their prior undignified behavior temporarily weakened their reputations—although ultimately, it was judged to be normal college behavior. Avoiding an initial evaluation that would have shown that he bought into the validity of various stereotypes, Nifong gave the impression that the facts, and not any preconceived notions, would establish the truth. He would seek justice.

In some ways, Nifong's initial response—to take Mangum's allegations seriously and pursue an investigation (ostensibly) to reveal the truth—was more judicious than that of some others involved in the events, with the possible exception of Coach Mike Pressler, who always believed that the players were innocent. For example, some Duke faculty seemed to jump to the conclusion

---

59. *Id.* at 78.

that the players were guilty, and pressured Duke President Richard Brodhead to disband the team.[60] Brodhead had already incurred the wrath of many students because of his "tough" stance on student parties and his cooperation with Durham police to subdue them.[61] His primary concern seemed to be to minimize the harm to Duke, and he was angry that the lacrosse students had put the university in such a position.[62] Feeling that he had no choice—tensions were mounting between residents and students, some faculty were becoming more irate, and Finnerty's altercation in D.C. hit the news—Brodhead eventually canceled the team's season.[63]

Although Brodhead cautioned against making the lacrosse team the scapegoat for Duke's wild-party persona,[64] he ultimately chose to distance Duke from the players. His administration did not stand by them until the investigation was over. Rather, it forced the coach to resign,[65] suspended McFadyen immediately after the email became public,[66] and left the players to fend for themselves. As far as one can tell, Duke's evaluation of the situation had nothing to do with Mangum or her credibility. Reportedly, Brodhead repeatedly refused to look at exculpatory evidence that was offered to him.[67] He seemed to base his judgment of the situation primarily on the lacrosse team's record and reputation of engaging in bad conduct. From this perspective, it did not matter whether the allegations were true because the damage was already done.

Within the gown community, where social and inherent dignity are common variables, one way to distinguish among the members is through their conduct. Although Duke understandably did not want to make the town-gown divide worse, it also did not want to lose status in the elite nationwide gown community. The idea that Duke's lacrosse team had "gang-raped" a black stripper could do immeasurable damage to Duke's reputation both locally and nationally. It probably would cause Duke to lose standing to compete with Stanford, MIT, and the Ivies. Duke's response—to distance itself from the players because of their undignified behavior—not only accepted the existing hierarchy, but, ironically, reinforced it. Duke might have even believed that it had no choice

---

60. *Id.* at 63.

61. *Id.* at 131–32.

62. *Id.*

63. *Id.* at 139.

64. *Id.* at 134 ("Brodhead warned against making an example of the lacrosse players if it meant treating them more harshly than Duke had treated other students in the past for similar conduct, including hiring strippers and racial slurs.").

65. *Id.* at 141–42. He reportedly had to resign or he would have been fired.

66. *Id.* at 139.

67. *Id.* at 129–51.

but to essentially punish the team *as if* the allegations were true in order for the gown community to preserve its position in the dignity hierarchy.

Similarly, some members of the town community also rushed to judgment and concluded that the players were guilty. Members who took this position, however, had to rely on the truth of the allegations. They desperately needed Mangum to be telling the truth because she became their collective voice, crying out for racial justice. This was their chance to challenge the validity of the hierarchy and obtain some long-overdue racial justice.

Thus, for the town community, the stakes were very high because if Mangum's story turned out to be a lie it would justify, in the eyes of both the gown community and the broader national community, the ordering of the dignity hierarchy that places all town communities at the bottom of every town-gown relationship. If Mangum turned out to be a liar, then many of the negative stereotypes that attach to women, to blacks, to black women, to strippers, to poor people, to townies, would all become "true." Her bad conduct would become inextricably bound up with her social and inherent dignity, making the latter invisible and irrelevant. Closely related, because she was a member of the town community, and especially the black town community that stood up for her, its members' inherent dignity was also on the line.

Analytically, once the focus shifts to inherent and social dignity, the players' inherent and social dignity also resurfaces. At this point, their bad conduct fades away, and the hierarchy that defines the town-gown relationship between Durham and Duke becomes more tension-filled than ever. From this perspective, achieving justice, particularly racial justice in Durham, would come from the further entrenchment of the hierarchy (serves "Mangum and them" right), and not from its dislodgement (it is possible for a white Duke athlete to violate a black women's inherent dignity by raping her). This would be an enormous price for the town community to pay.

Nifong understood these dynamics so well that he was able to exploit them for his personal gain.[68] Pivotally, he decided that he needed to win the election for District Attorney, partly because he wanted the job to secure his pension.[69] Probably no one takes issue with the legitimacy of that motive. *How* he ensured he would win the election, however, is quite problematic because, among other consequences, his exploitive conduct to secure his own personal agenda corrupted the political process, did immense damage to the players,

---

68. Nifong also had input from other officials who seemed to conduct their investigation in ways that were highly prejudicial to the players, reflecting an animosity toward Duke. *See generally id.* at 36–76.

69. *Id.* at 82.

and also played perhaps irrevocable havoc with the—already racially charged—town-gown relationship.

How did Nifong manipulate the dignity dynamics to meet his personal goals? First, he had to make sure that he won the election and to do that, he needed the town's black residents' support. Prior to the allegations, their votes seemed to be going to Keith Bishop, a black candidate. Moreover, Bishop was in a tight race with Freda Black, a white attorney who was a personal rival of Nifong's because he had fired her from a position in the District Attorney's office. If she became the new District Attorney, he feared she would do the same to him.[70]

The emergence of the Duke rape case made Nifong's path to victory clear. Like the players and members of the gown community, Nifong was also imbued with all kinds of dignity—social, inherent, and conduct. Because members of the town community, especially the African American community, had vocally and adamantly aligned themselves behind Mangum, Nifong decided to exploit their vulnerability, for the reasons explained above, and use his power as the sitting District Attorney to state repeatedly, and against the evidence, that Mangum was telling the truth. That is just what they wanted to hear.

Nifong did not woo their votes simply by insisting he had a real case against the players, though. He played into the dignity dynamics in other ways as well. Most pathetically, he exploited the need of the town community to get some affirmation of the history of racial injustice inflicted upon it by the very existence of the town-gown relationship and all of the inequality surrounding it. Toward this end, Nifong emphasized that the events of that evening were racially motivated. He related to the media that he personally wanted to handle the case partly because of the "general racial hostility" involved in the incident.[71]

Significantly, Nifong seems to have been right about his evaluation on this point. Racial slurs had been exchanged. The players who hired the strippers did have a preference for white women. Race is highly relevant to the town-gown dynamics between Durham and Duke. All of this is true. The problem, then, is not that Nifong was inaccurate in reporting that the evening was filled with "racial hostility." Rather, because relations between blacks and whites in Durham were already tense, even hostile, Nifong was wrong to exacerbate that divide in his media messages even when he was becoming fully aware that there were serious flaws in Mangum's allegations.

What else could Nifong use to win the town vote? He could expand his attack on the gown community by reminding voters of the huge economic gap

---

70. *Id.*
71. *Id.* at 87.

between the two communities. He could press that hot button simply by suggesting that the struggle to achieve *true* justice in the case would be that much harder because the players' rich "daddies" would be able to buy the best lawyers.[72] How inflammatory was that, especially in the context of Durham's and Duke's relationship and history?

Nifong's strategy rattled everyone and got many people who were called upon to evaluate the situation to doubt themselves and instead rely on his judgment because he had the power position in the hierarchy. Presumably, he had the facts. He was supposed to be trustworthy. He was supposed to conduct an investigation with the utmost of care and dignity. He was supposed to be able to diplomatically foster healthy town-gown relationships and not exploit them. Authors Stuart Taylor and KC Johnson explain this dynamic in their book, *Until Proven Innocent.* Nifong fooled the gown community:

> "If a prosecutor gets up and says, 'I know that certain things happened,' the white middle-class norm is to believe that it must have happened," Peter Lange, Duke's provost, later explained. "Could we really believe that Nifong would be out making stuff up to help his election? Look at the damage he'd be doing to our community, to Duke, to these kids. Could he really be that morally corrupt? It was hard to believe that."[73]

He also fooled the town community:

> No white prosecutor would act this way with white boys unless he had really solid evidence, many blacks, thought: White prosecutors never do that.[74]

He won the election.

But Nifong's perch atop the hierarchy was to be short-lived. Eventually, his extremely unethical and unprofessional conduct would cause him to fall from grace. He surrendered his license to practice law, spent one day in jail for criminal contempt, and has filed for bankruptcy.[75] North Carolina refused to help him pay his legal fees to defend himself against the charges that he conducted this case in gross violation of ethical standards, because he engaged in "fraud,

---

72. *Id.* at 85.

73. *Id.* at 89.

74. *Id.*

75. Mike Nifong, Wikipedia, http://www.wikipedia.org/wiki/Mike_Nifong (last visited Mar. 9, 2008).

corruption, [and] malice."[76] Astonishingly, he responded to the state's refusal by saying, "I don't know why I continue to expect people to do the right thing."[77]

Summary

The inextricable intertwining of the different ideas of dignity offer a way to try to understand a situation that barely makes sense. Dignity's different meanings provide an overlay to the town-gown relationship between Durham and Duke that is tenaciously tied to the historical subordination of blacks as slaves, and later, as less-than-human under the separate-but-equal doctrine. Many of white society's learned ideas about race have yet to be dislodged. With respect to the players, their social and inherent dignities were well-fortified before that evening. Regardless of the conduct they might have engaged in, their social and inherent dignities were virtually beyond reproach, contributing to the "shock value" of the allegations. Moreover, and significantly, Mangum's position on the dignity hierarchy was also well-established prior to that evening. Whatever conduct she engaged in, it was inevitable that she would be judged according to the diminished social and inherent dignity that dominant society had attached to her and to the town community more generally. In this way, undignified conduct on her part merely reinforced preconceived ideas that she was incredible because she lacked social dignity and had much less, if any, inherent dignity compared to members of the gown community, including the lacrosse players.

Nifong used these larger dynamics to set himself up as the most powerful attorney in the Durham area. By exploiting these dynamics, he could champion the town's cries for racial justice and, simultaneously, undermine Duke's status as a bastion of gifted athletes and scholars who are beyond engaging in conduct unbecoming their Duke identities. Without a doubt, Mangum was wrong to accuse the players of rape. Her accusations are inexcusable. But only Nifong is responsible for exploiting her lies and trying to destroy the players and Duke. Ironically and fortunately, because of their positions on the dignity hierarchy, the players and Duke will survive this. Hopefully, they also will have learned something about dignity—and all of its different meanings. Unfortunately, however, Nifong might have succeeded in setting back what little good-faith had been established between the Durham and Duke communities for a long time to come.

---

76. *Id.*
77. *Id.*

CHAPTER FOUR

Alcohol Consumption on College Campuses

George W. Dowdall

The Duke lacrosse case has been told in several versions.[1] Among the themes in the story is the role of alcohol abuse in the specific incident and the allegedly high level of alcohol use at Duke, set against growing national concern about college drinking. After reviewing the lacrosse-team incident, this chapter looks at alcohol use at Duke, comparing it to what is known about national patterns of college drinking (and the consequences of this drinking, such as intoxicated rape and party rape), and efforts to figure out what to do about the problem. Finally, the chapter examines the lessons that can be learned about college drinking from the Duke lacrosse case.

The Lacrosse Rape Case

For the Duke lacrosse team, March 13, 2006, began as another day of spring break. Soon after team members (some under twenty-one) arrived at 610 North Buchanan Street in Durham, beer drinking began in the back yard and some students played Beirut, a popular drinking game.[2] Gatherings like this one often occurred in the neighborhoods surrounding the Duke campus since the university had banned on-campus keg parties and moved fraternities out of the quad.[3]

---

1. *See* STUART TAYLOR & KC JOHNSON, UNTIL PROVEN INNOCENT: POLITICAL CORRECTNESS AND THE SHAMEFUL INJUSTICES OF THE DUKE LACROSSE RAPE CASE (2007), and DON YAEGER, IT'S NOT ABOUT THE TRUTH: THE UNTOLD STORY OF THE DUKE LACROSSE CASE AND THE LIVES IT SHATTERED (2007).
2. TAYLOR & JOHNSON, *supra* note 1, at 21.
3. *Id.*

American colleges and universities have struggled with what to do about college drinking for some time. Many undergraduates are under twenty-one, the minimum drinking age mandated by all U.S. states. Colleges and universities are required by federal law to inform their students about the prohibition on underage drinking and to tell them what the penalties are for violating associated laws and college regulations.[4] Duke's current policy bans underage undergraduates from using alcohol on its campus.[5]

The Duke administration's efforts to clamp down on alcohol parties on campus lead inevitably to tension. As a student observed,

> Deans, cops, neighbors, nerds, and the shadow of the Ivy League have gradually and systematically pulled the rug out from underneath the backbone of the school's identity: fun…. [T]his is about a change in priorities for a university stuck between a rock and a hard place without a clue as to what made my class and I want to come down South instead of going to goddam Harvard.[6]

On March 13, most of the lacrosse team members "sat around drinking and listening to music…. A few had partied hard for most of the day."[7] The only other substance abuse engaged in that night was apparently by one of the strippers, who appeared to be "dead drunk or on drugs."[8]

The enormous controversy over the alleged rape and the media firestorm that surrounded it focused primarily on whether a rape occurred. But, arguably because of prior concerns about substance abuse on the Duke campus and specifically about the image of alcohol consumption by the lacrosse team, much of the discussion following the incident also centered on Duke's undergraduate culture, including concerns about alcohol use and the broader issue of student conduct and comportment. For example, when Duke's President Richard Brodhead was interviewed by the CBS newsmagazine *60 Minutes* about the evening, "Brodhead reacted with deep, visceral disgust to the nature of the stripper party…. 'From our point of view, … this was an evening of highly unacceptable behavior whether or not the rape took place.' As a wry observer

---

4. For current requirements, see http://www.higheredcenter.org/dfsca/ (last visited Jan. 20, 2008).

5. For Duke's current alcohol policy, see Office of Judicial Affairs, Alcohol, http://judicial.studentaffairs.duke.edu/policies/policy_list/alcohol.html (last visited Jan. 20, 2008).

6. Taylor & Johnson, *supra* note 1, at 22.

7. *Id.* at 23.

8. *Id.* at 24.

noted: "it was like he'd never been to a college campus. Drinking! Strippers! Wild parties!"[9]

After the arrests of two of the team members, Brodhead told the Durham Chamber of Commerce, "If our students did what is alleged, it is appalling to the worst degree. If they didn't do it, whatever they did is bad enough."[10] But if there had been no rape, what out of the ordinary had taken place? A party with a stripper, racist language, and drinking by students, some of whom were under twenty-one? As two writers observed, "If every Duke student who'd ever done [things] like that were suspended, the place would almost be empty."[11]

Alcohol and Duke Lacrosse

The reactions at Duke to the stripper party shed a great deal of light on alcohol use by the lacrosse team and the broader Duke undergraduate student body. Several weeks after the incident, Duke's president asked James E. Coleman, a professor in the School of Law, to chair an ad hoc committee to review the lacrosse team members' conduct. Because the criminal investigation was still going forward, however, the committee didn't consider questions relating specifically to the alleged rape.[12] Coleman's group found that the team members were "academically and athletically responsible students" with no disciplinary problems with their professors. It concluded,

> Paradoxically, in contrast to their exemplary academic and athletic performance, a large number of the members of the team have been socially irresponsible when under the influence of alcohol. They have repeatedly violated the law against underage drinking. They have drunk alcohol excessively. They have disturbed their neighbors with loud music and noise, both on-campus and off-campus. They have publicly urinated both on-campus and off. They have shown disrespect for property. Both the number of team members implicated in this behavior and the number of alcohol-related incidents involving them have been excessive compared to other Duke athletic teams.

---

9. *Id.* at 129.
10. *Id.* at 190.
11. *Id.* at 191.
12. Report of the Lacrosse Ad Hoc Review Committee (2006), http://news.duke.edu/mmedia/pdf/lacrossereport.pdf.

Nevertheless, their conduct has not been different in character than the conduct of the typical Duke student who abuses alcohol. Their reported conduct has not involved fighting, sexual assault or harassment, or racist behavior. Moreover, even the people who have complained about their alcohol-related misconduct often add that the students are respectful and appear genuinely remorseful when they are not drinking.[13]

Most of the incidents of team member misconduct involved alcohol, including underage possession and public urination, with one incident involving ten students playing a drinking game in a dorm room while hosting a high-school recruit.[14]

Similarly, a Durham police captain reported that

lacrosse players did not represent a special or unique problem in District 2; in fact, none of the houses rented by lacrosse players was among the worst of those whose loud parties attracted hundreds of disorderly Duke students on weekends. Although lacrosse players rented a large house at 1206 W. Markham, Captain Sarvis said it was not among the top 10 houses about which neighbors complained the most. Nor did lacrosse players as a group stand out as the worst student offenders. Captain Sarvis said the fraternity-affiliated houses presented a greater challenge to police than any of the houses rented by athletes.[15]

The Ad Hoc Committee found that Duke student-affairs administrators were aware of "the irresponsible conduct of lacrosse players associated with drinking." But, except for the Office of Judicial Affairs, none was alarmed by the conduct, and none communicated with Coach Pressler about it.[16] The Committee concluded that Duke's process for dealing with "non-academic and non-suspendable athlete misconduct (and student misconduct generally) is hampered by an approach that is informal to the point of being casual. The result is a process that is arbitrary and often ineffective."[17]

For present purposes, the most important finding of the Ad Hoc Committee centers on Duke's stance toward alcohol:

---

13. *Id.* at 6–7.
14. *Id.* at 7–8.
15. *Id.* at 13.
16. *Id.* at 17.
17. *Id.* at 22.

The University's ability to deal fully with the problem of alcohol is undermined by its own ambivalence toward drinking and the conduct it spawns.

Alcohol is the single greatest factor involved in the unacceptable behavior of Duke students in general and members of the lacrosse team specifically, both on- and off-campus. Drunkenness is the cause of behaviors that represent a serious nuisance to the community and a source of significant personal danger for the student. The University's alcohol policy is reasonable, but it is inconsistently enforced and only ineffectually disciplined. The University's ambivalence is most obviously manifested in the University's tolerance of egregious violations of its own policies at events such as Tailgate and Last Day of Classes, as outlined in the Report of the Committee to investigate the Judicial Procedure. While the alcohol related misconduct by members of the lacrosse team is deplorable, the University is, by its lack of leadership in this area of deep concern, implicated in the alcohol excesses of lacrosse players and of Duke students more generally.[18]

The Ad Hoc Committee came up with four recommendations, the first three of which focused on athletics:

1. Continuance of the Men's Lacrosse Team with appropriate oversight.
2. Code of Conduct for Athletes.
3. Need for Improved Communication between Student Affairs and Athletics.[19]

The fourth recommendation sought a new approach to alcohol issues:

4. Need for a Clearly Articulated and Enforced Alcohol Policy
The university's own apparent ambiguity regarding underage alcohol consumption conveys inconsistent messages and confuses expectations regarding alcohol. Duke University has fostered a number of problems among its undergraduates, including lacrosse players, by its ambivalent policies toward underage and over-consumption of alcohol at Duke. This problem needs serious review and remediation within the University.[20]

---

18. *Id.* at 24.
19. *Id.* at 25.
20. *Id.*

The Duke Alcohol Scene

In the recent past, Duke had acquired a reputation as a major party school, with Greek life, big-time athletics, and a campus culture supportive of alcohol abuse. Observers within the Duke community confirmed that reality matched reputation. In the mid-1990s, while Duke was shifting toward a much more restrictive alcohol policy on its campus, its alumni magazine reported that the university had a binge-drinking rate slightly higher than the national average.[21] Duke's Dean of the Chapel William Willimon had issued a widely noted report, "Work Hard, Play Hard," that captured the prevailing Duke ethic of the 1990s.[22]

Duke's current national reputation as a party school, albeit one with strong academics, appears in several college guides. For example, the Princeton Review's 2007 *The Best 361 Colleges*, published before the lacrosse incident, describes Duke as "the fun younger brother of the aging Ivies," quoting a student who claims the campus has "top-ten academics, a beautiful campus, wonderful climate, a fun social scene...."[23] Noting that Duke has "lots of beer drinking," the guide goes on to comment, "Duke has a party scene, or rather, several (centered on the Greek houses, dorms, and off-campus apartments), although this may be changing, as strict alcohol policies are pushing a lot of weekend activity off campus." Duke balances academics with "cultivating sociable, friendly people who will be able to succeed in all future life situations."[24]

The *Fiske Guide To Colleges 2007*, published after the first stories about the Duke lacrosse rape allegations, mentions Duke's policy requiring freshmen to live on the dry East Campus as a way of "insulating them from the wilder aspects of Duke's social scene, which attracted national attention for a scandal involving off-campus behavior of members of the lacrosse team."[25] *Fiske* reports a freshman as saying, "alcohol, it seems, is quite easy to find."[26] The guide also notes how Greek life has been pushed off campus and how town-gown relationships are strained. *Fiske* gives Duke the highest rating for its academics, but slightly lower ones for "social" and "quality of life."

---

21. Bridget Booher, *A Move Toward Moderation: Drinking at Duke*, Duke Univ. Alumni Mag., http://www.dukemagazine.duke.edu/alumni/dm11/moderate.html (last visited Oc. 29, 2008).

22. *See also* William H. Willimon & Thomas H. Naylor, The Abandoned Generation (1995).

23. Robert Franek et al., The Princeton Review: The Best 361 Colleges, at 200 (2006).

24. *Id.*

25. Edward B Fiske, with Robert Logue, Fiske Guide To Colleges 2007, at 215 (2006).

26. *Id.* at 216.

What was the reality of alcohol use at Duke at the time of the stripper party? Some evidence suggests that, if anything, Duke was apparently making some progress in dealing with alcohol issues. A profile of Duke published in 2001 noted, "Data collected at Duke have shown that changes are occurring in desired directions. Emergency-room admissions data have shown decreases in alcohol-related accidents and alcohol overdoses. Core Surveys have been conducted at Duke every two years; survey results have shown that the binge-drinking rate has decreased, although Duke is still slightly above the national norm. The negative consequences of drinking assessed by the Core Survey have also decreased, and the incidence of negative consequences at Duke is below national norms."[27]

The 1999 death of Duke student Raheem Bath from aspirational pneumonia as the result of a night of very heavy drinking was a turning point for the university. Policies were changed, but the problem continued. By 2003, Duke's student newspaper would report: "Last year, 47 students were transported to the hospital for alcohol-related incidents, down from 2000–2001's high of 57, including 38 students hospitalized in fall 2000. Alcohol-policy violations also remained roughly the same as in fall 2001."[28]

More recent data also hint at a slightly different reality than Duke's party-school image:

> It turns out that Duke isn't really the party school everyone seems to think. According to the American College Health Association National College Health Assessment, Duke students believe that the use of drugs and alcohol on campus is more prevalent than it actually is. The study—which is conducted at Duke every two years—was last reported in Fall 2006. The results revealed fairly large discrepancies between what students perceive and what students actually do. At Duke, 15.5 percent of students reported never drinking alcohol, though students predicted that only 2.3 percent of the student body were nondrinkers. Although the perceived percentage of alcohol use, at 70.8 percent, is on par with what is actually consumed, 74.6 percent, the perceived prevalence of starting heavy drinking upon coming to Duke is not accurate.[29]

---

27. Higher Educ. Center, *Case Study: Duke University* (2001), http://www.highered-center.org/casestudies/duke-a.html.

28. Kevin Lees, *Alcohol Remains Back-Burner Issue*, CHRONICLE (Duke University), Jan. 17, 2003.

29. Emmeline Zhao, *Drug Use Misperceived on Campus*, CHRONICLE (Duke University), Sept. 21, 2007.

A more comprehensive view of Duke's alcohol scene was presented in reaction to the stripper party incident. Duke launched an extensive review of its undergraduate-campus culture by the Campus Culture Initiative (CCI) Steering Committee.[30] Although the results of the review were necessarily controversial, the report suggests how one set of Duke students and faculty viewed campus alcohol issues:

> Alcohol issues are not one single problem, but rather a series of three, interrelated problems that are viewed in multiple ways: "bad behavior," "impaired health," and "lost weekends." All three tend to involve heavy drinking—drunkenness—rather than drinking *per se*. With regard to bad behavior, drinking is a factor in much of the serious misbehavior, assault, property damage, injury, unwanted sex, and neighborhood disruption involving undergraduates. Drinking also creates a substantial legal liability to the University and is a significant risk to Duke's reputation. In terms of impaired health, a large minority of undergraduates engage in heavy drinking on a regular basis, putting their academic performance and their health at risk. Recent biomedical research on adolescent brain development underscores that heavy drinking can cause brain damage. The immediate threat is that students will be injured while drunk. Overdose appears to be a particular problem for first-year students: 37 were transported to the Emergency Room last year, and there were 7 transports of first-year students just during orientation week this year. The risk of another alcohol-related death in the Duke community is very real. Furthermore, several dozen students are seen in CAPS every year with serious symptoms of alcoholism, and far more than that will graduate with a heavy-drinking habit. Alcohol use also complicates other mental-health problems and heightens impulsive behavior, both contributing to and creating high risk in vulnerable students. Beyond bad behavior and impaired health is the problem of alcohol-induced lost weekends; much weekend social life at Duke is organized around getting drunk, an activity that is alluring for many students, but ultimately unsatisfying. Where, how, and with whom Duke students socialize are important influences on campus culture.[31]

The CCI Report presented data comparing Duke undergraduates with peers at comparable institutions:

---

30. REPORT OF THE CAMPUS CULTURE INITIATIVE STEERING COMMITTEE (2007), http://news.duke.edu/reports/ccireport.pdf.

31. *Id.* at 19.

Duke students report higher levels of drinking in college and more frequent binge drinking (three or more occasions of 5 or more drinks in the last 2 weeks) than their peers at comparable institutions. It is, however, Duke students in Greek letter organizations, not independents, who set Duke apart from its comparison schools. (For example, in the 2003 survey, binge drinking was reported by 43% of Duke fraternity members and 29% of sorority members compared to 14% non-fraternity and 8% non-sorority members.)[32]

The report also showed Duke students studying less and partying more than at the other schools.

The CCI Report noted the difficulty of dealing with these issues, including not enough clinical capacity to treat those with alcohol problems and inadequate monitoring of trends in use. The CCI offered the following recommendations about alcohol, designed "to promote a more responsible approach to the culture of campus drinking":

1. *Re-orient social life on campus to reduce the centrality of alcohol and enable more non-alcohol events and venues*
2. *Establish attractive venues for controlled distribution of alcohol for students of age, including a large space able to accommodate 300–400 people*
3. *Clarify alcohol regulations and enforce these regulations consistently. Specifically, target disorderly and disrespectful behavior and dangerous drinking*
4. *Increase staffing and resources for the oversight of policies and practices and for alcohol/substance abuse prevention and treatment services*
5. *Implement an evidence-based approach, based upon public-health principles, to alcohol policy, initiatives, and accountability.*[33]

Thus, the present Duke alcohol scene, like that of many other colleges across the country, appears to feature some percentage of students heavily engaged in binge drinking, with a majority of students either occasionally or never binging. But its image has now become the thing of "sex and scandal," to borrow the title of a widely-read *Rolling Stone* profile; Duke's undergraduate image, unfair or not, is a sum of "Lacrosse players, sorority girls and the booze-fueled culture of the never-ending hookup on the nation's most embattled campus."[34] As a Duke student observed,

---

32. *Id.*

33. *Id.* at 21.

34. Janet Reitman, *Sex & Scandal at Duke*, ROLLING STONE, June 1, 2006.

Indeed, our current policy's most unfortunate consequence is that it consistently allows a small minority of students, on the order of 15 to 20 percent, to ruin things for the rest of us; their involvement in things like baby oil-wrestling matches sullies the good name of all Duke students, especially those of us who have never found it necessary to urinate publicly.[35]

National Patterns of College Drinking

Drinking problems at Duke are neither new nor unique. A pioneering study of dozens of colleges and universities in 1953 found drinking to be widespread, although the report did not include evidence connecting drinking to a significant range of problems.[36] Recent investigations present a complex and troubling picture. To answer the question of how much drinking goes on at American colleges, social scientists have used survey research.[37] Henry Wechsler led the Harvard School of Public Health College Alcohol Study (HSPH CAS), which conducted four large-scale surveys from 1993 to 2001. The initial survey was done at 140 colleges and universities, using a representative sample.[38] (Participating institutions were promised confidentiality, so it is impossible to say whether Duke was involved.) In each survey, over 17,000 students completed a detailed twenty-page questionnaire about their drinking and other behaviors.

The HSPH CAS introduced a gender-specific definition of binge drinking (also known as heavy episodic drinking). Binge drinking was defined for men as drinking five or more drinks in a row in the two weeks before the survey was done (which was during the spring semester); for women, the definition included drinking four or more drinks in a row. Students with three or more episodes of binge drinking in the two-week period were considered to be frequent binge drinkers.[39] Later research by other investigators confirmed that an

---

35. Kristin Butler, *Our Inconvenient Truth*, CHRONICLE (Duke University), Sept. 8, 2006.

36. ROBERT STRAUS & SELDEN D. BACON, DRINKING IN COLLEGE (1953).

37. George W. Dowdall & Henry Wechsler, *Studying College Alcohol Use: Widening the Lens, Sharpening the Focus*, 67 J. STUD. ALCOHOL (2002).

38. Henry Wechsler et al., *Health and Behavioral Consequences of Binge Drinking in College: A National Survey of Students at 140 Colleges*, J. AM. MED. ASS'N, (1994).

39. Henry Wechsler et al., *A Gender-Specific Measure of Binge Drinking Among College Students*, 85 AM. J. PUB. HEALTH 982 (1995).

important subgroup of students drinks well above the binge threshold.[40] Other researchers have suggested refocusing attention at students who drink at this much-higher level and frequency.[41]

Table 1
Drinking of American College Students, 1993–2001* (percent)

Drinking Behavior	Year 1993	1997	1999	2001
Abstainer	16.4	19.6	19.8	19.3
Drank in past year	83.6	80.3	79.8	80.7
Binge drinking	43.9	43.2	44.5	44.4
Frequent binge drinking	19.7	21.0	22.6	22.8
Drank on ten or more occasions in the past thirty days	18.1	21.1	23.1	22.6
Was drunk three or more times in the past thirty days	23.4	29.0	30.2	29.4
Drinks to get drunk	39.9	53.5	47.7	48.2

* Ann L. Pastore & Kathleen Maguire, Sourcebook of Criminal Justice Statistics (2003).

Table 1 presents data about trends in college drinking from 1993 to 2001 based on the HSPH CAS data. The data show little change in binge or frequent binge drinking over this period, during which college drinking received considerable attention in the media and universities directed substantial effort toward the problem. If anything, there is evidence of a polarization over the time period, with a bit more binge drinking and an increase in abstention. The most striking change is the rise in getting drunk three or more times in the last month (from 23 to 29 percent) and drinking to get drunk (40 to 48 percent).

What factors shape college drinking? Many studies have been carried out, and a great deal is now known about how to study college drinking.[42] Table 2

40. Aaron M. White, Courtney L. Kraus & Harry Scott Swartzelder, *Many College Freshmen Drink at Levels Far Beyond the Binge Threshold*, 30 Alcoholism: Clinical and Experimental Res. 1006 (2006).

41. Cherly A. Presley, C.A. & E.R Pimental, *The Introduction of the Heavy and Frequent Drinker: A Proposed Classification to Increase Accuracy of Alcohol Assessments in Postsecondary Educational Settings*, 67 J. Stud. Alcohol 324 (2006).

42. *See, e.g.*, Dowdall & Wechsler, *supra* note 37.

presents a picture of the most important factors that have been found helpful in understanding college drinking, sorted into pre-college and college issues. Variations within colleges were considerable, but some factors—such as being male, white, young, living in fraternities or sororities, and having a party-centered lifestyle—predicted binge drinking.[43] Other lifestyle issue were important as well: being an athlete, or being involved in athletics, also predicted binge drinking.[44]

Among the most important findings of the HSPH CAS focused on the great variation across colleges in levels of binge drinking. Figure 1 shows that a few colleges have almost no binge drinkers in their student populations, while a handful of colleges have more than 70 percent of their student body made up of binge drinkers. Roughly a third of the colleges have more than 50 percent binge-drinking rates.

Figure 1
Distribution of Colleges by Percentage of Binge Drinkers[*]

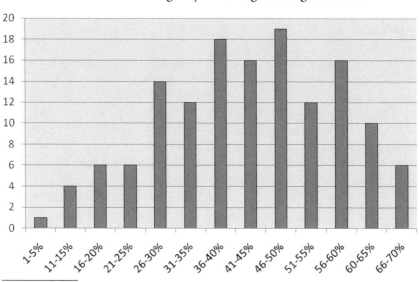

* *See* Wechsler et al., *supra* note 38, at 1674.

43. Henry Wechsler et al., *Correlates of College Student Binge Drinking*, 85 Am. J. Pub. Health 921 (1995).

44. Henry Wechsler, Andrea Davenport, George Dowdall, S. Grossman & S. Zanakos, *Binge Drinking, Tobacco, and Illicit Drug Use and Involvement in College Athletics*, 45 J. Am. College Health 195 (1997).

Table 2
Factors Shaping College Drinking[*]

Before College	During College
Family Factors	**Individual Factors**
• Genetics	• Age of drinking onset
• Parental drinking behavior	• High-school drinking
• Social class	• Drug or tobacco use
• Race or ethnicity	• Gender
• Religion	• Race
Public Policy	**College Environment**
• National laws	• Peer norms
• State laws	• Residential system
• Enforcement of minimum	• Greek life
drinking age	• Athletics
• Local community ordinances	• Academics
	• Community service
	• Religious involvement
Alcohol Environment in Community	**Alcohol Environment on Campus**
• Price of alcohol	• Dry or wet campus
• Advertising	• Availability
• Marketing practices	• Price
• Outlet density	• Alcohol policy
• Hours of sale	
Social and Institutional Structures	**Alcohol Environment Off Campus**
• Neighborhood	• Retail Price
• Middle and high school	• Outlet Density and Proximity
• Church, synagogue, or mosque	• Advertising
• Subcultures	• Marketing

[*] Dowdall & Wechsler, *supra* note 37, at 14.

Health and Behavioral Consequences of College Drinking

As part of the HSPH CAS, students were asked a series of questions about whether they had experienced one or more problems because of their own drinking. Table 3, based on data for the period 1993–2001, shows that the impact of drinking is substantial. Other data (not presented here) show that, for any one of the problems studied, frequent binge-drinking students had the highest risk of a problem while nonbinging students had the lowest risk. Some of the problems show the academic costs of binge drinking, such as getting behind in schoolwork or missing classes as a result of one's own drinking. Other consequences were behavioral, such as doing something one regrets or arguing with friends, having unplanned or unprotected sex, or getting injured or hurt. Almost half of the frequent binge drinkers reported experiencing five or more problems as a result of their own drinking since the beginning of the school year.

Table 3

Alcohol-Related Problems among College Students, 1993–2001* (percent)

Problem	1993	1997	1999	2001
Missed a class	26.9	31.1	29.9	29.5
Got behind in schoolwork	20.5	24.1	24.1	21.6
Did something you regret	32.1	37.0	36.1	35.0
Forgot where you were or what you did	24.7	27.4	27.1	26.8
Argued with friends	19.6	24.0	22.5	22.9
Engaged in unplanned sexual activities	19.2	23.3	21.6	21.3
Did not use protection when you had sex	9.8	11.2	10.3	10.4
Damaged property	9.3	11.7	10.8	10.7
Got into trouble with campus or local police	4.6	6.4	5.8	6.5
Got hurt or injured	9.3	12.0	12.4	12.8
Required medical treatment for an overdose	0.5	0.6	0.6	0.8
Drove after drinking alcohol	26.6	29.5	28.8	29.0
Had five or more different alcohol-related problems	16.6	20.8	19.9	20.3

* Ann L. Pastore & Kathleen Maguire, Sourcebook of Criminal Justice Statistics (2003).

Binge drinking also affects those in the immediate environment whether or not they themselves binge. Wechsler and his colleagues introduced the term "secondhand binge effects" to capture the issues.[45] These data are based on non-binging students living in residence halls or in Greek housing. Unwanted sexual advances or being pushed, hit, or assaulted were more likely to occur to students at colleges with high rates of binge drinking than at institutions with lower rates.

The HSPH CAS data helped to focus attention on the problem of college drinking. Student deaths at the Massachusetts Institute of Technology, Louisiana State University, and other institutions were given considerable attention in the media. The lead federal research agency on alcohol, the National Institute on Alcohol Abuse and Alcoholism (NIAAA), set up a task force to assess the problem of college drinking, commission detailed summaries of what was known about the problem, and recommend solutions.[46] In its 2002 report, the NIAAA Task Force concluded that college drinking was a serious public-health problem, as the following snapshot (updated with current estimates) indicates:

> The consequences of excessive and underage drinking affect virtually all college campuses, college communities, and college students, whether they choose to drink or not.
>
> **Death:** 1,700 college students between the ages of 18 and 24 die each year from alcohol-related unintentional injuries, including motor-vehicle crashes.
>
> **Injury:** 599,000 students between the ages of 18 and 24 are unintentionally injured under the influence of alcohol.
>
> **Assault:** More than 696,000 students between the ages of 18 and 24 are assaulted by another student who has been drinking.
>
> **Sexual Abuse:** More than 97,000 students between the ages of 18 and 24 are victims of alcohol-related sexual assault or date rape.
>
> **Unsafe Sex:** 400,000 students between the ages of 18 and 24 had unprotected sex and more than 100,000 students between the ages of 18 and 24 report having been too intoxicated to know if they consented to having sex.
>
> **Academic Problems:** About 25 percent of college students report academic consequences of their drinking including missing class,

45. Henry Wechsler et al., *The Adverse Impact of Heavy Episodic Drinkers on Other College Students*, 56 J. STUD. ALCOHOL 628 (1995).

46. TASK FORCE OF THE NAT'L ADVISORY COUNCIL ON ALCOHOL ABUSE AND ALCOHOLISM, A CALL TO ACTION: CHANGING THE CULTURE OF DRINKING AT U.S. COLLEGES (2002).

falling behind, doing poorly on exams or papers, and receiving lower grades overall.

Health Problems/Suicide Attempts: More than 150,000 students develop an alcohol-related health problem ... and between 1.2 and 1.5 percent of students indicate that they tried to commit suicide within the past year due to drinking or drug use.

Drunk Driving: 2.1 million students between the ages of 18 and 24 drove under the influence of alcohol last year.

Vandalism: About 11 percent of college-student drinkers report that they have damaged property while under the influence of alcohol.

Property Damage: More than 25 percent of administrators from schools with relatively low drinking levels and over 50 percent from schools with high drinking levels say their campuses have a "moderate" or "major" problem with alcohol-related property damage.

Police Involvement: About 5 percent of four-year college students are involved with the police or campus security as a result of their drinking ... and an estimated 110,000 students between the ages of 18 and 24 are arrested for an alcohol-related violation such as public drunkenness or driving under the influence.

Alcohol Abuse and Dependence: 31 percent of college students met criteria for a diagnosis of alcohol abuse and 6 percent for a diagnosis of alcohol dependence in the past twelve months, according to questionnaire-based self-reports about their drinking.[47]

This snapshot of college-drinking consequences was a notable achievement of the Task Force Report because it helped advance professional consensus about the negative consequences of college drinking.

Intoxicated Rape

Among the most serious issues tied to college drinking is rape. Table 4 presents data on the prevalence of rape in 1997, 1999, and 2001. A separate analysis of the HSPH CAS data revealed that one out of every twenty college women

---

47. Nat'l Inst. on Alcohol Abuse and Educ., *A Snapshot of Annual High-Risk College Drinking Consequences*, http://www.collegedrinkingprevention.gov/StatsSummaries/ snapshot.aspx (last visited Oct. 28, 2008).

had experienced sexual intercourse without consent (since the beginning of the school year, in a survey conducted during the spring semester). Nearly three quarters (72 percent) of those women had been too intoxicated to give consent.[48] Some of the correlates of intoxicated sex show that the routine activities of some women raise the risk of crime victimization. For example, women who were under 21 years of age, white, lived in sororities, consumed illicit drugs, and binge drank in high school had a higher risk of rape while intoxicated. Women who attended colleges with high rates of binge drinking also had higher risk of this type of rape.

Table 4
Prevalence of Rape since the Beginning of the School Year* (percent)

	Year			
Type	1997 (n=8,567)	1999 (n=8,425)	2001 (n=6,988)	All years (n=23,980)
While intoxicated	3.6	3.4	3.2	3.4
Forced	2.1	1.8	1.7	1.9
Threatened	0.5	0.3	0.3	0.4
Any type of rape	5.1	4.5	4.3	4.7

*Meichun Mohler-Kuo et al., Correlates of Rape While Intoxicated in a National Sample of College Women, 65 J. STUD. ALCOHOL 37, 40 (2004).

Heavy drinking by both men and women has become part of "hooking up," a sexual script widely practiced on college campuses, as a recent study by Kathleen Bogle explains.[49] Binge drinking facilitates hooking up, and hooking up meshes with heavy alcohol consumption. Among affluent college students in particular, hooking up and heavy drinking are often part of a partying-centered subculture.[50]

Some part of having sex without consent because of intoxication involves sex between individuals who are both too drunk to give consent. But some part also involves the deliberate use of alcohol as a date-rape drug designed to get women drunk enough to have nonconsensual sex. A detailed portrait of

48. Meichun Mohler-Kuo et al., *Correlates of Rape While Intoxicated in a National Sample of College Women*, 65 J. STUD. ALCOHOL 37 (2004).

49. KATHLEEN BOGLE, HOOKING UP: SEX, DATING, AND RELATIONSHIPS ON CAMPUS (2008).

50. For a detailed picture of that subculture at another elite university with a mixture of athletics, parties, and fraternities, see DAVID GRAZIAN, ON THE MAKE: THE HUSTLE OF URBAN NIGHTLIFE (2008).

this type of behavior at a fraternity house has been reported at another elite university much like Duke.[51] A Department of Justice report defines "party rape" as one that "occurs at an off-campus house or on- or off-campus fraternity and involves … plying women with alcohol or targeting an intoxicated woman."[52]

A study of undergraduate life at a major public research university pointed to the central value of "friendly fun" for the understanding of that life.[53] A recent study of a similar university helps to understand how party rape is produced by the very same forces that generate friendly fun. The authors note that "the vast majority of heterosexual encounters at parties are fun and consensual."[54] But their data show how the organization of everyday life for freshmen women helps facilitate party rape:

> Party rape is accomplished without the use of guns, knives, or fists. It is carried out through the combination of low level forms of coercion—a lot of liquor and persuasion, manipulation of the situation so that women cannot leave, and sometimes force (e.g., by blocking a door, or using your body weight to make it difficult for women to get up). These forms of coercion are made more effective by organizational arrangements that provide men with control over how partying happenings and by expectations that women let loose and trust their party-mates. This systematic and effective method of extracting nonconsensual sex is largely invisible, which makes it difficult for victims to convince anyone—even themselves—that a crime occurred. Men engage in this behavior with little risk of consequences.[55]

The Culture of College Drinking

To better understand college drinking and its correlates and consequences, recent research on the subject has tended to frame the problem in environmental and cultural terms. The NIAAA Report argued persuasively for a view

---

51. PEGGY REEVES SANDAY, FRATERNITY GANG RAPE: SEX, BROTHERHOOD, AND PRIVILEGE ON CAMPUS (1990).

52. RANA SAMPSON, ACQUAINTANCE RAPE OF COLLEGE STUDENTS. PROBLEM-ORIENTED GUIDES FOR POLICE SERIES, NO. 17 (2002).

53. MICHAEL MOFFATT, COMING OF AGE IN NEW JERSEY (1991).

54. Elizabeth A. Armstrong, Laura Hamilton & Brian Sweeney, *Sexual Assault on Campus: A Multilevel, Integrative Approach to Party Rape*, 53 SOC. PROBS. 483 (2006).

55. *Id.* at 492.

of college drinking as a *culture*, not merely something that can be understood in terms of individual pathology or personal troubles:

> The tradition of drinking has developed into a kind of culture—beliefs and customs—entrenched in every level of college students' environments. Customs handed down through generations of college drinkers reinforce students' expectation that alcohol is a necessary ingredient for social success. These beliefs and the expectations they engender exert a powerful influence over students' behavior toward alcohol.
>
> Customs that promote college drinking also are embedded in numerous levels of students' environments. The walls of college sports arenas carry advertisements from alcohol industry sponsors. Alumni carry on that alcohol tradition, perhaps less flamboyantly than during their college years, at sports events and alumni social functions. Communities permit establishments near campus to serve alcohol, and these establishments depend on the College clientele for their financial success.
>
> Students derive their expectations of alcohol from their environment and from each other, as they face the insecurity of establishing themselves in a new social milieu. Environmental and peer influences combine to create a culture of drinking. This culture actively promotes drinking, or passively promotes it, through tolerance, or even tacit approval, of college drinking as a rite of passage.[56]

Perhaps the most innovative part of the report is its framework for assessing which interventions have worked against excessive college drinking. The Task Force brought together leading experts on both the understanding of the college-alcohol problem as well as interventions that seek to moderate the problem. Considerable disagreement over possible solutions had marked the field of college alcohol. The Task Force argued "that to achieve a change in culture, schools must intervene at three levels: at the individual-student level, at the level of the entire student body, and at the community level. Research conducted to date strongly supports this three-level approach."[57]

The Task Force reviewed what it deemed "creditable research" to compile tiers of strategies that were effective among college students (such as offering brief motivational-enhancement interventions in student-health centers or emergency rooms); strategies effective among general populations and there-

---

56. TASK FORCE, *supra* note 44, at 8.
57. *Id.* at 2.

fore likely to work for college students (such as increased enforcement of min-imum-drinking-age laws); and those strategies deemed promising but not yet fully evaluated (such as adopting campus policies to reduce high-risk use like eliminating keg parties). A fourth tier, labeled "ineffective," included "infor-mational, knowledge-based values clarification interventions when used alone."[58] (This last category includes many of the practices that colleges had been using in the previous decade, presumably with little or no effect.)

Five years later, the NIAAA released an update to its Task Force Report, *What Colleges Need to Know Now.*[59] The NIAAA argued:

> The news is mixed. Among college students and other 18- to 24-year-olds, binge drinking … and, in particular, driving while intoxicated (DWI), have increased since 1998. The number of students who re-ported DWI increased from 2.3 million students to 2.8 million. The number of alcohol-related deaths also has increased. In 2001, there were an estimated 1,700 alcohol-related unintentional injury deaths among students 18–24, an increase of 6 percent among college students (that is, per college population) since 1998. In addition, it is estimated that each year, more than 696,000 students between the ages of 18 and 24 are assaulted by another student who has been drinking, and more than 97,000 students between the ages of 18 and 24 are victims of alcohol-related sexual assault or date rape. Clearly, alcohol-related problems on campus still exist.[60]

The NIAAA also reported that it had moved forward in redefining binge drinking, a term that had attracted considerable discussion since its use by Henry Wechsler in the HSPH CAS. The new definition: "[A] pattern of drink-ing alcohol that brings blood alcohol concentration (BAC) to 0.08 gram-per-cent or above. For a typical adult, this pattern corresponds to consuming 5 or more drinks (male), or 4 or more drinks (female), in about 2 hours."[61]

Finally, the NIAAA update summarized the results of two special reports that assessed progress in both individual and environmental prevention strate-gies for college students.[62] The NIAAA concluded,

58. *Id.* at 25.

59. Nat'l Inst. on Alcohol Abuse and Alcoholism, What Colleges Need to Know Now: An Update on College Drinking Research (2007).

60. *Id.* at 1.

61. *Id.* at 2.

62. Mary E. Larimer & Jessica M. Cronce, *Identification, Prevention, and Treatment Re-visited: Individual-Focused College Drinking Prevention Strategies 1999–2006,* Addictive

Research shows that several carefully conducted community initiatives aimed at reducing alcohol problems among college-age youth have been effective, leading to reductions in underage drinking, alcohol-related assaults, emergency department visits, and alcohol-related crashes. A close collaboration between colleges and their surrounding communities is critical. This includes environmental approaches (such as more vigorous enforcement of zero tolerance laws, other drinking and driving laws, and strategies to reduce the availability of alcohol) as well as approaches that target the individual drinker (such as wider implementation of alcohol screening, counseling, and treatment programs).[63]

Lessons Learned from the Lacrosse Rape Case

What lessons can be learned from the Duke lacrosse case about college drinking? In one sense, none; the case is a "false positive": no rape happened, and any discussion of the role alcohol played in the case obviously can't explain what didn't happen. But the case opened up discussion of alcohol problems at Duke, and may help raise more general questions about the role of alcohol in current undergraduate life.

Reports of the alleged rape by the Duke lacrosse team members frequently mentioned drinking and underage drinking, drug use by the alleged victim, and a "culture of excess" that marked some part of Duke undergraduate life. Some members of the team were under twenty-one, and so plans to go to a bar or strip club were shelved; the party the team attended had been moved to a private house off-campus because of a university crackdown on on-campus drinking. Reactions to the alleged rape included investigation into the conduct of the lacrosse team members and a critical assessment of Duke's culture, both raising the issue of alcohol abuse as a common problem at the university.

Duke has some of the institutional characteristics that make it likely to exhibit a culture of heavy college drinking. Big-time athletics, an active Greek life, and a reputation for a vibrant social life are often associated with that culture. But its own data show that most Duke students don't frequently binge drink, and even the lurid and sensational reporting after the stripper party

BEHAVIORS (2007). Traci L. Toomey, Alexander C. Wagenaar & K.M. Lenk, *Environmental Policies to Reduce College Drinking: An Update of Research Findings*, 68 J. STUD. ALCOHOL 208 (2007).

63. NIAAA, *supra* note 57, at 2.

indicates that only a minority of its students were part of the "Duke 500."[64] As some measure of how the alcohol issues raised by the stripper party were eclipsed by the furor over prosecutorial misconduct, a Duke Alumni Magazine "one year later" story did not even mention student drinking.[65] Media stories about the stripper party also have dropped the student-drinking theme.[66]

In the end, the Duke lacrosse rape case proved to be an example of egregious prosecutorial misconduct, because the lacrosse players were innocent of rape. Nevertheless, the students involved did engage in some heavy drinking that day, including playing drinking games. Some were underage. And, of course, they hired strippers and a few voiced crude racist remarks. So in this case, the underage and immoderate drinking ended up being linked to boorish and immature behavior, not an uncommon outcome. A minority of Duke's students appear to live in a subculture in which heavy drinking, hooking up, Greek life, and involvement in athletics mark their behavior off from other students. This same subculture exists at many other colleges and universities.

Extensive public-health evidence has shown that heavy episodic or binge drinking is associated with a host of health and behavioral consequences, including intoxicated or party rape. As one scholar of college sexuality observed of the Duke incident, "Regardless of the outcome of the criminal investigation, it was clear that members of this team were engaging in heavy alcohol consumption and creating a sex-charged atmosphere by hiring two exotic dancers. It is this type of behavior that has concerned many scholars who have studied binge drinking, fraternity life, and rape."[67] There is little evidence that college drinking has changed much across the country (if anything, it may have increased and intensified), and so one assumes that some of its correlates or consequences will continue—1,700 deaths, and one in twenty women raped, almost three-quarters because they are too intoxicated to give consent.

It is too early to assess the lasting consequences of the Duke episode (as reports circulate of continuing legal actions by the team members). The episode helped focus attention on how a culture that mixes alcohol, sex, and sports at an elite university raises both the risk of serious and criminal outcomes as well as troubling questions about alcohol use yet to be answered effectively by higher education. But raising the risk is not the same thing as certainty: no rape hap-

---

64. Reitman, *supra* note 32.

65. Robert J. Bliwise, *One Year Later*, DUKE ALUMNI MAG., May–June 2007.

66. David Aldridge, *Duke Lacrosse: Life After the Rape Scandal*, PHILADELPHIA INQUIRER, Mar. 4, 2008.

67. BOGLE, *supra* note 47, at 162.

pened at the Duke stripper party, though thousands do at colleges across the country, most of them because of too much alcohol.

CHAPTER FIVE

Invisible Criminality: Male Peer-Support Groups, Alcohol, and the Risk of Aggressive Sexual Behavior

Michelle S. Jacobs

Introduction

For the public, the experience of the Duke lacrosse players who were accused of participating in a gang rape was a nightmarish tale of a group of innocent, young, white scholar-athletes being dragged through the criminal-justice system on the basis of a false complaint by a black sex worker. The notion that these young men's lives would be irrevocably damaged by a spurious rape accusation was too horrible to contemplate. Fortunately, the players had access to resources—financial, political, and emotional—that ultimately created an avenue for their stories to be heard in the judicial arena. The resolution, or one might say dissolution, of the case was relatively quick as their parents had the money to pay for investigative assistance and legal expertise. The backlash against the prosecutor was equally quick and severe, with ethics proceedings commencing prior to the cases' dismissal and the decision to disbar him following shortly thereafter. The reality is that for the Duke players the criminal-justice system worked just as it should have. They were unjustly charged and wholly vindicated. There are many poor defendants for whom the same cannot be said, but that is not the focus of this chapter.[1]

---

1. It is, however, the focus of Chapter Ten (Uphoff), *infra*.

The Duke defendants found themselves facing false allegations of gang rape as a result of a party held in a private residence, where the team was participating in a bonding experience. There was an ample supply of alcohol within the apartment and the cocaptains had hired two exotic dancers to entertain the team. All of the risk factors that can lead to acquaintance rape, particularly of the gang-rape variety, were present that night. Although theories explaining why college-age men rape vary, four factors can generally be used to identify a heightened risk for male sexual aggression: stereotypical views of male and female role orientation, membership in a male peer-support group, alcohol consumption, and lack of deterrence. It is clear that at least three of these factors were present in the Duke scenario. This chapter will use the Duke lacrosse case as a lens through which to examine the phenomenon of acquaintance rape, particularly gang rape by college athletes; the risk of exposure to violence for exotic dancers; and finally, the prickly issue of false rape allegations in the acquaintance-rape context.

Athletes, Fraternities, and Sexual Assault

Masculinities and Male Peer Support

Sexual assault by strangers and acquaintance-rape are problems that exist on all college campuses today.[2] Judging by their actions, college administrators appear to consider stranger rape to be the more serious of the two. Colleges spend millions of dollars every year securing their physical campuses to protect coeds against strangers lurking in their midst. The majority of sexual assaults against college women, however, are committed by someone they know.[3] They are acquaintance rapes. Estimates are that from 10 to 25 percent of college-aged women have experienced an acquaintance rape prior to or during college.[4]

Two populations that are consistently identified as being "high risk" with regard to perpetrating sexual violence are fraternity members and athletes. Al-

---

2. *See* Bonnie Fisher, Francis T. Cullen & Michael G. Turner, Bureau of Justice Statistics, U.S. Dep't of Justice, The Sexual Victimization of College Women (2000), http://www.ncjrs.gov/pdffiles1/nij/182369.pdf.

3. Rana Sampson, Office of Community Oriented Policing, U.S. Dep't of Justice, Acquaintance Rape of College Students, Problem-Oriented Guide for Policing Series 3 (2002), http://www.cops.usdoj.gov/pdf/e03021472.pdf (citing statistics demonstrating that 90 percent of college women who were victims of rape or attempted rape knew their assailant).

4. *Id.* at 2.

though studies do not support a correlation between college athletics and violence against women, they do demonstrate that, for those men who were inclined to abuse women prior to entering college, the culture of athletics can help sustain and reinforce their negative attitudes toward women by promoting competitiveness, aggression, and male privilege.[5] The language of coaching and male bonding adds to the problem by frequently denigrating women.[6] Moreover, there is an emerging body of data suggesting that men who participated in aggressive high-school sports engage in more psychological aggression, physical aggression, and sexual coercion toward dating partners than other men. Studies also show that former high-school athletes cause their partners more physical injuries, are more accepting of violence, have more sexist attitudes and hostility to women, are more accepting of rape myths, and are less tolerant of homosexuality than average.[7] In short, taking part in aggressive high-school sports has been identified as one of the multi-dimensional pathways leading to relationship violence.

Researchers Jeffrey Benedict and Todd Crossett studied sexual assaults reported on ten college campuses. Their data revealed that male athletes were responsible for 20 percent of assaults, despite constituting only 3 percent of the male student population. One third of the athlete assaults involved multiple perpetrators—that is, they were gang rapes.[8] Upon a closer analysis of the data on athletes and rape, Benedict concluded that, although football players committed a disproportionate number of individual rapes on campus, the assailant's membership in a high-prestige male group was a more salient factor for predicting participation in a gang rape than involvement in a violent sport. According to Benedict's statistics, 35 percent of campus gang rapes were committed by fraternity men, 15 percent by basketball players, and the remainder by lacrosse, basketball, and hockey teammates.[9] The elite status of these groups appears to provide its members with a sense of entitlement that condones lawlessness.

Fraternities and sports teams are male peer-support groups. The central elements of membership in a male peer-support group have been identified as

---

5. Gordon Forbes et al., *Dating Aggression, Sexual Coercion, and Aggression-Supporting Attitudes Among College Men as a Function of Participation in Aggressive High School Sports*, 12 VIOLENCE AGAINST WOMEN, 441, 443–44 (2006). Lacrosse was not specifically mentioned in the study, and it is unknown whether the authors included it as one of the sports that the study participants could identify.

6. *Id.*; *see also* JEFF BENEDICT, PUBLIC HEROES, PRIVATE FELONS 26 (1998).

7. Forbes et al., *supra* note 5.

8. BENEDICT, *supra* note 6, at 4.

9. *Id.*

holding a narrow conception of masculinity, believing in group secrecy, and objectifying women sexually.[10] There are several socialization factors that foster a gang-rape mentality among such groups, including both childhood socialization and socialization to the group. Among the more interesting group-socialization factors include competition over "outrageous" behavior, such as risky or antisocial acts, to establish a valued identity; hazing to create loyalty to the group and rebirth with a new identity as a "brother"; cultural practices of misogyny; and sharing each other's heterosexuality.[11]

Members of male peer-support groups who are at risk for committing sexual aggression share a narrow and traditional view of manhood. The traditional view of male and female sex roles is heavily influenced by patriarchy. There are various definitions of patriarchy, and it is clear that it is a complex phenomenon that exists in a variety of settings. Authors Martin Schwartz and Walter DeKeseredy identify three systems of patriarchy that help inform their research: societal patriarchy (overall systems within North American society that maintain male-domination patterns); familial patriarchy (systems that maintain male control in domestic settings); and courtship patriarchy (rules and customs of patriarchy playing out within the context of a dating relationship). The systems inform men on how to become masculine. Scholars argue that in North America there is one hegemonic view of masculinity. Inherent in that view is that men should avoid all things feminine, restrict their emotions severely, show toughness and aggression, exhibit self-reliance, strive for achievement and status, exhibit nonrelational attitudes towards sexuality, and actively engage in homophobia.[12]

Benedict also noted the importance of masculinity to male athletes, asserting that they can be particularly vulnerable to fears that their manhood is being challenged. Male athletes' concern with masculinity was also identified by Sarah McMahon in her research on student athletes and rape. She reported that many male athletes participating in her survey became visibly uncomfortable when asked to define "masculinity." They were likely to describe it as being the opposite of femininity.[13]

---

10. MARTIN D. SCHWARTZ & WALTER S. DeKESEREDY, SEXUAL ASSAULT ON CAMPUS: THE ROLE OF MALE PEER SUPPORT 115 (1997).

11. Chris O'Sullivan, *Lady Killers: Similarities and Divergences of Masculinities in Gang Rape and Wife Battery*, *in* MASCULINITIES AND VIOLENCE 82, 85 (1998).

12. *Id.* at 69.

13. SARAH McMAHON, DEP'T SEXUAL ASSAULT SERVS., RUTGERS UNIV., STUDENT-ATHLETES, RAPE-SUPPORTIVE CULTURE, AND SOCIAL CHANGE 11 (2004), http://sexualassault.rutgers.edu/pdfs/student-athletes_rape-supportive_culture_and_social_change.pdf.

Sharing each other's masculinity is one of the group-socialization factors that can foster a gang rape mentality among male peer-support groups. Sharing heterosexuality most often comes about through reporting sexual experiences to the group and even watching other group members engage in sex. Thus it is not uncommon for members of male peer-support groups to videotape their sexual liaisons, usually without the knowledge of their partner, and share the tape with their peers.[14] Both the issue of masculinity, as well as sharing heterosexuality, were factors that arose in the context of the Duke case. Twice, stripper Roberts made comments to some players suggesting that the size of their penises were small, thereby questioning their masculinity.[15] The first occasion prompted the team member to pick up a broomstick and suggest it be used as a "toy." On the second occasion, the reference to the player's genitals led to a racially derogatory exchange. The hiring of the exotic dancers and the willingness of some team members to engage in explicitly sexual verbal exchanges with them in front of members are examples of their willingness to share heterosexuality.

Support of the Rape-Myth Risk Factor

At the same time that male peer-support groups endorse traditional conservative views of masculinity, they also are more likely to endorse rape myths. Rape myths are "attitudes and beliefs that are generally false but are widely and persistently held, and that serve to deny and justify male sexual aggression."[16] Individuals subscribing to rape myths shift blame for sexual aggression from the rapist onto the victim. Examples of persistent beliefs reflective of rape myths include: most women who report a rape are lying; when women talk or act sexy they are inviting rape ("asking for it"); even though a woman may call it rape, she probably enjoyed it; women tend to exaggerate how much rape affects them; and if a woman doesn't want to have sex she can always resist a man's efforts. The greater acceptance a person has of rape myths, the more likely he will act aggressively in sexual relationships. In a study of college stu-

---

14. O'Sullivan, *supra* note 11, at 85.

15. *See supra* Chapter One (Luck & Seigel), at 6–7.

16. Anne Marie Chicorelli, *Rape Myth Acceptance Among Intercollegiate Student Athletes: A Preliminary Examination*, AM. J. HEALTH STUD. (Dec. 2002) (citing Lonsway & Fitzgerald, 1994). The original Rape Myth Survey was created by Burton and is known as Burtons Rape Myth Acceptance Scale (BRMAS). The instrument was modified by Lonsway & Fitzgerald to help differentiate rape-myth acceptance from attitudes that more appropriately reflect hostility towards women.

dents across five campuses, 50 percent of male athletes reported believing that "almost half" of women who report being raped are lying. In contrast, female athletes who completed the study were far more likely to respond that "very few" women who report rape are lying.

Acceptance of rape myths can also lead the holder to have a very narrow definition of rape and its likely victims. To them, rape is something that strangers do and potential victims are limited to one's own mother or a woman who has never had sex before.[17] Women who fall outside of this narrow definition cannot be victims. Men who endorse rape myths develop psychological devices to convince themselves that, regardless of the level of their sexual aggression, they are normal men acting out normal impulses. Thus, when they claim they did nothing wrong and raped no one, they actually believe this to be so.[18] Benedict cites as an example the University of Massachusetts football players who gang-raped a woman after she had accepted a ride from them. The woman was a prostitute, but had not agreed to engage in any sexual activity. Not only did they rape her, but they beat her so badly her teeth were fractured and left on the side of the road. When questioned, all of the players said the sex was consensual.[19]

Unfortunately, it is not just rapists or athletes who endorse rape myths. North America has been labeled as having a rape-supportive culture. When potential rapists live in a rape-supportive culture, they may get reinforcement or sense approval from nonrapists who also endorse rape myths. In studies, boys and girls in the eighth grade already demonstrated awareness and endorsement of some rape myths. In another study, high-school students who were asked to evaluate vignettes of dating violence were more likely to blame the victim when they were shown a picture of a woman dressed provocatively than when they were shown no picture at all or a picture of a woman dressed conservatively.[20] Because women are socialized in the same cultural context as men, even women can endorse rape myths, which can lead them to question whether their experience with sexual violence actually constitutes rape. This inability to classify an assault as rape occurs even when the acts committed against them meet the legal definition of rape.[21] As will be demonstrated below, a woman's confusion over whether she has been raped may give law enforcement a reason to classify her report, should she make one, as unfounded.

---

17. SCHWARTZ & DEKESEREDY, *supra* note 10, at 79–80.

18. *Id.* at 80.

19. BENEDICT, *supra* note 6, at 82. They apparently believed that, since the woman was a prostitute, she could not be raped.

20. SCHWARTZ & DEKESEREDY, *supra* note 10, at 81.

21. *Id.* at 89.

The Role of Alcohol as a Risk Factor

The defendants in the Duke case were exonerated in the criminal proceedings against them. They are now perceived as innocents whose lives and reputations will forever be ruined by the false rape accusation. There is little statistical support for the claim that rape allegations ruin a defendant's life. In fact, the number of convictions obtained in high-profile rape cases is very low and Benedict's research indicates that athletes suffer few permanent repercussions from being accused of rape, even when a plea is obtained.[22] Moreover, although the team members were not guilty of the rape, they did engage in criminal conduct on the night in question and on other nights as well. The team members had, by their own admission, gone to a strip club as a "bonding" experience on previous occasions.[23] The trips included all members of the team, even those who were underage. They later gained admission to a facility where alcohol was served by using fake identification and, presumably, some of them drank while there.[24] Thus, they violated two distinct laws of North Carolina, one prohibiting fraudulent use of identification to gain entry to a place where alcohol is served, and the other prohibiting the purchase of alcoholic beverages by anyone under twenty-one.[25] On the night in question, the team captains decided to have the strippers come to their private home so that all members could enjoy the "bonding" experience (and drink) without having to sneak into the club.[26] Although these actions are far less significant than the rape allegation, they nevertheless constitute criminal conduct punishable by a range of sentences, including incarceration.[27]

Of course, college students and members of certain male peer groups engage in this kind of conduct with unabashed impunity all the time. As a result, some people have a tendency to excuse it as mere low-level criminality to be

---

22. Benedict, *supra* note 6, at 149.

23. *See supra* Chapter One (Luck & Seigel), at 3.

24. *See id.* at 5.

25. N.C. Gen. Stat. 18B-302(c), (e) (2007).

26. *Id.* § 18B-302(a1), (b), (c). NCGSA also provides for a lower level misdemeanor, class three, if the purchase, possession, or consumption was by a person who was nineteen or twenty years old.

27. *See* N.C. Gen. Stat. 15A-1340.13. Section 15A-1340.13 provides a range of penalties depending on the number of prior convictions and class of misdemeanor. All of the offenses could have been resolved with community service, however a jail term was also possible. Assuming the men had no priors they were exposed to a possibility of forty-five days in jail for a Class One misdemeanor, thirty days for a Class Two, and ten days for a Class Three. Fines could run as low as $200 for a Class Three offense to an amount at the judge's discretion for Class One.

waved off by saying "boys will be boys." In addition to constituting serious violations of the law, however, the lacrosse players' use of fraudulent identification and underage drinking reveal their penchant for dishonesty and willingness to exempt themselves from the obligation to obey the law. Additionally, the use of alcohol by college students significantly heightens the risk that a sexual assault will occur.

Alcohol consumption, including binge drinking, is a nationwide problem on college campuses; it is particularly prevalent within social networks such as fraternities and sororities.[28] Campus and off-campus parties organized by men in social networks have some of the highest levels of alcohol consumption and are also often the sites for abuse of women. Although current literature refutes any claim of a causal connection between alcohol use and violence toward woman, research does show an as-yet-unexplained correlation between the two. A number of possibilities exist for the connection. Men may have different reasons for social drinking than women, with men expecting alcohol to help facilitate the procurement of sex while women may drink to enhance group socialization.[29] Alternatively, men may have different views of women who drink versus their view of men who drink. They may see men who drink as normative while viewing women who drink as loose and promiscuous—demonstrating by their drinking in public that they are available for sexual conquest or, in other words, are "asking for it." In all situations, alcohol impairs judgment. In the context of sexual aggression, alcohol can reduce both parties' ability to analyze stimuli, such as ambiguous cues of sexual intent. Finally, some men may understand that intoxication can be used down the road as an excuse for misbehavior or allegedly criminal conduct.[30]

By the factual account of what transpired on North Buchanan Boulevard, members started assembling at the house at two in the afternoon and participated in "beer pong" and other drinking games.[31] Mangum and Roberts did not arrive until approximately eleven that night; at that point, the players had been consuming alcohol for nine hours. As the facts of the case indicated, inappropriate conduct and language did occur while the two dancers were present and, at one point, a player suggested the drunken Mangum be sodomized with a broomstick.[32] This caused Roberts to put an end to the engagement,

---

28. SCHWARTZ & DEKESEREDY, *supra* note 10, at 99. The issue is explored in detail *infra* in Chapter Four (Dowdall).

29. SCHWARTZ & DEKESEREDY, *supra* note 10, at 99.

30. *Id.* at 123.

31. *See supra* Chapter One (Luck & Seigel), at 4.

32. *See id.* at 6.

gather their belongings, and leave. Heavy alcohol consumption cannot be discounted as having played a role in sparking the events that led to the creation of conditions that fueled the false report of rape.[33]

The law's treatment of the role of intoxication in assessing criminal liability for rape can be divided into two parts: the intoxication of the alleged perpetrator and the intoxication of the complainant. In common-law jurisdictions, rape was a general-intent crime.[34] Case law prior to the development of the Model Penal Code commonly held that voluntary intoxication on the part of the alleged perpetrator did not constitute an excuse for the commission of a general-intent crime, therefore voluntary intoxication would not be admissible to prove lack of criminal intent. Today, although some cases still hold that voluntary intoxication is not a defense to a general-intent crime, the better view is to determine whether the defendant's intoxication made him incapable of forming the requisite intent or of possessing the required knowledge.[35] Under the Model Penal Code, when recklessness is the requisite mens rea, if an intoxicated defendant is unaware of a risk of which he would have been aware had he been sober, his unawareness is immaterial and his voluntary intoxication will not excuse him from the crime.[36] Therefore, assuming that the mens rea that attaches to the element of consent in rape cases is recklessness or lower, a defendant's voluntary intoxication would not be a valid defense. He could not claim, in effect, that his drunkenness made him unaware of the victim's lack of acquiescence.

Sexual intercourse with a woman without her consent is rape. However, there are situations in which there may be ambiguity as to whether consent exists, and alcohol can factor into the creation of that ambiguity. As an initial matter, having sex with someone who is incapacitated is rape because, by definition, such a person is incapable of giving consent. A victim may be incapacitated because she is asleep, unconscious, suffering from a mental defect—or because she is intoxicated or under the influence of drugs. Criminal responsibility for the alleged perpetrator is strongest when the complainant is unconscious or involuntarily intoxicated as a result of some action on the part of the al-

---

33. Alcohol has been a factor in a number of high-profile sexual assaults on campuses throughout the country, including within the state of Florida, including Pi Kappa Alpha, Sigma Alpha Epsilon and Delta Chi.

34. *See* Wayne LaFave, Criminal Law 852 (2003).

35. *Id.*

36. *See* State v. Cameron, 514 A. 2d 1302, 1304–09 (N.J. 1986) (presenting a succinct discussion of the development of the law regarding intoxication and mental states from pre-Code common law through the present).

leged perpetrator himself, such as when he plies her with alcohol or slips a drug into her drink.[37]

The strength of a legal case against an alleged perpetrator becomes less certain when the woman's intoxication is self-induced.[38] Objectively it should not matter whether the complainant is voluntarily intoxicated or involuntarily intoxicated. The only question should be whether she is capable of consenting. If she's not, then sexual intercourse with her should constitute rape. For a host of reasons, however, including the cultural understanding of rape within society, the issue of whether the complainant is voluntarily intoxicated can negatively impact the prosecution of a rape case at three different stages.

In the first instance, if the complainant decides to file a rape report, her rendition of events must pass the scrutiny of law enforcement. A police officer may not interpret the facts relayed by the complainant as a sexual assault once it becomes apparent to the officer that the complainant had been drinking at the time of the offense. Members of law enforcement may carry the same cultural stereotypes that prevail in society and may themselves endorse the rape myths. They may share the belief that women who drink in public are sexually promiscuous, or that it is unfair to put the burden on the male for nonconsensual sex when the complainant has voluntarily placed herself in a condition in which her judgment is impaired. The officer may harbor doubts as to whether the complainant was assaulted or whether she engaged in sexual relations while drunk and subsequently regrets the interaction.

Should the complaint survive scrutiny by the police, the prosecutor assigned to the case may question whether he or she can convince a jury beyond a reasonable doubt that the complainant's voluntary intoxication incapacitated her to the degree required by law. The prosecutor may believe that the complainant was drunk enough to be vulnerable to unwanted sexual contact, but may question whether she was too drunk to be able to give consent. The prosecutor may actually believe that a sexual assault took place but, if he or she does not believe it is possible to convince a jury, the case will likely not go forward.

Finally, the jurors who ultimately decide the facts of the case may view the woman's intoxication as an indication that she was a willing participant in the sexual activity. Jurors come to deliberations with all of the influences, biases, and stereotypes they carry every day. In general, jurors have difficulty reaching a determination that sex between acquaintances was nonconsensual. Even

---

37. *See* LaFave, *supra* note 34, at 866–67, 871.
38. *Id.* at 873.

the presence of significant injuries to the complainant may be insufficient to convince jurors to convict.[39]

At the same time that the letter of the law prohibits sexual intercourse with incapacitated women and disallows intoxication as a defense, men in college learn contrary messages through their interactions with male peer-support groups. In fraternities, for example, new brothers may learn that providing alcohol to a woman is a good way to loosen her up so that she will not resist sexual overtures. Moreover, fraternity culture may encourage men to believe that it is acceptable to have sex with someone who is so intoxicated that she has passed out.[40] The latter is clearly rape and the former is arguably rape as well.

The administrators at Duke University became aware that there was trouble brewing in connection with the lacrosse team's party on March 15, two days after the event. The Dean of Students, Sue Wasiolek, knew there had been underage drinking by team members.[41] At that point, the University should have brought the lacrosse cocaptains in and suspended them for providing alcohol to underage team members and for hiring strippers. By failing to take forceful action on the matters that were not in dispute, the university failed both the team members and the greater university community. It failed to use the incident as an opportunity to remind students of the danger of underage drinking and to send a message to the entire community that even low-level law breaking would not be tolerated. Perhaps early action on the known violations would have provided a pressure release from the media onslaught and would have provided the university with the time needed for the sexual assault charge to be developed or dismissed. Instead, the administration chose to do nothing until March 25, when media pressure forced the cancellation of the game with Georgetown.

Although we now know it did not occur, the risk factors for sexual assault were in place. The lacrosse team was an elite men's sport with high visibility on campus. They were coming off a very successful season and had high expectations for a championship run. The team constitutes a male peer-support group. As highly competitive athletes, it is likely that they subscribed to traditional stereotypes of masculinity and endorsed at least some of the rape myth. Certainly, the reactions to references about the size of their genitalia suggest that classic concerns about masculinity were present. Alcohol was also present and

---

39. *See* JEFFREY R. BENEDICT, ATHLETES AND ACQUAINTANCE RAPE x–xi (1998); *see also* SCHWARTZ & DEKESEREDY, *supra* note 10, at 139 (discussing the difficulty of finding jurors who were willing to hold college athletes accountable for their behavior).

40. SCHWARTZ & DEKESEREDY, *supra* note 10, at 105.

41. *See supra* Chapter One (Luck & Seigel), at 23.

apparently the team's habitual use of alcohol and low-level criminality was known and tolerated by the university. The combination of these factors was combustible.

Exotic Dancers and the Danger of Violence in the Workplace

Just as the Duke lacrosse team members were college students, so too was Crystal Mangum, although this fact will likely be lost in the historical telling of the Duke tale, because she was a 31 years old single mother of two, hardly society's idea of a naïve and vulnerable coed. More importantly, it will be lost in the telling because she was an exotic dancer, a woman who earned money through sexual titillation. Although many college students do in fact earn money by engaging in exotic dancing, both the law and society's view of them is shaped by what they do as opposed to who they are. The adult-entertainment industry is experiencing unbelievable growth in the Unites States.[42] Operating a strip club or an escort service is a legitimate form of commercial enterprise. It is legal to work in such establishments; however, while the men who own these establishments are considered legitimate businessmen, the women who work in them have a heavier burden to bear. They are generally viewed as sex workers—individuals who exchange sex for money—regardless of whether they engage in this practice or not.[43] There is, of course, nothing inherent about the job of dancing or stripping that requires the performer to exchange sex for money. Nonetheless, some exotic dancers and strippers are, indeed, sex workers—which stigmatizes them all.

Allegations of rape are difficult to prove in most acquaintance-rape situations, but they are even more difficult to prove when the complainant works in the adult-entertainment industry or is a sex worker—or both. Women's claims for protection, which are already weak, are further reduced because the

---

42. Devi Maria Schmidt, *An Inside Look at the Life of an Exotic Dancer*, at 2, http://www.law.uoregon.edu/faculty/cforell/docs/ lifeofexoticdancer.pdf (last visited Oct. 28, 2008).

43. Lisa E. Sanchez, *Boundaries of Legitimacy: Sex, Violence, Citizenship, and Community in a Local Sex Economy*, 22 Law & Soc. Inquiry 543, 552 (1997) ("What the law treats as legal sexual commerce and conduct as a matter of official policy often contradicts the way it handles these spaces and the women who occupy them in practice. Moreover, while the law sanctions some sexual conduct, cultural attitudes tend to stigmatize all sex trade participants and treat them as noncitizens without rights.").

dancer's social status and behavior usually lead to false presumptions that they have consented to whatever happens to them. As former exotic dancer and prostitute Robin Few stated, "Most people would think a woman who goes into a stranger's home alone to bare it all for groups of intoxicated rowdy men is like a woman walking down a dark alley alone at 2 am. You don't do [it]…."[44] In his study of elite college athletes and professional sports figures, Benedict documented examples of sexual assault against exotic dancers. In one instance, a woman who had associated with professional athletes for years was raped by a group of athletes with whom she had no relationship. The woman was thirty-eight years old and had worked in a "legitimate" service field for all of her adult life. Eight months before the sexual assault she started performing nude dancing to earn more money. She was gang-raped by members of the New Orleans Saints and reported the rape to the police. The prosecutor assigned to the case decided not to go forward with it. The extensive media coverage of the case focused only on the fact she was an exotic dancer, ignoring the fact she had no criminal record, did not do drugs, and was a successful single parent—all equally relevant to the case and her credibility.[45] A second example is that of Dallas Cowboy player, Erik Williams, who sexually assaulted a seventeen-year-old topless dancer who had been hired to perform in his home. He raped the girl, confined her against her will and, when the police came to investigate, denied that he was detaining her. Fortunately, the police observed the girl signaling for help from the bedroom window and were able to rescue her.[46]

The available facts in the Duke case do not reveal whether Crystal Mangum or Kim Roberts were simply adult-entertainment workers or whether they were in fact sex workers. The DNA analysis for Mangum indicated the presence of semen from several unidentified men,[47] which suggests either that she had had multiple consensual partners prior to the lacrosse party, had engaged in sexual acts in exchange for money, or had been raped somewhere else. Nothing suggested that Roberts was anything other than a private dancer in the adult entertainment industry.

It is entirely possible that Mangum had been assaulted at a different location. Exotic dancers and women who engage in other indoor activity, whether in adult entertainment or in sex work, are at risk of being subjected to sexual

---

44. Megan Scott, *Exotic Dancers Face Real Dangers*, July 7, 2006, http://www.desiree alliance.org/Exoticdancersfacerealdangers.htm.

45. BENEDICT, *supra* note 6, at 58.

46. *Id.* at 63.

47. *See supra* Chapter One (Luck & Seigel), at 23.

violence. The work itself and stereotypical notions about women who engage in it lead many to question whether a sex worker or adult-entertainment worker can be raped. On the face of it, the question should be absurd—any woman who is forced to have sex against her will has been raped—but examples abound where prosecutors (such as in the New Orleans Saints case), judges, and jurors have difficulty concluding that a rape has occurred.[48] Law enforcement is often unwilling to take rape claims made by prostitutes seriously. In her work with prostitutes in Oregon, Sanchez quotes one of them:

> I flagged [an officer] down after I had been raped, and he didn't even give me the time of day. He said, 'It's your fault you're out here. I've got other things to do than worry about that.' I think it's wrong.... It's a crime that was committed, and every crime should be looked at the same—just because he was an *honorable citizen* doesn't give him the right to hurt me.[49]

In a study of indoor sex work, which included escort services, exotic dancing, and private dancing, half of the women in escort services reported being forced to have sex and 51.2 percent of the women working as exotic dancers reported being threatened with a weapon.[50] The authors stated that 19 percent of exotic dancers had been threatened with rape or threatened with a weapon between five and ten times. Customers were identified as being primarily responsible for the violence against these two groups.[51]

Workplace safety is one of the issues about which groups seeking to unionize sex workers or adult-entertainment workers have complained. Many strip clubs post signs explicitly prohibiting any touching of the dancers. Yet many dancers report incidents of customers touching them or even grabbing their crotches. In a well-run club, a dancer can ask the bouncer to eject an offending customer, but in many establishments the club owner may pressure dancers to allow customers to violate prohibitions on touching, give lap dances, or en-

---

48. Municipal-court judge Theresa Carr Deni set off a firestorm of criticism in October 2007, when she ruled that an African American prostitute gang-raped by four men had been robbed rather than raped. The judge suggested that the prostitute's allegation of rape "demeaned rape of real women." Jill Porter, *Hooker Raped and Robbed—By Justice System?*, Phila. Daily News, Oct. 12, 2007, at 6.

49. Sanchez, *supra* note 43, at 5. The speaker was fourteen years old at the time.

50. Jody Raphael & Deborah L. Shapiro, *Violence in Indoor and Outdoor Prostitution Venues*, 10 Violence Against Women 126, 131 (2004).

51. *Id.* at 135.

tertain in private booths where the dancer is secluded with the customer in an environment fostering intimate contact and placing the dancer at a heightened risk of sexual assault or other injury.[52]

As the adult-entertainment industry grows and the number of strip clubs increases, the working conditions for dancers have deteriorated, leading many women to minimize the time they spend in clubs and instead choose to work bachelor parties and one-on-one events.[53] The more private settings, however, can create situations conducive to coerced sex.[54]

Mary Anne Layden, a psychotherapist who counsels strippers, prostitutes, and sex offenders has stated that strippers make up a disproportionate share of rape victims. "Even when dancers are sent by an escort service, they are at risk of walking into a dangerous situation."[55] In addition, despite the fact an exotic dancer may be employed by an agency, there is no guarantee that the agency will send a bodyguard with the woman, and, even when a bodyguard is hired, there is no guarantee that he will enter the residence with the dancer as opposed to waiting outside in the car.[56] Layden argues that a stripper inadvertently sends a message to a man that, because he can invade her visually, it's acceptable to do so physically.[57] The very nature of the dancer's job is to excite the customer and for him to imagine that she is dancing just for him. Some customers engaging in the fantasy can blur the line between being a customer and being the imaginary boyfriend of the dancer. This blurring can lead the customer to justify touching or harassing the dancer in an inappropriate way.[58]

In the Duke case, the agency sent the dancers without a bodyguard. Exotic dancers have few workplace protections and cannot demand a bodyguard. Normally, agencies treat exotic dancers as independent contractors and thus they are not required to provide the dancers with any level of protection.[59] Most agencies can help a dancer obtain the services of a bodyguard, but the dancer

---

52. Sanchez, *supra* note 43, at 557.

53. *Id.*

54. *Id.* One of Sanchez's informants, who worked for a bachelor-party agency, said that some of her peers engaged in prostitution at "almost every party." While, not defining the work as prostitution, as the informant put it, "they would just "give 'em a hand job or something and get the money out of them that way."

55. Scott, *supra* note 44.

56. *Id.*

57. *Id.*

58. *See* Ann C. McGinley, *Harassment of Sex(y) Workers: Applying Title VII in Sexualized Industries*, 18 YALE J. L. & FEMINISM 65 (2006).

59. Marot Rudman, *Exotic Dancers' Employment Law Regulation*, 8 TEMP. POL. & CIV. RTS. L. REV. 515, 519–21 (1999).

must pay for this service herself.[60] Due to the nature of the work, it is unclear whether, even if dancers were employees of an agency or a club, they would be entitled to protection from sexual harassment in the workplace.

This is the context in which Roberts and Mangum performed their work. The conditions at the lacrosse team's party exemplified the many ways in which a dancer can be placed at risk. Alcohol consumption had been ongoing for nine hours; indeed, Mangum herself had something to drink while waiting to begin the show. At one point, the combination of alcohol and a muscle relaxant she had taken caused her to be unstable on her feet. Roberts later reported that Mangum was tripping and falling over herself and even collapsed to the floor, at which time Roberts simulated an oral sex act on her.[61] One of the lacrosse players inquired whether they had brought any toys. When Roberts indicated that they had not, the player picked up a broom and suggested it be used. The inference was clear: he was suggesting that the broom either be used to sodomize the incapacitated Mangum or be inserted into her vagina. Roberts refused to engage in the suggested conduct. One could easily imagine that, had Roberts been more intoxicated, the situation could have spiraled out of control and she or Mangum could have been assaulted.

Exotic dancers do not fit the stereotype of a traditional rape victim. By the account of many, an exotic dancer is a "bad" woman who is "asking for it." In reality, however, exotic dancers classically fall into the category of vulnerable women whom aggressive males seek out.[62] Victims tend to be individuals who are either outnumbered and overmatched physically, or especially vulnerable. Vulnerability can come from instability as a result of mental impairment through alcohol or drug consumption—or through employment in the adult-entertainment industry, exactly where prostitutes and exotic dancers are found.

A similar incident at the Delta Chi house at the University of Florida in 1999 demonstrates the difficulty of having a stripper's claims of rape taken seriously by law enforcement. The fraternity held an initiation party at which a female stripper claimed she had been raped.[63] Initially, officers went to the fraternity to interview the men and obtain a videotape of the event. After reviewing the tape, the police concluded that the sex was consensual. The State

---

60. Scott, *supra* note 44.

61. *See supra* Chapter One (Luck & Seigel), at 6.

62. BENEDICT, *supra* note 6, at 4; O'Sullivan, *supra* note 11, at 101.

63. *See* Adam Smith, *Volatile '99 Case a Test for Candidate*, St. PETERSBURG TIMES, June 26, 2006, http://www.sptimes.com/2006/06/25/State/Volatile__99_case_a_t.shtml (providing the details of the case in the context of how it would affect the gubernatorial candidacy of former State Attorney, Rod Smith).

Attorney General then charged the stripper with filing a false report. A local judge released the videotape to the public, deciding that nothing he saw on the tape that "would deem her a victim." The campus chapter of the National Organization for Women protested, stating that the tape actually showed the woman resisting penetration by slapping the man away, pushing him, and saying, "Stop. Stop. Stop." The fraternity members can be heard shouting "rape, rape, rape" while sexual acts were committed on the stripper. After the tape was made public and pressure mounted on the State to take action, six fraternity members were charged with soliciting a prostitute and lewdness. The false-report charge against the stripper was eventually dropped in exchange for a guilty-plea for running an escort service with an expired license. The men were placed on probation, paid fines, and the university placed the fraternity on disciplinary probation for two years.

In 2006 Delta Chi returned to campus of the University of Florida. Although newspaper accounts mentioned the 1999 incident, two articles erroneously stated that no charges had been brought against fraternity members;[64] a third stated that fraternity members were accused of soliciting a prostitute and having an unregistered party, although it is not clear whether the article was referring to charges the University brought as opposed to criminal charges.[65] All three articles mentioned that the stripper had been charged with filing a false report, without noting that the charge had been dropped. A documentary of the event entitled *Raw Deal* was made and shown at the Sundance Film Festival in 2001, but even at the conclusion of the documentary, which incorporated portions of the video taken at the fraternity, many viewers were uncertain as to whether a rape had occurred.

False Rape Reports

For most observers, the analysis of criminality in the Duke lacrosse case begins in the evening of March 13 and the morning after, when Crystal Mangum made her allegation that she had been raped. The final chapter on the issue of what occurred in that house has been written and the case will go down as a

---

64. Jack Stripling, *UF Fraternity Attempts a Daunting Task: Reform*, GAINESVILLE SUN, Feb. 14, 2006, at 6A (discussing Delta Chi's return to campus after a four-year suspension over the stripping incident); Deborah Swedlow, *Banquet Welcomes Delta Chi Fraternity Back to UF*, INDEP. FLA. ALLIGATOR (Gainesville, Fla.), Feb. 18, 2008, http://www.alligator.org/articles/2008/02/18/news.greeks_affairs/080218_deltachi.txt.

65. Kyle Craig, *Delta Chi Returns After Long Hiatus*, INDEP. FLA. ALLIGATOR (Gainesville, Fla.), Jan. 30, 2006, http://www.alligator.org/pt2/060130deltachi.php.

false rape claim. No doubt it will be forever cited as proof that rape complainants cannot be viewed as credible.

The issue of the prevalence of false rape reports is a complex one that has defied concrete measurement. The Duke case will likely instigate a new round of articles in academic journals alleging that false rape claims are rampant in the criminal-justice system. All scholars and criminal justice administrators acknowledge that unfounded claims of rape can be and are made. There is nothing unique about false rape reports: all categories of crime, including murder, have a percentage of claims that constitute false reports. It does appear to be the case, however, that the rate of false reporting for rape exceeds that for other crimes.[66] The actual percentage of unfounded rape claims is subject to debate. Estimates range from a low of 2 percent (which is frequently cited by many feminists and appears to be based on early FBI data) to a high of 41 percent, advocated by Eugene Kanin.[67] Both of these extremes have been the subject of methodological critique.[68]

Neither local police nor the FBI maintains separate statistics for false rape reports. Rather, the FBI tracks a category labeled "unfounded," which includes reports where the elements of the incident could not be established as well as incidents were the report was revealed to be false.[69] The two categories are not the same. For example, "unfounded" includes cases in which there may be a reasonable difference of opinion over whether consent was given. The complainant never recants her statement and continues to believe that she was raped. A false report, on the other hand, occurs only when the complainant withdraws her allegations and, in most instances, admits that they were falsely made. Currently, the FBI lists unfounded rape reports at slightly less than 9 percent.[70] It is impossible, however, to determine the portion of this that is constituted by false reports. In addition, law-enforcement personnel use different criteria from jurisdiction to jurisdiction to make the determination that a case is unfounded, making it difficult to compare rates of unfounded accusations across jurisdictions.[71]

---

66. David P. Bryden & Sonja Lengnick, *Rape in the Criminal Justice System*, 87 J. CRIM. L. & CRIMINOLOGY 1194, 1304 (1997) (citing an argument by Alan Dershowitz pointing to FBI statistics that "unfounded" rapes represent 8.4 percent of rapes reported as compared to 3.8 percent for burglary or 4.2 percent for motor-vehicle theft).

67. Eugene Kanin, *False Rape Allegations*, 23 ARCHIVES SEX. BEHAV. 81, 81 (1994).

68. Bryden & Lengnick, *supra* note 66, at 1309.

69. *Id.* at 1305; *see also* Sampson, *supra* note 3, at 5.

70. Sampson, *supra* note 3, at 5.

71. Bryden & Lengnick, *supra* note 66, at 1295, 1305.

Some police officers believe that there is an unusually high rate of false rape reporting by both college women and women generally. A published account lists some of the reasons why officers may think a case is unfounded or false:

> The victims had a prior relationship with the offender; the victim used drugs or alcohol at the time of the assault; the victim fails to immediately label her assault as rape and/or blames herself; there is no visible evidence of injury.[72]

As was discussed earlier, these reasons may be explainable as results of adherence to rape myth by society at large and by the victim herself. One indication of this is the fact that rape claims are far more likely to be labeled unfounded in acquaintance cases than in stranger ones. For acquaintance-rape allegations, the unfounded rate is four times higher than that for other rape crimes.[73]

Examples of police failure to investigate rape allegations seriously have been documented in several major metropolitan areas. An investigation by the *St. Louis Post-Dispatch* uncovered a two-decade-old policy within the St. Louis Police Department to maintain most rape complaints on paper (as opposed to on the computer), avoid reporting rape as part of the Uniform Crime Statistics, and collect but not process rape kits.[74] In addition, after a period of time, the police shredded the paper memorandum, the only evidence of the complaint, effectively ruining any chance that the alleged perpetrator could be prosecuted. On top of all this, when complaints were initially taken, officers frequently downgraded the allegation to a less serious crime.[75] When these practices were disclosed in the newspaper, the chief of police ordered the paper files remaining to be reviewed and the complaints listed as crimes. After the order, some of the reports were filed and dismissed as unfounded. An audit of the St. Louis records performed by an official who had helped resolve similar problems in Philadelphia noted that the St. Louis police were using their own definition of unfounded instead of following generally accepted reporting standards set forth for law enforcement agencies.

---

72. Sampson, *supra* note 3, at 6.

73. Bryden & Lengnick, *supra* note 66, at 1233.

74. For a in-depth discussion of this scandal, see Jeremy Kohler's ten-part series written in 2005 for the *St. Louis Post-Dispatch*, http://www.dartcenter.org/dartaward/ 2006/newspaper/hm1/toc.php.

75. *Id.*

Similar problems had been uncovered in both Philadelphia and Atlanta. The inability of sex workers to be considered credible was exemplified in the problems identified in the Atlanta police department. There, the police tended to mark as "unfounded" any allegation of rape made by a prostitute or drug-addicted woman. The police admitted that, as a result of the failure to investigate these claims, a serial murderer-rapist remained undetected and at large in the Atlanta area for years.[76]

The existence of false rape reports is clearly a serious matter, both for the protection of defendants who might be falsely accused as well as for those women whose complaints are valid. To the extent that law-enforcement personnel and prosecutors suspect the statistics on false reports are depressed, they are less likely to support women whose complaints are valid. Some writers and men's organizations allege the existence of a feminist conspiracy to artificially reduce the statistics on the occurrence of false reports of rape.[77] Such allegations defy logic. Feminists are concerned about the prevalence of sexual assault, particularly in the acquaintance context. For years the push has been to help the law defining rape evolve from old common-law rules of credibility and evidence that operated against the complainant in a rape case.[78] Creating an environment in which women's credibility is evaluated fairly is of major concern to feminists. Fostering or encouraging women to file false reports of rape would not work to their benefit.

Much more research needs to be done to uncover how law-enforcement departments keep statistics on rape allegations. As in other areas of the law, the federal government could be helpful in setting standards for differentiating unfounded reports from false ones and establishing uniform definitions for both categories. Until such measures are taken, determining the true rate of false reporting will remain elusive. As a result, women whose complaints are valid will continue to have their claims discounted by those who believe the rate of false reporting is higher than it may actually be.

---

76. Jeremy Kohler, *In Atlanta, Fallout Over Policy Ended in Disciplinary Action*, ST. LOUIS POST-DISPATCH, Aug. 31, 2005, http://www.dartcenter.org/dartaward/2006/newspaper/hm1/.08.php.

77. *See, e.g.*, False Allegations—False Accusations—Recovered Memories, http://www.falseallegations.com (last visited Oct. 28, 2008); Most Rape Allegations Are False, http://www.angryharry.com/esMostRapeAllegationsAreFalse.htm (last visited Oct. 28, 2008).

78. Lord Hale's Rule is the best example of the oppressive nature of the old approach to rape law. Lord Hale believed that a woman's report of rape was inherently suspicious and that the jury should be given instruction to scrutinize her testimony more carefully than other witnesses'. "It is the victim, not the defendant, who is on trial." LaFave, *supra* note 34, at 848.

Conclusion

It is fortunate for the Duke players that the system worked in the end and the charges against them were dropped. They will be free to continue their lives unblemished and with substantial financial security as a result of their lawsuits against Duke and the City of Durham. Their good fortune is somewhat ironic in view of the fact that, in many instances, defendants who are exonerated after lengthy periods of incarceration and whose lives have been permanently ruined receive little if anything for the miscarriage of justice. Nonetheless, the reality is these students dodged a bullet; the factors that put athletes at risk for committing gang rape were in place that evening. The team skirted uncomfortably close to a line that they could easily have crossed. Fortunately for the team, Roberts, at least, was able to make an assessment that she and Mangum were at risk of being subjected to violence and she left the party, dragging Mangum along. In addition, some of the team members had enough courage and strength to resist groupthink and were instrumental in keeping the situation from escalating beyond a verbal attack against the dancers. Rather than celebrate this particular group of athletes and hold them up as victims, the public, universities, and lawmakers should use the case as a cautionary tale of the potential for tragedy when college athletes and other male peer-support groups have the privilege of engaging in conduct that is both criminal and immoral with impunity.

PART THREE

LESSONS LEARNED ABOUT RACE

Sarah Baartman, the Hottentot Venus, 1810[*]

---

[*] http://www.westminster.gov.uk/libraries/archives/blackpresence/16.cfm (last visited Oct. 23, 2008).

Black Venus Hottentot Revisited: Gratuitous Use of Women of Color's Bodies and the Role of Race and Gender in Campus and Academic Reactions

Michèle Alexandre

Introduction

The Black Venus Hottentot[1] was the name given to Saartjie Baartman, an African woman whose body and body parts were exhibited for years in Europe

---

1. *See generally Hottentot Venus: The Story*, http://www.theimageofblack.co.uk/2_feature.htm (last visited Oct. 28, 2008). This site discusses Baartman's life:

Saartjie Baartman was a Quena (or Hottentot) woman brought to Europe in 1810, to be exhibited for public inspection as an example of her tribe.... Indigenous tribes around the world provided cultural and intellectual challenges to European notions of civilization, spiritual belief, and human body ideals—beauty and health.... When she arrived in Britain and later France, Saartjie was confronted with the astonishment, curiosity and cruel heckling of a public that had limited contact with native Africans, but already had preconceived notions about them. In London Saartjie was displayed as a freak show display piece amidst the hairy women, vitiligo sufferers and obese people of the time.... African women in particular were viewed as exotic and represented a 'native' eroticism, relative to 'forbidden' sexual life. In France, black women were used to promote brothels and their visual presence amidst white prostitutes on postcards and later in photo-for people to ogle, appropriate, and dissect; Europeans at the time perceived her body parts as particularly anomalous.[2] Confined to prostitution after being exhibited at *Le Musée de l'Homme* in Paris, Baartman died of complications from sexually transmitted diseases in 1816.[3] Although society has generally marginalized women throughout history, black women's bodies, because of their initial categorization as property, have been particularly commodified and sexualized—as Baartman's tragic fate demonstrates.[4] This derogatory treatment has been endured not only by black women but, to some degree, by women of color in general.

By now the dust has settled, somewhat, on the turmoil that was the Duke lacrosse rape case.[5] In the meantime, much energy has gone into decrying the procedure used to investigate the rape allegations.[6] Many have felt vindicated on behalf of the once-accused players by the scrutiny and punishments bestowed upon prosecutor Mike Nifong.[7] Yet, in the midst of all the debates about guilt, innocence, procedure, and DNA evidence, important facts have generally been overlooked: the lacrosse students' participation in the sex industry, the ease with which they contacted the escort service, the apparent absence of security provided to the sex workers,[8] and the appar-

---

graphs, usually ensured successful patronage. Saartjie's extreme physical difference to the established black prostitutes in Paris made her an instant target for lurid sexual advances. Saartjie died of an infection in 1816 after prostitution and excessive alcohol abuse had consumed her body. Following her death, Cuvier made a cast of her body and dissected her brain and genitalia to be pickled in jars for ethnographic display at the Musee de l'homme in Paris. The jars remained on public display there until 1985, when they were finally put into storage. *Id.*

2. *See* Brigham A. Fordham, *Dangerous Bodies: Freak Shows, Expression, and Exploitation*, 14 UCLA Ent. L. Rev. 207, 215–16 (2007) ("Like many San women, Baartman had steatopygia, which appeared strange and primitive to European audiences. During her lifetime, Baartman had been paraded around in beads, feathers, and in tight clothes matching her skin color while a barker exclaimed that Baartman was 'wild as a beast' and invited viewers to stare at and poke her unusually large buttocks.").

3. *See* Lucille Davie, *Sarah Baartman, at Rest at Last*, SouthAfrica.info, Aug. 12, 2002, http://www.southafrica.info/ess_info/sa_glance/history/saartjie.htm.

4. *See* Jean Young, *The Re-Objectification and Re-Commodification of Saartjie Baartman in Suzan-Lori Parks's* Venus, 31 Afr. Am. Rev. 699, 699–700 (1997).

5. *See* Lara Setrakian, *Charges Dropped in Duke Lacrosse Rape Case*, ABC News, Apr. 11, 2007, http://abcnews.go.com/US/story?id=3028515.

6. *Id.*

7. *Id.*

8. Although this chapter primarily discusses the dangers and challenges faced by female sex workers, the author acknowledges that the risks faced by male and transgendered sex workers are also important issues.

ent lack of value attached to the bodies of the women of color involved.[9] Ultimately, the story of the rape allegations is much more than a legal narrative of culpability and innocence.[10] Beyond that much-exploited dichotomy, the sensationalism surrounding the media's portrayal of the case recalls the narratives of women whose stories are often relegated to the margins of history.[11]

The Duke case tests our ability to look beyond stereotypes triggered by occupation, gender, and race.[12] Thoughtful analysis leads us to consider the scope of protections that escort services afford to sex workers and whether the failure to provide adequate protection should give rise to equitable if not legal contractual claims. Furthermore, this case should lead us to evaluate seriously the level of accountability exhibited by the university's administrators in the face of reports that students commonly hired sex workers. How far should we extend universities' recognized duty to promote gender and racially unbiased practices, and how should that goal be balanced with the desire to encourage free speech and independence on college campuses?

This chapter will analyze the class, race, and gender implications of the campus reactions to the rape allegations as well as explore the potential for added protections for women employed in the erotic-labor force. The first section of the chapter discusses the perception of women of color's bodies, both historically and in modern times, the latter examination focusing on media-perpetuated stereotypes. The second focuses on sexual profiling in the erotic-labor force and discusses how such profiling is an especially great burden for women of color. Section three explores the race, class, and gender issues that the events and narratives surrounding the Duke rape allegations have raised. The fourth section analyzes the Duke administration's reaction to students' hiring of sex workers. Finally, the fifth considers how legal accountability should be imputed to employers to ensure the safety of the erotic workers on their payroll.

---

9. *See* Kimberlé Crenshaw, *Mapping The Margins: Intersectionality, Identity Politics, and Violence Against Women of Color*, 43 STAN. L. REV. 1241, 1242 (1991).

10. *See* Susan Hanley Kosse, *Race, Riches & Reporters—Do Race and Class Impact Media Rape Narratives? An Analysis of the Duke Lacrosse Case*, 31 S. ILL. U. L.J. 243, 259–61 (2007).

11. *Id.*

12. *Id.*

Perception of Women of Color's Bodies, Both Historically and in the Era of *Flavor of Love* and *I Love New York*

Historically, women's legal status in the United States was not protected, but enslaved African women faced an even more marginalized state: they were not viewed as persons in the eyes of the law.[13] Instead, it saw them as property, beasts, and animals.[14] As such, enslaved African women were completely the physical and sexual subjects of their owners.[15] The rape of African-American women was justified by rhetoric that labeled them as "animalistically hyper-sexual"[16] and thus "responsible for their own rapes."[17] This was so pervasive that an article written by a southern white woman in a popular periodical on March 17, 1904, declared that:

> Degeneracy is apt to show most in the weaker individuals of any race; so Negro women evidenced more nearly the popular idea of total de-pravity than the men did. They are so nearly lacking in virtue that the color of a Negro woman's skin is generally taken as a guarantee of her immorality.... I sometime read of a virtuous Negro woman, hear of them, but the idea is absolutely inconceivable to me.[18]

This stereotyping was nothing new. For centuries, black women had to battle images of themselves as licentious, herculean, and amoral.[19] The unfairness of the unequal juxtaposition of black women to their white counterparts prompted Sojourner Truth's famous "Ain't I a Woman"[20] speech:

---

13. *See* Sarah Gill, *Dismantling Gender and Race Stereotypes: Using Education to Prevent Date Rape*, 7 UCLA Women's L.J. 27, 36 (1996).

14. *Id.*

15. *Id.*

16. *Id.*; Sander Gilman, *Black Bodies, White Bodies: Toward an Iconography of Female Sexuality in Late Nineteenth-Century Art, Medicine, and Literature, in* "Race," Writing, and Difference (Henry Louis Gates, Jr. ed., 1985).

17. Paula Giddings, *The Last Taboo, in* Words of Fire: An Anthology of African-American Feminist Thought XX (Beverly Guy-Sheftall ed., 1995).

18. Anne Firor Scott, *Most Invisible of All: Black Women's Voluntary Associations*, 56 J. So. Hist. 10 (1990).

19. *See* David Pilgrim, *Jezebel Stereotype*, Jim Crow Museum of Racist Memorabilia, July 2002, http://www.ferris.edu/jimcrow/jezebel.

20. Sojourner Truth delivered this powerful speech at a women's-rights convention in Akron, Ohio, in 1851. It is famous for illustrating the feminist movement's initial failure to address the needs of black women.

Dat man ober dar say dat womin needs to be helped into carriages, and lifted ober ditches, and to hab de best place everywhar. Nobody eber helps me into carriages, or ober mud puddles, or gibs me any best place.... And ain't I a woman? ... I have borne thirteen chillern and seem 'em mos' all sold off to slavery, and when I cried out with my mother's grief, none but Jesus heard me! And ain't I a woman?[21]

In contemporary times, black women have continued to struggle with being labeled as "promiscuous" and "mules of burden."[22] In addition, new stereotypes, like those of black women as "emasculators," "superwomen," "welfare mothers," and "negligent mothers," have filled the airwaves and popular discourse.[23] Most recently, several reality shows have exacerbated these negative stereotypes.[24]

---

21. O. GILBERT, NARRATIVE OF SOJOURNER TRUTH 133 (1878); *see also* Henry Louis Gates, Jr., *To Be Raped, Bred, or Abused*, N.Y. TIMES, Nov. 22, 1987, at 12 (reviewing HARRIET JACOBS, INCIDENTS IN THE LIFE OF A SLAVE GIRL (J. Yellin ed., 1987)); *see* D. WHITE, AREN'T I A WOMAN? FEMALE SLAVES IN THE PLANTATION SOUTH 27–29 (1985).

22. *See* Mark Anthony Neal, *(White) Male Privilege, Black Respectability, and Black Women's Bodies*, SEEINGBLACK.COM, May 23, 2006, http://www.seeingblack.com/ article_38.shtml.

23. *See* Michèle Alexandre, *Dance Halls, Masquerades, Body Protest and the Law: The Female Body as a Redemptive Tool Against Trinidad's Gender-Biased Laws*, 13 DUKE J. GENDER L. & POL'Y 177 (2006) ("Shows like *The Jerry Springer Show* and *The Maury Povich Show* have capitalized on some women's economic despair and social challenges, and deliberately depict poor black women as morally loose and unfit parents. At no time do these shows ever analyze the socio-economic elements affecting these women's lives. Instead, these women are presented to the public as caricatures and as objects of the public's moral judgment.").

24. *See Flavor of Love: About the Series*, VH1.COM, http://www.vh1.com/shows/dyn/flavor_of_love/series_about.jhtml (last visited June 10, 2008) ("In 'Flavor of Love,' 20 single women from all walks of life, selected for their expressed love for Flav [a black male rapper], will move into a 'phat crib' in Los Angeles and vie for his affection. With help and advice from Big Rick, Flav's gigantic body-guard and chauffeur, Flavor Flav will date all of the women, weed out the ones who are only after his fame and fortune ... and in the end will choose his one true love."); *see also* Teresa Wiltz, *Love Him, or Leave Him? Flavor Flav's Popular Show Sets Off Passionate Debate on Comedy and Race*, WASH. POST, Nov. 2, 2006, at C0.

"I Love New York" is a similar show, but with twenty single men vying for the affection of one black woman. *See I Love New York: About the Series*, VH1.COM, http://www.vh1.com/shows/dyn/i_love_new_york/series_about.jhtml (last visited June 10, 2008) ("[New York] will put 20 men through the paces, testing them on everything from their physical prowess to their 'daddying' skills to their earning potential. The men who impress New York and her mother will get dates with the ladies. The men who don't will get the door. And in the end, the man who loves New York the most will win a very special prize ... her heart.").

For example, VH1's reality-television shows *Flavor of Love* and *I Love New York* predominantly feature women of color, all eager to achieve notoriety. The women's private sexual lives are showcased and their body parts constantly made the focus of the camera. Millions of viewers tune in each week to watch the outrageous sexual behaviors and demeaning acts that take place on the show. Reality shows that objectify women are not out of the ordinary, of course, but those that focus on women of color have had remarkable ratings in light of the secondary networks on which they appear. The latter shows are not aberrations or manifestations of recent phenomena.[25] They are simply the modern versions of the same voyeuristic exhibitions in which museums, like *Le Musée de l'Homme,* showcased black women such as Saartjie Baartman two centuries ago.[26] Though not in physical bondage like Baartman, these women are similarly lured into participating in demeaning activities by the possibility of fame.[27] Producers and networks, well aware of the appeal of negative stereotypes, encourage them to behave as outrageously as possible.[28] Society's tendency to depreciate women' bodies in general, and black and brown bodies in particular, explains the Duke lacrosse players' casual decision to hire exotic dancers, and the escort service's apparent need to send women of color to the team's party (after the players had expressly asked for white dancers), that fateful night.[29] Moreover, according to reports, other Duke students had also hired exotic dancers in the past.[30]

---

25. *See id.* ("[*Flavor of Love* is] like watching the Hottentot Venus on display.... It's without redeeming value.... It's just about exploitation. It's like having slaves fight for your amusement.") (quoting Debra Dickerson).

26. *See Hottentot Venus: The Story, supra* note 1.

27. *See* Alessandra Stanley, *No Accounting for Taste: Jail Brides and Would-Be Rap Molls,* N.Y. TIMES, Aug. 8, 2006, at E1 (discussing the reality shows *Flavor of Love* and *Secret Lives of Women*).

28. *Id.*

29. STUART TAYLOR, JR. & KC JOHNSON, UNTIL PROVEN INNOCENT: POLITICAL COR-RECTNESS AND THE SHAMEFUL INJUSTICES OF THE DUKE LACROSSE RAPE CASE 17 (2007) ("[The hiring of exotic dancers] was not uncommon at Duke.... Over the 2005–2006 academic year, fraternities, sororities, and athletic teams hired strippers for more than twenty parties. This tally never challenged by Duke was computed by a lacrosse player's father.... The father did some old fashioned investigative reporting.... He opened the yellow pages, found 'four' escort agencies, called them up, and asked what services they offered and what experience they had with Duke parties.").

30. *See* Adam Hochberg, *Duke University Calls for an Attitude Adjustment,* NPR.ORG, Mar. 25, 2007, http://www.npr.org/templates/story/story.php?storyId=9131243.

Sexual Profiling and the Erotic-Labor Force

The Duke lacrosse rape case is a story that is crucially centered on our inability to address and undo our longstanding assumptions about women of color's bodies.[31] It is also a story about the inability of nontraditional women, such as exotic dancers and prostitutes, to have a safe space in our society to address verbal and physical abuses that do not always meet accepted legal definitions but, nonetheless, perpetually dehumanize women and stagnate society's progress.[32] The ease with which many dismissed the verbal assaults directed toward the exotic dancers the night of the lacrosse party is evidence of this stagnation.[33] Worse, the very setting of the rape allegations, a house owned by Duke University,[34] occupied primarily by privileged white students, which was the site of a party featuring two exotic black dancers for the audience to watch and mentally dissect, is an eerie throwback and sad re-enactment of Saartjie Baartman's experience.[35]

The objectification of women's bodies is, of course, not limited to the bodies of women of color.[36] Nonetheless, as a result of ideals perpetuated through slavery and colonization, women of color have been more common and more accepted targets of this practice.[37] Baartman's experience, and those of others like her, has made women of color in general, and black women in particular, keenly aware of society's historical perception of their bodies and of the prevailing assumption that there exists a greater right of access to their bodies

---

31. *See* Camille A. Nelson, *American Husbandry: Legal Norms Impacting the Production Of (Re)Productivity*, 19 YALE J.L. & FEMINISM 1, 3 (2007) ("[W]hile 'sexuality is the linchpin of gender inequality,' it is also the lynch-pin of racial injustice for black women.")

32. *See* Rosenberg and Associates, Victims of Sexual Abuse, Am. Acad. of Experts in Traumatic Stress, http://www.aaets.org/article123.htm (last visited Oct. 29, 2008).

33. *See* William L. Anderson, *Duke Lacrosse: The Players Were Already Vindicated*, LEWROCKWELL.COM, May 30, 2007, http://www.lewrockwell.com/anderson/anderson187.html.

34. TAYLOR & JOHNSON, *supra* note 29, at 22 ("Duke next decided to block students from renting in Trinity Park by buying houses from landlords, putting them under owner-occupancy covenants and then reselling them to nice, quiet adults. The purchase of fifteen houses, including 610 North Buchanan, went through on February 28, two weeks before the lacrosse team annoyed the neighbors with its stripper party.").

35. *See* Mark Reynolds, *NEGRITUDE 2.0: Modern Day Hottietots*, POP MATTERS, Mar. 10, 2006, http://www.popmatters.com/columns/reynolds/060310.shtml.

36. *See* Michelle R. Adelman, *International Sex Trafficking: Dismantling the Demand*, 13 S. CAL. REV. L. & WOMEN'S STUD. 387, 387 (2004) ("The objectification of women as sexual beings in the public and private spheres is not a new phenomenon and, despite political and media portrayals, is in no way unique to any one culture, society, or religious sect.").

37. *See* Vednita Carter & Evelina Giobbe, *Duet: Prostitution, Racism and Feminist Discourse*, 10 HASTINGS WOMEN'S L.J. 37, 40 (1999).

than to those of women in general.[38] This fact has caused many women of color, in overt rejection of negative stereotyping, to embrace traditional ideals of propriety.[39] Still, women of color who choose to work in the sex industry, including the exotic dancers involved in the Duke case, are doubly vulnerable[40] : they face danger from their participation in the sex trade as well as from their status as women of color.[41] They often risk ostracism, and even physical harm, from members of both the white community and communities of color.[42] Worst yet, these women are more likely to experience neglect and indifference even when it is clear that their bodies have been violated.[43] This vulnerability was illustrated by the sheer indifference to the dancers' needs in the aftermath of the Duke lacrosse party.

This neglect is also explained by society's tendency to sexually profile[44] women based on their choice of clothing or occupation. Sexual profiling manifests itself in private interactions, as well as legal indifference for these women's welfare. "The white racist view of Black women as 'unrape-able' from slavery forward works like the marital rape preclusion: for women effectively owned, sexual possession and use is assumed, making rape inconceivable."[45]

---

38. *See* Sander L. Gilman, *Black Bodies, White Bodies: Toward an Iconography of Female Sexuality in Late Nineteenth-Century Art, Medicine and Literature,* 12 Critical Inquiry 206, 212 (1985).

39. *See* Robert S. Chang & Adrienne D. Davis, *The Adventure(s) Of Blackness in Western Culture: An Epistolary Exchange on Old and New Identity Wars,* 39 U.C. Davis L. Rev. 1189, 1202 (2006) (discussing the negative reaction of black actresses, and the subsequent backlash faced by Halle Berry and artist Kara Walker, for their portrayal of "popular and subordinating fantasies of black female sexuality").

40. *See* Carter & Giobbe, *supra* note 37, at 40 ("Today sex-oriented businesses are typically zoned in Black neighborhoods. Poor, Black communities have become de facto combat zones where street prostitution is highly visible and readily available. The implicit message to white men is that it is all right to solicit Black women and girls for sex, that we are all prostitutes.").

41. *See* Karin S. Portlock, *Status On Trial: The Racial Ramifications of Admitting Prostitution Evidence Under State Rape Shield Legislation,* 107 Colum. L. Rev. 1404, 1412 (2007) ("[P]articular, societal conceptions of black women traditionally placed them in the unprotected group: Rape in the black community was perceived as something other than a violation of the sexual purity that common law rape jurisprudence sought to defend. As a result, black women were historically excluded from the protection of early rape laws.").

42. *Id.*

43. *Id.*

44. Alexandre, *supra* note 23, at 180 ("Sexual profiling is rooted in the gender stereotypes historically associated with women's bodies.").

45. Catharine A. MacKinnon, Sex Equality 831 (2007).

Across cultures, a woman's worth and society's eagerness to protect her usually relate closely to how she chooses to express herself physically and the value that the society attaches to her body.[46] The widespread method of judging a woman's character based on her way of dressing is alarming and infrequently questioned.[47] In addition, the ways in which mainstream black women still fall prey to verbal and oppressive assaults demonstrates the fundamental vulnerability of black women to objectification and dehumanization.[48] Don Imus's hateful words[49] towards the Rutgers women's basketball team and Isiah Thomas's hateful and routine statements to his black employee[50] are examples of the vitriol that one's status as a black woman can trigger. Even more, when a black woman works in a nontraditional occupation, like exotic dancing or prostitution, the activity obliterates any remnants of humanity that were once accorded these women.[51] This reality demands that we, as a society, prioritize the dis-

46. *See* Sakthi Murphy, *Rejecting Unreasonable Sexual Expectations: Limits on Using a Rape Victim's Sexual History to Show the Defendant's Mistaken Belief in Consent*, 79 Cal. L. Rev. 541, 564 (1991) ("Throughout history, our culture has made assumptions about people based on certain physical characteristics.").

47. *See* Theresa M. Beiner, *Sexy Dressing Revisited: Does Target Dress Play a Part in Sexual Harassment Cases?*, 14 Duke J. Gender L. & Pol'y 125, 125 (2007).

48. Judith Olans Brown, Lucy A. Williams & Phyllis Tropper Baumann, *The Mythogenesis Of Gender: Judicial Images of Women in Paid and Unpaid Labor*, 6 UCLA Women's L.J. 457, 522 n.284 (1996) ("[T]he frequency with which sexual insults ... are coupled with "black," "nigger," or "jungle" explains the higher number of sexual harassment cases brought by black women.").

49. *Imus Sparks Controversy with Comments About Rutgers Team*, Apr. 5, 2007, http://www.nbc10.com/news/11536642/detail.html ("Imus started out talking about the Rutgers team as, 'some rough girls from Rutgers. They got tattoos,' and then went on to call them 'some nappy-headed hos.'"). Imus also compared them to the Tennessee team, saying "[t]he girls from Tennessee—they all looked cute." The conversation then went on to refer to the game as "the jigaboos versus the wannabes." *Id.*

50. *Trial Starts in Isiah Thomas Sex Harassment Suit*, N.Y. Daily News, Sept. 11, 2007, http://www.nydailynews.com/sports/basketball/knicks/2007/09/11/2007-09-11_trial_starts_in_isiah_thomas_sex_harassm.html ("'Bitch, I'm here to win basketball games,' Browne Sanders quoted Thomas as saying in the workplace. In another discussion about season ticket holders, she claimed Thomas said, 'Bitch, I don't give a (expletive) about these white people.'"). These statements carry the same meaning whether white or black individuals utter them. The ease and repetitive ways in which they are used in our society against black women demonstrate again the vulnerable positions in which women of color in all sectors find themselves. The fact that the Madison Square Garden did not take immediate actions learning of Thomas's behavior shows the unfortunate social acceptance of this kind of language against women of color.

51. *See* Kosse, *supra* note 10, at 264 ("[T]he media and public feel less sympathy for a stripper than a student possibly because of an entrenched perception that certain women may be more at fault than others for the rape.").

mantling of these debilitating stereotypes.[52] Otherwise, the judgment of women on their race, gender, occupation, and dress will continue to facilitate inequity.[53]

In the aftermath of Duke lacrosse rape allegations, the crucial questions are: What are Duke's[54] and the city of Durham's responsibilities in this matter? How can they work to implement policies and procedures that can help topple and eradicate these nefarious race and gender based assumptions?

Much of the debate in the Duke case primarily centered on race and class.[55] The sharp contrast between the privileged ivy coated lacrosse players and the seemingly working class[56] black accuser raised questions of white and class privilege that were important.[57] The controversial reactions that this debate

---

52. *See* Carter & Giobbe, *supra* note 37, at 55 ("White society's standards and definitions have defined our sexuality as African-American women. Although the master no longer holds us captive on the plantation, we still carry the chains of slavery by virtue of our slave mentality. For Black women to reclaim what has been stolen, we must begin to name ourselves. We must realize that we no longer have to accept the many labels that have been engraved in our minds.").

53. *Id.*

54. *See* Karla FC Holloway, *Coda: Bodies of Evidence*, The Scholar and Feminist Online, Published by The Barnard Center for Research on Women, http://www.barnard.edu/sfonline/sport/holloway_01.htm (last visited June 11, 2008). Holloway describes her ambiguous position as a black woman and a member of Duke faculty, called to serve on a committee created to address the effects of the rape allegations on Duke University:

> I write these thoughts, considering what it would mean to resign from the committee charged with managing the post culture of the Lacrosse team's assault to the character of the university. My decision is fraught with a personal history that has made me understand the deep ambiguity in loving and caring for someone who has committed an egregious wrong. It is complicated with an administrative history that has made me appreciate the frailties of faculty and students and how a university's conduct toward those who have abused its privileges as well as protected them is burdened with legal residue, as well as personal empathy.

Id.

55. *See* Gitika Ahuja, *Duke Rape Allegations Challenge Booming Sport*, ESPN News, Mar. 29, 2005, http://abcnews.go.com/Sports/story?id=1784378 ("The investigation is focused on three white male Lacrosse players, and the allegations have enflamed passions about race and class.")

56. Taylor & Johnson, *supra* note 29, at 19 ("Daughter of an African-American retired mechanic who still works on cars in his front yard, [Mangum's] parents lived together in the house where she and her (then) two children also lived.").

57. *See* Peter Bradley, *Racism 101 at Duke*, Apr. 12, 2006, http://www.realclearpolitics.com/articles/2006/04/racism_101_at_duke.html ("Before the results of the DNA tests came back negative on Monday evening, most of the amateur detectives hyping the case had already convicted the whites. The general theme was that the alleged rapes represent 'white skin privilege.'"). Bradley went on to quote several observers:

elicited, furthermore, demonstrated that the allegations were mere triggers which created room for people to express already-existing grievances.[58] The legal resolution of the case will not cure these existing problems. If they remain unaddressed, they will continue to fester, only to erupt with violence again during the next controversy.[59]

Class-, Race-, and Gender-Based Dynamics in Events and Narratives Relating to the Rape Allegations

Although a number of details are in dispute, one fact has not been controverted: a group of Duke students, mostly white males, at a regular college student party, were so accustomed to gaining access to bodies with money that they placed a routine call to an escort agency, "ordered" two white[60] dancers, and were sent two women of color instead. After the dancers appeared, one report states that "one of the older players went into the living room and said that the

---

"The issues here," said Chandra Y. Guinn, director of the Mary Lou Williams Center for Black Culture, "go far deeper than a single incident. There are pockets of white privilege on this campus...."

"There's an embedded white supremacy here," said Travis Simons, a Duke divinity student.

"For me, this is not simply a case of sexual violence or just a case of racism. It's a case of racialized sexual violence, meaning if it had been a white woman in that room, it would not have gone down the same way," claimed Mark Anthony Neal, an African-studies professor.

"Last weekend was Duke's minority recruitment," said local resident Betty Greene. "What a welcome for minority students to walk into this story. I'm trying not to call it racial terrorism, but that's really what it is."

Id.

58. *See* Rachel Smolkin, *Justice Delayed*, Am. Journalism Rev., Aug.–Sept. 2007, http://www.ajr.org/Article.asp?id=4379 (referring to fellow journalist Daniel Okrent's reprimand of the media for subscribing to the public's preconceived notions regarding the Duke rape allegations: "It conformed too well to too many preconceived notions of too many in the press: white over black, rich over poor, athletes over non-athletes, men over women, educated over non-educated. Wow. That's a package of sins that really fit the preconceptions of a lot of us.").

59. *See* Gretchen Parker, *Dealing With Issues of Race in America*, Tampa Bay Online, Mar. 30, 2008, http://www2.tbo.com/content/2008/mar/30/dealing-issues-race-america/?news-politics.

60. Taylor & Johnson, *supra* note 27, at 24.

women had both arrived but were not as expected."[61] The dancers did not bring bodyguards, as such dancers usually do, and they were not white or Hispanic, as the agency had promised.[62] The lacrosse players had paid $800 for the service.[63] The extent of the players' disappointment at the fact that the women were not racially what they expected is not clear. What seems clear is that the women noticed the difference; one of the players went to deliver the news to his fellow party attendees, which demonstrates that there might have been at least a fear that some attendees would be disgruntled.

Furthermore, in at least one witness account, the fact that the dancers' race did not conform to the players' expectations resurfaced when the nights' activities later turned acrimonious. When Kim Roberts, the other dancer, headed back to her car at 12:50 a.m. through a crowd of the team members still complaining about being scammed, she called one player, who had earlier made a rude comment, "a little dick white boy, who could not get his own and had to pay for it." She stated that in response, "he was mad and it ended with him calling me the N-word."[64] Player Matt Zash recalled hearing second hand that the comment was "we wanted white girls, not n_____[s]."[65]

Although some, including Roberts herself in a *60 Minutes* interview, have described her first comment as provoking the player's retort, the two comments do not seem to be proportionate. The N-word is a racial slur loaded with hundreds of years of deadly and dehumanizing meaning. It seems disproportionate in any context. In addition, this racial slur unveils centuries-old stereotypes about the value of black women's bodies. It is interesting that the comment about the offending player's genitalia triggered a racial slur, a statement about the value of black dancers compared to the white dancers they initially requested. Furthermore, as Roberts was driving away from the premises, one of the guys was heard yelling, "Hey bitch, thank your grandpa for my nice cotton shirt."[66] This, too, was a deeply problematic comment that should not be dismissed as light-hearted banter. The ease with which these types of insults come to mind in times of anger is evidence of the steadfastness of racial and gender stereotypes in our psyche. Even more troubling,

---

61. Durham County Superior Court, Office of The Attorney General of North Carolina SUMMARY OF CONCLUSIONS (2007), http://www.newsobserver.com/content/news/ crime_safety/duke_lacrosse/20070427_AGreport.pdf.

62. TAYLOR & JOHNSON, *supra* note 27, at 24.

63. *Id.*

64. Durham County Superior Court, *supra* note 61, at 8.

65. TAYLOR & JOHNSON, *supra* note 27, at 29.

66. *Id.*

the students' choice of words indicates that our younger generations might be using these stereotypes with as much unchecked ease as generations before them. The comment regarding the woman's grandfather and the cotton shirts intersects both racial and class stratifications. The reference to the grandfather as providing the cotton shirt evidences an awareness of class and race privilege that in this context was used as a taunt rather than as mean of bridging differences.

What is equally disturbing in the many accounts of the event is that one of the players devalued the dancers by suggesting the use of a 'broomstick' on the women.[67] The threat of battery and the suggestion that the women's bodies be violated with a foreign object seems a grossly disproportionate reaction to an insult.

As the discourse centered on culpability and non-culpability, the students' use of an escort service has been accepted as customary behavior.[68] In the mass media, as well as the books and articles written about this controversy, the descriptions of the transaction to hire the dancers have read like descriptions usually accorded to the ordering of pizza or Chinese food.[69] One narrative written by a self-described "Dukie," described how the poor and tired athletes, who were usually robbed of their spring break, sought entertainment:

> The incident began during spring break of 2006, when three of the four captains of the nationally ranked Duke lacrosse team … threw a party at their small, off-campus house. Throwing a party had become a ritual over the years because spring break usually occurred during the middle of the Lacrosse season and the team had to remain on campus to practice. Since this team could not take advantage of spring break like the other students, they attended a party. As part of the evening's entertainment, Dan Flannery googled an escort service and hired two strippers to dance for the team…."[70]

The explanation that the students had to stay on campus for spring break, included here to justify the search for "entertainment," does not explain why

---

67. *Id.* at 25.

68. *See* Dahlia Lithwick, *At Duke, Just Pick Your Facts*, WASH. POST, Apr. 23, 2006, at B02.

69. *See Duke Lacrosse Scandal Sheds New Light on the Stripper Industry: A Campus Trend?*, ABCNEWS.COM, Apr. 24, 2006, http://abcnews.go.com/US/LegalCenter/ Story?id=1882072 (discussing the commonality of students "ordering" strippers for events).

70. NADER BAYDOUN & R. STEPHANIE GOOD, A RUSH TO INJUSTICE: HOW POWER, PREJUDICE, RACISM, AND POLITICAL CORRECTNESS OVERSHADOWED TRUTH AND JUSTICE IN THE DUKE LACROSSE RAPE CASE 9 (2007).

the students' definition of proper entertainment resulted in the hiring of two exotic dancers. Another narrative of the reasons for the decision states:

> By now you know the truth.... First a stripper who was hired to dance at a party thrown by the members of the Duke University Lacrosse team claimed to have been brutally gang raped, sodomized and beaten.... It began on Monday night, March 13, 2006, when about forty young men were crammed into a tiny rented house on 610 North Buchanan Boulevard. Mostly members of the Duke University lacrosse team, they could not participate in the usual spring break festivities because of conflicts with their practice schedules. They had to celebrate by other means. A blowout party had become something of a tradition. But this year, the entertainment would leave team members with a night they would never forget.[71]

By many accounts, Duke students commonly hired exotic dancers.[72] This fact is deeply concerning. In the lacrosse team's case, the explanation that the students hired the dancers because they "could not participate in the usual spring break activities" leaves more questions than answers. What does this practice say about a university that tolerates such transactions? Why ignore the fact that these students thought the hiring of dancers was essential to a basic threshold definition of "entertainment"? In addition, the fact that the dancers have been routinely referred to as "strippers," the common vernacular that devalues and minimizes those who work in that profession, juxtaposes the privileged position of the Duke students to the vulnerable position of the dancers in even starker contrast.[73] These facts painted in their best light present many reasons for a university to be concerned.

These facts also illustrate our society's obsession with instant gratification, the disproportionate sense of entitlement that great purchasing power often confers, and the distortion of judgment that a mob mentality can create.[74] These are issues that logically stem from the students' decision to hire exotic dancers at the rate of $800 a night. The act of hiring exotic dancers, once thought of as ex-

---

71. *Id.* at 3.

72. Taylor & Johnson, *supra* note 29, at 17.

73. Kosse, *supra* note 10, at 259 (discussing the effect of the media's portrayal of Crystal Mangum as a stripper rather than as a student and mother of two).

74. *See* Sally Kalson, *Collegians Too Special for Their Own Good,* Pittsburgh Post-Gazette, Mar. 2, 2007, *available at* http://www.postgazette.com/pg/07061/766267-51.stm (discussing the effect of self-esteem touting and the ramifications of associated instant gratification and the rising rate of narcissism among college students).

traordinary, is now so commonplace that college students pay high sums of money for the gratification.[75] More important, however, the students' comments to the dancers reflect the ease with which women's bodies can be commodified and how quickly they can be classified as conforming versus nonconforming goods.[76] So does the dismissive label of "stripper" used in many narratives describing the event.[77]

In addition, the racist and sexist nature of the comments directed toward the women was confirmed by the e-mail sent a few hours later by team member Ryan McFadyen. As reported, his

> e-mail rant about killing strippers and cutting their skin off in his Duke University dorm room has started a chain reaction resulting in his coach's resignation, the season's cancellation and an internal probe into the university's response to alleged violence by athletes.[78]

This e-mail raises a serious question about the types of behaviors and language that had come to be considered acceptable within the players' environment.[79] Why did McFadyen apparently not think twice before sending such an ugly e-mail? Initially, at least, the university administration appeared to recoil with horror at the e-mail's content: it suspended McFadyen from school. But the administration's decision to reinstate him just three months later, in June 2006,[80] morphed the original punishment into a feeble slap on the wrist. Regardless of the legal status of the case, the fact that a student sent an e-mail using university resources in which he expressed such violent, racist, and sexist threats should have prompted Duke to send a clear message that it would

---

75. *See* Stuart Taylor, Jr., *An Outrageous Rush to Judgment*, Nat'l J., Apr. 29, 2006, http://www.theatlantic.com/doc/200604u/nj_taylor_2006-05-02.

76. *See* Scott Jaschik, *Anger and Consequences*, InsideHigherEd.com., Mar. 29, 2006, http://www.insidehighered.com/news/2006/03/29/duke; *see also* Charlene Israel, *Taking Back the Music*, CBN News, http://www.cbn.com/special/BlackHistory/news_takingbackmusic.aspx (last visited Oct.29, 2008) (discussing the demeaning nature of hip-hop lyrics).

77. *Id.*

78. *See Duke Rape Case E-mail Shocker*, The Smoking Gun, Apr. 5, 2006, http://www.thesmokinggun.com/archive/0405061duke1.html (hereinafter "*E-mail Shocker*") ("Shortly after an exotic dancer claimed she was raped at a Duke University lacrosse team party, a member of the squad sent an e-mail announcing that the following night he planned 'to have some strippers over' and would be 'killing the bitches' as soon as they walked into his dorm room.... The e-mail from McFadyen's account notes that, after the strippers were killed, they would be skinned while the author was 'cumming in my duke issue spandex.' The e-mail is signed '41,' which is McFadyen's jersey number.").

79. *Id.*

80. *See, e.g.,* Timeline in Duke Lacrosse Investigation, NBC Sports, Apr. 11, 2007, http://nbcsports.msnbc.com/id/18054818.

not tolerate such behavior by students.[81] Instead, by commuting the punishment, the university sent a dubious message about its commitment to eradicating hateful and threatening speech.[82]

The Accountability and Ethical Responsibilities of University Administrators

The Duke incident showed how catalysts, such as rape allegations, can cause dormant racial and gender wounds to erupt in an already polarized community.[83] The racial dichotomy and rivalry existing between North Carolina Central University (NCCU) and Duke University became apparent in the types of comments made by students from the respective schools during the investigation.[84] For example, a NCCU student stated: "If it was a Duke student and it was Central's football's team, the situation would have been handled totally differently,"[85] while, in the same spirit, a Duke University student explained "that the allegations ... put a new strain on the already delicate relationship between the school and the community in Durham."[86] Although the rape allegations were eventually dropped and are no longer the subject of such intense scrutiny, it is worthwhile to explore the ways that the racial- and gender-biased environment created an atmosphere of dread in the community.

Almost immediately after the rape allegations became public, student's comments to the media made it clear that—for the Durham community—the rape allegations were not just one isolated incident, but the culmination of slights and abuses of privilege that many hoped would be punished.[87] The very fact that a group of young lacrosse players thought hiring two African American strippers an acceptable form of entertainment corroborated this exasperation.[88]

---

81. *See E-mail Shocker, supra* note 78.

82. *Id.*

83. *See* Kosse, *supra* note 10, at 243.

84. *See* William L. Anderson, *What If the Duke 3 Had Been Black?*, LEWROCKWELL.COM, Dec. 11, 2006, http://www.lewrockwell.com/anderson/anderson155.html.

85. *See E-mail Shocker, supra* note 78.

86. *Id.*

87. *See* Dan Abrams, *Students Speak About Duke Rape Case*, MSNBC.COM, Mar. 30, 2006, http://www.msnbc.msn.com/id/12080770/.

88. *See* Jaschik, *supra* note 76.

This raises a critical issue: how should an institution go about promoting non-biased behavior and protecting students and other community stakeholders?[89] The standard to which an institution holds its members becomes apparent by looking at the ease, or lack thereof, with which the members violate rules.[90] Based on the type of language that the lacrosse students freely used on campus property, not to mention their behavior, Duke certainly appears to need stricter policies on the issue of basic respect.[91] Also, the students' perceptions of having an absolute right to access entertainment at any cost and their engagement in excess need to be questioned openly.[92] Criticisms voiced against this environment of excess are not made moot simply because of the dismissal of the rape case.[93] On the contrary, we should regard the case as an opportunity to devise practices and policies that can help combat the centuries of assumptions that guide our decisions.[94] The first step to achieving that goal at the university level would be to organize real discussions from the freshman year forward about gender and racial assumptions and how the students can begin to dismantle them.

The following criticism made during the investigation, for example, still applies to the type of behaviors and assumptions exhibited by McFadyen's e-mail and the team's hiring of exotic dancers. Houston Baker, then an English professor at Duke, told a *CBS News* correspondent,

> There's a kind of macho, cock-of-the-walk, boys culture that is characterizing this administration now and I hope there will be purges in

---

89. *See* Stephanie Schmid, *A Perfunctory Change? Harvard University's New Sexual Misconduct Complaint Procedure: Lessons from the Frontlines of Campus Adjudication Systems*, 18 Berkeley Women's L.J. 265, 272 (describing a female student's negative experience with her university administration following a date rape). The female student stated that the administration took the position that she would have sought help if she needed it, so the school did not need to take any affirmative steps. *Id.*

90. *See generally id.* (chronicling the impact of Harvard's limited-adjudication system for student violators). Schmid also gives a brief history of date-rape policies at Harvard: "[S]ome highly publicized event arouses the attention of activist students. The administration agrees, under pressure, to consider new policies. Eventually the activist students graduate and the policies remain essentially unchanged." *Id.* at 269. Consequently, Harvard's lack of policy perpetuates the violence that it was meant to quell.

91. *See* Jaschik, *supra* note 76.

92. *See* Katherine L. Hatfield, *A Dialogic Approach to Combating Hate Speech on College Campuses*, 13 Atlantic J. Comm. 41, 45–46 (2005).

93. *See* Lisa Bennett & Jessica Hooper, *Media Put Accuser on Trial in Duke Rape Case*, NOW.org, June 15, 2006 (discussing the ongoing struggle to "help create a less hostile environment for women and rape survivors").

94. *See generally* Kosse, *supra* note 10.

the administration as there have been voluntarily, we're told, in the sports department with the resignation of the lacrosse coach.[95]

President Brodhead initially had a similar reaction to the rape accusations. According to reports, "he demanded Pressler's resignation, cancelled the lacrosse season, and issued a statement anchored by a lament on the evils of rape. ..."[96] While President Brodhead subsequently apologized for these actions, the concerns motivating his initial reactions should lead to the enactment of policies and methods designed to delve into the issues of race, gender, privilege, and entitlement showcased by the behavior of the lacrosse team.[97]

Indeed, the fact that the rape issue has been settled allows more space for a critical look at institutional and societal norms:

> Justice inevitably has an attendant social construction. And this parallelism means that despite what may be our desire, the seriousness of the matter cannot be finally or fully adjudicated in the courts. The appropriate presumption of innocence that follows the players, however the legal case is determined, is neither the critical social indicator of the event, nor the final measure of its cultural facts. Judgments about the issues of race and gender that the lacrosse team's sleazy conduct exposed cannot be left to the courtroom. Just as aspects of their conduct that extend into the social realms of character and integrity should not be the parameters of adjudicatory processes, the consequence of that conduct will not be fully resolved within a legal process.[98]

The legal system is just the first place where accountability and awakening must take place with regard to these issues. In addition, the permissiveness

---

95. *See E-mail Shocker, supra* note 78.

96. Durham in Wonderland: Comments and Analysis about the Duke/Nifong Case, Case Narrative, http://durhamwonderland.blogspot.com/2006/10/case-narrative.html (last visited Oct. 29, 2008).

97. *See* James D. Gordon III & W. Cole Durham, Jr., *Toward Diverse Diversity: The Legal Legitimacy of "Ex Corde Ecclesiae,"* 25 J.C. & U.L. 697 (1999). Gordon states:

> It is also clear that academic freedom is not unlimited at any university. At most universities, there are at least four categories of official limitations on individual academic freedom.... Many universities have adopted harassment policies or campus speech codes prohibiting faculty and students from engaging in expression that harasses or demeans others because of race, ethnicity, religion, gender, or sexual orientation.

98. *See* Holloway, *supra* note 54.

and latitude that institutions accord to athletic bodies should be tackled.[99] Otherwise,

> the 'event' is phased back into the subaltern spaces of university life and culture.... The intersection of race, gender and culture of privilege, either class based or constructed by athletic hierarchy, if not checked, unfailingly results in verbal or other abuses of those perceived as freely accessible and fungible.[100]

In exploring ways to dismantle these assumptions, athletic teams as well as members of the mainstream community should be called to be the leading participants in these efforts.[101] The conversation will be most fruitful if the members of the privileged sectors lead the charge of reform and learn to hold each other accountable for dismantling stereotypes.[102] Otherwise, the task will be left to the very people in the institution who regularly suffer the effects of these stereotypes. As Professor Karla Holloway, a Duke faculty member, described, the disproportionate participation of women and community members of color in efforts to solve perceived race and gender problems poses an inherent problem:

> When, in the last year of President Nannerl Keohane's presidency, a report on the status of women at Duke discovered evidence of cultural and social practices that disadvantaged women, a commission of women faculty and administrators, a group of women student scholars, and an alumni group of women (legates of the Duke Women's

---

99. *See* Christopher M. Parent, *Personal Fouls: How Sexual Assault by Football Players Is Exposing Universities to Title IX Liability*, 13 FORDHAM INTELL. PROP. MEDIA & ENT. L.J. 617, 618–21 (2003) (chronicling a lawsuit arising from the sexual assault of a student by members of a football team and discussing the responsibility of universities more effectively establishing and enforcing conduct requirements for athletes).

100. *See* Holloway, *supra* note 54 ("Until we recognize that sports reinforces exactly those behaviors of entitlement which have been and can be so abusive to women and girls ... the bodies who will bear evidence and consequence of the field's conduct will remain, after the fact of the matter, laboring to retrieve the lofty goals of education, to elevate the character of the place, to restore a space where they can do the work they came to the university to accomplish.").

101. *See* Yafit Cohn, *Affirmative Action for Women in the Workplace at Home and Abroad: A Comparison of* Johnson v. Transportation Agency *and* Abrahamsson v. Fogelqvist, 37 COLUM. J.L. & SOC. PROBS. 277, 309 (2003) ("[T]he duty to correct institutional discrimination and to contribute to the cost of the remedy is shared by all members of the privileged class, not merely those who personally discriminated against minorities and women in the past.").

102. *Id.*

College) were charged with discovering the "fix" to the problem. This flurry of restructuring and response came after a committee of women faculty, students, and administrators labored to uncover the gendered issues of disparate treatment and its consequences. As if a prelude to the events of spring 2006, the bodies that mattered, those who were the objects of inquiry, were also the bodies whose labor was required to fix the inequity.[103]

The default method of choosing the very members of an aggrieved group to fix the problem by which they were victimized guarantees that the rest of the community will continue to feel disconnected and removed from the reform process.[104] As a result, the internal work necessary to effect change rarely takes place.[105] The Duke lacrosse rape allegations and the nefarious behaviors that they unveiled should serve as an incentive for change. The institution should commit itself to the creation of committees composed of members from diverse gender and racial backgrounds and encourage heavy student involvement.[106] Other institutions with similar problems should follow suit.

Possible Equitable or Contractual Claims for Added Protections for Erotic Workers

The Duke rape case is also significant as a showcase for the dangers that exotic dancers and other erotic workers face. Much has been written about the vulnerable status of sex workers.[107] The facts surrounding the Duke rape alle-

---

103. *See* Holloway, *supra* note 54.

104. *See* Reginald Leamon Robinson, *Poverty, the Underclass, and the Role of Race Consciousness: A New Age Critique of Black Wealth/White Wealth and American Apartheid*, 34 IND. L. REV. 1377, 1443 (2001) ("[B]y simply reacting, we signal our usual, but discomforting, impotence to change who we really are. In part, we remain in this stagnant place because we do not realize that reactions enslave us to our tragically suffering minds.").

105. *Id.*

106. *See* Hatfield, *supra* note 92, at 46–48.

107. *See* Eleanor Maticka-Tyndale & Jacqueline Lewis, *Escort Services in a Border Town*, Sept. 16, 2000, http://www.walnet.org/csis/papers/lewis-escorts.html (literature and policy summary). These authors note:

> The Prostitutes' Rights Movement became visible in North America, Europe and Australia in the 1970's with the founding of organizations such as COYOTE. Members of this movement have challenged researchers and policy-makers to shift attention away from an individualistic, single issue approach to sex work. Specifically, they have called for a shift of focus to the level of the political, social and eco-

gations indicate, however, that there is still a need for legal and social advocacy to help eliminate the risks to erotic workers' security.[108] In addition, the treatment of many exotic dancers as independent contractors often minimizes the level of employment protections afforded to them.[109]

While much is still in dispute regarding the Duke event, it is uncontested that the dancers left in the midst of great contention. The idea of two sex workers alone in a room full of inebriated male students emphasizes the need to provide erotic workers with adequate protection.[110] Furthermore, there is a need for serious discussions about the safety measures that agencies should provide to dancers, as well as about the need to hold agencies accountable for failing to protect them.[111] Aside from the rape issue, the fact remains that two erotic women alone in a room full of intoxicated men can often lead to abuse and transgression;[112] even the students were surprised by the fact the dancers came without bodyguards.[113]

---

nomic factors, such as the influence that women's relative poverty, low status, and disempowerment have, not only in drawing women into sex work, but in the way the work is conducted and dealt with by the community. As several sex worker/activists and researchers have noted: research, programmes and policies need to view sex work as work.... In response to the call for this paradigm shift, some recent research has begun to focus on the impact of policy and legislation on the conduct of sex work and the health and well-being of sex workers.

Id.

108. *See* Sarvenaz Kermanshahi, *Decriminalizing Sex Industry: Former Exotic Dancer Says Safety and Exploitation Need to Be Addressed*, GAZETTE (Univ. W. Ontario, Can.), Oct. 20, 2006, http://www.gazette.uwo.ca/articles.cfm?articleID=818&day=31&month= 11&section=news&year=2006.

109. *See* Andrew Gilden, *Sexual (Re)consideration: Adult Entertainment Contracts and the Problem of Enforceability*, 95 GEO. L.J. 541, 545 (2007); *see also* Margot Rutman, *Exotic Dancers' Employment Law Regulations*, 8 TEMP. POL. & CIV. RTS. L. REV. 515, 519 (1999); Holly J. Wilmet, *Naked Feminism: The Unionization of the Adult Entertainment Industry*, 7 AM. U. J. GENDER SOC. POL'Y & L. 465, 468–69 (1999) ("The courts have become an active partner in the continuing financial exploitation of adult entertainers ... by legally classifying various types of ... entertainers as independent contractors, and thus denying these workers protection of the labor laws enacted for their benefit."); *see also* 29 U.S.C. §157 (2000).

110. *See* Kermanshahi, *supra* note 108 ("Many women working in the sex industry get sexually assaulted, but are not taken seriously by police.").

111. *Id.*

112. *See* DAVID A. SCOTT, BEHIND THE G-STRING: AN EXPLORATION OF THE STRIPPER'S IMAGE, HER PERSON AND HER MEANING (2004).

113. *Id.*

Exotic dancers sometimes are regular performers at specific clubs or lend their services to escort agencies, as in the Duke case.[114] Agencies typically recruit escort workers through advertisements.[115] They commonly place such advertisements in local newspapers, phone books, weekly entertainment magazines, or on the Internet.[116] Though the advertisements do not explicitly mention sex, their wording, pictures, and descriptions usually imply that sexual services are part of the job.[117] They also frequently specify the status of the potential dancers as independent contractors. For example, an ad placed by an agency in Virginia stated:

> Affordable Pleasures has been successfully serving the Virginia area for the last 10 years. We have an excellent reputation as well as an international following. Due to our unique success we have been featured in several adult publications. We receive well over 3,500 phone calls each week from clients responding to our vast advertising. This is why those who work with Affordable Pleasures make such an incredible average income of $2,000–5,000 per week. Independent Contractors set their own schedules and rates. Income potential is unlimited. You are your own Boss. No employment contract.[118]

The treatment of exotic dancers as independent contractors, instead of as employees, purposefully limits their on-the-job legal protections. As employees, for instance, they would be covered under most states' workers' compensation statutes. As a typical example, Tennessee's statute provides: "Every employer and employee subject to the Workers' Compensation Law ... shall, respectively, pay and accept compensation for personal injury or death by accident arising out of and in the course of employment without regard to fault as a cause of the injury or death"[119] Even working as independent contractors, however, erotic workers should be given some legal and equitable redress if their agency fails to protect their safety by providing inadequate security per-

---

114. *Id.*

115. *See* Scott, *supra* note 112.

116. *See* Maraya Mullen, *Escort Agencies: Going High Tech*, US Web Pros, http://www.uswebpros.com/?Escort_Agencies__Going_High_Tech_186&a=10812 (last visited Oct. 29, 2008) (noting that escort agencies are highly prolific, and discussing the move toward cyber advertisements).

117. Maticka-Tyndale & Lewis, *supra* note 107.

118. Dancer Job Openings, http://www.getdancerjobs.com/dancer-exotic-escort-virginia-beach-virginia-11.htm (last visited June 11, 2008).

119. Tenn. Code Ann. § 50-6-103 (2007) (dealing with compensation for personal injury or death and exemptions).

sonnel or an unsafe worksite (in the Duke case, the party location). In fact, some state agencies, such as the Vermont Department of Labor & Industry (DLI), have become increasingly critical of the independent-contractor label when used by a prospective employer to avoid responsibility. Under DLI's analysis, an employer might be liable for workers' compensation even when an independent-contractor agreement is in effect. DLI expanded its standard in exploring issues of liability by looking to see whether the injury happened as part of the nature of the business promoted by the would-be employer (the "nature of the business test"), in addition to the more common "right to control" test.[120]

For instance, in the 1997 decision *Workers' Compensation Division v. Playmate Entertainment, Inc.* ("PEI"),[121] the court found that exotic dancers who were contracted out by PEI—a company engaged in the entertainment business—were found to be employees despite the fact that neither they nor their drivers were paid by PEI and the company didn't control how the dancers danced or the drivers drove. In addition, both the dancers and the drivers "provided their own equipment and instruments."[122] The "nature of the business" test better pierces the veil of alleged independent-contractor status, thereby placing the responsibility to protect dancers on the shoulders of the hiring agency. Employers cannot simply invoke the fact that they did not control the particular circumstances of a performance to evade liability.

Other courts have found would-be employers liable to independent contractors based on traditional negligence theory. The Texas Supreme Court, for example, recently outlined the elements of an employer's potential liability to independent contractors in *D. Houston, Inc. v. Love.*[123] According to the Texas court,

---

120. Workers' Comp. Div. v. Playmate Entertainment, Inc., Vermont Dep't of Labor and Indus., Findings of Fact and Conclusions of Law, Opinion No. 29-97PEN, Conclusions of Law, Sept. 29, 1997, para.19, http://www.labor.vermont.gov/Default.aspx?tabid=676 ("[Courts] appear to be looking today less as to who controls the work than whether the work being done is in the nature of the [company's] business. If the latter is so, the person performing that work should be considered an employee for workers' compensation purposes, even though that person might be deemed an independent contractor under common law.").

121. Workers' Comp. Div. v. Playmate Entertainment, Inc., Vermont Dep't of Labor and Indus., Findings of Fact and Conclusions of Law, Opinion No. 29-97PEN, Conclusions of Law, Sept. 29, 1997, http://www.labor.vermont.gov/Default.aspx?tabid=676.

122. *Id.* at ¶ 7.

123. 92 S.W.3d 450 (Tex. 2002).

A cause of action for negligence in Texas requires three elements. There must be a legal duty owed by one person to another, a breach of that duty, and damages proximately caused by the breach. Proximate cause requires both cause in fact and foreseeability. Foreseeability exists when 'the actor as a person of ordinary intelligence should have anticipated the dangers his negligent act creates for others.'[124]

The court further explained,

> An employer may breach a duty to its independent contractor by failing to exercise its retained control over the contractor with reasonable care. An employer may retain control either by contract or by exercising actual control over the contractor's work. When disputed, control is an issue for the trier of fact.[125]

An escort service that regulates the manner of payment and retrieves a share of the earnings for each call could satisfy this standard if it failed to protect the dancer from foreseeable danger.

In *Love*, the employer was found liable under the Dram Shop Act for requiring the plaintiff, an exotic dancer, to consume alcohol while working and failing to provide safe transportation for her after work.[126] While working one night, Melissa Love consumed at least twelve alcoholic beverages with

> the customers and became intoxicated. She performed her last table dance at about 1:00 a.m. As Love was leaving Treasures about thirty minutes later, the club manager asked if she was alright. She replied that she was "fine." But while Love was driving herself home, her car struck a guardrail and she suffered serious personal injuries. At 4:00 a.m., Love's blood alcohol level as measured at the hospital was .225, more than twice the then-applicable .10 legal limit.[127]

The plaintiff sued for injuries suffered in the accident. The Texas Supreme Court affirmed the court of appeals' granting summary judgment to the plaintiff.[128] It held that the employer had retained control over the dancer while she was performing, because she was not paid unless she brought her money in after the dance.[129] Accounts of the Duke events described Mangum and

---

124. *Id.* at 454.
125. *Id.*
126. *Id.* at 451.
127. *Id.* at 454.
128. *Id.* at 451.
129. *Id.* at 455.

Roberts as being concerned with collecting the money properly for that very reason. In addition, the fact that most agencies retain a share of their dancers' money is also evidence of control that should trigger a duty to exercise reasonable care.

An agency may also be negligent by dispatching its dancers to a site without providing proper security.[130] The provision that the agency will hire security guards is crucial; it minimizes the need for the dancers to seek protection through means that would most likely expose them to predatory behaviors.[131] For example, in the accounts reconstructing Mangum's whereabouts the nights and days before the Duke events, she is described as "having had four private hotel engagements with various escort customers"[132] and as making "at least 20–25 calls to at least eight escort services that week-end for jobs.... [According to some accounts], one of her 'drivers' (some called them pimps) took her to the Holiday Inn at 2:20 p.m., picking her up half an hour later...."[133] Assuming all these facts are true, Mangum had to rely on a number of "drivers" for transportation and security. This opened the door for these individuals to make predatory demands in exchange for protection. The risks of vulnerability would consequently be minimized if the cost of providing security were shifted to the escort agencies, which would have an incentive to screen and police bodyguards as a result.[134]

Conclusion

As seen above, the infamous Duke lacrosse rape allegations unveiled many stereotypical and privileged views and attitudes. Still, one of the stories that is left untold is that of Crystal Gail Mangum, the dancer who became most known as the accuser in the case.[135] Her status as a black exotic dancer gave her ignominy that would have only been shattered in the eyes of the mainstream media if she had fulfilled their need for a story with clear binaries, i.e. poor black woman raped by rich white men. Her linear function prevented us from learning about who she was and to investigate what happened to her that night outside of the rape context or what her life was like.[136] Everything we know of her

---

130. *See* Scott, *supra* note 112.
131. *Id.*
132. Taylor & Johnson, *supra* note 29, at 21.
133. *Id.*
134. *See* Scott, *supra* note 112.
135. *See* Bennett & Hooper, *supra* note 93.
136. *Id.*

confirmed ready-made stereotypes about black exotic dancers.[137] For example, in a Jerry Springer-like episode, Fox News interviewed Mangum's cousin to explore whether Mangum was pregnant.[138] Later the pregnancy was confirmed and paternity test ordered, again in Springer and Maury Povich fashion.[139] Also, the pictures of Mangum while she was performing the night of the Duke party apparently revealed that "she had several bruises on her body."[140] Still, beyond the obvious stereotypes that these accounts conjure, these facts seemed to give us a glimpse of a woman who at some point suffered some trauma and might have been in need of help. If that is the case, it is tragic that her need was buried through the stereotypical maze that became Duke rape allegations.

The allegations demonstrated a disconnect between the "body protest,"[141] real or imagined, that women sometimes engage in when participating in the erotic labor force and society's unwillingness to conceive of these erotic workers as "employees" deserving of legal protection. This absence of protection often thrusts these workers in a state of vulnerability, which they sometimes try to mitigate on their own by transacting for a male protector or by befriending coworkers.[142] It is notable that in the midst of the mass obsession with the culpability or non-culpability of the three players, no one took time to question how, in a community so racially polarized, women of color could be so objectified and subjugated without any remonstrance from the university administration. This seeming indifference to the dancers' actual wellbeing during the heat of the Duke controversy, as well as the deeper labor issues involved, illustrate the need for more layered discussions of race, class, and gender.[143] These discus-

---

137. *Id.*

138. *See* Accuser in Duke Lacrosse Rape Case—Having BABY, YouTube.com, Dec. 14, 2006, http://www.youtube.com/watch?v=RrnjA3umkEM.

139. *See Duke Lacrosse Accuser Gives Birth to Baby Girl*, WRAL.COM, Jan. 4, 2007, http://www.wral.com/news/local/story/1107413/.

140. BAYDOUN & GOOD, *supra* note 70, at 41.

141. Alexandre, *supra* note 23, at 178–79 ("Body protest consists of the use of women's bodies by women to challenge gender restrictions and to activate women-centric legal reforms."). It also encompasses the therapeutic goals of asserting dominance over one's body and of facilitating one's expression of womanhood in revolt against a patriarchal society. Instances of body protest include, but are not limited to, women's use of their bodies through dance, dressing, or performance art. For example, certain women choose to dance suggestively, dress contrary to societal standards of propriety, perform sexually explicit artistic roles, bring attention to specific body parts, and adopt sexually explicit personas in order to highlight the societal restraints imposed on them.

142. *See* SCOTT, *supra* note 112.

143. *See* Bennett & Hooper, *supra* note 93.

sions cannot take place without the acknowledgement of the role that the accuser's profession as an exotic dancer played in our original limited analysis. In the aftermath of the controversy, I contend that the Duke lacrosse rape case can help eradicate assumptions about the right of access to women's bodies generally, and women of color's bodies in particular. The case can also be instrumental in helping to identify more structured legal protections for the benefit of erotic workers.

CHAPTER SEVEN

Racial Politics and Discretion in Criminal Law

Janine Young Kim

Case Background

Race and crime are profoundly entwined in the American imagination. Watching the nightly news, we are simultaneously inured to, and riveted by, dissonant portrayals of black criminality and white victimization, black victimization and white oppression. But the link between race and crime extends beyond familiar television images of victims and perpetrators in various contexts; the law itself is indelibly marked by race, both in the very definition of crimes as well as in their uneven enforcement. Add rape, which in its own right is a politically charged social and legal issue, and we are sure to get a volatile combination. It should come as no surprise, then, that the allegations made by a young black local college student, who also worked part-time as an exotic dancer, against three white members of the Duke University lacrosse team stirred controversy and commanded close media scrutiny.[1]

---

1. Susan Hanley Kosse has conducted an interesting study of the effects of media narrative on this case in an effort to provide further data on the widely held consensus that the media tends to be more sympathetic to the victim when she is a middle-class white woman than when she is a lower-class woman of color, particularly if the assailant is black. Susan Hanley Kosse, *Race, Riches & Reporters—Do Race and Class Impact Media Rape Narratives? An Analysis of the Duke Lacrosse Case*, 31 S. ILL. U. L.J. 243 (2007); *see also* Jeffrey J. Pokorak, *Rape as a Badge of Slavery: The Legal History of, and Remedies for, Prosecutorial Race-of-Victim Charging Disparities*, 7 NEV. L.J. 1, 4 (2006) (discussing the disparate media treatment of Latoyia Figueroa and Laci Peterson, two young, attractive, and pregnant women who disappeared).

News about the alleged rape broke on March 24, 2006, when local newspapers reported that DNA tests were ordered for the members of the Duke lacrosse team related to an alleged gang-rape during an off-campus party on March 13.[2] Although this first story did not make any racial references, it did not take long for such details—not all of them accurate, as it turned out—to emerge. Just one day later, the press reported that the accuser was one of two black dancers hired to strip at a small bachelor party for five, and that the party was actually attended by dozens of white men who "surrounded" the dancers and "shouted" racial insults during and after the performance.[3] From that point forward, race occupied center stage in the media coverage of this case. Even already-reported events, like the DNA collection from the team, were retold with a racial angle that emphasized the exemption of the sole black member of the lacrosse team.[4]

The racial aspects of the case grew increasingly explicit and disturbing over time. It was later revealed that the lacrosse players specifically agreed to have a white woman and a Hispanic woman dance at the party,[5] and that the players might have been upset, or at least disappointed, when two black women arrived to perform.[6] When the party broke up early and as the women were leaving the house, more racial comments were made (indeed, first by a dancer, then by some of the attendees at the party). In particular, one unidentified man reportedly yelled, "We asked for whites, not niggers,"[7] and another unidentified partygoer was heard shouting, "Thank your grandpa for my cotton shirt."[8] Perhaps the most disturbing piece of information—that is, besides the alleged rape itself—was an e-mail sent by one of the players after the party that detailed his plans to hire strippers for a party of his own, kill them, and cut their

---

2. *See* Samiha Khanna & Anne Blythe, *DNA Tests Ordered for Duke Athletes*, News & Observer (Raleigh, N.C.), Mar. 24, 2006, at A1.

3. *See* Samiha Khanna & Anne Blythe, *Dancer Gives Details of Ordeal*, News & Observer (Raleigh, N.C.), Mar. 25, 2006, at A1.

4. *See id.*; Susannah Meadows & Evan Thomas, *What Happened at Duke?*, Newsweek, May 1, 2006, at 40.

5. *See* Joseph Neff, *"Weird Evening" Was Just the Start*, News & Observer (Raleigh, N.C.), May 11, 2006, at A1. Kim Roberts, the other dancer at the party, is biracial. *See id.*

6. *See* John Moreno Gonzales, *Dancer: Race an Issue at Duke Party*, Newsday, Jun. 6, 2006, at A19.

7. *See* Susannah Meadows & Evan Thomas, *That Night at Duke*, Newsweek, Apr. 23, 2007, at 40.

8. *See* Khanna & Blythe, *supra* note 3.

skin off.[9] Although the e-mail did not explicitly mention race, its particular reference to skin-mutilation is both gruesome and troublingly suggestive.[10]

The particulars of the case prompted the media to broaden its narrative to include the social and economic dichotomies between Durham and Duke, or as some residents called Duke, "the plantation."[11] The people and events surrounding the case seemed tailor-made to illustrate the divide that apparently existed between the largely white, elite Duke University where the accused lacrosse players were enrolled and the largely black, underfunded North Carolina Central University (NCCU) attended by the accuser; between the privileged lacrosse captains who occupied the house on Buchanan Street and the poor residents who lived around them; between the young men from Duke, who had bright futures ahead of them on Wall Street, and the young woman from NCCU, a single mother who had to dance at a gentlemen's club to make ends meet.

The media surely did its part to sensationalize the case against the Duke lacrosse players, and so did the district attorney. Michael Nifong's motives for using this case to his own political advantage are, by now, well-documented.[12] Facing a close primary election to remain in office and needing the black vote to win, Nifong courted the local African-American community (which accounts for approximately 44 percent of Durham's population[13]) with aggressive public statements about the merits of the accuser's claims. Nifong's comments to the press not only expressed his personal belief that the accuser was in fact raped at the party, but also his desire to make a more general statement for social justice.[14] On at least one occasion, he declared that he would

---

9. *See* Duff Wilson & Viv Bernstein, *Duke Cancels Season and Begins Inquiries*, N.Y. TIMES, Apr. 6, 2006, at D1.

10. The e-mail's language also evokes the public mutilations that took place during and after spectacle lynchings in the South, in which spectators often took away pieces of the victim as souvenirs. *See* Emma Coleman Jordan, *A History Lesson: Reparations for What?*, 58 N.Y.U. ANN. SURV. AM. L. 557, 589–93 (2003).

11. Interestingly, some news stories reported that white Southerners resent Duke because it is seen as "the school of elite Northerners." John Moreno Gonzales, *A Divide Grows Deeper*, NEWSDAY, Apr. 2, 2006, at A8. Jesse Jackson also noted: "Durham ... is not the old South. Its mayor is black, as are its police chief and the majority of its city council." *See* Jesse Jackson, *Duke Accusations Reopen Old Wounds*, CHI. SUN-TIMES, Apr. 18, 2006, at 39.

12. During Nifong's disbarment hearing, the chairman of the disciplinary committee concluded that Nifong's decisions could only be explained by his "political ambitions." *See* Aaron Beard, *Prosecutor to be Disbarred for Duke Lacrosse Case "Fiasco"*, CHI. TRIB., Jun. 17, 2007, at 6.

13. *See* Gonzales, *supra* note 11, at A8.

14. In a series of editorials, Thomas Sowell has been critical of this case, concluding that Nifong's only strategy was to be reelected by "conjur[ing] up all the racial injustices of

not allow "Durham's view in the minds of the world to be a bunch of lacrosse players at Duke raping a black girl from Durham,"[15] and suggested that the alleged rape may have constituted a hate crime.[16] Nifong also explained that, to send the message that the rape allegations were being taken seriously, he was personally handling the case.[17] He further accused his critics of trying to intimidate either him or the accuser to drop the charges—a common problem in rape prosecutions.[18]

It is difficult to measure how much of the outrage displayed by the media and the district attorney was genuine and how much of it was simple opportunism. But amid the legitimate criticism about how this case was mishandled by both, it is important to remember that the underlying racial conflicts in this case were and continue to be real. Although there was no rape, and community divisions were fueled by those who sought to capitalize on the incident, Nifong and the others who reflexively blamed the lacrosse players for the alleged rape did not, and could not, wholly manufacture the tension manifest in Durham and the rest of the nation. In fact, the media and the district attorney were, to a significant extent, also reacting to the public's growing anger over the alleged incident and its demand for justice for the accuser. So, although the media and the prosecutor have borne most of the blame for agitating racial animosity and for their "rush to accuse,"[19] a complete explanation for what happened must entail an acknowledgment that the rape allegations illuminated preexisting issues that implicate the longstanding tension between racial justice and criminal justice in the United States. Indeed, the Duke lacrosse rape case was ripe for sensationalism and

---

the past, which he would now vow to fight against in the present." Thomas Sowell, *Justice Was Never Goal of Nifong in Duke Case*, BALT. SUN, Jan. 4, 2007, at 11A. Nifong's former campaign manager has said, however, that Nifong did not act for political gain but rather because "[h]e got caught up in the media." David Zucchino, *D.A. in Duke Case Gives up the Fight*, L.A. TIMES, Jan. 13, 2007, at A1.

15. *See* Duff Wilson, *Duke Rape Shadows an Unusual Race*, N.Y. TIMES, Nov. 1, 2006, at 20. Nifong also stated that the defendants showed "contempt ... for the victim based on race." *See* David Zucchino, *Problems Detailed in Duke Case*, L.A. TIMES, Apr. 28, 2007, at 9.

16. Nifong asserted that the rape had "a deep racial motivation ... mak[ing] a crime that is by its nature one of the most offensive and invasive even more so." Aaron Beard, *Rape Allegations Divide Duke*, CINCINNATI POST, Mar. 29, 2006, at B1.

17. *See* Benjamin Niolet, *15 Players Had Prior Charges*, NEWS & OBSERVER (Raleigh, N.C.), Mar. 28, 2006, at A1.

18. *See* Wilson, *supra* note 15, at 20.

19. *See* Duff Wilson & David Barstow, *Duke Prosecutor Throws Out Case Against Players*, N.Y. TIMES, Apr. 12, 2007, at A1.

exploitation precisely because race has always played a central role in the criminal law.

Historical and Legal Context

The rape of a black woman by a privileged white man resonates deeply in American historical consciousness. For a significant period of American history, nonconsensual intercourse between black women and white men was not considered to be rape at all.[20] Instead, it was viewed as an exercise of the master's (illicit) sexual prerogative over his slave, as well as a legitimate means of reproducing property in the form of slave-children born from the nonconsensual encounter.[21] To rationalize white-male behavior, black women were simultaneously demonized as temptresses and degraded as property. Thus, it was legally impossible to recognize any black slave, including the ravished black woman, to be the victim of a violent crime, particularly when her victimizer was her own master.[22]

Of course, this is no longer the law; today, there is no explicit distinction between black and white women within the law of rape, or any other law. But the Duke lacrosse rape allegations instantly revived the memory of those days in the mind of some segments of the public, whose outrage was clearly attuned to the sociohistorical meaning of white-on-black rape. Soon after the case went public, numerous protests in support of the accuser (and against the lacrosse-team members, who remained free) took place in Durham and on the campuses of Duke and NCCU. In an interview during one of these events, a Durham resident noted that the racism, sexism, and elitism of this case "take[] you so far back."[23] At another march, an African-American woman

---

20. *See* Pokorak, *supra* note 1, at 8.

21. *See id.* at 9–10; Dorothy E. Roberts, *Crime, Race, and Reproduction*, 67 Tul. L. Rev. 1945, 1970 (1993).

22. The well-known case of *State v. Mann*, 13 N.C. 263 (1829), illustrates this legal attitude toward slaves. In that case, the court dismissed a battery charge brought against John Mann, who had beaten Lydia, a slave that was hired out to him by her owner, Elizabeth Jones. Instead, the court discussed the possibility of restitution by Mann to Jones for impairing Lydia's value. *See also* George v. State, 37 Miss. 316 (1859) (explaining that the criminal law does not protect slaves, even from violent acts by third parties); *cf.* State v. Hale, 9 N.C. 582 (1823) (holding that battery upon a slave by a third party is an indictable offense only because it is a "great provocation to the owner").

23. *See* Anne Blythe, *NCCU Students Back a Classmate*, News & Observer (Raleigh, N.C.), Apr. 4, 2006, at B1.

observed: "Our history is full of sexual violence. It's not new to us."[24] While acknowledging that the truth about what happened at the party was still unknown, Jesse Jackson lamented how the case evoked for him "bad memories" of slavery.[25] On the one hand, it may have surprised some to hear how readily these individuals recalled the legal and social structure of the antebellum South. On the other hand, it appears that the past was not buried very deep in Durham, as evidenced by Duke's nickname ("the plantation") among the city residents and the comment by one of the partygoers about the origins of his cotton shirt ("Thank your grandpa….").

One need not go that far back in history, however, to observe the disparate treatment of black and white victims of crime. Black rape victims, in particular, have garnered a significant amount of scholarly interest because they continue to be neglected by the media and the criminal-justice system. Although the criminal law now ostensibly protects black women as much as white ones, there still remains a significant gap in the enforcement of crimes committed against each group.[26] This problem begins with the fact that black women tend to underreport rape, especially when the rapist is white, because they think that the police will not believe them.[27] Furthermore, prosecutors decline to pursue black women's rape allegations for a variety of reasons, ranging from their own prejudice to the prejudice of juries that may render such cases unwinnable.[28] As a result, the legal system generally confines itself to addressing "believable and atypical" rape cases, for instance, those of white women raped by black strangers, even though most rapes are intraracial and committed by a person known to the victim.[29] This, in turn, feeds a paradigm of rape that systematically excludes black women (along multiple axes,

---

24. *See* Ames Alexander et al., *Outcry at Assault Grows in Durham*, CHARLOTTE OBSERVER, Mar. 30, 2006, at 1A.

25. Jackson, *supra* note 11, at 39.

26. *See* Pokorak, *supra* note 1, at 43. It should be noted that underenforcement and underreporting is a general problem in rape law, apart from the special problems raised by race. *See* Michelle Anderson, *All-American Rape*, 79 ST. JOHN'S L. REV. 625, 627–28, 642 (2007).

27. *See* Erin Edmonds, *Mapping the Terrain of Our Resistance: A White Feminist Perspective on the Enforcement of Rape Law*, 9 HARV. BLACKLETTER L.J. 43, 65 (1992).

28. *See* Pokorak, *supra* note 1, at 38–43 (discussing how prosecutors make decisions based on (1) their personal biases about what constitutes a typical rape, and (2) anticipated jury outcome); *see also* Edmonds, *supra* note 27, at 70 (describing how race is one of five factors that impact rape-charging decisions in Washington state).

29. *See* Edmonds, *supra* note 27, at 66; Anderson, *supra* note 26, at 627 (describing the typical rape).

which also often includes class[30]) and sustains the historical but false assumption that they either cannot be, or are rarely, raped.[31] In fact, the opposite is true: blacks are far more likely to be victims of violent crime, including rape, than whites.[32]

High-profile cases of white rape victims, such as the Central Park jogger in 1989, further accentuate the fact that countless black victims go quietly unacknowledged. Few are aware that on the same night that the white jogger was raped in Central Park, a black woman was raped and thrown down an elevator shaft in the Bronx.[33] In fact, some of the biggest crime stories in recent years have involved the victimization of white women and girls—for example, the murders of JonBenet Ramsey and Laci Peterson and the disappearance of Natalee Holloway. But, if noticed at all, the stories of black women and girls who have been similarly victimized are hardly remembered.[34] All this tends to suggest that injuries to black women have been of little social and legal concern throughout most of American history, which helps to explain not only Nifong's move to frame this case in terms of social, and specifically racial, justice, but also the black community's demand for "justice" based upon what Nifong was telling them.

The neglect of black victims reflects only one side of the fraught relationship between African Americans and the criminal law. It turns out that black women tend to underreport rapes by black men as well, in part because black women believe that the law treats black men unfairly.[35] This underreporting phenomenon also has deep historical roots in a time when states enacted and enforced race-specific criminal codes aimed at preserving slavery and white supremacy. Through these laws, blacks were forbidden from exercising basic rights and privileges, such as learning how to read or write, on pain of crim-

---

30. *See generally* Kosse, *supra* note 1 (discussing this issue in the context of media coverage).

31. *See* Angela Y. Davis, Women, Race, and Class 182–83 (1981); Pokorak, *supra* note 1, at 8–10, 22–23, 39.

32. *See* David Cole, No Equal Justice 5 (1999).

33. Edmonds, *supra* note 27, at 62.

34. In the critique against the media's emphasis on white women, many have emphasized the stories of their black counterparts. For example, less than a month after JonBenet Ramsey's death, a nine-year-old black girl was "repeatedly raped, beaten, choked, poisoned with gasoline, and left for dead in a stairwell of the Cabrini Green housing project in Chicago." Ann Scales, *Disappearing Medusa: The Fate of Feminist Legal Theory?*, 20 Harv. Women's L.J. 34, 45 (1997); *see also* Pokorak, *supra* note 1, at 4 (discussing the media's disparate treatment of Latoyia Figueroa and Natalee Holloway, two young, attractive women— one black and Hispanic, the other white, respectively—who disappeared in 2005).

35. *See* Edmonds, *supra* note 27, at 65–66.

inal punishment;[36] the law also prohibited blacks from congregating freely for fear that they might conspire to rebel against their oppression.[37] Blacks were also subjected to special, harsher forms of punishment than whites. Most notable of these were the enslavement of free blacks who committed crimes,[38] and the imposition of the death penalty on any black person convicted of a crime for which a white person would be imprisoned three or more years.[39] Even after the formal end of slavery, and despite the passage of the Fourteenth Amendment that guaranteed equal protection of laws to former slaves, the Black Codes of the American South continued to define crimes that only blacks could commit, for example, breach of an employment contract or the making of "insulting gestures."[40] And well into the twentieth century, research has shown that black men convicted of rape were much more likely to suffer the death penalty than whites convicted of the same crime.[41]

Despite the dismantling of *de jure* race discrimination during the Second Reconstruction, an impressive array of studies on criminal-law enforcement reveals that the law continues to be applied unequally.[42] It is well-documented that young black men are often targeted for closer scrutiny by police forces

---

36. *See* Roberts, *supra* note 21, at 1954–55.

37. *See* N. Jeremy Duru, *The Central Park Five, the Scottsboro Boys, and the Myth of the Bestial Black Man*, 25 Cardozo L. Rev. 1315, 1323 (2004) (discussing the Virginia slave codes).

38. *See* Roberts, *supra* note 21, at 1955 n.41.

39. *See* Corinna Barrett Lain, *Furman Fundamentals*, 82 Wash. L. Rev. 1, 25–26 (2007).

40. *See* Andrew E. Taslitz, *Slaves No More!: The Implications of the Informed Citizen Ideal for Discovery Before Fourth Amendment Suppression Hearings*, 15 Ga. St. U. L. Rev. 709, 746 (1999); Pokorak, *supra* note 1, at 14–15. The lynching of Emmett Till in 1955 appears to be a more contemporary instance of the latter "violation," aggravated by sexual implications, in which the fourteen-year-old boy from Chicago allegedly whistled at a white woman in Mississippi. *See* Duru, *supra* note 37, at 1329.

41. Death was applied both legally and extralegally. In *Coker v. Georgia*, 433 U.S. 584 (1977), which abolished the death penalty for the rape of an adult woman, the Supreme Court received data indicating that "since 1930, ... 48 whites, 405 blacks, and 2 members of other minorities have been put to death for [the crime of rape]." Brief of Petitioner at 53–57, Coker v. Georgia, 433 U.S. 584 (1977) (No. 75-5444). Many scholars have noted that after slavery was abolished, an informal death penalty often was meted out by lynch mobs seeking to protect white womanhood from black rapists. *See* Edmonds, *supra* note 27, at 52–53; Duru, *supra* note 37, at 1325–27.

42. *See* Christian Halliburton, *Neither Separate Nor Equal: How Race-Sensitive Enforcement of Criminal Laws Threatens to Undo* Brown v. Board of Education, 3 Seattle J. Soc. Just. 45, 52–53 (2004) (arguing that there are currently two separate systems of criminal law based on race).

through the use of race-based profiles,[43] and are more exposed to the usual scrutiny due to the nature of their criminal activities.[44] In addition, studies indicate that encounters between law-enforcement officers and blacks tend to be more violent more often; indeed, blacks are four times more likely to be killed in the course of such encounters than whites are.[45] Black men are also generally imprisoned and executed at a significantly disproportionate rate (particularly when their victim is white). According to Professor David Cole, African-Americans make up about 12 percent of the population in the United States but more than 50 percent of the prison population.[46] The mass incarceration of black men has led to, among other things, the significant fracturing of the black family, cultivating socioeconomic conditions that breed more crime.[47] This, in turn, contributes to a vicious cycle that confirms the widespread belief that "crime has a black face,"[48] leading to easier convictions and longer prison sentences for blacks who are caught up in the criminal-justice system.

---

43. *See* Russell L. Jones, *A More Perfect Nation: Ending Racial Profiling*, 41 Val. U. L. Rev. 621 (2006) (discussing the problematic nature of racial profiling).

44. For example, narcotics crimes in poor, inner-city neighborhoods are more easily detected and arguably more dangerous because they take place in the streets, leading to more exposure and thus are more likely to be accompanied by intimidation and violence. *See* Donald Braman, *Criminal Law and the Pursuit of Equality*, 84 Tex. L. Rev. 2097, 2118 (2006); *cf.* R. Richard Banks et al., *Discrimination and Implicit Bias in a Racially Unequal Society*, 94 Cal. L. Rev. 1169, 1177–78 (2006) (noting that blacks also commit violent and drug-related crimes at a disproportionate rate).

45. *See* Banks et al., *supra* note 44, at 1173.

46. Cole, *supra* note 32, at 4; *see also* U.S. Dep't of Justice, Bureau of Justice Statistics, Prison Statistics (Summary Findings) (2006), *available at* http://www.ojp.usdoj. gov/bjs/prisons.htm ("At year end 2006, there were 3,042 black male sentenced prison inmates per 100,000 black males in the United States, compared to 1,261 Hispanic male inmates per 100,000 Hispanic males and 487 white male inmates per 100,000 white males."); Banks et al., *supra* note 44, at 1177 (reporting that young black men are more than seven times more likely to be imprisoned than young white men). Cole also writes that from 1976 to 1998, only seven white men were executed for killing black victims while 115 black men were executed for killing white victims. Cole, *supra* note 32, at 132.

47. *See generally* Invisible Punishment: The Collateral Consequences of Mass Imprisonment (Marc Mauer & Meda Chesney-Lind eds., 2002) [hereinafter Invisible Punishment]; *see also* Cole, *supra* note 32, at 5 ("Nationally, for every one black man who graduates from college, 100 are arrested."); Braman, *supra* note 44, at 2115–17.

48. Jody Armour, *Race Ipsa Loquitur: Of Reasonable Racists, Intelligent Bayesians, and Involuntary Negrophobes*, 46 Stan. L. Rev. 781, 787 (1994); *see also* Banks et al., *supra* note 44, at 1172–73 (reporting that experiments suggest people associate criminality with individuals who possess highly stereotypical racial features such as wide noses, thick lips, or dark skin).

Thus, race has a dual impact on the criminal law. Black victims of crime suffer from underenforcement of the criminal law; their victimhood is downplayed or ignored, and they are left exposed to increasing violence. For this reason, Harvard Professor Randall Kennedy has argued that underenforcement of the criminal law is the central dilemma for blacks in the United States.[49] At the same time, black perpetrators of crime suffer from overenforcement of the criminal law, with all of the attendant social problems that it creates for the community. For commentators like David Cole, this is the principal problem not only for the black community but also for the law itself, which faces a crisis of legitimacy because of its dependence on racial inequality to preserve the rights of the wealthy and white at the expense of the poor and black.[50] In the end, however, under- and overenforcement are only symptoms of an underlying sickness: an entrenched racism within the criminal-justice system that expresses itself in numerous strategic as well as opportunistic ways.[51]

Not surprisingly, both symptoms were present in the Duke lacrosse rape case. Nifong's failure to identify and quickly arrest the alleged culprits was widely seen as just another example of underenforcement on behalf of a black victim, especially in light of his aggressive rhetoric regarding the strength of the case. Skepticism and discontent did not subside until mid-April 2006, when indictments against two players and the promise of a third finally "indicated to the black community [that Nifong] would be fair."[52] The police, too, claimed

---

49. Randall Kennedy, *The State, Criminal Law, and Racial Discrimination*, 107 HARV. L. REV. 1255, 1259 (1994). Kennedy also writes: "The most lethal danger facing African-Americans in their day-to-day lives is not white, racist officials of the state, but private, violent criminals (typically black) who attack those most vulnerable to them without regard to racial identity." *Id* . Some have noted that neglect of a community may lead to increased violence in that community as individuals are forced to engage in self-help. *See, e.g.,* FRANKIE Y. BAILEY & ALICE P. GREEN, "LAW NEVER HERE": A SOCIAL HISTORY OF AFRICAN AMERICAN RESPONSES TO ISSUES OF CRIME AND JUSTICE, at xvi (1999) (suggesting that violent self-help is a form of resistance to oppression); Alexandra Natapoff, *Underenforcement*, 75 FORDHAM L. REV. 1715, 1772 (2007) (describing how a young man with an illegal firearm may become a victim of both under- and overenforcement).

50. *See* COLE, *supra* note 32, at 4–9; *see also* Braman, *supra* note 44, at 2120 ("It is hard to argue that broader police powers will help crime-ridden communities unless one has a more detailed conception of the consequences that follow from enforcement.").

51. This is not to suggest that the debate surrounding the relative significance of under- and overenforcement is irrelevant. From a practical perspective, we may indeed have to choose to focus our limited attention and resources on combating one or the other for the optimal benefit of the affected community.

52. *See* Michael Biesecker, *Study Says Black Vote Aided Nifong*, NEWS & OBSERVER (Raleigh, N.C.), May 6, 2006, at 1B (quoting a black community leader).

that it would be "relentless in finding out who committed [the] crime,"[53] implying that a crime was, in fact, committed. But a search of the house where the party took place was not made until two days after the alleged rape occurred, and a search of the suspects' dorm rooms did not happen until two weeks after the suspects were identified.[54] These facts did not go unnoticed by some segments of the watchful public. As one cynical Durham resident succinctly put it, "We already know they're going to get off."[55] Even after the tide of public opinion turned against the prosecution of the case, another Durham resident insisted that the accuser should get her day in court, whatever the strength of the evidence.[56]

The delays and weaknesses of the case also raised the specter of overenforcement. Frustrated by the slow progress of the case, the public compared the treatment that the Duke lacrosse players were receiving to the treatment that a black man would have hypothetically received in a similar case. The African-American community took as an affront the fact that the accused players remained free for weeks after a rape allegedly occurred. Several individuals bitterly observed that had this case been about three NCCU athletes accused of raping a Duke student, the athletes would have been promptly arrested.[57] This sentiment was so strong that one student at NCCU argued that the lacrosse players should be prosecuted for rape "whether it happened or not ... [as] justice for things that happened in the past."[58]

Despite these issues, the Duke lacrosse rape case demonstrated that significant changes have been wrought in racial discourse and, consequently, in the role of race in criminal law. Considering its historical and geographical context, the case against the Duke lacrosse players constitutes a noteworthy departure; the zealous prosecution of three wealthy, educated, white men for the rape of a black exotic dancer in the South, apparently backed by both popular and institutional support, is indeed an unusual event in the annals of American criminal law.[59] This is not to say that race is no longer relevant to the criminal law. Rather,

---

53. *See* Khanna & Blythe, *supra* note 3, at A1.

54. *See* Joseph Neff, Michael Biesecker & Samiha Khanna, *DA, Police to be "Tried," Too*, NEWS & OBSERVER (Raleigh, N.C.), Apr. 30, 2006, at A1.

55. *See* Andrea Stone, *Rape Allegations, Race Divide a Community*, USA TODAY, Feb. 28, 2007, at 8D.

56. *See id.*

57. *See* Gonzales, *supra* note 6, at A19; Blythe, *supra* note 23, at B1.

58. *See* Meadows & Thomas, *supra* note 4, at 40.

59. Of course, the fact that the allegations turned out to be false may cause an unfortunate backlash.

the Duke case reveals that the role of race has become much more sophisticated and less predictable than ever before as the criminal justice system adjusts to changing national demographics, politics, and awareness of racial oppression.

Moreover, there is promise in unpredictability. It demonstrates that the law need not always be an instrument of oppression used by whites against blacks; those days, we hope, have passed never to return. Today, the law may be more properly seen as a contested site fought over by many different races, classes, and backgrounds. Although the groups are by no means evenly matched, the moral claims of African-Americans resonate in ways that they have never done before. Who could have imagined such an outpouring of sympathy even fifteen years ago, let alone 150, towards an alleged rape victim who also happened to be poor, black, and a stripper? Who could have predicted that the prosecution of three well-to-do white students for rape would be described by a black editorialist as a "mob lynching"?[60] Or that a white prosecutor's success in a Southern election could turn on the votes of the black community over a white-on-black rape allegation? Sadly—unforgivably—the case against the lacrosse players was hollow and false; nevertheless, this remarkable instance of race-reversal also offers significant insights about the modern relationship between race and the criminal law.

Some Lessons from the Case

Let us proceed from the more obvious to the less. The Duke lacrosse rape case clearly demonstrates how destructive racial stereotypes can be, especially when they are utilized in the context of a powerfully coercive institution like the criminal law. The myth of the black man as criminal and lascivious has contributed to the subordination of blacks for centuries,[61] but it is no less problematic when applied to demonize white men. The Duke lacrosse team members were certainly no angels; several of them had records of criminal charges for misdemeanors (mostly underage drinking and public urination), and no one disputes that some of them used racist insults at the party. But they were not rapists, and no amount of bias—or, for that matter, history—can change that fact. Even more important than abiding by the legal principle that indi-

---

60. *See* Thomas Sowell, *DA Plays Politics with Suspects in Lacrosse Rape Case*, TEN-NESSEAN (Nashville, Tenn.), Apr. 26, 2006, at 17A.

61. *See* Duru, *supra* note 37, at 1321–23 (tracing the myth of the "Bestial Black Man" to the 16th century).

viduals accused of crimes are presumed innocent until proven guilty, we must always take care to examine whether our rush to judgment and outrage is backed by legitimate reasons based in law and fact, or by illegitimate criteria and stereotypes like race, gender, and class.

Fortunately, the Duke lacrosse rape case had a just outcome: the young men never had to face a trial or conviction. Although they undoubtedly suffered an extraordinary ordeal, the accused players spent no more than a few hours in jail and were vindicated with much media fanfare, including the state attorney general's declaration of their innocence and condemnation of the "tragic rush to accuse" by an "unchecked" and "overreaching" prosecutor.[62] They also received a public apology from Nifong,[63] and experienced the satisfaction of seeing the district attorney disbarred for his misconduct in this case.[64] Their brush with the criminal law is over, and they emerged from it victims turned heroes.[65]

Sadly, not all wrongfully accused defendants are able to prove their innocence and avoid punishment. In contrast to the Duke lacrosse players, many other innocent individuals—all too often, poor minorities—end up convicted and imprisoned because they do not have the resources necessary to vindicate themselves.[66] For these innocent criminal defendants, race plays an insidious, multifaceted role: it depresses economic status, thereby depriving them of the means to dispute the charges; it raises suspicion of guilt, so that minorities are singled out for investigation, and pleas and convictions are easier to obtain; and it renders such cases (which are also appalling, if not "tragic") routine, trivial, and invisible. The exoneration of these innocent prisoners—which comes rarely, if at all—is often treated as unimportant by the media, which tends to relegate their stories to the back pages of newspapers.[67] Public outrage, apology, and legal sanctions against prosecutors are certainly not the norm; in-

---

62. *See* Wilson & Barstow, *supra* note 19, at A1.

63. *See* Duff Wilson, *Prosecutor in Duke Case Apologizes*, Int'l Herald Trib., Apr. 14, 2007, at 5.

64. *See* Beard, *supra* note 12, at 6.

65. During Nifong's disbarment hearing, it was revealed that the three accused players were "looking for ways they can help other wrongly accused people." Ann Givens, *Ex-Player Now on the Accuser's Team*, Newsday (New York, N.Y.), Jun. 15, 2007, at A16.

66. *See, e.g.*, Tonja Jacobi & Gwendolyn Carroll, *Acknowledging Guilt: Forcing Self-Identification in Post-Conviction DNA Testing*, 102 Nw. U. L. Rev. 263, 292 (2008) (describing the prohibitive cost of DNA testing); Stephen B. Bright, *Turning Celebrated Principles into Reality*, Champion, Feb. 27, 2003, at 6 (discussing how the poor have difficulty obtaining effective criminal-appeals lawyers).

67. *See, e.g.*, Ralph Blumenthal, *15th Dallas County Inmate Since '01 is Freed by DNA*, N.Y. Times, Jan. 4, 2008, at A11 (recounting the exoneration of Charles Chatman, a black man misidentified by the victim, who was in prison for twenty-seven years for a rape he did

deed, officials often refuse to admit their mistake, or vow to pursue an appeal.[68]

Perhaps the most significant insight from the Duke lacrosse rape case relates to the role of discretion in the criminal law. Shortly after all charges were dismissed, one of the accused lacrosse players marveled at how he had been "railroad[ed] ... with absolutely no evidence whatsoever."[69] He described how the prosecution exposed "a tragic world of injustice [he] never knew existed."[70] But, as many commentators have observed, Nifong's abuse of discretion toward the Duke students is what blacks (and Latinos) typically experience in the criminal justice system.[71] Scholars writing in the criminal law field have long recognized the growing power of the prosecutor; the public, perhaps, had not been as familiar with this phenomenon until the Duke lacrosse rape case exposed it with startling clarity. In fact, prosecutors enjoy a great deal of discretion to pursue cases, choose the charges, negotiate pleas and sentences, and affect releases.[72] The legislatures and courts that make and interpret law, respectively, have done little to restrain such powers. On the contrary, at least one prominent criminal-law-and-procedure scholar has observed that legislatures have ceded more power and discretion to prosecutors by making broad, overlapping laws that become relevant in the real world only as the prosecutor de-

---

not commit); Rodney Foo, *Judge Wipes Out Wrongful Conviction*, SAN JOSE MERCURY NEWS, Apr. 6, 2007, at B1 (discussing a man, freed after eleven years in prison, whose case also raised questions of prosecutorial misconduct). In contrast, the Duke lacrosse rape case generated thousands of articles, was featured on the front pages of newspapers, and graced the covers of numerous national magazines.

68. *See, e.g.*, Duru, *supra* note 37, at 1318 (discussing how some members of the media and police continue to believe that the five men exonerated in the Central Park-jogger rape case are guilty); Frank Green, *Prison Now a Memory*, RICHMOND TIMES-DISPATCH, Jan. 24, 2002, at A1 (describing Earl Washington, Jr.'s pardon from death row based on DNA evidence and the persistent belief among some officials that he committed the crime); Ellen Barry, *Georgia's Supreme Court Reverses 10-Year Sentence*, L.A. TIMES, May 4, 2004, at 16 (reporting that the district attorney planned to file an appeal after a court reversed Marcus Dixon's conviction for aggravated child molestation in a racially charged statutory-rape case).

69. *See* Wilson & Barstow, *supra* note 19, at A1.

70. *See id.*

71. *See, e.g.*, Victor Goode, *If They'd Been Black*, COLORLINES MAGAZINE, Nov. 1, 2007, at 42 (suggesting that "Nifong's real offense was not misconduct, but rather treating three middle-class white defendants as if they were poor and Black").

72. *See* Angela J. Davis, *Prosecution and Race: The Power and Privilege of Discretion*, 67 FORDHAM L. REV. 13, 20–25 (1998).

cides.[73] Countless legal articles on plea bargaining and sentencing guidelines, especially, are devoted to examining this troubling development.[74]

None of this suggests that prosecutors are particularly prone to abusing their authority. But the fact remains that the possibility of prosecutorial overreaching exists, with only a small likelihood that it will be discovered, followed by little to no consequence when it is.[75] Such illegitimate exercises of discretion, moreover, are most likely to occur in cases involving those least likely to discover, or dispute, them: poor people of color.[76] And because of the high stakes involved, abuse of discretion can easily lead to ruinous results for a criminal defendant.[77]

There is, moreover, some evidence to suggest that prosecutorial misconduct occurs with more frequency than we realize or acknowledge. Exoneration of innocent prisoners often involves serious prosecutorial mistakes and misconduct, ranging from poor judgment to deliberate withholding of evidence (one of the ethics charges made against Nifong).[78] Prosecutorial decision-making is also commonly thought to be influenced by race, whether consciously or subconsciously.[79] But rarely do prosecutors suffer any penalty,

---

73. *See* William Stuntz, *The Pathological Politics of Criminal Law*, 100 MICH. L. REV. 505, 506–10 (2001).

74. *See, e.g.*, Andrew Taslitz, *Sentencing Lessons from the Innocence Project*, 21 CRIM. JUST. 6, 11–12 (2006) (discussing prosecutorial discretion in plea bargaining generally, in particular the racial disparities involved); Kate Stith & Jose A. Cabranes, *To Fear Judging No More: Recommendations for the Federal Sentencing Guidelines*, 11 FED. SENT. R. 187, 188 (1999) (arguing that sentencing guidelines have resulted in a power shift toward prosecutors who operate largely unchecked). Some of this prosecutorial power may have dissipated after the Supreme Court held that sentencing guidelines are advisory rather than mandatory. *See* United States v. Booker, 543 U.S. 220 (2005). *But see* Rosemary Barkett, *Judicial Discretion and Judicial Deliberation*, 59 FLA. L. REV. 905, 918–19 (2007) (suggesting that the *Booker* effect may be "more imagined than real").

75. *See* Pokorak, *supra* note 1, at 36; Davis, *supra* note 72, at 20–21; Adam Liptak, *Prosecutor Becomes Prosecuted*, N.Y. TIMES, Jun. 24, 2007, at 4.

76. *See* Pokorak, *supra* note 1, at 6; Taslitz, *supra* note 74, at 11–12; Liptak, *supra* note 75, at 4.

77. As Angela Davis points out, the prosecutor herself need not have abused her discretion to create problematic results. Because the prosecutor often gets involved in the case after arrest, the case may already be infected by racial discrimination from the improper use of police discretion at an earlier, investigative stage. *See* Davis, *supra* note 72, at 31.

78. *See* Mark Johnson, *N.C. Lawyers: Disbarment of Nifong Rare Move by Bar*, CHARLOTTE OBSERVER, Jun. 26, 2007, at 1A (discussing the rarity of disciplinary sanctions against prosecutors even for grave allegations of misconduct); Liptak, *supra* note 75, at 4 (discussing the frequency of prosecutorial misconduct).

79. *See* Davis, *supra* note 72, at 32–38.

let alone the drastic sanction of disbarment, as a result of their behavior.[80] In this sense, Nifong's well-deserved fall from grace is a spectacle that misleads. The harsh and public reproach that he received seemed to suggest that his abuse of discretion, based on race and other illegitimate considerations, was an aberration in the criminal process: that he was, indeed, a "rogue prosecutor."[81] The Duke lacrosse rape case is a reminder—one given to us largely because the defendants were white and well-off—that prosecutorial misconduct can occur too easily.

The Duke case also starkly demonstrates the role of politics in the dynamic between race and the criminal law. Nifong's critics decried what they believed to be his unprincipled pandering to Durham's African-American community to win a close race for the district-attorney seat. But the pressure that Nifong experienced is not unusual in the sense that all elected prosecutors must please their electorate to win and hold office (or advance to a higher one). This is usually accomplished by an overall winning record and a few high-profile convictions. It is easy to see how these considerations can harm minorities: as noted above, compared to their white counterparts, black defendants tend to be more easily convicted, and black victims are less likely to garner media attention or remain in the public's mind.[82]

A less obvious lesson from the Duke lacrosse rape case is the fact that the impact of racial politics reaches beyond the prosecutor's use of discretion. Legislators—those who create and define the criminal law—are also elected officials beholden to their constituencies (which largely do not include convicted criminals).[83] In our world of tough-on-crime politics, legislators vie to be the toughest, creating more and more criminal offenses and using stronger and

---

80. *See* Goode, *supra* note 71, at 42; Liptak, *supra* note 75, at 4; *see also* Barry Saunders, *Justice Blunted?*, NEWS & OBSERVER (Raleigh, N.C.), Apr. 16, 2007, at B1 (discussing the exonerations of Darryl Hunt and Alan Gell in North Carolina, the latter of whom was wrongfully prosecuted by Roy Cooper, the attorney general of North Carolina who called Nifong a "rogue prosecutor"). One reason why sanctions are difficult to obtain is because it is difficult to prove that a prosecutor had malicious intent. *See* Liptak, *supra* note 75, at 4.

81. *See* Wilson & Barstow, *supra* note 19, at A1 (quoting North Carolina Attorney General Roy Cooper).

82. *See* Alan Hirsch, *Why Good Lawyers Become Overzealous Prosecutors*, L.A. TIMES, Jun. 21, 2006 at B13 (discussing the frequency of prosecutorial misconduct and the incentives that drive it).

83. *See* Marc Mauer, *Mass Imprisonment and the Disappearing Voters, in* INVISIBLE PUNISHMENT, *supra* note 47, at 50, 51 (observing that 2 percent of the adult population in the United States is disenfranchised as a result of a criminal conviction, and that 13 percent of African-American males cannot vote for this reason).

stronger rhetoric in favor of harsh punishment for offenders.[84] Moreover, there are very few limitations on lawmakers' ability to create new crimes and attach severe punishments to them.[85] Even if they appear racially neutral, these laws can disproportionately affect minorities in a number of complex, interrelated ways. For example, the law can criminalize conduct that is more commonly associated with one minority group, thereby disproportionately impacting that group merely through the law's routine enforcement.[86] More often, however, criminal laws have a disproportionate effect on minority groups because of racially uneven enforcement by the police, who—like prosecutors—have been granted a wider realm of discretion in recent years. Armed with a vast array of laws, a police officer enjoys the flexibility to enforce the law against everyone (which is impractical), or against only some individuals as he or she chooses. The data on racial profiling, and the demographics of the prison population in the United States, suggest that these choices have fallen especially hard on African-Americans.[87]

The abuse of discretion by legislators, police, and prosecutors, moreover, need not turn on their expressed personal biases. Although some may harbor overt prejudice against racial minorities, it is more likely that each of these actors operates under "common sense,"[88] that is, unconscious assumptions[89] about race and moral characteristics that influence his or her discretionary decisions. Thus, the myths and stereotypes of race, even when acknowledged to be myths and stereotypes, persistently affect outcomes in the criminal process in predictable patterns that are all too recognizable for the victimized communities. As a former gang member has written: "Prison loomed in my future like wisdom teeth; if you lived long enough you got them."[90]

---

84. *See* ALAN ELSNER, GATES OF INJUSTICE 12–13 (2004); JAMES Q. WHITMAN, HARSH JUSTICE 3–4 (2003); Stuntz, *supra* note 73, at 509.

85. *See* Janine Young Kim, *Rule and Exception in Criminal Law (Or, Are Defenses Necessary?)*, 82 TUL. L. REV. 247, 273–74 (2007).

86. The most recent, controversial example of this kind of lawmaking is the one-hundred-to-one sentencing-guideline discrepancy between crack and powder cocaine. *See* William Spade, Jr., *Beyond the 100:1 Ratio: Towards a Rational Cocaine Sentencing Policy*, 38 ARIZ. L. REV. 1233, 1267–68 (1996). Many people associate the "crack epidemic" that prompted these guideline rules with inner-city black males. *See id.* at 1255–56.

87. *See supra* text accompanying notes 42–48.

88. *See* MICHAEL OMI & HOWARD WINANT, RACIAL FORMATIONS 59–61 (1994).

89. *See* Charles R. Lawrence III, *The Id, the Ego, and Equal Protection: Reckoning with Unconscious Racism*, 29 STAN. L. REV. 317, 322–23 (1987).

90. ELSNER, *supra* note 84, at 13 (quoting SANYIKA SHAKUR, MONSTER 163 (1994)).

To be sure, the Duke lacrosse rape case did not follow this well-worn path. Discretion led to the zealous and wrongful prosecution of white men, not black, for the alleged rape of a black woman, not white. The significance of this race-reversal should not be exaggerated, however. Although some pundits have argued that the case signals a change in the tide of racial politics—that is, racial politics (or political correctness) now persecutes white males as racist politics once persecuted black males—this conclusion overstates the racial meaning of this case.[91] The reason why we noticed this case, and why the reversal matters, is that it was *atypical*. The reason why the black community clamored not only for justice in this case, but also for a gesture of atonement for so many others, is not just because of the inequality of the past but also that of the present. Without recognizing this backdrop of racism and the criminal law, and their impact specifically on the black community, we cannot truly understand what happened at Duke.

Nor should we mistake this case as proof that politics trump race. The Duke lacrosse rape case was a revelation, not a catharsis. Nifong's disbarment and public disgrace, the excoriation of the media, and the celebration of the young lacrosse players fall far short of purging the legal system of its racialized operation. If anything, the case confirms critical race theory's premise that race is itself political (as opposed to essential) and hence, race's role in the criminal law is similarly complex, fluid, and significant—but often unseen. When we do bother to see it by reading the back pages of newspapers—or when it is thrust upon us at the supermarket checkout line as the Duke lacrosse rape case was—it should prompt us to question what kind of justice the criminal law can achieve in an unequal society burdened by its own devastating history.

---

91. *See* Wilson & Barstow, *supra* note 19 (reporting that some believe the case represented "justice run off the rails by political correctness"); Mary Laney, *Innocent Duke Lacrosse Players Stuck in P.C. Nightmare*, CHI. SUN-TIMES, Jan. 22, 2007, at 29 (quoting Charles Osgood as saying, "Being politically correct is always having to say you're sorry.").

PART FOUR

LESSONS LEARNED ABOUT THE CRIMINAL-JUSTICE SYSTEM

CHAPTER EIGHT

The Duke Lacrosse Players and the Media: Why the Fair Trial-Free Press Paradigm Doesn't Cut It Anymore

Andrew E. Taslitz

Introduction

The Duke lacrosse case, in which false rape allegations against four Duke University lacrosse team players were ultimately dismissed, long captured the media's imagination. The prosecutor who eagerly pursued these questionable charges, and who likely did so for political reasons (namely, to capture the black vote in a tough election campaign), Mike Nifong, has been disbarred for his misconduct. Among his many other wrongs, Nifong made false statements to the press, including expressing absolute confidence in the lacrosse players' guilt when he knew of strong contrary evidence; insisting that the purported crime was racially motivated when there was no credible evidence to that effect; and proclaiming that the players were conspiring to hide the truth when they in fact had been extraordinarily cooperative with investigators. While wildly exaggerating the case against the players, Nifong also hid exculpatory evidence from the defense and the press. Apart from the untruth of his public statements, he also violated provisions of the North Carolina ethical code that bar statements "hav[ing] a substantial likelihood of ... materially prejudicing an adjudicative proceeding" or "heightening public condemnation of the accused." Yet the press did eventually turn on Nifong, he has been banished from the public scene, and the formerly reviled lacrosse players are now lauded as poster boys for the innocence movement, so justice has been done, right?[1]

Wrong. The injury done to the team members—the destruction of their reputation—had material and psychological consequences for them that the law systematically undervalues. Moreover, especially given the racially charged atmosphere in which these allegations were made, these reputational injuries had much broader consequences than just the harm to the individual team players: they harmed the city of Durham, the nation, and the public's perception of the legitimacy of the American criminal-justice system. The law does not, of course, ignore reputational harms in criminal prosecutions. But legitimate concerns about free speech and a relatively unfettered free press have led to undue caution about muzzling the sort of public statements by prosecutors that can devastate individual lives and inflict grievous community harms. Yes, there are ethics codes governing prosecutors' statements to the press, but these largely focus on the danger prosecutorial media-manipulation poses to the fairness of trials. The Duke case starkly illustrates the ill consequences that can occur from prosecutor-fed media coverage in a high-profile case, *even if it never goes to trial or results in a guilty plea.*

At the individual level, the players' education and future careers were delayed, their sense of physical safety dampened by threats of violence, their bank accounts depleted, and their standing in society for a long time lost. Although their claims of innocence were vindicated, their names will forever be connected to the scandal, their lives redefined. At the community level, a university's reputation was stained—causing concrete damage to its student-recruitment efforts, and risking its access to financial resources and public good will—election results cynically manipulated, racial tensions heightened, and interracial-communication efforts further stymied. Worrying only about the harm to a fair trial is to blind one's self to other, equally serious harms that an errant, unchained prosecutor can inflict via the media. Worrying only about free speech can undermine the legal system, the vibrancy of which is a prerequisite for the useful and vigorous public debate we so value.[2]

The key point here turns on the power of the prosecutor. Part of the very point of a criminal conviction is to visit public condemnation upon the guilty—that is, to justifiably tarnish their reputations. It is partly for this reason that a prosecutor's words have such weight in the public mind. Prosecutors also usu-

---

1. *See generally* N.C. Rules of Prof'l Conduct R. 3.6(a), 3.8(f); *supra* Chapter One (Luck & Seigel).

2. *See supra* Chapter One (Luck & Seigel).

ally have much greater access than the defense to both information and the means to disseminate it; this is especially true in the initial phases of a case, when public impressions are most manipulable. These observations do not mean that prosecutors should never be allowed to speak to the press, nor that they should be shackled in responding to the defense's efforts to control the public debate. But the prosecutor wields special power with the media, power rooted in the ability to wound reputations. That power must be controlled, especially given the reasons that it is granted: to impose proportional reputational harms on the guilty through a criminal *conviction*. Absent a conviction, however, the justification for risking undue reputational harm is significantly diminished.

This chapter's narrow task is, using the details of the Duke lacrosse case as a springboard, to defend the idea that the law gives insufficient weight to prosecutor-inflicted reputational harm. In practice, it does so partly by its excessive reliance on ethics codes that focus more on trial fairness than on the distinct importance of avoiding reputational injury, which merits protection in its own right. It also embraces a vague, First Amendment jurisprudence that too readily risks reputational injury to the accused. The chapter is too brief to offer thoroughly worked-out solutions; instead, I hope to highlight the urgency of debating such solutions—of putting them on policymakers' radar screens. Nevertheless, the chapter concludes by briefly outlining a few illustrative suggestions to jump-start future discussion.[3]

After this introduction, Part II explains the social function of reputation. Part III concisely summarizes the social-science literature on the media's impact on fair trials as the most analogous literature available to show how media coverage of high-profile cases can wound reputations and what, if anything, can be done to fix the problem. Part IV moves from the general to the specific, recounting the reputational injuries done to, and their consequences for, the Duke lacrosse players and the larger community. Part V reviews the leading relevant free-speech case law and ethics codes, examining their strengths and weaknesses, including the need for recognizing the unique reputation-controlling power wielded by prosecutors—who simultaneously serve as lawyers, law-enforcement officers, and elected officials. The chapter concludes with some ruminations about potential solutions.

---

3. For an excellent summary of the enormous power of the prosecutor relative to the defense, see Angela J. Davis, Arbitrary Justice: The Power of the American Prosecutor (2007).

Part II: Undervaluing Reputational Injury

Social status is an important good. Individuals with high social status gain readier access to money, jobs, and political power. Those of higher status, numerous empirical studies show, are perceived as more competent and credible, are allowed more speaking time, and are more effective persuaders in public settings. As a consequence, they are more likely to be hired for desirable jobs, make their voice heard on public political questions, and attract the resources needed for extended political combat. High-status individuals frequently receive deference from lower-status persons, live longer and healthier lives, and more easily attract similarly situated mates. High status is also inherently valuable, bringing psychological rewards that add satisfaction to life while correspondingly encouraging more confident, aggressive social-interaction styles that bring yet more material, social, and psychological benefits.[4]

There are a number of determinants of social status, such as race, gender, class, education, likeability, and meritorious behavior. An individual's reputation—what others in his neighborhood, church, class, job, or broader community say about him—is a powerful contributor to an individual's social status. Reputation can vary among different settings. For example, one can be a very good worker, but a lousy neighbor. Reputation for particular traits may also be valued more in one setting than others; a perfectionist may be known as an annoying acquaintance but also as an excellent accountant. Reputation may be deserved or not but, either way, it is a real social fact that can alter the path of lives for better or worse. Overconcern with reputation can lead to stultifying conformity, to behaving as you believe others wish you to do simply because they wish it, not because it reflects your own deeply held values. But a good reputation can also bring joys, new experiences, and new friends. Humans are social beings bred for hierarchy. Everyone, therefore has a reputation, whether she wants one or not. Moreover, our reputation affects our self-conception, thus becoming, sometimes against our will, part of who we are. That is, reputation also affects our identity because we are in part what we do, and whether others

---

4. *See, e.g.,* Geoffrey Brennan & Philip Petit, The Economy of Esteem 26–27, 29–33 (2004) (detailing the individual benefits from, and biological roots of, gaining the esteem of others); Devah Pager, Marked: Race, Crime, and Finding Work in an Era of Mass Incarceration (2007) (analyzing the relationship among status, race, and employment opportunities); Andrew E. Taslitz, Rape and the Culture of the Courtroom 112–13 (1999) (discussing status generally, deference, and voice).

trust or distrust us, like us or loathe us, our reputation alters what we can and will do with our lives.[5]

The book of Proverbs recognizes reputation's critical role in our lives, declaring, "A good name is rather to be chosen than great riches."[6] John Proctor, a character in *The Crucible*, Arthur Miller's iconic play based on the Salem Witch Trials, refuses to confess to crimes of witchery "[b]ecause it is my name! Because I cannot have another in my life!" Proctor laments, "How may I live without my name? I have given you my soul; leave me my name!"[7]

Perhaps the most famous literary paean to reputation is William Shakespeare's play, *Othello*. Among Shakespeare's many themes is how ruined reputations destroy lives. Most poignant is the fate of the reputation of Desdemona, Othello's wife. Iago, seeking revenge on Othello for perceived slights, falsely convinces Othello of his wife's adultery. In the oft-cited speech,[8] Iago summarizes reputation's power:

> Good name in man and woman, dear my lord,
> Is the immediate jewel of their souls:
> Who steals my purse steals trash; 'tis something, nothing;
> 'Twas mine, 'tis his, and has been slave to thousands:
> But he that filches from me my good name
> Robs me of that which not enriches him
> And makes me poor indeed.[9]

Believing himself cuckolded, Othello murders Desdemona for her supposed betrayal, only thereafter learning that Iago lied about it. Othello's violence seems motivated partly by jealousy but also by concern for his own reputation as a great military hero, in charge of his own house as much as of the forces under his command. Upon learning that he has wronged his wife, he takes his own life, as much from grief as from fear of public shame for his ill judgment

---

5. *See* BRENNAN & PETIT, *supra* note 4, at 2–4, 26–33, 70–72, 197–200, 222–39, 311–21 (analyzing the nature and importance of esteem and competition for it via publicity and the creation of reputation); STEVEN FRIEDLAND, PAUL BERGMAN & ANDREW E. TASLITZ, EVIDENCE LAW AND PRACTICE 103–08 (3d ed. 2007) (defining "reputation" and explaining its role in the law of evidence).

6. *Proverbs* 22:1.

7. ARTHUR MILLER, THE CRUCIBLE 133 (Penguin Books 2003) (1953).

8. *See* WILLIAM SHAKESPEARE, *Othello*, *in* 3.3 THE OXFORD SHAKESPEARE (Stanley Wells & Gary Taylor eds. 1988) (1622); *see also* DANIEL J. KORNSTEIN, SHAKESPEARE'S LEGAL APPEAL 156–60 (1994) (summarizing the portions of *Othello*'s plot that are relevant to the concept of reputation).

9. *See* SHAKESPEARE, *supra* note 8, at 160–66.

and for the ease with which he was deceived by Iago. Iago's gossip killed two people; good reputation, therefore, is portrayed as necessary even to physical, as much as social and spiritual, survival. To cabin such violence and injustice, many religions have, like the great Jewish rabbis of the Talmud, roundly condemned gossip.[10]

The law also often recognizes the importance of protecting reputation. Defamation and privacy-invasion suits were, in part, created to protect reputations. Indeed, reputation-protection was the motivating force behind Samuel Warren and Louis Brandeis's seminal article arguing that tort law should recognize a right to privacy. Although some academics have argued that defamation and privacy actions should be banned because they chill free speech, neither courts nor legislatures have generally heeded this advice. The Supreme Court has repeatedly recognized the value of reputation to an individual and to a free society; for example, it declared in 1966 that, "Society has a pervasive and strong interest in preventing and redressing attacks upon reputation." As Justice Potter Stewart put it in a separate opinion in that same case, the individual's "right to the protection of his own good name reflects no more than our basic concept of the essential dignity and worth of every human being—a concept at the root of any decent system of ordered liberty."[11]

The Court has even recognized that groups and the individuals comprising them have reputational interests worthy of safeguarding, even at some cost to free speech. Notably, in *Beauharnais v. Illinois*,[12] the president of the White Circle League challenged his conviction under a criminal statute prohibiting the defamation of groups of people, arguing that his First Amendment right to free speech guaranteed him the freedom to distribute a pamphlet spewing race hatred. Said the pamphlet, "if persuasion and the need to prevent the white race

---

10. This reading of *Othello* is my own but is informed by, and in many ways tracks, that in KORNSTEIN, *supra* note 8, at 156–65. For a concise summary of the Talmudic view of gossip and related practices, see JOSEPH TELUSHKIN, A CODE OF JEWISH ETHICS: YOU SHALL BE HOLY 332–79 (2006).

11. *See* Rosenblatt v. Baer, 383 U.S. 75, 86 (1966) (Stewart, J., concurring); ROBERT C. POST, CONSTITUTIONAL DOMAINS: DEMOCRACY, COMMUNITY, MANAGEMENT 118–20, 127–34, 152–63 (1995) (discussing the social function of defamation law); DANIEL J. SOLOVE, THE FUTURE OF REPUTATION: GOSSIP, RUMOR, AND PRIVACY ON THE INTERNET 113, 116–26, 158–59, 191 (2007) (analyzing the relationship among reputation, privacy, gossip, and defamation); RUSSELL L. WEAVER & DONALD E. LIVELY, UNDERSTANDING THE FIRST AMENDMENT 34–43 (2d ed. 2006) (summarizing modern defamation law); Samuel D. Warren & Louis D. Brandeis, *The Right to Privacy*, 4 HARV. L. REV. 193 (1890).

12. 343 U.S. 250 (1952).

from being mongrelized by the Negro will not unite us, then the aggressions ... rapes, robberies, knives, guns, and marijuana of the Negro surely will."[13] The Supreme Court affirmed Beauharnais's conviction, rejecting his free-speech claims, explaining that,

> It would, however, be arrant dogmatism, quite outside the scope of our authority in passing on the powers of a State, for us to deny that the Illinois legislature may warrantably believe that a man's job and his educational opportunities and the dignity accorded him may depend as much *on the reputation of the racial and religious group to which he willy-nilly belongs as on his own merits.* This being so, we are precluded from saying that speech concededly punishable when immediately directed at individuals cannot be outlawed if directed at groups with whose position and esteem in society the affiliated individual may be inextricably involved.[14]

Beauharnais is, of course, several decades old, and the modern Court has arguably become increasingly solicitous of First Amendment free speech claims. Nevertheless, whatever the modern Court might decide today, this earlier case correctly gives substantial weight to the goal of protecting reputation. Of course, *undeservedly* tarnishing an otherwise-stellar reputation is perhaps the worst sort of reputational harm. But even fostering a bad reputation based on *truthful* reports of events does important damage. Others can never know a person's whole nature in all its complexity. Moreover, we rightly reveal parts of our nature in some settings but not others; for example, one might be calm in the office but known to slam-dance in nightclubs. Losing control over how much of ourselves we reveal to whom, at what time, and in what setting, would often expose us to a grave risk of misdefinition by others: they do not know all the facets of our personality. Yet observers are willing to make judgments about our entire nature, even our worth as human beings, from supposed knowledge of a single trait—and they often determine the existence of that trait itself from minimal evidence. Nonconsensual revelation of even truthful information about us also wounds the nature of our relationships, while exposing secrets meant to demarcate intimacy with another, thus putting us in faux relationships with strangers who have learned things about us that we would ordinarily reveal only to parents, spouses, or close friends.[15]

---

13. *Id.* at 252.

14. *Id.* at 262–63 (emphasis added).

15. Andrew E. Taslitz, *Condemning the Racist Personality: Why the Critics of Hate Crimes Legislation are Wrong*, 40 B.C. L. Rev. 739 (1999) (analyzing the precedential value of

In a complex modern world in which the internet can quickly and globally spread rumors, gossip, and tabloid-tales, these reputational concerns are heightened still further. Rapid dissemination is especially worrisome when the information concerns the criminal-justice system. One major function of that system is to identify those persons who, by their criminal acts, deserve extreme stigmatization and condemnation via powerful mechanisms (for example, imprisonment) thereby sending unequivocal messages designed to bring the offender "down a peg," tainting his reputation as the price he must pay for his arrogance in wounding another. For this reason, even the most minimal association with the criminal-justice system, whether by arrest or even merely by being investigated upon suspicion, can destroy previously positive reputations. Media reports can be especially pernicious because most readers know the suspects only from these reports, which, even when true, paint a radically incomplete picture. When false, however, such reports can have especially brutal consequences for individuals, groups, and institutions. Therein lies the tale of the Duke lacrosse players.[16]

Part III: Media Coverage in High-Profile Cases

Is Media Coverage Antidefendant?

Before turning to the players' story, however, we must ask: Why assume that media coverage will be *harmful* (rather than helpful or neutral) to a suspect's reputation? In other words, is the Duke case, in this respect, a fluke?

The assumption of harm to a suspect's reputation is indeed flawed in most cases, for the majority of crimes receive no press coverage whatsoever, and those few that do are covered only minimally. The minimal coverage these cases receive, moreover, may be barely noticed by the public given the declin-

---

Beauharnais); Andrew E. Taslitz, *The Fourth Amendment in the Twenty-First Century: Technology, Privacy, and Human Emotions*, 65 LAW & CONTEMP. PROBS. 125, 150–158 (2002) (discussing privacy invasions and misdefinition of individual identity).

16. *See* SOLOVE, *supra* note 11, at 1–49 (explaining and illustrating the impact of the internet on rumors, gossip, and the like); Andrew E. Taslitz, *A Feminist Fourth Amendment?: Consent, Care, Privacy, and Social Meaning in* Ferguson v. City of Charleston, DUKE J. GENDER L. & POL'Y 1, 4–5 (2002) [hereinafter Taslitz, *Feminist Approach*] (evaluating the "down a peg" function of the criminal-justice system); *see also* Andrew E. Taslitz, *The Inadequacies of Civil Society: Law's Complementary Role in Regulating Harmful Speech*, 1 MD. L.J. OF RACE, RELIGION, GENDER & CLASS 306 (2001) (making similar points and comparing stigma-imposing purposes of the criminal- and civil-justice systems); *infra* text accompanying notes 23–26 (evaluating the reputational effects of minimal criminal-justice-system contact).

ing readership and viewership for newspapers and television news and the audience's limited attention span. One recent study found that a market with four simultaneously broadcasting news stations captured at most a mere 25 percent of the potential viewers. To affect reputation, a story must be covered and reported by the media and noticed, processed, and remembered by the audience. The required combination of significant coverage and attentive audience is simply unlikely to occur in the vast majority of cases. But this combination does arise in a small subset of cases: the high-profile crimes that receive moderate-to-massive, extended media coverage like that in the Duke rape case.[17]

Just because high-profile crimes have a strong potential to affect reputation does not necessarily mean, however, that those effects will be antidefendant; there is no logical reason to presuppose that the media will say largely negative things about criminal suspects. But even if logic does not dictate this outcome, it is nevertheless the empirically documented reality, with a variety of social forces pushing coverage in an antidefendant direction—especially immediately after the media takes note of the case. These forces include law enforcement's earlier access to more case-specific information than defense counsel; the lurid nature of many high-profile crimes; and the media-generated atmosphere about crime in general, which makes pro-prosecution tales more credible to audiences than prodefendant counter-stories.[18]

Press Dependency on Law Enforcement

Police and prosecutors have more information about a crime at an earlier stage than do defense counsel, if only because the latter typically do not receive the limited discovery to which they are entitled (limited, that is, relative to civil cases) until shortly before trial. Reporters, on the other hand, often have limited short-term alternative sources of information and few resources to pursue them. Furthermore, the press understands that it has a continuing and symbiotic relationship with law enforcement: the same reporters repeatedly deal in different cases with the same police officers and prosecutors. Yet a reporter might cross a particular *defense attorney's* path but once, creating less

---

17. *See* Jon Bruschke & William E. Loges, Free Press vs. Fair Trials: Examining Publicity's Role in Trial Outcomes 81, 105 (2004). Steven Penrod, however, seems to question whether enough research has been done to make confident judgments about the average amount of coverage in particular cases. *See* Christina A. Studebaker & Steven D. Penrod, *Pretrial Publicity and Its Influence on Juror Decisionmaking, in* Psychology And Law: An Empirical Perspective 254, 259 (Neil Brewer & Kipling D. Williams eds., 2005).

18. *See infra* text accompanying notes 19–24.

incentive to curry favor with the defense. Crime sells newspapers. Reporters are thus dependent, at least early in a news cycle, on police and prosecutors for quick information that the reporters highly prize to meet pressing deadlines. The result is relatively one-sided, antidefendant coverage. Defense counsel may struggle to gain information to counter the media assault, but they are most likely to draw significant media attention by playing up deviant aspects of a case, an ultimately self-defeating strategy.[19]

Savvy defense counsel in high-profile cases must nevertheless try to foster good press relations while being patient, accepting that short-term media successes will be elusive. But the short term can often prove determinative, for the defense might plea bargain precisely to reduce or avoid negative media coverage, which, should the case eventually go to trial and result in a conviction, can tighten the pressure for harsh sentences. In white-collar cases, especially, corporations and their officers may fear the media coverage more than the conviction; negative publicity can send stock prices plummeting, destroy fortunes, and even cause a company's demise. Sometimes, however, publicity can indirectly benefit resource-poor defendants by improving the quality of legal representation. An overworked public defender facing a television camera is likely to give the spotlighted case special attention. Moreover, in a high-profile case, top-flight counsel may see it as in their career interest to defend even a poor client, because it will get them in the news.

Still, the benefits of better counsel may bear fruit only in the long run because the prosecution's short-term media advantage is so substantial. Moderate coverage, interestingly, may harm a defendant more than very intense, extended pretrial publicity. Precisely because the crime press depends on the state for information, short-term, moderate coverage results in a very one-sided, antidefendant narrative. More intense, longer-lived publicity, however, is increasingly likely to embrace a two-sided narrative. Unfortunately, it can take a very long time for more-balanced coverage to kick in, with much damage done along the way.[20]

---

19. *See* Bruschke & Loges, *supra* note 17, at 100–04 (discussing media coverage); *see also* Richard G. Singer, Criminal Procedure II: From Bail to Jail 76–77 (2005) (evaluating limited discovery in criminal cases, relative to civil cases).

20. *See* Bruschke & Loges, *supra* note 17, at 11, 57–58, 107–08, 119–28, 148 (talking about the incentive effects of media coverage); Paul B. Wice, Public Defenders and the American Justice System, at x (2005) (stating that public defenders, who nationally represent three-quarters of all criminal defendants in serious cases, are often inexperienced, facing "staggering caseloads and inadequate resources"); Candace Zierdt & Ellen Podgor, *Corporate Deferred Prosecutions Through the Looking Glass of Contract Policing,* 96 Ky. L.J. 1, 2 (2007) (noting that corporations readily sign deferred-prosecution agreements as an alternative to the "corporate death sentence" that can result from the publicity accompanying an actual prosecution).

Another reason that the defense can find it hard to gain traction with the media is the lurid, deviant nature of the crime.

Cultivating Deviancy

The more "deviant" from social norms a tale seems to be, the more likely that the press will cover it—and cover those aspects of it that are most deviant. Deviance includes: "statistical deviance" (the unusual); "status deviance" (being of a lower-status race or deviating from the expected behavior of the higher-status race); "cultural deviance" (the alleged acts are seen as "unhealthy, unclean, or perverted"); and "normative deviance" (the degree to which the act violates social standards—the greater the degree of deviancy, the more likely the potential sentence will be higher to properly account for the crime's severity). The type of alleged crime thus affects the intensity of media coverage as well.[21]

Merely reporting the fact of arrest can harm a suspect's reputation, especially if there is a "perp walk" before the cameras. The media also seems to create a "cultivation effect"—a vision of crime, criminal justice, and criminals cultivated by the daily onslaught of portrayals of criminality found in novels, films, news reports, television shows, and other media outlets.[22] The result is that this generalized pretrial publicity can

> make some narratives offered by the prosecution and defense more plausible and some more incredible. Jurors who are heavy viewers of television are the most likely to be exposed to any television coverage the crime in question did receive, but also the most likely to have developed beliefs about the world that are more consistent with the world of television than with reality. This combination may make such jurors more willing to believe that people can't be trusted and that crime is common and ever-threatening.[23]

These "scary-world beliefs seem biased against a criminal defendant," although there may be some important exceptions, like making the defendant's self-defense claims more plausible than they really are. Crime coverage that applies these stereotypes to a particular defendant is most likely to trigger "pe-

---

21. *See* Bruschke & Loges, *supra* note 17, at 101; D. Pritchard & K. D. Hughes, *Patterns of Deviance in Crime News*, 47 J. of Comm. 49 (1997).

22. *See* Bruschke & Loges, *supra* note 17, at 104, 108–09; Ray Surette, Media, Crime, and Criminal Justice: Images, Realities, and Policies 31–55, 125–40 (3d ed. 2007) (discussing how the media socially constructs crime and its connection to pretrial publicity).

23. Bruschke & Loges, *supra* note 17, at 109.

ripheral processing" in which categorical media-primed thinking supersedes the audience's careful analysis of the evidence in the case. Antidefendant news, especially early in a case, thus gets more coverage and attention than its opposite. The next questions raised, however, are these: how damaging is this coverage, and can its ill effects be cured? The bulk of the research on this question, to which we now turn, has addressed the media's impact on trial deliberations and verdicts.[24]

The Impact of Media Coverage

There are two views on the impact of media publicity on the pretrial process—the pessimistic view and the optimistic one—each with analogous implications for the Duke rape case.

The Pessimistic View
The Media's Ill Effects

Social scientists holding the pessimistic view have concluded that pretrial publicity has "broad effects," influencing the defendant's likeability, the sympathy he elicits, potential jurors' perceptions of him as a "typical criminal," their pretrial judgments of his guilt, and the likelihood of his being convicted. However, there are a number of factors that affect the degree to which pretrial publicity affects a defendant.[25]

The amount of coverage varies geographically and with the nature of the crime and the particular set of alleged facts. Field and laboratory studies suggest a "dosage effect" in which reporting a combination of prejudicial information—such as the seriousness of the offense, the race of the accused, unfavorable statements by the prosecutor, a confession, and retention in custody—is more likely to result in a guilty verdict than any one item presented in isolation. "Emotional," as opposed to "factual," information is also more likely to produce a conviction.[26] One team of authors, discussing the disparate impact between emotional and factual information, declared,

> Overall, these studies reveal that information casting doubt on the character of the defendant is one of the principal vehicles through which [pretrial publicity] exerts its effects. Jurors who have heard

---

24. *See id.* at 109–10.
25. *See* Studebaker & Penrod, *supra* note 17, at 254–55.
26. *See id.* at 258–59, 262, 268.

about prior bad acts by a party or who have reason to question the character of a party are more likely to convict or find fault with that party.[27]

Indeed, this team concluded, pretrial publicity increases juror recall of damaging pretrial information, biases that recall against the accused, enhances pre-existing relevant negative attitudes (for example, that fraternities promote licentiousness), and ultimately encourages jurors to believe that the defendant is culpable for the alleged wrongs. The heinous nature of the crime, particularly if it involves sexual abuse or violence, may also increase the antidefendant effect of press coverage.[28]

There can be many sources of pretrial publicity, including gossip, rumor, and the media. Although the research is limited, social scientists espousing the pessimistic view speculate that the impact of publicity increases with the credibility of the source and that the media are likely to be perceived as relatively neutral, thus relatively more credible. Media impact is also greater when pretrial publicity focuses on the particular defendant rather than on a class of similar defendants or similar crimes. A minimal threshold for publicity to have an impact, of course, is that the audience hears the message in the first place. This suggests that tales of more lurid crimes are more likely to reach potential jurors than more mundane or run-of-the-mill criminal behavior. To the pessimists, therefore, the impact of antidefendant press coverage is deeply troubling.[29]

The Lack of an Effective Cure

Perhaps the most pessimistic thing about the pessimists, however, is their conclusion that

> the effects of [pretrial publicity] can find their way into the courtroom, can survive the jury selection process, can survive the presentation of trial evidence, can endure the limiting effects of judicial instructions, and can persevere not only through [jury] deliberation, but may also actually intensify.[30]

---

27. *Id.* at 262.

28. *See id.* at 257–58, 262–6, 268.

29. *See id.* at 267–71; *supra* text accompanying notes 21–29 (discussing lurid tales' "cultivating deviancy"). Psychologists Neil Vidmar and Valerie Hans remind us that it is not only media content, but gossip and "the formation of community solidarity against a trial participant" that contribute to antidefense public perceptions in high-profile cases. *See* Neil Vidmar & Valerie P. Hans, American Juries: The Verdict 122–23 (2007).

30. Studebaker & Penrod, *supra* note 17, at 265–70.

As one of the leading pessimists has pointed out, setting aside preconceived notions of guilt requires a juror consciously to identify earlier-received information as biasing, knowing how it was processed and memorized, while reversing or controlling any resulting bias, three challenging tasks given the "integrative nature of human information processing"—that is, "mak[ing] connections between various pieces of information and [bas]ing decisions on overall impressions rather than on specific pieces of information." Yet "prejudgments guide our attention, our interpretation of new and old information, and our memories." Moreover, jurors reason by constructing stories that fit trial evidence into the existing stock tales that they bring with them into the courtroom. These stories create the framework in which jurors will place trial evidence. Pretrial publicity, by influencing the salience of certain stock tales from films, news reports, and TV shows, and by aiding in the early construction of the specific case story as a variant on that stock, alters how trial jurors interpret new evidence. This can create a "primacy effect," supported by some experimental evidence, in which jurors ignore testimony conflicting with prior evidence or reinterpret the conflicting evidence to make it and other evidence tending to show guilt consistent.[31]

This state of affairs puts defense counsel in an awkward position in responding. Attitude change is least likely if the new evidence and its interpretation differ dramatically from the old. Audience members will also resist attitude change on matters of great importance to them, or when they doubt the credibility of the discrepant source. Pretrial publicity in high-profile cases may form initial attitudes and involve hot-button issues of race, class, and gender that symbolize matters of deep juror importance. Defense counsel cannot, therefore, craft a tale straying too far from the initial antidefendant media-crafted script, and must overcome the script's symbolic, unconscious power while substituting equally compelling alternative symbols. Doing so is no mean feat.[32]

Some thinkers, albeit relying on sparse and conflicting research, have suggested, however, that negative media impacts might be diluted over time because of differences in emotional and more-reasoned forms of cognitive

---

31. *See* Studebaker & Penrod, *supra* note 17, at 257–58, 265–66. On storytelling theory in jury reasoning more generally, see Taslitz, *Feminist Approach*, *supra* note 16.

32. *See* ROBERT M. ENTMAN, THE BLACK IMAGE: MEDIA AND RACE IN AMERICA 60–106 (2000) (analyzing the treatment of race and class in the news media); Studebaker & Penrod, *supra* note 17, at 270; Andrew E. Taslitz, *Patriarchal Stories I: Cultural Rape Narratives in the Courtroom,* 5 S. CAL. REV. L. & WOMEN'S STUD. 387, 433–39 (1996) [hereinafter Taslitz, *Patriarchal Stories I*] (noting a similar problem for the *prosecution* in crafting workable victim narratives in rape cases).

processing. Less-educated persons are more likely to rely on emotional reactions, while those who are more educated are likely to rely on conclusions attained through reason. The media's audience is initially quite ignorant about the facts of a particular case, and thus may at first judge guilt from the heart. But extended coverage, *at least if offering multiple perspectives on the evidence and if still carefully watched by the audience*, makes the audience more informed about the case, and thus more likely to use reason.[33]

But pessimists rely instead on research purportedly demonstrating that time passage *increases* the negative effect of pretrial publicity, rendering continuances counterproductive, and that jury deliberations strengthen bias rather than overcoming it. Furthermore, say the pessimists, extended voir dire is no more effective in overcoming bias than is ordinary voir dire, and jurors who claimed in voir dire to be unbiased were, at least in some studies, just as likely to convict as those admitting their own lack of impartiality and were much more likely to convict when exposed to damaging publicity. Moreover, the pessimists would argue, even the few studies supposedly suggesting that extended media coverage can cure short-term prejudicial effects assume that long-term reports are balanced and attended to closely. In reality, these assumptions are far from guaranteed. Pessimists suggest, therefore, that the only truly effective way to avoid pretrial publicity's biasing effect on verdicts is to avoid the publicity in the first place.[34]

The Optimistic View

Those who view pretrial publicity optimistically rely partly on a critique of the pessimists' methodology that need not be reviewed here. Several of the optimists' conclusions are, however, relevant to the Duke case. First, optimists reject the idea that there is any general pretrial publicity effect on verdicts. They agree, however, that in unusual cases of intense media scrutiny, press reporting of information with probative value concerning guilt is the most likely sort to lead jurors who closely follow the case to presume guilt. But, they say, even then the effect is often modest.[35]

That the effect is modest does not necessarily make it unimportant. For example, psychologist John Bruschke and his co-author note that one pessimist's study revealed a purportedly modest publicity effect accounting for only 2.5 percent of the variance. In laymen's terms, this means that when two jurors, one aware of media coverage and the other not, are exposed to the same trial evi-

---

33. *See* Studebaker & Penrod, *supra* note 17, at 268–70.
34. *See id.* at 264–65.
35. *See* Bruschke & Loges, *supra* note 17, at 74–75, 80, 89.

dence but react to it differently, 2.5 percent of the difference in their reactions can be attributed to pretrial publicity. In most cases, this means that both jurors would vote guilty, one just being 2.5 percent more confident in that verdict than the other. In close cases, however, that 2.5 percent might alter outcomes, leading one juror to be just over the "beyond a reasonable doubt" conviction threshold, the other just under it. Pretrial publicity is thus most likely to matter when the coverage is intense and the evidence of guilt versus innocence is otherwise sufficiently balanced as to leave jurors just a bit uncertain or divided about whether the state has made its case. The more probative the evidence revealed by the media, such as seemingly strong confessions, eyewitness identifications, or fingerprints, the greater the likelihood that the publicity will influence the verdict. Moreover, research in other contexts consistently shows that the strength of the evidence is the most important determinant of jury outcomes. Although studies on the strength of the evidence in the pretrial-publicity context are few, there is reason to believe that publicity will only affect verdicts when evidence of innocence is weak.[36]

Optimists defend, however, the "cumulative remedies hypothesis." Most research finding remedies ineffective examined only one remedy at a time. But optimists find strong reason to believe that combining these remedies will counteract any biasing pretrial publicity. Accordingly, careful voir dire, effective defense counsel, cautionary instructions, jury deliberation, and presentation of trial evidence under real-world conditions should cumulatively minimize or even entirely erase media coverage's negative effects. Furthermore, the optimists suggest that psychological theory and research support a number of alterations in these remedies to improve their effectiveness: giving jury instructions on how to process evidence early in the trial, explaining to jurors the rationales for evidentiary rules, presenting instructions in narrative form, giving rules a "soft sell" that downplays limitations on jurors' freedom, paying attention to "face" concerns so that jurors identifying a bias will not feel foolish admitting and addressing it, stressing the presumption of innocence, and requiring public juror pledges to seek fairness and eliminate bias.[37]

---

36. *See id.* at 25, 89–92. Bruschke and Loges' illustration seems to concern a civil case using the preponderance of evidence burden of persuasion, but their logic readily extends to criminal cases and the beyond a reasonable doubt standard. *See also* Nancy M. Steblay et al., *The Effects of Pretrial Publicity on Jury Verdicts: A Meta-Analytic Review*, 23 Law & Hum. Behav. 219 (1999) (source of the 2.5 percent study interpreted optimistically by Bruschke and Loges but more pessimistically by Steblay and cohorts).

37. *See* Bruschke & Loges, *supra* note 17, at 17–18, 57, 61, 65, 70–71, 74, 92–98, 135–36.

Implications for the Duke Rape Case

What these studies were really testing was the impact of media publicity on trial outcomes, but what is publicly said about defendants by definition affects their reputations. Perhaps more precisely, reputation is better thought of as the sum of what is said and believed about a person. Yet these studies suggest that negative things said about a person in the press in criminal cases, at least early on in a high-profile case, will indeed be believed. Additionally, they will be believed so strongly that they will alter assessments of a person's character and change jury verdicts. Furthermore, early impressions made about character and guilt will be hard to overcome.[38]

Where researchers part company is in what they believe can be done about this state of affairs. Pessimists believe that the answer is little or nothing, short of preventing media coverage in the first place or perhaps a change of venue if coverage has been entirely local. The few and most extreme optimists believe that *in the long run* more balanced coverage will restore reputations. But, even under this rosy picture, much damage will be done along the way. For the bulk of the optimists, it is the aggressive use of cumulative trial remedies that saves the day.

The Duke case, however, never got to trial, so trial remedies had no chance to do their work. It does seem to be true that a combination of effective defense counsel, a strong North Carolina open discovery statute, and media coverage did eventually bring the truth to light, as other commentators have explained in great detail. This long-delayed outcome came about, however, only after grave, and in some ways irreparable, reputational harm was inflicted on the lacrosse players.[39]

Part IV: Pretrial Publicity and Reputational Harms in the Duke Rape Case

The Antidefendant Content of the Press Coverage

The same processes that may taint the public's attitude toward the case as time passes also taints their views of the standing—the moral worth—of the

---

38. *See supra* text accompanying notes 4–13 (defining "reputation").

39. *See* Robert M. Mosteller, *The Duke Lacrosse Case, Innocence and False Identifications: A Fundamental Failure to "Do Justice,"* 76 FORDHAM L. REV. 1331 (2007) [hereinafter Mosteller, *Innocence*]; Robert M. Mosteller, *Exculpatory Evidence Ethics, and the Road to Disbarment of Mike Nifong: The Critical Importance of Open-File Discovery,* 15 GEO. MAS. L. REV. 285–306 (2008) [hereinafter Mosteller, *Exculpatory Evidence*].

accused. Even if the optimists are right—that the effects of pretrial publicity are small—even small effects, as they concede, can tip close verdicts. Such effects are thus likely to do the same thing to tip public opinion about a suspect's reputation, especially when the accused did not have a good "public" reputation to work in his favor. The media-created public reputation of the lacrosse players was, for a long time, tipped radically against them, because they had no broader "public" reputation to speak of—beyond that on the Duke campus or among family and friends—until the media spoke. Yet what the media had to say was initially strongly negative and one-sided.[40]

The research summarized above suggests that a number of factors present in the Duke rape case created a powerful media-poisoned, antidefendant atmosphere that ravaged the students' reputation. The crime alleged, rape, was a heinous one, and the press' suggestion that the rape was racially motivated because the students allegedly specifically requested only African-American strippers (an allegation later proven to be false), heightened the taint of evil, painting the students' behavior as a particularly violent and insulting hate crime. Interracial, interclass sex is still taboo to many Americans, at least subconsciously, adding to the picture of the students as deviants. Moreover, the press readily reported and distorted prior bad acts by the students, most notably by falsely stating that Collin Finnerty had previously been arrested for gay bashing. (He had been arrested on a minor assault charge, but homophobia had nothing to do with it.) Additionally, the press portrayed the lacrosse players as privileged brats (a charge clearly false as to at least some, and perhaps most, of the players), feeling entitled to take whatever they wanted, whenever they wanted it, heedless of the harm they caused others.[41] In *Newsweek*'s words:

---

40. *See generally* STUART TAYLOR, JR. & KC JOHNSON, UNTIL PROVEN INNOCENT: POLITICAL CORRECTNESS AND THE SHAMEFUL INJUSTICES OF THE DUKE LACROSSE RAPE CASE (2007) (giving a book-length defense of the proposition that the Duke students suffered unfair reputational injuries).

41. *See id.* at 6–7, 13–14, 40–41, 64–66, 85, 87–88, 96, 103, 106, 128, 144, 244–48, 273–74, 292; PETER WALLENSTEIN, TELL THE COURT I LOVE MY WIFE: RACE, MARRIAGE, AND LAW—AN AMERICAN HISTORY 249–50 (2002) (noting the reduced, but remaining, bias against interracial marriage); DON YAEGER, IT'S NOT ABOUT THE TRUTH: THE UNTOLD STORY OF THE DUKE LACROSSE CASE AND THE LIVES IT SHATTERED 99–105, 147–64, 183–92 (2007); Taslitz, *Patriarchal Stories I, supra* note 32, at 453–55 (discussing the continued taboo against interracial sex). I am not arguing that every lacrosse player was an angel, nor even that none of them made racially insensitive or insulting comments. At least one of the students did so. *See* TAYLOR & JOHNSON, *supra* note 40, at 138. But it is unfair to taint all the players with these sins, and it is quite a leap from one player making a racially charged comment to there being evidence of a racially motivated crime.

Strutting lacrosse players are a distinctive and familiar breed on elite campuses across the Eastern Seaboard. Because the game until recently was played mostly by prep schools and in the upper-middle-class communities on New York's Long Island and outside Baltimore, the players tend to be at once macho and entitled, a sometimes unfortunate combination.[42]

Concluded *Newsweek*, these lacrosse players "sometimes behave like thugs."[43]

That the story the media told was long one-sided is indisputable and was amplified by the prosecution's steady refusal to release exculpatory evidence, its false insistence that the suspects were not cooperating with the investigation, and its repeated pandering to unsubstantiated claims of racial bias by an entire team gone wild with beer bashes, noisy parties, and public humiliation of women. The prosecution went even further, lying to the press about how much credible evidence there really was of the students' guilt; creating, apparently intentionally, misleading evidence of culpability, particularly by arranging photospreads populated solely by lacrosse players so that any photo picked by the alleged victim was the "right" one; and distorting public reports of what true evidence did exist. Nifong himself gave fifty to seventy interviews to the press in the first week after the rape allegations were made public, vigorously attacking the character and motivations of the lacrosse players. In short, this was a lurid tale of sex, drugs, and rock-and-roll by a violent bunch of wealthy hooligans, a one-sided drama certain to grip the public imagination. Both pessimist and optimist social scientists would likely agree that the Duke case was a powerful example of just the sort of case that can ravage accused's reputations as they await trial.[44]

Tainting the Team: The Publicity's Negative Effects

Many of the Duke lacrosse players seemed well on their way to successful business careers before the rape allegations hit the press. Some, like David Evans, were described in glowing terms by those who knew them well. Evans's coach, for example, described Evans as "mature, serious, thoughtful, well-liked, and really respected." Residents of Reade Seligmann's hometown gave glowing re-

---

42. TAYLOR & JOHNSON, *supra* note 40, at 8 (quoting *Newsweek*).

43. *Id.*

44. *See id.* at 85–89, 96–97, 100, 143–44, 220, 230–32, 239–41, 248–49, 279–80; YAEGER, *supra* note 42, at 99–105, 147–58, 177–92, 233–43, 262–66; Mosteller, *Innocence*, *supra* note 39, at 1348–64; *see generally* discussion *supra* Chapter One (Luck & Seigel).

ports of his character, as did his teachers. Seligmann volunteered to help the needy in Appalachia and in poor sections of New York City. His high school gave him the Fighting Spirit Award for the strength of his character, integrity, and drive to excel. Collin Finnerty, although he had one prior, minor run-in with the law, was routinely described as sweet-tempered, warm, self-effacing, and calm. None of these descriptions are offered here to glorify the team members. But they do show that many of the student-athletes started out with generally strong reputations working to their benefit. The rape allegations changed all that.[45]

Nifong and the media portrayed the lacrosse players as racist brutes. Some media reports used animalistic metaphors, describing the players as moving in a "pack." Nifong consistently overstated the strength of his case, expressing absolute certainty in the lacrosse players' guilt. He labeled the entire team a "bunch of hooligans," who made rampant use of racial slurs and were protected by the expensive lawyers hired by their "daddies." The local Durham newspaper, the *Herald-Sun*, joined the drumbeat, claiming that the players brought frat-boy culture to a "whole new sickening level." Campus protests sprouted. One candlelight vigil involved signs declaring, "Real Men Don't Protect Rapists," while protesters chanted "shame." A second, later group of protesters banged on pots to draw attention to the players' alleged wrongdoing. Further protests expressly labeled the players as racists.[46]

Even Father Joe Vetter, during a Catholic Mass held at Duke Cathedral, gave a sermon condemning the players. The local paper for nearby Raleigh, the *News and Observer*, suggested that a large percentage of the lacrosse team were loud drunkards. One Duke civil-rights professor portrayed the students as modern-day slave masters, while several professors in classes in which the players sat denounced them as racist rapists. Cable-news commentators Nancy Grace and Joe Scarborough, certainly no liberals, likewise labeled the players racist. CNN and Professor Houston Baker portrayed the players as unclean, frequent lawn-urinators, who made a habit of slinging racist slurs.[47]

Protesters also plastered the campus with wanted posters with all the players' photos, chanting "Time to Confess!", and waving signs advocating the players' castration. Legal costs for the players were enormous; the savings of Reade Seligmann's family, for example, were thoroughly drained both by the lawyers and the need to post the $400,000 bond to keep Reade out of jail prior to the trial.[48]

---

45. *See* TAYLOR & JOHNSON, *supra* note 40, at 12–15.

46. *See id.* at 64–66, 85–88, 103; YAEGER, *supra* note 41, at 99–105, 147–59.

47. *See* TAYLOR & JOHNSON, *supra* note 40, at 75, 87–88, 106, 108–11, 122–23, 143–44.

48. *See id.* at 145, 182, 189.

Judge Titus, after Nifong and the media had flooded the news with anti-lacrosse-players tales, imposed a gag order on all lawyers and potential witnesses, handcuffing defense efforts to present counterstories. Some of the players fled Durham, fearing violence, and some of them were either suspended or chose not to return to Duke. The local NAACP hailed the gag order and also insisted on the racist motivations of the lacrosse players. Even when an early DNA report revealed no evidence of the accused lacrosse players' semen in or on the alleged victim, Nifong explained this evidence away with the theory that the players had used condoms—despite the victim herself denying any condom use. Many in the media nevertheless still uncritically stuck with Nifong's version of events, although some dissenting voices began to be heard.[49]

Duke's President, Richard Brodhead, later sought to explain his own condemnation of the players and the general witch hunt-like atmosphere that Nifong had created:

> In the early days of this story DA's were people who carried a certain amount of credibility. So you have reputable papers reporting what the DA said about the likelihood the crime had occurred, and speaking with considerable confidence. And if a lot of people then formed the conclusion that they knew what had happened how could one be surprised? One other thing I'd ask you to remember is, it was a long time before the students made the case for their innocence in any effective way. They made no public statement about it for several days.[50]

Nifong went so far as to reenact on MSNBC "how one of the players had supposedly choked Mangum during the rape." Yet Mangum, in most of her stories, "never ever claimed to have been choked much less described the act with any specificity." Even as continuing revelations poked holes in Nifong's case, he stubbornly insisted on the players' guilt and continued making inflammatory public statements. Many in the media omitted or downplayed reports of exculpatory evidence, continuing the assault on the players' good names. President Brodhead eventually fired the lacrosse team's coach, adding to the public sense that something bad must have happened.[51]

The tide slowly and eventually did start to turn in the players' favor, but that turn was indeed slow, and the prospect of lengthy prison sentences and the ac-

---

49. *See id.* at 87, 96–97, 103–05, 248–52; YAEGER, *supra* note 41, at 177–82, 233–43.

50. TAYLOR & JOHNSON, *supra* note 40, at 89 (quoting Brodhead).

51. *See id.* at 100, 118–19, 122–23, 125–26, 211, 220–22; YAEGER, *supra* note 41, at 147–59.

tuality of continued, public humiliation still hung over the lacrosse players' heads.[52] Reade Seligmann explained well the impact all this had on the players:

> To see my face on TV, and that, you know, in those little mug shots, and above it saying, you know, "Alleged rapists." You don't know what that does to me and to my family and to the people who care about me.... Your whole life, you try to, you know, stay on the right path, and to do the right things. And someone can come along and take it all away, just by going like that. [He pointed a finger.] Just by pointing their finger. That's all it takes.[53]

Nifong had at one point publicly assailed the players' exercise of their Sixth Amendment right to counsel. He asked why the players were "so unwilling to tell us what, in their words, did take place that night? And one would wonder why one needs an attorney if one was not charged and had not done anything wrong?" Yet it was those lawyers, aided by North Carolina evidentiary rules, access to a judge who finally enforced them, and a bravura media performance by the team captain that ultimately turned the tables on Nifong.[54]

Nifong had—as part of a pattern of delaying production of exculpatory evidence under the state's discovery rules—long resisted producing all the data underlying the various DNA-test results. Finally, Judge Smith ordered production of what turned out to be 2,000 pages of raw data from the DNA testing, and hundreds more pages from the state's DNA lab. Defense counsel studied this highly technical data and discovered something that Nifong had long known and hidden: DNA from four unidentified males—not one molecule of which was from a Duke lacrosse player—had been found in Mangum's panties, rectal swabs, and pubic hair comb. All of this DNA must have been deposited *before* the party at which the rape allegedly took place. Meanwhile, the inconsistencies in Mangum's story continued to multiply, as did growing countercurrents of support for the players among the Duke student body. When combined with the state bar association's investigation of Nifong's misconduct, and with some media outlets' decisions finally to defend the players, the public story shifted in the players' favor.

Nifong was eventually disbarred for his misconduct; the case was transferred to the state's Attorney General's Office, which ultimately dropped the charges;

---

52. *See* TAYLOR & JOHNSON, *supra* note 40, at 225–26, 216–17, 232–33, 235, 239–41, 245, 254–59, 269–84, 312–31; YAEGER, *supra* note 41, at 203–12, 224–31, 247–66.

53. *See* TAYLOR & JOHNSON, *supra* note 40, at 182 (quoting Seligmann).

54. *See id.* at 100; Mosteller, *Exculpatory Evidence, supra* note 39; Mosteller, *Innocence, supra* note 39.

and the lacrosse players began living their lives again—but all this came about only after one year of the psychic pain, public ostracism, emptied family coffers, interrupted educations, truncated sports participation, and diverted career plans that stemmed from the grievous wounds to their reputations.[55]

The law acted late to correct these wrongs, using the cumbersome and rarely exercised ethics-review process. Whenever the law seeks to prevent or punish speech, of course, First Amendment free-speech and free-press concerns arise, even when the speakers are lawyers. Designing remedies for the danger of prosecutor-inflicted reputational harm thus requires examining how the courts have balanced free speech with other justice-system-generated harms in the past. Usually that balance has been struck after weighing the benefits of free speech against the harms to a fair *trial*, a dichotomy that this chapter argues oversimplifies the true complexity of the problem.[56]

Part V: Fair Trial-Free Press

The Tension

In the bulk of the relevant Supreme Court case law interpreting the First Amendment, two rights often come into conflict: the right of the press and the trial participants to speak their minds versus the accused's right to a fair trial. When the press is involved, the Supreme Court has weighed this balance heavily in favor of the media, all-but-prohibiting gag orders silencing pre- or post-trial coverage of a case.[57] For example, in *Nebraska Press Association v. Stuart*,[58] the Court overturned a gag order prohibiting media publication of confessions or statements against interest purportedly made by a defendant charged with murdering a ten-year-old girl and a number of her family members in a farming community of 850 people. In doing so, the Court adopted a "clear and present danger to the administration of justice" test for justifying gag orders (which are generally disfavored as "prior restraints" on speech). The Court seemed at

---

55. *See* Taylor & Johnson, *supra* note 40, at 230–31, 279–80, 301–05; Yaeger, *supra* note 41, at 259–66; Mosteller, *Exculpatory Evidence*, *supra* note 39, at 285–306; Duff Wilson, *Lawyer Says Two Duke Lacrosse Players Are Indicted in Rape Case*, N.Y. Times, Apr. 18, 2006; Duff Wilson & David Barstow, *All Charges Dropped in Duke Case*, N.Y. Times, Apr. 12, 2007.

56. *See infra* text accompanying notes 58–87.

57. *See* Jerome A. Barron & C. Thomas Dienes, First Amendment Law in a Nutshell 391 (2d ed. 2000).

58. 427 U.S. 539 (1976).

first to suggest, however, that this version of the "clear and present danger" test was a relatively lenient one, not requiring an imminent danger to justice yet permitting suppression if the evil feared from pretrial publicity was sufficiently large, though its occurrence be quite improbable. But the Court articulated several details of this test that set the bar for meeting it high: first, a court must conclude that pervasive, intense pretrial publicity that might impair a fair trial *would occur* absent suppression; second, that less-restrictive alternatives would be inadequate to protect the defendant's rights; and third, that the gag order would succeed in halting prejudicial publicity. The Court found that, in the grisly case before it, the risk of massive prejudicial publicity fell short of meeting these three requirements. Although this was not a per se bar on gag orders, it was a "virtual death knell."[59]

Yet, a decade earlier, in *Sheppard v. Maxwell*,[60] the Court had expressed a readiness to reverse convictions stemming from unduly prejudicial media coverage as denying an accused a fair trial. In part, the Court did so because there were, it insisted, a catalogue of trial-judge options for promoting trial fairness without silencing the press, including intense voir dire, jury sequestration, continuances to allow community anger to soften, and even a change of venue. *Stuart* reaffirmed, rather than rejected, the importance of the availability of these options "to mitigate the effects of pretrial publicity."[61]

When the speech of lawyers, rather than the press, is involved, however, the Court has suggested that even-more-aggressive measures may be taken to avoid infringing upon the accused's fair-trial rights, including, under certain circumstances, silencing the attorneys with a gag order. The press, of course, is likely to object to silencing lawyers, a primary source of relevant information about a case, thus indirectly silencing the press itself. But these entreaties have not seemed to trouble the Court because of the special role of lawyers in our adversarial system of justice.[62] In *Florida Bar v. Went For It, Inc.*,[63] the Court seemed

---

59. Barron & Dienes, *supra* note 57, at 391; *see Stuart*, 427 U.S. at 541–42, 563–67; Barron & Dienes, *supra* note 57, at 59–72, 387–97 (giving the background and similar analysis).

60. 384 U.S. 333 (1966).

61. *Stuart*, 427 U.S. at 555.

62. *See* Douglas S. Campbell, Free Press v. Fair Trial: Supreme Court Decisions Since 1807 (1994); Mattei Radu, *The Difficult Task of Model Rule of Professional Conduct 3.6: Balancing the Free Speech Rights of Lawyers, the Sixth Amendment Rights of Criminal Defendants, and Society's Right to the Fair Administration of Justice*, 29 Campbell L. Rev. 497, 500–01, 510–19 (2007) (analyzing and discussing the major Supreme Court decisions addressing the notions of free press and fair trial).

63. 515 U.S. 618 (1995).

to embrace implicitly the special role that lawyers play in our system of justice, upholding a Florida bar rule prohibiting personal-injury lawyers from sending targeted direct-mail solicitations to victims and their relatives for thirty days following an accident. The Florida Bar's brief to the Court was more explicit on this point than the Court's opinion itself; it argued that the Court "has historically recognized that the exercise of free expression is subject to reasonable limitations when the nature of such exercise is detrimental to, or inconsistent with, the mission of the public institution within which the expression is exercised,"[64] offering examples from public employment, penal institutions, the armed forces, and educational institutions.[65] Indeed, the Bar noted, the Court itself recognized that "lawyers are essential to the primary government function of administering justice, and have historically been 'officers of the courts.' "[66] The Bar recognized that this was part of lawyers' dual role as self-employed businesspeople *and* "assistants to the court in the search of a just solution to disputes."[67] The brief then concluded:

> While lawyers are not public employees, the analogy is valid. As "officers of the court" lawyers perform an essential role in the administration of justice. Courts have always recognized that a lawyer's speech within the courtroom is subject to considerable judicial oversight in order to protect the integrity of the judicial process. The fact that advertising the availability of legal services takes place outside the courtroom is of little consequence in this context. Such advertising deals solely with an essential aspect of the administration of the public function. To the extent that it may adversely affect the mission of the judicial system, the State has no less interest in its regulation than it does in any employment situation.... The public's perception of, and confidence in, its system of justice and those who administer it is critical to the stability of a democratic society.[68]

The Florida Bar thus accurately synthesized the Court's decisions on lawyers' special role, in particular how it had embraced the "officer of the court" rationale in an earlier case, *Gentile v. State Bar*,[69] which specifically involved pre-

---

64. Brief of Petitioner, Fla. Bar v. Went For It, Inc., 512 U.S. 1289, No. 94-226 (Nov. 4, 1994), 1994 WL 614916, at *15.

65. *Id.* at *15–17.

66. *Id.* at *17 (quoting Goldfarb v. Va. State Bar, 421 U.S. 773, 792 (1975)).

67. *Id.* at *17.

68. *Id.* at *19.

69. 501 U.S. 1030 (1991).

trial publicity. There, Dominic Gentile held a press conference about a case mere hours after his client had been indicted on criminal charges. The State Bar of Nevada had a rule in force similar to the then-operative version of Rule 3.6 of the ABA's *Model Rules of Professional Conduct* that governed what lawyers could tell the press about pending cases. After a hearing, the State Bar Disciplinary Board recommended a private reprimand, finding a Rule 3.6 violation. The Nevada Supreme Court agreed with this conclusion, but the United States Supreme Court eventually reversed. The Court held that the discipline imposed violated the First Amendment because the state's "safe harbor" provision in its equivalent to Rule 3.6 permitted the speech in question and, if it did not (as the state supreme court had held), then the rule violated constitutional bars on undue vagueness and selective enforcement.

Although there were numerous opinions in *Gentile*, the decision's significance lies in five members of the Court agreeing that the state may regulate speech by lawyers representing clients in pending cases more readily than it may regulate the press. Moreover, those five did so because they concluded that lawyers, serving a special role, are "different." Thus, Chief Justice Rehnquist, in an opinion for the Court, stressed "that lawyers in pending cases [are] subject to ethical restrictions, on speech to which an ordinary citizen would not be."[70] Indeed, he concluded, "[e]ven in an area far from the courtroom and the pendency of a case," lawyers are not protected to the same extent as individuals in other professions.[71] This was so because a lawyer is "an officer of the court, and, like the court itself, an instrument ... of justice."[72] Thus the speech of "lawyers in pending cases may be regulated under a less demanding standard than that established for regulation of the press."[73] Justice O'Connor reaffirmed these principles in her concurrence.[74] Furthermore, five Justices concluded that Nevada's Rule 3.6 equivalent, which prohibited lawyer speech that created a "substantial likelihood [of] material prejudice" at trial, met this more deferential First Amendment test.[75]

The rationale for this deference to the Rule 3.6 drafters was, once again, that lawyers, as officers of the court, have a "fiduciary responsibility not to en-

---

70. *Id.* at 1071.

71. *Id.* at 1073.

72. *Id.* at 1074 (quoting Cohen v. Hurley, 366 U.S. 117, 126 (1961)).

73. *Id.*

74. But on this point Justices Marshall, Blackmun, Stevens, and Kennedy disagreed. *See id.* at 1034–37 (noting that the speech at issue was critical of the government and thus lay "at the very center of the First Amendment").

75. *Id.* at 1074.

gage in public debate that will redound to the detriment of the parties or ...
the fair administration of justice."[76] The Rule 3.6 equivalent "substantial likelihood" test was, the Court concluded, designed precisely to "protect the integrity
and fairness of [the s]tate's judicial system."[77] Moreover, the limitations the
rule imposed were narrow and necessary to achieve the state goals of avoiding
improper influence on the likely outcome of the trial and avoiding tainting or
prejudicing the jury venire. The Court found that the state had an adequate interest, even if an untainted panel could ultimately be found.

The Court found the tailoring sufficiently narrow, even though other options to protect a fair trial were available, such as sensitive voir dire or a change
of venue. The Court concluded that these methods impose "serious costs" on
the state and litigants, a substantial harm the state can legitimately avoid. The
Court found narrow tailoring even though it admitted that other options like
voir dire might have completely avoided any impact of the publicity on the
trial outcome in particular cases, without the need to muzzle the lawyers or
the parties.[78]

This is not the kind of "narrow tailoring" associated with a compelling-state-
interest analysis. It is more like requiring "less restrictive" than "least restrictive" alternatives, a form of middle scrutiny.[79]

Furthermore, the Court found a "substantial government interest," even
though the defense attorney sought to counteract allegedly prejudicial statements
first made to the press *by prosecutors*. The defense attorney responded in the
media (1) in order to protect his client's reputation and (2) because the defense had information that the prosecution lacked.[80]

Despite the Court's strong defense of the state's regulatory authority over the
lawyer's speech in *Gentile*, the Court ultimately held that the discipline imposed there violated the Constitution because the state's safe-harbor provision
was unduly vague. But the *Gentile* Court's logic provided ample ground for

---

76. *Id.* at 1074–75 (quoting Neb. Press Ass'n v. Stuart, 427 U.S. 539, 601 n.27 (1994)).

77. *Id.* at 1075.

78. *See id.* at 1075–76.

79. *See* JOHNSON E. NOWAK & RONALD P. ROTUNDA, CONSTITUTIONAL LAW (4th ed. 1991).

80. *See Gentile*, 501 U.S. at 1043–48. The Court also found it significant that the lawyers' comments were merely postponed until after trial—effectively a time, place, and manner restriction. *Id.* at 1076. This observation could potentially be understood to *only* permit limiting lawyers' speech to protect trial fairness. This chapter, however, rejects the wisdom of that approach: it underestimates the harm done by the lawyers', especially prosecutors', ravaging of the accused's reputation, particularly when the accused is acquitted or never even tried.

upholding better-drafted restrictions on lawyers' speech as a means to promote fair trials untainted by pretrial media coverage. Indeed, the ABA redrafted Rule 3.6 in light of *Gentile* to achieve this goal. The revised rule retained the general bar on a lawyer involved in "investigating or litigating a matter making extrajudicial statements that he reasonably should know will be disseminated by means of public communication and will have a substantial likelihood of materially prejudicing an adjudicative proceeding."[81] It also contains a clearer safe-harbor provision which lists narrow classes of information, such as facts already in the public record, which a lawyer may publicize. Furthermore, the rule provides for additional, narrow safe harbors in criminal cases and a narrow right of response to counteract unduly prejudicial statements made by others (including prosecutors and the media) so long as the response is "limited to such information as is necessary to mitigate the recent adverse publicity."[82]

Moreover, although the Court found inadequate defense counsel's asserted justification for his statements in *Gentile*—that they were an act of self-defense needed in part to restore the damage done to his client's reputation by the prosecutor—that conclusion is best understood as an application of the principle that "two wrongs do not make a right." It cannot sensibly be read as condoning the prosecutor's reputation-wounding statements themselves or minimizing the weight of protecting against reputational harm as a justification for limiting or gagging prosecutors' public statements.

To the contrary, the prosecutor, unlike defense counsel, has a "duty to do justice." Whatever this highly contested term means, at the very least it includes taking steps to affirmatively provide the accused with a fair trial, and certainly entails avoiding efforts to deny the accused such a trial. This greater burden of responsibility is imposed on the prosecutor because of the enormous power he wields on behalf of the state against the usually weaker defendant.[83]

---

81. Model Rules of Prof'l Conduct R. 3.6.

82. *Id.*; *see* Ann M. Murphy, *Spin Control and the High-Profile Client—Should the Attorney-Client Privilege Extend to Communications with Public Relations Consultants?*, 55 Syracuse L. Rev. 545, 584–85 (2005) (explaining how the *Gentile* decision led the ABA to modify Rule 3.6).

83. *See* Model Code of Prof'l Responsibility EC 7–13 (1980) ("duty to seek justice"); Model Rules Of Prof'l Conduct R. 3.8 ("Minister of Justice"); Michael Cassidy, *Character and Context: What Virtue Theory Can Teach Us About A Prosecutor's Ethical Duty to "Seek Justice,"* 82 Notre Dame L. Rev. 635 (2006); Stanley Fisher, *In Search of the Virtuous Prosecutor: A Conceptual Framework*, 15 Am. J. Crim. L. 197, 236 (1988) (safeguarding the substantive and procedural rights of the accused); Bruce Green, *Why Should Prosecutors "Seek Justice"?*, 26 Fordham Urb. L.J. 607 (1999); Abbe Smith, *Can You Be a Good Person and a Good Prosecutor?*, 14 Geo. J. Legal Ethics 355, 378–79 (2001); Fred Zacharias, *Struc-*

The ABA recognizes the prosecutor's special responsibilities in Rule 3.8(f) of the *Model Rules of Professional Conduct.* This rule mandates that, except for statements necessary to inform the public of the nature and extent of the prosecutor's action and that serve a legitimate law enforcement purpose, prosecutors must "refrain from making extrajudicial comments that have a substantial likelihood of heightening public condemnation of the accused." Moreover, the prosecutor has an affirmative obligation to exercise reasonable care to prevent investigators, law-enforcement personnel, and similar persons from making extrajudicial statements barred to the prosecutor. Because Rule 3.8(f) refers to avoiding "heightening public condemnation" of the accused rather than merely preventing prejudice in a potential adjudicatory proceeding, the Rule's text may be read as recognizing "guarding against harm to the accused's reputation" as an important interest, distinct from ensuring a fair trial. Comment 5 to Rule 3.8 indeed explains that paragraph (f) of that rule "supplements" Rule 3.6's protections against biasing jurors through pretrial publicity because "[i]n the context of a criminal prosecution, a prosecutor's extrajudicial statement can create the *additional problem* of increasing public condemnation of the accused."[84] Still, there is little evidence that Rule 3.8(f) is enforced more than sporadically. In addition, it does not expressly address the greater need for gag orders to prevent reputational injury because, unlike jury prejudice, there are not even arguably adequate systemic counterweights for reputational harm; the rule does not alter the general focus of the ethical rules and case law on protecting the right *to a fair trial.* As criminologist Ray Surette has explained, appeals courts rarely, if ever, recognize prejudicial publicity as a mitigating factor at sentencing and have "[l]eft unaddressed ... cases in which a defendant is found innocent of criminal charges but has his or her career or reputation permanently ruined by publicity."[85] Surette continues:

> The concern is that live television coverage incites such negative feelings against defendants that, even if they are later acquitted, the feelings are irreversible. The modern mass media have constructed a new

---

turing the Ethics of Prosecutorial Trial Practice: Can Prosecutors Do Justice?, 44 Vand. L. Rev. 45 (1991).

84. *See* Model Rules of Prof'l Conduct R. 3.8(f) & cmt. 5; Restatement (Third) of the Law Governing Lawyers § 109 (2000); Am. Bar Ass'n, ABA Standards for Criminal Justice: Prosecution and Defense Function 3-1.4, 3-1.5 (3d ed. 1993); Am. Bar Ass'n, ABA Standards For Criminal Justice: Fair Trial and Free Press 8-1.1 (3d ed. 1991); Ray Surette, Media, Crime, and Criminal Justice: Images, Realities, and Policies 139 (3d ed. 2007).

85. Surette, *supra* note 84, at 139–40.

verdict: legally innocent but socially guilty. In the process, media coverage confounds the concepts of legal guilt (is the defendant legally responsible for a crime?) and factual guilt (did the defendant actually commit the criminal behavior?). Factual guilt is not always equivalent to legal guilt, and the general public little understands and is poorly instructed by the media in the differences between the two. If defendants who have been found innocent are subsequently still punished by losing their career or reputation because of publicity, then the criminal justice system loses legitimacy with those who identify with these defendants.[86]

The Duke lacrosse players were never tried, but they were effectively found innocent—*both* legally and factually—by North Carolina's Attorney General. The reputational injuries they suffered may not all be permanent—in some circles they are even lauded as heroes—but the injuries are still profound, and they still undermine the justice system's legitimacy in the eyes of those who identify with the painful consequences of the prosecutor's victimization of the lacrosse players.[87]

The Elected Nature of Most Prosecutors: A First Amendment Wrinkle?

Professor Michael Cassidy suggests, however, that the State has no adequate justification for preventing prosecutors from making statements harmful to the accused's reputation absent a corresponding effect on the fairness of the judicial proceedings. Cassidy insists that his position is strongest concerning prosecutors, like Nifong, who make such statements as part of an electoral campaign. A candidate's expressing views on public policies and pressing public events is, argues Cassidy, essential to informed public choices in an election, and there is no reason to treat prosecutors differently from other elected officials.

In support of his position, Cassidy relies on *Republican Party of Minnesota v. White*,[88] which, he maintains, supersedes "officer of the court" language like that in *Gentile*.[89] *White* held unconstitutional under the First Amendment Min-

---

86. *Id.*

87. *See supra* text accompanying note 55 (describing the actions of the North Carolina Attorney General); discussion *supra* in Chapter One (Luck & Seigel).

88. 536 U.S. 765 (2002).

89. Michael Cassidy, *The Prosecutor and the Press: Lessons (Not) Learned from the Mike Nifong Debacle*, 71 LAW & CONTEMP. PROBS. (forthcoming 2008). Cassidy's focus on the elected prosecutor may partly be explained by the Supreme Court's willingness to allow

nesota's state constitutional provision that prohibited candidates for judicial office, including sitting judges, from announcing their views on disputed legal or political issues (Minnesota's so-called "announce clause"). The Minnesota Supreme Court limited the apparently broad meaning of the announce clause, declaring that it only reached disputed issues likely to come before the candidate were he to be elected a judge. Comments on past judicial decisions were, therefore, permissible, although the rule prohibited a candidate from public insistence on ignoring the stare decisis effect of such decisions.

In *White*, Gregory Wersal withdrew from his 1996 campaign for a judgeship after a complaint was filed against him for, among other things, distributing literature criticizing Minnesota Supreme Court abortion, crime, and welfare decisions. When he ran again in 1998, he sought an advisory opinion from the Lawyers' Professional Responsibility Board on whether it planned to enforce the announce clause. When Wersal received an equivocal answer, he filed suit in federal district court, along with other plaintiffs, seeking a declaration of the announce clause's unconstitutionality as violative of free speech under the First Amendment. Upon the filing of cross-motions for summary judgment, the district court ruled against the plaintiffs, concluding that the announce clause was indeed constitutional. The Supreme Court reversed.

The Court concluded that the announce clause permitted content-discrimination against speech at the core of First Amendment protections, and therefore subjected it to strict scrutiny. But the Court found that the clause, even as narrowly interpreted by Minnesota's Supreme Court, was not narrowly tailored to serve the allegedly compelling state interests of preserving the actual and apparent impartiality of the state judiciary.

There were, said the Court, three possible meanings of "impartiality" in this context. First, impartiality might mean a lack of preconception in favor of a particular view of the law. But such a goal, insisted the Court, was "neither possible nor desirable"; impossible psychologically, and undesirable because it would reflect a "complete *tabula rasa*," hardly the sort of learned mind sought in a judicial candidate. To pretend otherwise, to lie, for the sake of creating a false appearance of this sort of impartiality could not constitute a compelling interest.[90]

A second meaning of impartiality might be "open-mindedness," a willingness to remain open to persuasion, at least in a pending case, even on legal

---

elected chief prosecutors to impose substantial limits on the speech of their prosecutor employees. *See* Garcetti v. Ceballos, 547 *U.S.* 410 (2006) (affirming a chief prosecutor's authority to discipline a subordinate-attorney whistleblower).

90. *White*, 536 U.S. at 776–778.

questions for which the judge holds a preconceived position. The Court concluded, however, that, under the strict-scrutiny test, the state had not met its burden of establishing that campaign position statements are uniquely destructive of open-mindedness. The Court noted that candidate *promises* to take a particular action were banned by separate state laws, but such promises were not before it, and it simply was not persuaded that nonpromissory statements of legal and policy positions would psychologically operate as promises committing the former candidate to action once on the bench.[91]

The third sense of impartiality examined by the Court was bias for or against a particular *party* to the proceeding. The correct position, according to the Court, was that the judge who hears a case should "apply the law to ... [one party] in the same way he applies it to any other party."[92] On this point too, however, the Court declared:

> We think it plain that the announce clause is not narrowly tailored to serve impartiality (or the appearance of impartiality) in this sense. Indeed, the clause is barely tailored to serve that interest *at all*, in as much as it does not restrict speech for or against particular *parties*, but rather speech for or against particular *issues*. To be sure, when a case arises that turns on a legal issue on which the judge (as a candidate) had taken a particular stand, the party taking the opposite stand is likely to lose. But not because of any bias against that party, or favoritism toward the other party. *Any* party taking that position is just as likely to lose. The judge is applying the law (as he sees it) evenhandedly.[93]

The Court rejected any rigid distinction between judicial and legislative elections in a country, like ours, where courts can "make" common law, set aside laws enacted by the legislature, and alter the shape of state constitutions. Accordingly, any abridgement of the right to speak in the electioneering context turns First Amendment jurisprudence upside down, for "[d]ebate on the qualifications of candidates is at the core of our electoral process and of the First Amendment freedoms.... It is simply not the function of government to select which issues are worth discussing or debating in the course of a political campaign."[94]

Professor Cassidy, relying partly on post-*White* lower-court cases concerning alleged *judicial* misconduct, argues that *White* squarely protects *prosecutor* electioneering statements, even those made about pending cases or investiga-

---

91. *See id.* at 778–80.
92. *Id.* at 775–76.
93. *Id.* at 776–77.
94. *Id.* at 781–82 (citations omitted).

tions, including many of the statements made to the media by Nifong.[95] Cassidy never fully explains why comments on pending cases should be treated the same as ones made about broader legal issues, largely seeing it as self-evident that this distinction does not survive a "close reading of *White* or its progeny."[96] He does suggest that the distinction may be unsupportable because there is no bright-line divide between issues of law and those of fact. Furthermore, whichever definition of "impartiality" is used in the prosecutorial context, insists Cassidy, any resulting ill effects can be cured by stricter voir dire, change of venue, or additional remedies other than silencing the prosecutor.[97]

But Cassidy too-readily dismisses the Court's insistent distinction between speech about *parties* versus speech about *issues*. Many of Nifong's comments portrayed several of the defendants as wild, animalistic hooligans. He sought indeed to turn the public against them, inflaming the public's anger as a crass tactic to garner additional votes. The distinction between issues of law and case-specific fact may not be an analytically sharp one, but it is a necessary one routinely recognized by our justice system. To publicly smear the Duke defendants as spoiled, racist kids pampered and protected by their rich daddies and thus undeserving of the benefit of the doubt is unquestionably an effort to arouse ill feeling against parties on key questions *of fact*—whether a rape occurred and whether they committed it.[98]

Cassidy also dismisses concerns about reputational harms, arguing that if defendants are acquitted, the acquittal largely cures the harm, and any remaining injury can be redressed via civil suit. On the other hand, says Cassidy, if the defendants are convicted, that shows that they deserve the harms imposed on them. The latter point ignores the risk that pretrial reputational harms create of convicting the innocent. The former point severely underestimates, as argued above, the individual and social harms wrought by undeserved reputational injury. It smugly ignores the severe obstacles to civil recovery in such cases, and the limitations of such lawsuits in addressing broader social harms emanating well beyond the parties to the community and the justice system at large.[99]

---

95. Cassidy, *supra* note 89, draft at 9–10.

96. *Id.* at 10.

97. *See id.* at 11–12.

98. *See supra* text accompanying notes 1, 46, 51 (concerning Nifong); *see generally* Ronald J. Allen & Michael S. Pardo, *The Myth of the Fact-Law Distinction*, 97 Nw. U. L. Rev. 1769 (2003).

99. *See* Cassidy, *supra* note 89, draft at 14; Peter J. Henning, *Prosecutorial Misconduct and Constitutional Remedies*, 77 Wash. U. L.Q. 713, 818–19 (1999) (discussing the many

Prosecutors, of course, are not judges. Rather, they are advocates, but advocates of a special kind. Only the prosecutor, among all lawyers, has an overriding duty to "do justice"—a phrase fraught with ambiguity but clearly requiring, at a minimum, ensuring procedural fairness to all parties. Increasingly, prosecutors are recognizing an affirmative duty on their part to prevent constitutional violations by others, such as the police, and to take strong steps to avoid convicting the innocent. Growing numbers of prosecutors are also coming to recognize that their general polices and procedures, and their cumulative behavior in many individual cases, can prevent or cause broader social harms, including fostering or hindering the public's perception of law-enforcement legitimacy, the level of racial tension in a community, and the public's willingness to obey the law.

Moreover, the prosecutor has enormous and growing power, prosecutorial discretion having been substituted for judicial discretion in many cases, a trend only moderately arrested recently in a few discrete areas of the law. This power dwarfs that of the defense in most cases. Recognition of this power is why Robert H. Jackson, later a United States Supreme Court Justice and a prosecutor at the Nuremburg trials, opined as long ago as 1940 that "[t]he citizen's safety lies in the prosecutor who tempers zeal with human kindness, who seeks truth and not victims, who serves the law and not factional purposes, and who approaches his task with humility."[100] It is also why Justice Kennedy argued in *Gentile*, as Cassidy concedes, that "a state may have a more compelling interest in regulating prosecutor speech than defense attorney speech for reasons of power disparities and greater access to insider information."[101]

---

obstacles to civil recovery against prosecutors); Andrew E. Taslitz, *Wrongly Accused Redux: How Race Contributes to Convicting the Innocent: The Informants' Example*, Sw. U. L. Rev. (forthcoming 2008) (explaining how long-term group-reputational harms inflicted by the criminal-justice system can raise the risk of convicting innocent members of that group); *supra* text accompanying notes 4–16, 25–39, 98 (discussing risks from reputational harms).

100. Robert H. Jackson, *The Federal Prosecutor*, 31 J. Crim. L. & Criminology 3, 6 (1940).

101. *See* Am. Bar Ass'n, Achieving Justice: Freeing The Innocent, Convicting The Guilty, The Report Of The ABA Criminal Justice Section's Ad Hoc Innocence Committee To Ensure The Integrity of the Criminal Process (2006) (discussing prosecutors' recognition of obligations to protect the innocent against conviction, including by advocating systemic procedural and institutional changes in how crimes are investigated); David W. Neubauer, America's Courts and the Criminal Justice System 126 (2004) (discussing the increase in prosecutorial, relative to judicial, power); David Luban, Lawyers and Justice: An Ethical Study 44 (1988) (noting that prosecutorial power usually dwarfs that of the defense); Cassidy, *supra* note 89, draft at n.15 (summarizing Justice Kennedy's argument); *supra* text accompanying notes 83, 100 (discussing a prosecutor's duty to do justice).

Therefore, a prosecutor does have both a duty akin to that of impartiality in the particular case, and an affirmative duty to safeguard the overall integrity of the prosecutor's office as a component of the criminal-justice system. Moreover, when there is a pending case, unjustifiable risks to the accused's reputation arise—risks far more severe than when a prosecutor taints the reputation of someone not expected to be prosecuted and risks that, if realized, do grave individual and social harm, even if no conviction results.[102]

To grant Nifong First Amendment cover for his assault on the Duke lacrosse players' character serves no legitimate goal of free speech, does not aid the search for truth, and does not promote a more unified political community or greater procedural fairness. Instead, it would merely sanction vindictive, entirely self-interested prosecutorial action that undermines the values of the rule of law upon which the survival of a robust system of free debate depends.[103]

Conclusion

I have sought in this chapter to use the Duke lacrosse players' case as a vehicle for challenging what I see as the law's undervaluation of reputational injuries inflicted by too-loose prosecutorial lips. I have suggested that this observation justifies significant limits on the free speech of even elected prosecutors when it unnecessarily taints an accused's reputation in pending criminal charges or investigations. But I cannot, in this brief chapter, delineate the precise contours of these free-speech limits nor significantly explore potential solutions. I have, however, suggested that remedies designed to repair reputational injury for cases that never reach trial are few, and are likely to be of limited effectiveness; preventing harmful prosecutorial speech in the first place may thus be an unavoidable part of any solution. Ethics rules are often paper tigers, and even if they weren't, it is a difficult job crafting one that burdens free speech without being too heavy-handed or sweeping too broadly. Accordingly, my instinct is that institutional solutions—such as internal prosecutor units to counsel chief prosecutors on public media comments in high-profile cases, and independent "audits" of prosecutorial files when complaints are made about unwarranted publicity—be pursued first, with a next-best alternative being a mechanism for ready pre-indictment judicial intervention upon com-

---

102. Cassidy, *supra* note 89, draft at 9 (comparing a prosecutors' duty of impartiality to that of judges).

103. *Id.* at 14; *see generally* Vincent Blasi, Ideas of the First Amendment (2005) (analyzing the various purposes arguably served by protections for free speech).

plaint. What is clear, however, is that business as usual in this area should be a business forced quickly to shut its doors.[104]

---

104. *Cf.* Andrew E. Taslitz, *Eyewitness Identification, Democratic Deliberation, and the Politics of Science*, 4 CARDOZO J. PUB. L., POL'Y & ETHICS 271 (2006) (suggesting and illustrating institutional rather than legal-rule-based solutions to prosecutor contributions to convicting the innocent); Andrew E. Taslitz, *Racial Auditors and the Fourth Amendment: Data with the Power to Inspire Political Action*, 66 LAW & CONTEMP. PROBS. 221–98 (2003) (suggesting auditing procedures involving the local lay public as a way to discourage law-enforcement from abusing its power).

CHAPTER NINE

When Prosecutorial Discretion Meets Disaster Capitalism

Lenese Herbert

"Many heroic actions and chivalrous adventures are related to me which exist only in the regions of fancy."[1]

She never called 911,[2] nor told the same story twice.[3] For weeks, she failed to identify accurately her purported assailants or their specific deeds. She had no bruises, no tearing, nor bleeding; she was virtually free of signs of a violent sexual assault, including the DNA of the accused.[4] She never quite pieced together all of what she said in a coherent, consistent fashion, no doubt a result of her history of, among other things, substance abuse[5] and psychological problems.[6]

---

1. Susan Faludi, The Terror Dream: Fear and Fantasy In A Post-9/11 America 256 (2007).

2. *See supra* Chapter One (Luck & Seigel), at 7 (identifying Ms. Mangum's dance partner, Kim Roberts, as the party who called 911); Robert P. Mosteller, *The Duke Lacrosse Case, Innocence, and False Identifications: A Fundamental Failure to "Do Justice,"* 76 Fordham L. Rev. 1337, 1345 (2007) (detailing Ms. Roberts's call to 911).

3. Stuart Taylor & KC Johnson, Until Proven Innocent: Political Correctness and the Shameful Injustices of the Duke Lacrosse Rape Case 30–31 (2007); *Officer Describes Woman in Duke Case as Drunk*, N.Y. Times, Apr. 14, 2006, at D7.

4. *See supra* Chapter One (Luck & Seigel), at 8, 12.

5. Taylor & Johnson, *supra* note 3, at 84–85; *Officer Describes Woman in Duke Case as Drunk*, *supra* note 3, at D7.

6. Crystal Mangum may suffer from some sort of bipolar disorder. Several observers have opined, for example, that Mangum may have believed her ever-shifting accounts about what happened that March night. *See, e.g.*, Thom Weidlich, *When the Truth Was Violated*, Newsday, Sept. 23, 2007, at C27 (criticizing authors Taylor and Johnson for "[d]ownplay-

Nevertheless, in her, he saw promise. She presented an unexpected potential windfall, a timely opportunity to radically reconfigure what otherwise would have been his certain political and professional defeat. Her case overlapped his election campaign, which had not only stalled, but was significantly threatened by a popular rival[7] and a newly recruited challenger.[8] So, he used her. He mined her anger, confusion, and image, straddling her trope, "push[ing] the window of opportunity that opened up after the shock"[9] of alleged gang rape. He seized upon her story—a poor, single, young Black mother sexually assaulted by privileged, wealthy, White lacrosse players—flung it into the public sphere for community consumption, and made her reported violation the focus of his political campaign. Her community had already been ignored.[10] Via this horror, it was now savaged.[11] Suddenly, the Black vote was now up for grabs.[12]

The unusual combination of factors that brought together District Attorney Mike Nifong and Crystal Mangum can obscure what actually occurred in the Duke lacrosse case. Although many commentators have weighed in on the seemingly bizarre and blatant bungling of Nifong, as well as his dénouement,[13] few have spoken directly to the methodology of his intent.

---

ing Mangum's bipolar disorder"); *see also* Mosteller, *supra* note 2, at 1338 (opining that Mangum's story was "either a hoax or ... based on delusion"); Craig Jarvis, *Mangum's Life: Conflict, Contradictions*, News & Observer (Raleigh, N.C.), Apr. 13, 2007, at 1A (noting Mangum's multiple contacts with mental-health providers and facilities). Presumptions regarding Mangum's mental health also may account for why, when faced with the opportunity, North Carolina Attorney General Roy Cooper declined to prosecute her. *See id.*

7. *See* Mosteller, *supra* note 2, at 1355 (describing how Nifong was challenged by Freda Black, a popular candidate who had received positive and widespread publicity for her prosecution of novelist Michael Petersen for the death of his wife).

8. *See id.* (noting how Keith Bishop was recruited to run as a voice of the local community of color).

9. Naomi Klein, *The Shock Doctrine*, Democracy Now!, Sept. 17, 2007, http://www.democracynow.org/article.pl?sid=sid=07/09/17/1411235.

10. *See supra* Chapter One (Luck & Seigel), at 1 (characterizing Durham as "the poor, red-headed step-child" of nearby cities Raleigh and Chapel Hill).

11. *See id.* at 22 ("I'm not going to allow Durham's view in the minds of the world to be a bunch of lacrosse players at Duke raping a black girl from Durham." (quoting Mike Nifong)).

12. *See id.* at 33 ("[Nifong] pandered to the community." (quoting Professor James Coleman, *60 Minutes* interview)).

13. *See, e.g.,* Weidlich, *supra* note 6, at C27 (noting that the case "offered the great American powder keg of race, class, and sex" and that the players "represented the chasm between privilege (including race privilege) and poverty in our country"); Myron Magnet, *In the Heart of Freedom, in Chains*, City Journal (Vol. 17, No. 3) 12–27 (2007) (characterizing the case as "a political godsend" for Nifong); Duff Wilson and Jonathan D. Glater,

Mike Nifong's recognition and nearly successful exploitation of Mangum to further his self-interest over and above the rights of the players and the public constituted an unfettered, unchecked rush to accuse falsely in order to prosper personally. In other words: the Duke lacrosse case is a primer in disaster capitalism.[14]

Prosecutorial Discretion

The job of the prosecutor is often misunderstood. The public regards prosecutors as public servants hired to throw people in jail, seek guilty verdicts, and win criminal convictions at all costs. This is incorrect. A prosecutor is, foremost, oath-bound to do justice. That is as it should be, as prosecutors are considered by many to be the most powerful public officials in the American criminal-justice system, given their ability to determine and control the initiation, direction, conclusion, or dismissal of criminal cases. Prosecutors truly make life-and-death decisions for the myriad individuals who come to their professional attention through alleged criminal wrongdoing.[15]

A significant portion of the prosecutor's power arises from the ability to make numerous unchecked and unreviewable decisions about cases for which they are responsible. This power is called prosecutorial discretion. Prosecutors exercise their discretion in the charging decision (which, above and beyond

---

Files From Duke Rape Case Give Details But No Answers, N.Y. TIMES, Aug. 25, 2006, at A1 (calling the episode "yet another painful chapter in the tangled American opera of race, sex and privilege"); Dick Meyer, *The Devils at Duke*, CBSNEWS.COM, Apr. 6, 2006, http://www.cbsnews.com/stories/2006/04/06/opinion/meyer/main1480683.shtml (drawing on dichotomies of "Black and White, town and gown, rich and poor, privilege and plain, jocks and scholars"); David Whitley, *Ex-Duke Coach Is the Fall Guy in Lacrosse Scandal*, ORLANDO SENTINEL, Jan. 25, 2007, at D1 ("Preppy Duke and privileged white boys were inviting targets."); Mosteller, *supra* note 2, at 1337 (characterizing the case as "a disaster" and a "caricature"; also quoting North Carolina State Bar Chair, Lane Williamson, who described the case as "a fiasco").

14. Mosteller, *supra* note 2, at 1337 (quoting North Carolina Attorney General Roy Cooper).

15. *See* Brady v. Maryland, 373 U.S. 83, 87 n.2 (1963) ("[T]he Government wins its point when justice is done in its courts" (quoting Judge Simon E. Sobeloff, a former solicitor general)); *see also* Berger v. United States, 295 U.S. 78, 88 (1935) (noting the "peculiar and very definite" status of prosecutors as servants of the law); Mosteller, *supra* note 2, at 1366 ("[Nifong's role is] a minister of justice ... whose most important duty and responsibility is to seek justice, not merely to convict" (quoting North Carolina's Doug Brocker, the lead prosecutor in the Nifong disbarment proceedings)).

law enforcement's power to arrest, officially places the individual into the criminal-justice system),[16] the grand-jury process (which is solely the province of the prosecutor), plea bargaining (which the prosecutor may initiate, entertain, or foreclose), jury selection, trial strategy, and recommendations for sentencing. Prosecutorial discretion can be influenced by considerations both significant (for example, an uncooperative or unreliable witness, fairness, weak or compelling evidence, or an alternative disposition) and insignificant (for example, a chief prosecutor's pet peeve or campaign promise, office workload, triviality of the property damage or loss, defendant remorse, identification or empathy with the defendant or victim, or the collegiality (or lack thereof) of opposing counsel).

Prosecutorial discretion is necessary to the smooth operation of the criminal-justice system on both the federal and state levels. With it, prosecutors are free to decide who and what should be charged, based upon social, evidentiary, economic, and political considerations—weighed, of course, against the legislature's determination that certain behaviors should be punished as criminal. Just as police officers possess the power to decide whom to investigate and arrest, and judges possess the power to decide who, pending trial, shall be held, receive bond, or be released on their own recognizance, prosecutors must have the power and freedom to disburse individualized justice when and where necessary. Justice demands consideration of individual facts and circumstances; not all criminal defendants, victims, witnesses, and societal harms are the same, even when the criminal code affixes the same name to the alleged criminal conduct.[17]

Prosecutors have been granted the power and responsibility to enforce the law. They are regarded and treated as experts in that realm and are presumed to act in accordance with their duty and its obligations. The Supreme Court expects that prosecutors receive deference in the exercise of their judgment, including discretionary decisions, as interference with prosecutorial duties will almost-certainly interfere with criminal-law enforcement:[18]

---

16. Professor Angela J. Davis reminds us that there is no law that requires a prosecutor to charge an individual with criminal conduct. The decision to do so, then, makes the decision to charge "the most important prosecutorial power and the strongest example of the influence and reach of prosecutorial discretion." ANGELA J. DAVIS, ARBITRARY JUSTICE 23–24 (2007).

17. See id. at 13–14 (noting that significant differences in the facts of each case should be considered in prosecutorial decision-making in order to effect a just outcome for a diverse group of criminal defendants).

18. See id. at 127 (citing Rose v. Clark, 478 U.S. 570, 582 (1986)). One commentator has characterized the standards for obtaining discovery of evidence that may prove prosecutorial misconduct as "nearly impossible." Moreover, even when such a standard is met

This broad discretion rests largely on the recognition that the decision to prosecute is particularly ill-suited to judicial review. Such factors as the strength of the case, the prosecution's general deterrence value, the Government's enforcement priorities, and the case's relationship to the Government's overall enforcement plan are not readily susceptible to the kind of analysis the courts are competent to undertake.... Examining the basis of a prosecution delays the criminal proceeding, threatens to chill law enforcement by subjecting the prosecutor's motives and decision-making to outside inquiry and may undermine prosecutorial effectiveness.[19]

Prosecutorial discretion has its fair share of critics. According to these critics, prosecutorial discretion is unlike that exercised by others in the criminal-justice system because public challenge or criticism of it is virtually nonexistent. This is becoming even more problematic, as the breadth of subjects over which prosecutors may exercise their discretion continues to increase, while the public's pressure on prosecutors to obtain more convictions and seek harsher penalties only seems to intensify. This combination is even more alarming when one is forced to reckon with the fact that all prosecutors do not always make decisions that are "legal, fair, and equitable."[20]

One might hope to draw more comfort in the case of elected prosecutors because, ostensibly, they are answerable to voters. Conventional wisdom holds that popular elections serve as a public check on prosecutorial power and guarantee some prosecutorial accountability. Moreover, prosecutors elected by popular vote are not beholden to political rainmakers or forced to curry favor with their jurisdiction's high court or governor. Instead, elected prosecutors are largely and near-exclusively accountable to "the people."[21]

Unfortunately, electoral accountability has proven a mirage. Electing prosecutors (as opposed to appointing them) actually *reinforces* unchecked prose-

---

and evidence is discovered, judicial review of the prosecutorial conduct shall be "extremely limited" and assessed under the "harmless error" standard—courts should not set aside convictions if the error was harmless beyond a reasonable doubt.

19. Wayte v. United States, 470 U.S. 598, 607 (1985).

20. *See* DAVIS, *supra* note 16, at 8–11, 127–30 (citing United States v. Russell, 411 U.S. 423, 435 (1973); United States v. Hasting, 461 U.S. 499, 506 (1983) (curtailing judicial review of judicial oversight even when convictions suffer from harmless error based on law-enforcement—including prosecutorial—misconduct). Davis finds civil lawsuits equally ineffective as a potential check or oversight of prosecutorial misconduct. *See id.* at 128.

21. *See id.* at 10–12, 163–77 (noting the failure of the electoral process to expose, much less check, prosecutorial discretion).

cutorial power, independence, and discretion. Although voters dissatisfied with their prosecutor may vote him or her out of office in the next election cycle, under the best of circumstances, such efforts tend to lose import and potency because they are untimely. Besides, decisions marred by inappropriately exercised prosecutorial discretion are often carried out behind the scenes and are usually discovered too late for effective action, if they are discovered at all.[22]

Concern regarding abuse of prosecutorial discretion is seldom based on a prosecutor's use of that discretion to effect a positive outcome for a defendant. Rather, the concern usually stems from prosecutorial decisions that impact criminal defendants negatively, given that useful standards, meaningful guidelines, effective penalties, and official accountability for prosecutors is generally lacking in our criminal-justice system. Specifically, prosecutorial discretion is criticized when it is morphs into prosecutorial abuse and prejudices the accused, who often has little or no opportunity to hold the prosecutor's power in check. Discerning how a prosecutor's various decisions were made is often an impossible task. Seldom is there a consistent, standardized methodology, explanation, or record.

When one takes into consideration the natural—some may even say mandated—competitiveness of the American criminal-justice system and criminal-trial work, as well as the challenge of thwarting prosecutors who intentionally exploit their discretion and power to engage in illegality, the task of checking that discretion is more daunting still. If even well-meaning prosecutors exercise their discretion in ways that produce unfair results, one can only imagine what ill-intentioned prosecutors are able to do, particularly because misconduct and abuse are rarely uncovered or punished.[23]

Disaster Capitalism

Disaster capitalism has been defined by investigative journalist, author, and filmmaker Naomi Klein, as one or more "orchestrated raids on the public sphere in the wake of catastrophic events, combined with the treatment of disasters as

---

22. *See id.* at 14–16 (citing the Wickersham Commission's criticism and others regarding the absence of a "meaningful check" regarding prosecutors' discretion, as well as the ineffectiveness of elections in this regard). Davis speaks generally of the failure of the electoral process to check or make more visible prosecutorial discretion. *See id.* at 163–177.

23. *See id.* at 17 (identifying the problems of prosecutorial discretion even when prosecutors attempt only to "do justice"); *see also id.* at 140–41 (criticizing prosecutorial career advancements and rewards as improper and positive reinforcements for "arbitrary, hasty, and impulsive" decisions that may lead to high conviction rates, but are derived without accountability or supervisory input).

exciting market opportunities."[24] The capitalistic opportunity arises because the disaster puts the entire population into a state of collective shock, allowing a corporate-supremacist ideology to pave the way for private interests to maximize for-profit disaster gains. According to University of Chicago economist Milton Friedman, the father of disaster capitalism, "[o]nly a crisis—actual or perceived—produces real change. When that crisis occurs, the actions that are taken depend on the ideas that are lying around."[25] In other words, once a disaster such as a war, earthquake, or terrorist attack occurs, disaster capitalists act quickly to impose "rapid and irreversible change before the crisis-wracked society slip[s] back into the tyranny of the status quo."[26] According to Friedman, since people are more susceptible to suggestion from leadership during a crisis and take some time to regain their post-shock emotional and intellectual bearings, politicians and their advisors should take advantage of the moment to push through all painful policies at once. This indispensable tactical nostrum may be regarded as the "Shock Doctrine." Although the shock does not have to be violent to disrupt or disorient, it must be traumatic. Additionally, subsequent shocks (such as harsh or widespread human-rights violations and physical torture) may need to be administered in order to break any remaining resistance to private interests blocking the public will. In sum, when the citizenry is suffering, it is ripe for manipulation.[27]

When disaster capitalism is discussed, most often the focus is upon private corporations and their reengineering of foreign countries, societies, and communities that are still reeling from shocks such as war, natural disaster, or terrorist attacks. Typically, disaster capitalists take advantage of public vertigo to pick the mental locks of public resistance to achieve private gain, most often by privatizing what had been state functions. Disaster capitalists have no interest in repairing what was. Harnessing societal shock for private, personal gain is the goal.[28]

---

24. Naomi Klein, *State-Sanctioned Torture and Disaster Response for the Chosen*, Democracy Now!, Nov. 7, 2007, http://www.democracynow.org/2007/11/7/shock_doctrine_author_naomi_klein_on.

25. Milton Friedman, Capitalism and Freedom, at ix (University of Chicago Press (1962). Naomi Klein deems Friedman the father and pioneering advocate of disaster capitalism. Naomi Klein, The Shock Doctrine: The Rise of Disaster Capitalism 6 (2007).

26. *See* Klein, *supra* note 25, at 6.

27. *See id.* at 10; *see also* Faludi, *supra* note 1, at 64 (discussing the frailties of hero-worshipping in the face of cultural crisis and created narratives that are, at bottom, false).

28. *See* Klein, *supra* note 24, at 17 ("Like the terrorized prisoner who gives up the names of comrades and renounces his faith, shocked societies often give up things they would otherwise fiercely protect.").

There are a number of historical examples illustrating the intersection between a megadisaster (for example, a coup, regime change, or foreign war) and corporate superprofits.[29] General Augusto Pinochet's September 11, 1973, defeat of the sitting, democratically-elected Chilean government by violent coup is a classic example. On its own, the coup shocked Chileans, who had enjoyed an overwhelmingly peaceful 160 years of democratic rule. In the days immediately following the initial coup, however, Pinochet administered additional shocks to the newly disoriented and politically kidnapped citizenry, including arresting approximately 80,000 civilians, thousands of whom "disappeared." He also authorized death squads, which publicly executed hundreds of high-profile prisoners throughout the countryside and freely "exhibited" their ravaged bodies, many of which ended up bloated and floating in canals. The message was delivered; the country was officially "shocked."[30]

The cowed citizenry was now amenable to economic shock-therapy. The radical and comprehensive capitalist transformation was based on privatization, deregulation, and skeletal social spending. State-owned companies, banks, and speculative-finance firms were privatized; imports were encouraged; price controls were removed; probusiness policies with the goal of complete free trade were enacted. Subsequent economic shocks were administered that required the eschewing of governmentally imposed economic controls or intervention in the free market's reign.[31] Disaster capitalists and their fans regarded the massive overhaul of Chile's economy and government during the post-shock "democracy-free zone" as a great success and model of societal transformation.[32]

Disaster capitalism has been carried out domestically as well. Recently, the United States witnessed two examples of disaster capitalism at work: (1) during the aftermath of Hurricane Katrina, and (2) during the aftermath of 9/11. Mere months after the disaster of Hurricane Katrina and, specifically, the failure of the levees in New Orleans, the New Orleans public school system was among the infrastructure that was in a state of utter destruction. In the finest tradition of disaster capitalism, Friedman virtually demanded "an educational land grab."[33] He noted the "tragedy" of the destruction of the New Orleans

---

29. *See generally id.* at 75–273 (detailing disaster-capitalism efforts in, among other places, Chile, Bolivia, China, and South Africa).

30. *See id.* at 76–77.

31. *See id.* at 77–78 (identifying Friedman's work as bearing a "striking resemblance" to "The Brick," the radical free-market economic counterrevolution).

32. *See id.* at 131 (citing Great Britain's Margaret Thatcher's praise of Pinochet's "remarkable success ... [regarding] the Chilean economy").

33. *Educational Land Grab,* Rethinking Schools, Fall 2006, http://www.rethinkingschools.org/archive/21_01/grab211.shtml. One observer described it as follows:

school system and its lack of children; however, he also characterized the crisis as "an opportunity to radically reform the educational system." Shortly thereafter, the New Orleans public-school system was, in fact, auctioned off with lightning speed and replaced in its entirety by privately owned and operated charter schools. The teachers' union was disbanded; its entire membership was fired.[34] Crowing about the successful private sale of this heretofore public function, a Friedman-inspired think tank remarked: "Katrina accomplished in a day ... what Louisiana school reformers couldn't do after years of trying."[35]

Similarly, after 9/11, disaster capitalists on the federal level seized upon the collective American shock inflicted by the multiple terrorist attacks that day. Almost immediately, the Bush administration immediately launched its massive, for-profit "War on Terror." This War on Terror, which was fueled by Americans' post-9/11 fear, as well as omnipresent insecurity and peril, was used by the Bush administration to increase dramatically the power of the executive branch via policing, spying, occupying, detaining (without due process or meaningful suspicion), and reconstructing.[36]

The War on Terror has generated a global security industry worth $200 billion and counting. It led to the creation of the Department of Homeland Security and spawned wars in Afghanistan and Iraq, cash cows for private corporations that have benefited from no-bid contracts with the federal government to produce and provide weapons; build high-tech structures and barriers; provide and mount security cameras; reconstruct foreign facilities; help occupy Iraq; assist in the care and feeding of American personnel and members of the military; and build and defend a brand new billion-dollar U.S. Embassy in Iraq. Thanks to disaster capitalists' exploitation of Americans' insecurity after 9/11, terror has become an incredibly lucrative market unto itself. In the name of national security and fighting terrorism, disaster capitalists have created "the disaster capitalism complex," what Klein calls "a full-fledged new economy in homeland security, privatized war[,] and disaster reconstruction

---

I believe we are witnessing a land grab of a magnitude not seen since America was first being settled by "civilized people." The predominantly black victims of Hurricane Katrina have been evacuated and housed in practically every state except Louisiana, and by no means is it a benign occurrence.

Anthony Davis, *Redistricting New Orleans,* CHI. SUN-TIMES, Oct. 20, 2005, at 44.

34. KLEIN, *supra* note 25, at 5–6; *see also* Milton Friedman, *The Promise of Vouchers,* WALL ST. J., Dec. 5, 2005, at 20.

35. Susan Saulny, *U.S. Gives Charter Schools a Big Push in New Orleans,* N.Y. TIMES, June 13, 2006, at 19.

36. KLEIN, *supra* note 25, at 295–303.

tasked with nothing less than building and running a privatized security state, both at home and abroad."[37]

Self-interest is not limited to denizens of the private sector.[38] In fact, disaster capitalists can and do operate in the public sector. Civil servants may appear uniquely insulated from the temptations of disaster capitalism;[39] however, they are not. Their goals may not be as grand, lucrative, or global as those of multinational corporations, world leaders, or dictators, but they are equally susceptible to the temptation to exploit postcrisis public shock to achieve self-interested private gain.[40] Few civil servants are in a better position to be a successful disaster capitalist than a prosecutor who is willing to break laws and rules to charge and prosecute the innocent.[41]

When Discretion Meets Disaster

In prosecuting the Duke lacrosse case until his ethical lapses forced him off, Durham District Attorney Mike Nifong used his personal brand of disaster capitalism to secure his reelection and—he thought—his eventual pension. He exploited the community's shock over what it thought had occurred on Buchanan Street that night. He was so determined to get what he wanted that he stirred up public sentiment, abused his prosecutorial power, violated his ethical and legal duties, and infringed upon the constitutional rights of the lacrosse players. He also grossly misused Crystal Mangum, who ultimately suffered widespread condemnation and national ire as a result of his actions. He was not, of course, the first man to use Mangum. He was, however, the most powerful one and, as a result, had the most devastating impact.[42]

---

37. Klein notes that Bush and his administration created the War on Terror, building it "to be private from the start." KLEIN, *supra,* note 25 at 13, 298–99; *see also* William Langewiesche, *The Mega-Bunker of Baghdad,* VANITY FAIR, Nov. 2007, http://www.vanityfair.com/politics/features/2007/11/langewiesche200711 (estimating the cost of building a new American embassy in Baghdad at $600 million and its annual operation at $1.2 billion).

38. *See* Klein, *supra* note 9 (noting that disaster capitalists' idea of exploiting crises is not unique to modern right-wingers: "[f]ascists have done it. State communists have done it").

39. Scott Shane & Ron Nixon, *In Washington, Contractors Take on Biggest Role Ever,* N.Y. TIMES, Feb. 4, 2007, at 1 (quoting David M. Walker, U.S. Comptroller General).

40. *See* KLEIN, *supra* note 25, at 51.

41. *See* Mosteller, *supra* note 2, at 1365 (citing Fred C. Zacharias, *Structuring the Ethics of Prosecutorial Trial Practice: Can Prosecutors Do Justice?*, 44 VAND. L. REV. 45, 50, 107 n.259 (1991)).

42. Others have also made this observation, including a mother of one of the accused players: "When I'm trying to get over the rage I am thinking about, so deeply, this young

Crisis

Crystal Mangum was born July 16, 1978, the youngest of three children in a working-class Durham family, headed by Mary and Travis Mangum. Her family lived across the street from one of the churches the family attended regularly. In 1996, she graduated from Durham's Hillside High School. Her soon-to-be husband, Kenneth N. McNeill, was fourteen years her senior and did not know how to read or write. He was, however, astute enough to know that Crystal "wanted to see the world." When he suggested that she "join the Navy," she did.[43]

In the summer of 1997, the Navy stationed Crystal in Dam Neck, VA, where she trained in radio operation and navigation equipment. In the fall of that same year, Crystal married Kenneth. The Navy then transferred Crystal to Concord, CA, and assigned her to an ammunition ship. According to Kenneth, their honeymoon was the cross-country drive to Crystal's new assignment.[44]

Lengthy days at sea caused tension in the marriage. Crystal developed interest in another sailor and began a relationship with him. Her seventeen-month-old marriage crumbled. The couple had no children. Crystal, however, had provided Kenneth with a most loving and enduring gift: she had successfully taught him how to read and write.[45]

Over the course of the next few years, Crystal's life destabilized. She was discharged from the Navy; records indicate that she was pregnant with her lover's son at the time. In 1998, Crystal filed a court complaint against Kenneth, accusing him of taking her into a wooded area and threatening to kill her. Kenneth denied the charges and Crystal never appeared in court for the hearing on them. As a result, the complaint was dismissed. In 2002, Crystal was arrested after getting drunk and fleeing in a car she stole from the parking lot of a strip club where she worked as a dancer—she had taken the keys from a customer's pocket while she gave him a lap dance. Before being apprehended, she led the police on a high-speed chase. She was charged with multiple felonies and misdemeanors. In 2003, Crystal pleaded guilty to four misdemeanors and was sentenced to three consecutive weekends in jail and two years' probation.

---

woman who has been abused by men all her life. And nobody has abused her more than Mike Nifong." 60 Minutes, *The Duke Case*, CBSNEWS.COM, Jan. 14, 2007, http://www.cbsnews.com/stories/2007/01/11/60minutes/main2352512.shtml (quoting Rae Evans, mother of player David Evans).

43. *See* Michael Y. Park, *Crystal Gail Mangum: Profile of the Duke Rape Accuser*, FoxNEWS.COM, Apr. 11, 2007, http://www.foxnews.com/story/0,2933,265374,00.html.

44. *See id.*

45. *Id.*

She paid court costs, restitution, and all of her legal bills. That same year, Crystal would find herself in court on another matter entirely: seeking child support from her ex-lover, the sailor, for their two children. By then, Crystal was the mother of three.[46]

For a short period of time, Crystal somehow managed to pull out of this tailspin. She enrolled in Durham Technical Community College and, in 2004, received an Associate's Degree. She then sought and gained admission to North Carolina Central University (NCCU), a historically Black college with a proud history,[47] robust curricular offerings,[48] an international student body,[49] and celebrated alumni.[50] NCCU "Eagles"[51] are expected to soar, and the school's alumni

---

46. *Id.*

47. NCCU was chartered in 1909 and began operations in 1910 as the National Religious Training School and Chautauqua. NCCU declared that its purpose was to prepare young men and women of character and sound academic education to serve the country. After a major reorganization in the early- and mid-1920s that would inure to the school's financial benefit, the General Assembly of North Carolina began the creation of the nation's first state-supported liberal-arts college for African-American students. The institution's name was changed to North Carolina College for Negroes (NCC). NCC's mission was changed to preparation of secondary-school teachers and principals in a liberal-arts education. In the late 1920s and through the 1930s, the institution's physical plant grew, thanks to generous private donors (including Durham philanthropist B.N. Duke). In 1937, the Southern Association of Colleges and Secondary Schools accredited NCC as an "A" class institution. In 1957, the association admitted NCC to membership. In 1969, North Carolina College became North Carolina Central University (NCCU). *See* North Carolina Central University, *NCCU at a Glance*, http://www.nccu.edu/About%20NCCU/index.cfm (last visited Jan. 20, 2008).

48. *See id.* (listing bachelor's degrees in over one-hundred fields of study and graduate degrees in approximately forty fields).

49. *See id.* (noting that NCCU's student body consists of students hailing from the United States, Liberia, India, Senegal, Sierra Leone, Nepal, China, the Czech Republic, Nigeria, South Korea, Russia, the Dominican Republic, Mexico, and South Africa).

50. *See id.* The university is committed to the fulfillment of its motto "Truth and Service," as well as the preparation and equipment of graduates capable of competing in the global marketplace. NCCU alumni include Maynard Jackson (J.D.), the first African American mayor of Atlanta; G.K. Butterfield (B.S., J.D), U.S. Congressman and former associate Justice of the North Carolina Supreme Court; Eva Clayton (M.S.), U.S. Congresswoman; Andre Leon Talley (B.A.), Editor-at-Large of Vogue Magazine; multi-millionaire Willie Gary, Esq., aka "The Giant Killer," (J.D.), whose settlements wrested from mega-corporations are legendary; The Honorable Wanda G. Bryant (J.D.); George Hamilton, Sr. (B.S.,), President, Dow Automotive; Ernie Barnes (B.A.), Father of American Neo-Mannerist art; Larry Black, Olympic Gold and Silver Medalist; and Samuel "Mr. Clutch" Jones (B.S.), NBA Hall of Fame Inductee. *Id.*

51. *See id.* NCCU's school mascot is an eagle.

prove that all manner of fame and achievement are possible. As a "B" student, Crystal was certainly poised to take flight, even with her shaky, but seemingly stabilized, trajectory. Employment as a sex worker[52] would be unthinkable and an inexplicable perversion.[53] How, then, did this young woman fall so far from the hallowed halls of higher learning, not only to become a sex worker, but to work as an employee of at least eight "escort agencies," including the likes of Angels Escort Service and Diamond Girls Service, a.k.a. "Bunny Hole Entertainment?" She was, on the one hand, a single mother and successful college student; yet, on the other hand, she not only stripped for money, but also fellated and had all manner of sexual intercourse with strangers for a living and acquaintances for whatever reason suited them or her.[54]

There seems to be no satisfactory reconciling of the noble commencement tassel with the ignoble tassel of the stripper's pasties. Crystal literally embodied the town-gown schizophrenia of Durham, which could accurately be described as "a very volatile mix of race, sex, and class."[55] Her "defiance narrative"[56] ultimately succumbed to the unacceptable metanarrative of the drug- or other-substance-addled Black stripper, stumbling and falling during an aborted routine after arriving late, talking incoherently to no one in particular, only to end up passed out a short distance away, in the parking lot of an all-night Kroger grocery store.[57]

Erik Erikson puts it pithily: "[she] who is ashamed would like to force the world not to look at [her], not to notice [her] exposure. [S]he would like to destroy

---

52. *See* Kimberly A. Yuracko, *Private Nurses and Playboy Bunnies: Explaining Permissible Sex Discrimination*, 92 Cal. L. Rev. 147, 172 (2004) (describing sex work as "including lap dancing, stripping, and acting as a sexualized gaze object").

53. Lane Williamson, chair of the North Carolina State Bar, characterized the events of the case as follows: "if it were applied in a John Grisham novel would be considered to be perhaps too contrived." Mosteller, *supra* note 2, at 1337.

54. *See, e.g.,* Craig Jarvis, *Mangum's Life: Conflict, Contradictions*, News & Observer (Raleigh, N.C.), Apr. 13, 2007, at 1A.

55. So much so that Mangum was characterized as the "Louvre of DNA" on a national late-night talk show because she had the sperm of three, separate men—none of which belonged to the accused players—who were all drivers for her dancing gigs, inside her vagina and anus. *See also* Robert P. Mosteller, *Exculpatory Evidence, Ethics, and the Road to Disbarment of Mike Nifong: The Critical Importance of Full Open-File Discovery*, 15 Geo. Mason L. Rev. 257, 286 (2008) (citing DNA Security, Inc., the firm that located male DNA profiles in samples taken from Mangum's panties, rectum, and pubic area).

56. *See* Anthony Alfieri, *Defending Racial Violence*, 95 Colum. L. Rev. 1301, 1335 (1995) (citation omitted).

57. *See* Joseph Neff & Anne Blythe, *Team Party Turned Sour Early*, News & Observer (Raleigh, N.C.), Apr. 28, 2007, at 18A; Mosteller, *supra* note 2, at 1342–45.

the eyes of the world."[58] March 14, 2006, was not the first time that Crystal had been looked up and down by paying, leering, insulting strangers. It was an indignity that she had suffered repeatedly and, on this occasion, one time too many. Her protectors—whoever they were—had failed her. Benefactors were nowhere to be found. Nice girls may finish last; however, last girls "don't finish nice."[59] Accordingly, it should come as little surprise that when Crystal was asked whether she had been violated, she not only answered "yes," but over the course of the next few days, falsely—but, perhaps, not inaccurately—also indicated that she had been violated in virtually every way one might imagine.[60]

Shock

There is a brief psychological interval or paralysis, akin to suspended animation, after shock is experienced. In this moment, those who are shocked are far more open to suggestion. They are more likely to comply with commands or directions; they are more willing to submit to another's imposed will. In the immediate aftermath of the shock, individuals and societies can become much more childlike, in that they are more willing to follow leaders who proclaim they shall protect. In such a state, there is a decreased ability to see or react clearly, allowing for, among other things, support of paternalistic leadership. The goal at this stage in a disaster capitalist's strategy is to stall or prevent those shocked from recovering their rational and intellectual footing prior to the leadership pushing through its self-interested programs and policies.[61]

Nifong faced an election fight in a district that was forty-percent African American. Durham's Black community—fueled by the local, regional, and national disgust at what the lacrosse players were alleged to have done—was particularly ripe for the apotheosization of Nifong. Properly manipulated, they were capable of lifting him and his campaign effort to a soaring success on Election Day. He grabbed the manufactured disaster, exploited community shock, and ran with it.[62]

---

58. Erik H. Erikson, Childhood And Society 252–53 (1963).

59. See Glenn C. Loury, The Anatomy Of Racial Inequality 105 (2002).

60. See Mosteller, *supra* note 56, at 286 (recounting Mangum's differing accounts of the "assault," including anally, vaginally, orally, perhaps without a condom, with an instrument, in a bathroom, car, or suspended mid-air); Jeffrey Rosen, The Unwanted Gaze: The Destruction of Privacy in America 18–20 (2001) (describing the injury to dignity from unwanted gazes).

61. See Klein, *supra* note 9.

62. See Mosteller, *supra* note 2, at 1354–55 (speculating Nifong's motivation was to take advantage of a racially charged allegation and, via "crass political calculation … pursue charges without being constrained").

Nifong's narrative was simple, yet powerful. He portrayed himself as a hero, a courageous prosecutor who was prepared to provide solace to a community that needed a champion of their cause. Likewise, he desperately needed them for his reelection bid.[63] On Mangum's behalf—and by extension, Black Durham's—Nifong

> challenged the players' manhood: "I'm disappointed that no one has been enough of a man to come forward";
> questioned their humanity: "I would like to think that somebody who was not in the bathroom has the human decency to call up"; and
> threatened their resolve: "My guess is that some of this stonewall of silence ... may tend to crumble once charges start to come out."[64]

Nifong also, at various times, verbalized his intention to avenge the wrong that had been done not only to Mangum, but to Durham as well—particularly to its Black residents:

> "[T]he reason I decided to take it over myself, was the combination gang-like rape activity accompanied by the racial slurs and general racial hostility";
> "I'm not going to let Durham's view in the minds of the world to be a bunch of lacrosse players from Duke raping a Black girl in Durham";
> "The circumstances of the rape indicate a deep racial motivation for some of the things that were done. It makes a crime that is by its nature one of the most offensive and invasive even more so";
> "[T]he contempt that was shown for the victim, based on her race was totally abhorrent. It adds another layer of reprehensibleness, to a crime that is already reprehensible."[65]

Of course, as he was purporting to stand in the shoes of a hero, Nifong was purposefully violating the accused players' constitutional rights when he failed to disclose exculpatory evidence, violating North Carolina law and the players' rights by ordering a suggestive lineup, and violating his ethical obligations through these actions and by trying the case in the press. But these were facts about which the voters were unaware and toward which Nifong appeared to manifest zero concern.[66]

---

63. *See* TAYLOR & JOHNSON, *supra* note 3.

64. Mosteller, *supra* note 2, at 1350 n.49 (citations omitted).

65. *Id.* at 1350–51 (citations omitted).

66. *See* Brady v. Maryland, 273 U.S. 83 (1963) (holding that due process requires prosecutors to provide exculpatory evidence to defense counsel). This prosecutorial obligation

Disaster Capitalism

Disaster capitalism relies upon the element of surprise. Klein puts it this way: "A state of shock, by definition, is a moment when there is a gap between fast-moving events and the information that exists to explain them."[67] Without a story, a description of what has happened, those in a state of shock are vulnerable to those poised to exploit them. Once a story describes what has occurred, shock dissipates; with a story, the world makes sense again. Narratives are more than useful; they are determinative.[68]

Nifong embarked on an ideological campaign to seal his electoral deal. He harnessed the shock of Mangum's "gang rape" and used it to ensure his electoral win on votes from a community in crisis. His message of protection, as well as his self-created identity as a powerful, avenging angel, allowed Nifong to profit from the fear by insinuating that he was uniquely positioned to save Black Durham from the wealthy, White power structure. Without the Duke lacrosse rape case, it is almost certain that Nifong would not have been able to win the election; proffering himself as the most meritorious candidate would not have otherwise been possible. In other words, he benefited from his successful manipulation of what he understood to be a useful "market opportunity."

Nifong won the primary (which, in North Carolina at the time, was tantamount to winning the general election). He finished with 45.2 percent of the vote; his nearest competitor, Freda Black, won 41.5 percent; Keith Bishop, an African-American candidate, garnered a mere 13.3 percent. Nifong's narrow victory—reportedly 883 votes—was attributed to the strong support he received from Durham's Black community. There, Nifong won 44 percent of the Black vote; Black 25.2 percent, and Bishop 30.8 percent.[69]

---

exists even when the defense fails to asks for it. *See* United States v. Agurs, 427 U.S. 97 (1976). This obligation is reiterated in each state—including North Carolina—and the District of Columbia, via various ethical and disciplinary rules for prosecutors. *See* Davis, *supra* note 16, at 130; *see also* N.C. Gen. Stat. §15A-901 (2007) (applying discovery statutes to cases within the superior court's original jurisdiction).

67. Klein, *supra* note 24, at 458

68. *Id.*

69. *See* Taylor & Johnson, *supra* note 3, at 201–23. It is reported that Nifong informed his campaign manager, "I'm getting a million dollars of free advertisements." *See* Mosteller, *supra* note 2, at 1355–56. Regarding non-Black Durham voters, the vote was as follows: 46.2, 50.6, and 3.2 percent for Nifong, Black, and Bishop respectively. *Id.*

Shockproof?

Ultimately, Nifong's self-interest and personal ambition "collided with a very volatile mix of race, sex, and class"[70] and he lost control of the situation. Perhaps Nifong's incomplete understanding of the narrative he offered, which the public initially accepted but ultimately rejected, doomed his political grab for power and destroyed his career. Ponder how very different an outcome there might have been if Nifong had been more skilled and retained his psychological edge over the lacrosse players by immediately jailing and separating them from all communication, sensory input, and, therefore, potentially useful narratives. An example of such a prosecution is in order.

The Central Park Jogger Case: Mission Accomplished

The boys never told the same story twice, nor were their stories consistent. Each one pleaded not guilty to a vicious rape and brutal assault. Those who had provided a videotaped confession claimed that the police coerced and concocted the stories. The DNA collected at the crime scene did not match the DNA of any of the boys.[71] The female victim was evidence-free when it came to the "attackers'" DNA.[72] She had no recollection of the crime or memory of the perpetrators. She never identified the boys as attackers.[73]

---

70. Mosteller, *supra* note 2, at 1337 (quoting North Carolina Bar Chair Lane Williamson).

71. Steven Drizin wryly notes: "It is often said that teenage boys can't make a peanut butter and jelly sandwich without leaving evidence." *See* Lynnell Hancock, *Wolf Pack: The Press and the Central Park Jogger,* Colum. Journalism Rev. (Jan./Feb. 2003), http://cjrarchives.org/issues/2003/1/rapist-hancock.asp.

72. *See* People v. Wise, 194 Misc. 2d 481, 489 (N.Y., Dec. 19, 2002).

73. Similar to the Duke lacrosse case, in the Central Park Jogger case, despite the inability to link forensically any of the teens to the DNA found at the crime scene, the prosecution remained undeterred and its "quest for convictions never wavered." Rivka Gewirtz Little, *Ash-Blond Ambition,* The Village Voice, Nov. 20–26, 2002, http://www.villagevoice.com/news/0247,little,40000,1.html; *see also Wise,* 194 Misc. 2d at 491–92. As four of the boys were under sixteen years old when they were convicted, they were sentenced under juvenile guidelines, requiring sentences of five to ten years. Because Kharey Wise was sixteen at the time he was convicted, however, he was considered an "adult" under New York law and was sentenced to five-to-fifteen years imprisonment. Trisha Meili revealed her identity to the public in her book, I Am the Central Park Jogger: A Story Of Hope And Possibility (2003). At the time of her writing, the convictions of the accused and convicted boys had not been vacated. In fact, the book retells the event from facts that have been discredited and rejected, given the confession of Reyes, as well as the DNA match of his semen with that found on Meili and at the crime scene. *See* Trisha

Yet, to the government prosecutors, she was an opportunity. They used her, capitalizing upon the shock created via the injuries inflicted on her violated and broken body. Her trope was seized, and a city's racialized fear of crime was stoked to epic levels.[74]

The Central Park Jogger case is one of the more modern and infamous miscarriages of justice in the United States. There, five Black and Latino teen boys, ranging in age from fourteen to sixteen years old, were wrongfully convicted of the vicious attack on Trisha E. Meili, the "Central Park Jogger," a young White woman who was raped, viciously beaten, and left to die in a ravine in Manhattan's Central Park.

That case represents an unfettered exploitation of a community's shock via the government's jettisoning the rights of the accused in order to advance key prosecutorial players' professional and pecuniary interests. Those responsible took full advantage of the city's tense racial and class climates of mistrust and loathing, as well as the shock of a brutal crime against an unsuspecting young White, middle-class, female Phi Beta Kappa investment banker at Salomon Brothers who jogged through Central Park at night. New York City was on edge, given a number of high-profile racial crimes.[75] All of the boys—Antron McCray, Kevin Richardson, Raymond Santana, Yusef Salaam, and Kharey Wise—were regarded as "dubious" students from fractured Harlem homes, itself then widely regarded as a marginalized, impoverished community of non-White New Yorkers.[76] That the assault occurred while she jogged through what was thought to be a space safe from the crime that otherwise plagued

---

Meili, *I Am the Central Park Jogger*, MSNBC.COM, Apr. 6, 2003, http://www.msnbc.msn.com /id/3080126 (excerpting Meili's preface and first chapter).

74. *See* Hancock, *supra* note 71 (quoting Northwestern University's Children and Family Justice Center Attorney Steven Drizin).

75. *See* Sydney H. Schanberg, *A Journey Through the Tangled Case of the Central Park Jogger: When Justice is a Game*, VILLAGE VOICE, Nov. 19, 2002, http://www.villagevoice.com/ news/0247,schanberg,39999,1.html (recounting violent, criminal cases which received extensive media coverage and were overtly racial, including the 1986 Howard Beach killing of a young black man chased by a group of bat-wielding white men; the 1989 Bensonhurst, Brooklyn, killing by white men of black teen Yusef Hawkins, after Hawkins had wandered onto their Italian-American "turf").

76. *See* Chris Smith, *Central Park Revisited*, N.Y. MAG., Oct. 14, 2002, http://nymag.com/ nymetro/news/crimelaw/features/n_7836/. As it turns out, this was untrue. Prior to this tragedy, each boy had a very good reputation. Most were from stable, two-parent, working-class homes. Words intimates used to describe the boys were "not aggressive," "very easy-going," "a straight-up guy," and "very shy, very respectable." *See* Hancock, *supra* note 71.

New York City at the time was a "bonus" for the Manhattan District Attorney's Office;[77] in fact, the site of the crime, considered by some "the city's premier greensward," exponentially bolstered "the theme of middle-class violation."[78] It was nothing, then, for motivated media outlets to complete the story with the specter of Black and brown male thugs marauding around the city, engaged in a "violent outburst of destruction, or beating, or assaulting"—also known as "wilding"[79]—in an orgy of gang rampage and rape.[80] This was the government's "theory" of the case.[81] Shock delivered.[82]

Given the trauma suffered and shared by New York City's ruling White class from the event, agents with an agenda began their violations of the civil and human rights of the accused teens. In a blatant power-grab, Linda Fairstein, head of the Manhattan District Attorney's Sex Crimes Unit, bested her supervisor in securing the case assignment by directly soliciting District Attorney Robert Morgenthau.[83] Fairstein not only authorized police interrogations of the boys, she also bullied and prevented one child's mother and another's friends—which included the child's mentor, an Assistant U.S. Attorney—from entering the interrogation room.[84] As if reading from the Shock Doctrine play-

---

77. Hancock, *supra* note 71 ("At the same time, middle-class white people were slowly moving back to midtown and reclaiming the symbol of the city, Central Park.").

78. *See* Smith, *supra* note 78 (characterizing Central Park as a "mythologized" locale).

79. *See* Hancock, *supra* note 71 (pondering the origins of the term "wilding," given that the case "planted 'wilding' into the English lexicon, a term that came to define the inhumanity of these kids").

80. *See id.* According to the *Columbia Journalism Review*, the press defined "wilding" as "a phenomenon not unlike the violent raves in *A Clockwork Orange*—'packs of bloodthirsty teens from the tenements, bursting with boredom and rage, roam the streets getting kicks from an evening of ultra-violence.'" *Id.*

81. *See* Smith, *supra* note 78. The police reported that the accused boys coined the term "wilding" to describe their acts on the evening of their arrest. "Wilding" purportedly involved "beating up random victims." *Id.* In fact, the government conceded in open court that its theory of the case was that the jogger "was set upon by a number of young men, gangraped by two or more of them, kicked and pummeled by the group, and beaten about the head with a pipe, a brick, and a rock." People v. Wise, 194 Misc. 2d 481, 494–95 (N.Y., Dec. 19, 2002).

82. One scholar characterized such young men as "teen superpredators" and predicted that their ilk would, by the millennium, overrun the streets. *See* Hancock, *supra* note 71.

83. *See* Schanberg, *supra* note 77.

84. Judge Titone, dissenting from his colleagues' affirmance of Saleem's conviction, spoke harshly of the police officers and Assistant District Attorney:

This case concerns a horrible and brutal crime that captured and held the public's attention for more than a year. It also involves the conduct of police officers

book, Fairstein's outrageous, unconstitutional, and unethical conduct was done to keep the vulnerable boys secluded and without the assistance of protective adults or legal counsel.[85] She intended that she and the police who worked under her authority and command would capitalize on the boys' youth and isolation, as "she had been informed by the interrogating detective that

---

and an Assistant District Attorney who obtained a confession from a fifteen-year-old boy by keeping him in isolation from the three concerned adults who came to the police station to help him.... represent[ing] a deliberate effort to keep him away from all responsible individuals who might have offered counsel or assistance.

....

In all, defendant was questioned for an hour and a half before the interrogation was terminated. During that entire period, unbeknownst to him, there were related and/or concerned adults who were present and could have provided him with helpful counsel.... What emerges from these facts is a picture of law enforcement officers who were so anxious to extract a full and complete confession that they did everything within their power to keep this youthful suspect isolated and away from any adults who might interfere with their exploitation of the awesome law enforcement machinery possessed by the State.

People v. Salaam, 83 N.Y.2d 51, 58, 60 (N.Y. 1993) (Titone, J., dissenting) (internal citations omitted).

85. The Shock Doctrine dovetails quite nicely with the U.S. Supreme Court's Fourth Amendment jurisprudence, which relies upon and encourages citizens' consent to relinquish their constitutionally protected rights against unreasonable governmental searches and seizures. In fact, citizen ignorance is essential to disaster capitalism, particularly given that it allows governmental actors to exploit their imprimatur, as well as the rights-holders' lack of comprehensive and accurate knowledge concerning their constitutional rights and personal options. Such disadvantages are to be exploited by law enforcement; such is the accepted way. *See, e.g.,* John M. Burkoff, *Search Me?,* 39 Tex, Tech L. Rev. 1109, 1120 (2007) (citing Daniel Williams, *Misplaced Angst: Another Look at Consent-Search Jurisprudence,* 82 Ind. L.J. 69, 80 (2007)). The target suspect's "disadvantages of ignorance, fear, and resignation are accepted as vulnerabilities we expect law enforcement to exploit to good effect." *Id.* Accordingly, waiver of constitutional rights simplifies law enforcement's need to comport with requirements such as probable cause, reasonableness, and restraint. Consent frees the government from constraints and spares it much administrative work and shoe leather. "Consent searches are the black hole into which Fourth Amendment rights are swallowed up and disappear." Craig M. Bradley, *The Court's Curious Consent Search Doctrine,* Trial, Oct. 2002, at 72, http://www.atla.org/publications/trial/0210/sct.aspx. With assent, the government simply talks its way into the desired evidence. *See, e.g.,* Burkoff, *supra,* at 1121. Although the Supreme Court's Fifth Amendment jurisprudence provides criminal suspects with prophylactic measures to protect their right against governmentally compelled self-incrimination, officers are often still capable of obtaining a waiver of that protection, leading to an incriminating confession.

the questioning was in a delicate phase where [one] had begun to make some admissions."[86]

How did the government wrongfully convict these boys? There are several reasons. The teens were alone. None had the experience or maturity to protect his rights—constitutional, human, civil, or otherwise—in the inherently coercive, adult environment of a police station's interrogation room. Each boy was questioned, and most had been awake, for two days before the government finally obtained their "confessions."[87] Each boy gave at least one self-incriminating statement, each of which was crucial to his conviction.[88]

Ultimately, in 2002, a confession by the actual perpetrator, serial rapist and murderer Matias Reyes, led to a motion for a new trial based on newly discovered evidence by stellar defense counsel and reinvestigation of the crime by the Manhattan District Attorney's Office.[89] As it turned out, Reyes' DNA

---

86. People v. Salaam, 83 N.Y.2d 51, 58, 63 (N.Y. 1993) (Titone, J., dissenting) ("Manifestly, an experienced adult could have disabused defendant of the naïve notion that there was anything he could say to police that would result in his release at this stage in the investigation. Certainly, a knowledgeable adult—or an attorney retained by such an adult—could have alerted him that he could not extricate himself from the most serious charges merely by denying having directly participated in the rape."); *see* Schanberg, *supra* note 77. Fairstein ultimately failed to keep Salaam's determined mother away; not surprisingly, Salaam was the sole suspect who did not sign a written statement or give a videotaped confession. *Id.*

87. *See* Hancock, *supra* note 71 (noting that police abuse, yelling, swearing, and deceiving were a large part of the protracted interrogations).

88. *See* People v. Wise, 194 Misc. 2d 481, 496 (N.Y., Dec. 19, 2002) ("These confessions were the quintessential evidence in the prosecution of the defendants. They laid the foundation for a course of action developed, followed, and relied on for the prosecution and conviction of the defendants. That course was based on a theory that the defendants were involved as a group in a single incident: a crime rampage, which included rape, robbery and other crimes. That theory also incorporated a logical 'guilt by association' to the crimes against the Central Park jogger inference.").

89. Bill Perkins, president of the Schomburg Plaza tenants' association, was responsible for being a "first responder" on hearing of Reyes' confession to committing the rape and beating. Three of the boys had lived in Schomburg Plaza during his tenure. After consulting with the families, Perkins contacted attorney Michael Warren. Warren found co-counsel, Roger Wareham. The attorneys then enlisted the assistance of a private investigator, Earl Rawlins, who interviewed Reyes. Rawlins was successful; his efforts led to a detailed, written, audiotaped statement. The work of counsel and their private investigator grounded the motion to dismiss the boys' convictions. *See id.* Additionally, Warren and Wareham attacked the convictions based on the police investigations as well as interrogations. Most importantly, Warren and Wareham's work led to matching Reyes' DNA to the only DNA found at the crime scene and on the jogger. *Id.*

matched the only DNA gathered from the victim and crime scene.[90] Acting Supreme Court Justice Charles J. Tejada vacated the convictions of the five falsely accused, prosecuted, convicted, and jailed individuals. Unfortunately, by that time, the boys had aged into men behind bars.[91]

Angela Cuffee, sister of one of the convicted boys, said it best: "people profited from our pain."[92] Ms. Cuffee was correct. In fact, several professional reputations were launched from the wrongful prosecutions and convictions of the young Black defendants. The pain suffered by the wrongfully convicted and their loved ones was particularly lucrative for Fairstein, who, despite lackluster reviews of her literary talent, left the Manhattan District Attorney's Office "to write novels about an assistant district attorney who prosecutes sex crimes"— thereby increasing her net worth by millions.[93]

The Duke Lacrosse Case: Disaster Capitalism, Demurred?

Initially, Nifong's attempt at disaster capitalism succeeded. Ultimately, however, it failed. Nifong was thwarted by, among other things, wealth—defendants with motivated and moneyed parents who were immediately able to retain quality defense counsel on behalf of their sons. Had Nifong successfully segregated the accused, he might have enjoyed the "success" obtained by the prosecutors in the Central Park jogger case, in which the convictions rested nearly

---

Reyes, a violent, serial rapist, had committed a rape two days before raping the Central Park jogger. *Id.* His modus operandi involved stalking lone, White, female joggers; brutalizing them; raping them; and stealing their portable stereo and headphones. *Id.*

90. *See Wise*, 194 Misc. 2d at 488–89 (finding that Reyes was the sole source of DNA identified at the crime scene "to a factor of one in 6,000,000,000 people"). Additionally, Reyes' statement and criminal history established that he habitually stalked and then attacked White female victims in their twenties; beat, raped, always robbed them, frequently stole their Walkmans, and tied them up. *Id.* at 491.

91. *See id.* at 482–83, 486.

92. *See Central Park 5 Are Cleared!*, Democracy Now!, Dec. 20, 2002, http://www.democracynow.org/2002/12/20/central_park_5_are_cleared_manhattan (reflecting upon the cost to the accused and their families from the improper imprisonment).

93. Oliver Jovanovic, formerly a Columbia University microbiology Ph. D. student, was wrongly convicted by Fairstein as a cybersex attacker. A court of appeals overturned his conviction, determining that crucial exculpatory evidence was withheld by the prosecution. The case was ultimately dismissed, but only after Jovanovic served two years in jail for a crime he did not commit. *See* Gewirtz, *supra* note 73. In commenting upon Fairstein's involvement in the Central Park jogger case, Jovanovic stated: "Each time one of these cases occurred, her books probably went flying off the shelves.... She used what happened in that unit to make money, and that is wrong." *Id.*

exclusively on the boys' "confessions"—which were, of course, extracted while they were not only sequestered from family and friends, but also abused by police.[94]

Additionally, accusing white men of rape across racial and class lines can be tricky. It seems that when white men are accused, scrutiny turns toward the woman and her "contribution" to any aspect of the sexual violence to ascertain how she caused and, therefore, deserved the assault. Further, when the purported victim is a Black woman, the stereotype of black female promiscuity decreases the perceived criminal culpability of the accused. Thus, Nifong's accusation of rich, white males on behalf of a working-class, Black, female stripper may have imploded on its own. Unlike the narrative enjoyed by the prosecutors in the Central Park jogger case, here the story already in place was a centuries' old narrative that did not recognize well-to-do White males' nonconsensual sexual conduct with a lower-class Black female as criminal.

Specifically, this American monomyth is of one sort and identity; it assumes an unyielding complexion and plays a particular role in the United States. Essentially, the monomyth is based on female peril and "the rescue of just one young girl."[95] Unfortunately for Nifong, American mythology, lore, and preoccupation with female rescue and retribution for womanhood defiled are based on "[t]he specter of the White maiden taken against her will by dark savages." Sexual predation by dark-skinned (Native Americans) and Black men of White women was the horror against which heroic White men came to the rescue of pure White women and avenged these victims defilement or endangered honor.[96] But American mythology has never had an affinity for Black female purity or protection.

Prosecutorial remonstrations regarding an impaired Black stripper with a checkered past and a criminal record who was paid to dance for wealthy White athletes were especially likely to meet with failure. Throughout much of American history, while mere allegation of the rape of a White woman by one or more Black men was punished "with especial violence,"[97] raping a Black woman

---

94. 60 Minutes, *supra* note 42. According to a mother of one of the accused players, Nifong's error was that he "messed with the wrong families" (quoting Rae Evans, mother of player David Evans). Mrs. Evans went even further, vowing that Nifong "will pay every day for the rest of [his] life." *Id.*

95. *See* FALUDI, *supra* note 1, at 200.

96. *See id.*

97. *See id.* at 212–14, 276–78 (chronicling white American rape hysteria regarding native and African men whose purported victims were White women). Even today, the names and faces of young White women proliferate the front pages of newspapers, tabloids, and television screens, which has been identified as the "White woman syndrome" or the "damsel in distress" factor, as the focus remains unerringly upon one class of missing person: "at-

was neither prohibited nor a crime. More difficult for Nifong, Mangum was no vulnerable maiden, no virginal, trembling waif, capable only of being taken, ravaged, and rescued; she was not a virtuous Black damsel in distress needing a savior. One cannot save what never was and, certainly, what no longer exists.[98]

This failure of narrative dovetails with Nifong's failure to capitalize on the initial shock of the accused lacrosse players and, in accordance with the tenets of disaster capitalism, isolate and force his narrative upon them. Shock does not last; it wears off, eventually. It is a temporary state. Those who are skilled in interrogation know this very well. The window of opportunity is small; the right effort at the right time is key to successful implementation of the Shock Doctrine. Given the nearly universal reaction of complete helplessness when faced with the government's awesome power, Nifong might have retained the ability to "break" the players, given the confusion, disorientation, and surprise of being jailed and isolated without explanation.[99] Instead, by allowing the players to remain in constant contact and communication not only with each other, but with their parents and counsel as well, they were able to resist and then combat Nifong's "shock." Unlike the Central Park jogger boys, these players were almost always cognizant of what was happening and why. Most importantly, their parents and counsel were available to offer counternarratives to Nifong's attempts to push his contrived indictments through the North Carolina criminal-justice system. The presence of these counternarratives brought a perspective on the crisis that explained the shocking event and reoriented the players' emotions and reason. The world as they once knew it now made sense again.[100]

---

tractive White women" and is "much more than happenstance." Jeffrey J. Pokorak, *Rape as a Badge of Slavery: The Legal History of, and Remedies for, Prosecutorial Race-of-Victim Charging Disparities*, 7 Nev. L.J. 1, 6–7 (2006).

98. *See* Pokorak, *supra* note 97, at 7–9.

99. *See* Klein, *supra* note 24, at 459, 465–66 (noting how CIA training materials stress the necessity for psychological and physical segregation of detainees to cut them off from anything that will assist in the creation of a counternarrative).

100. *See id.* at 458; *see also* Klein, *supra* note 9 (identifying resistance as key to combat disaster capitalism's shock doctrine).

Conclusion

It is a relief that this "rogue prosecutor" was stopped in his tracks.[101] Unfortunately, he was not stopped before wreaking substantial, additional damage not only to the accused—who have received significant sympathetic treatment—but also to Mangum, who suffered unfathomable humiliation. Damage was also done to the real victims of sexual assaults who, in the future, may be cowed into silence by the treatment of Mangum and the theatrical, public outcome: not only were all charges against the accused dropped, but their innocence was declared as well.[102]

The Duke case can be seen as a tale of limitation, perhaps, on the reach of disaster capitalism. Nifong's reaction to Mangum's allegations was that of a classic disaster capitalist, and he initially achieved his goal of reelection as a result. Ultimately, however, Nifong's malfeasance was detected and punished, given the moneyed families who were able to check and, ultimately, trump his hand. Nifong, though, was just unusually unlucky: the Duke defendants were atypical of those who usually enter the criminal-justice system. They had massive resources; most criminal defendants have few or none. They assembled a legal dream team, purchasing not merely an adequate, but a superior, defense. These attorneys spent literally thousands of hours and millions of dollars defending the accused. To the contrary, the overwhelming majority of the criminally accused are represented too often by overworked, underpaid assigned counsel.

"The system's legitimacy turns on equality before the law, but the system's reality could not be further from that ideal."[103] Until change occurs, "typical" criminal defendants will remain vulnerable to prosecutorial discretion that

---

101. *See* Mosteller, *supra* note 2, at 1338 (noting North Carolina Attorney General Roy Cooper's characterizations of Nifong).

102. *See* Kathleen Parker, *Nifong's Legacy, Feminism's Shame*, REALCLEARPOLITICS.COM, June 20, 2007, http://www.realclearpolitics.com/articles/2007/06/ unfinished_business.html. Parker notes that after the mishandling of this case, "real rape victims may be reluctant to come forward" and intimidated prosecutors may be reluctant to bring such prosecutions when faced with the possibility of persuading "jurors jaded by the Duke spectacle." *Id.* (characterizing Nifong's legacy as not only one that be long-lived, but also "ultimately may hurt women more than it does the falsely accused men"); *see also* Aaron Beard, *Durham: Don't Blame Us for Lacrosse Case*, SALON, Jan. 16, 2008, http://www.salon.com/wires/ap/us/ 2008/01/16/D8U78R7O1_duke_ lacrosse/index.html. Nifong was disbarred and spent one night in jail for North Carolina State Bar violations. Additionally, in January 2008, Nifong filed for bankruptcy.

103. DAVID COLE, NO EQUAL JUSTICE: RACE AND CLASS IN THE AMERICAN CRIMINAL JUSTICE SYSTEM 3 (1999).

borders on or veers into the realm of abuse. These individuals will continue to be sacrificed for the self-interest of those prosecutors whose personal aspirations—even in the public sector—draw their decisions away from doing justice and toward prosecutorial disaster capitalism.

The Duke Defendants Reaped the Benefits of a Zealous Defense—But Do Only the Rich Get Real Lawyers?

Rodney Uphoff

"This entire experience has opened my eyes up to a tragic world of injustice I never knew existed.... If police officers and a district attorney can systematically railroad us with absolutely no evidence whatsoever, I can't imagine what they'd do to people who do not have the resources to defend themselves."

Reade Seligmann[1]

Introduction

In many respects, Reade Seligmann and his codefendants in the Duke lacrosse case, Collin Finnerty and David Evans, were very unlucky. Admittedly, luck played no role in the decision that Evans and his fellow teammates and co-captains, Matt Zash and Dan Flannery, made to host a party at their house on March 13, 2006. Nor was luck a factor in the hosts' decision to hire two exotic dancers to perform for the partygoers. Unfortunately, a rude remark by one of the players, coupled with the intoxicated condition of one of those dancers, Crystal Mangum, led to an aborted striptease and, eventually, an exchange of angry words between Mangum's codancer Kim Roberts and several of the play-

---

1. *See* Duff Wilson & David Barstow, *Duke Prosecutors Throw Out Charges Against Players*, N.Y. TIMES, Apr. 12, 2007, at A1.

ers as Roberts drove away. Regretfully for Durham, Duke, and everyone caught up in this tragedy, approximately an hour later, Mangum chose to claim falsely that she was the victim of a violent gang-rape that occurred while she was at the Duke party.

It is not entirely clear why Mangum concocted this bogus rape story.[2] Whatever her motive, the assignment of Sergeant Mark Gottlieb to handle the investigation of the Mangum allegations also significantly contributed to the defendants' misfortune. The first investigator assigned to the case, B. S. Jones, thought that there was no evidence to go forward and concluded the file should be closed. Usually, that would have been the end of the matter. The case, however, was reassigned to Gottlieb, an officer characterized by the defense as a "Duke hater" with a history of "selective and malicious prosecution, false arrest, excessive use of force, manufacturing of evidence and filing of false police reports against students at Duke University."[3]

Despite Mangum's wildly inconsistent claims to medical personnel and various police officers, the fact she recanted the rape allegation when interviewed by Sergeant John Shelton, and the absence of any significant physical or medical evidence consistent with a violent attack, Gottlieb pressed ahead with his investigation. In doing so, he ignored the assessments of Sergeant Shelton and other Durham police officers who had spoken with Mangum in the early morning hours of March 14 that Mangum was not credible. Moreover, Gottlieb totally disregarded the statements of Evans, Flannery, and Zash about what happened at 610 N. Buchanan that night, disbelieving their version of events in spite of their cooperation, their willingness to submit to a sexual-assault-suspect kit, and their offers to take lie-detector tests.[4] He similarly ignored Kim Roberts's statement that Mangum's sexual assault claim was a "crock" and

---

2. Stuart Taylor and KC Johnson suggest several possibilities, including (1) that Mangum made up the rape claim to avoid being involuntarily committed to the Durham Access Center, or (2) that she wanted to extract a large sum of money from the players. *See* STUART TAYLOR & KC JOHNSON, UNTIL PROVEN INNOCENT 31, 35, 42 (2007). Her statement to Kim Roberts as they drove away from the party in her car—"Go ahead, put marks on me. That's what I want. Go ahead."—lends support to the notion that Mangum was motivated by money. *Id.* at 292. In contrast, North Carolina Attorney General Roy Cooper, focusing on her mental-health history and her mixing of drugs and alcohol, concluded that "her mentally imbalanced state suggested that she might actually believe her myriad tales." *Id.* at 352.

3. Complaint at 21, Evans v. Durham, North Carolina, No. 07-cv-00739 (M.D.N.C. 2007) [hereinafter *Civil Complaint*]. For a more comprehensive look at the basis for this characterization of Gottlieb, see TAYLOR & JOHNSON, *supra* note 2, at 36, 52–55.

4. *See* TAYLOR & JOHNSON, *supra* note 2, at 42–44 (describing the Gottlieb-led search at 610 N. Buchanan on March 16 and the players' cooperation).

brushed aside Mangum's bizarre, inconsistent allegations about Roberts's role in the attack. Instead, Gottlieb relied almost entirely on the opinion of Sexual Assault Nurse Examiner ("SANE nurse") Tara Levicy, who firmly believed that Mangum had been sexually assaulted. Remarkably, neither Gottlieb nor anyone else from either the Durham Police Department or the County Prosecutor's office ever interviewed Dr. Julie Manly, who had examined Mangum at Duke Hospital after she claimed she was raped.[5] Had a different sergeant with a more critical and unbiased eye headed the investigation, the case might well have been evaluated much differently from the outset.

Even if an overly aggressive police officer is pushing a weak case, charging decisions generally rest with the prosecutor. Often a conscientious prosecutor will decline to issue any charge if that prosecutor doubts that there is sufficient evidence to sustain a conviction. Unluckily for the defendants, the Duke case was not evaluated by an even-handed prosecutor committed to ensuring that the awesome power of the state is not used to convict the innocent.[6] Rather, Durham County District Attorney Mike Nifong took over the investigation of the case because its timing and circumstances presented him with a perfect vehicle to save his faltering election campaign.[7] Unfortunately for the defendants, Nifong used the case to generate an avalanche of local and national publicity that portrayed him as a noble champion of a black victim brutally gang-raped by privileged Duke hooligans.[8] Nifong made the decision to pursue the prosecution without ever having personally interviewed Mangum about her contradictory stories and without any conclusive (or even convincing) medical or physical evidence corroborating her claims. Moreover, he recklessly charged the defendants despite the existence of exculpatory DNA evidence and the serious problems Mangum had in identifying any of her supposed assailants. Fi-

---

5. TAYLOR & JOHNSON, *supra* note 2, at 47, 349.

6. *See* Bruce Green, *Why Should Prosecutors "Seek Justice,"* 26 FORDHAM URB. L.J. 609, 634–35 (1999) (sketching the historical development of the prosecutor's duty to seek or to do justice). For a thorough discussion of District Attorney Mike Nifong's failure to do justice in the Duke case, see Robert P. Mosteller, *The Duke Lacrosse Case, Innocence, and False Identifications: A Fundamental Failure to "Do Justice,"* 76 FORDHAM L. REV. 1337 (2007).

7. Mosteller, *supra* note 6, at 20–24; Amended Findings of Fact, Conclusions of Law, and Order of Discipline at paras. 4, 11, 12, N.C. State Bar v. Michael B. Nifong, No. 06 DHC 35 (Disciplinary Hearing Comm'n July 11, 2007) [hereinafter Amended Order of Discipline].

8. Amended Order of Discipline, *supra* note 7, at paras. 19–40. During the week of March 27, 2006, Nifong gave fifty to seventy interviews and devoted more than forty hours to reporters. John Stevenson, *DA Halting Interviews Until Update*, THE HERALD-SUN (Durham, N.C.), Apr. 4, 2006, at A1.

nally, Nifong marched forward and issued charges while refusing even to consider defense counsels' offers to show him evidence supporting their clients' innocence. Unquestionably, Nifong's upcoming election colored his decision-making. Had the case come to the prosecutor's office postelection, it is highly unlikely that it would have been handled in the same way.

Nonetheless, once Nifong unleashed the media monster, it was virtually impossible for him to rein it in. As the rally at North Carolina Central University on April 11 made abundantly clear, given the strong sentiments evoked by this case, if Nifong did not charge some Duke players he would lose the black vote—and the election.[9] Accordingly, Nifong saw to it that the grand jury indicted three players: Seligmann, Finnerty, and, later, David Evans. Unluckily for them, Mangum had picked them out of a photo lineup at a highly suggestive identification event staged on April 14. Given the discrepancies between her initial descriptions of her attackers and the features of Seligmann, Finnerty, and Evans, it appears that her selection of these three players was totally random. Indeed, any of the forty-six white lacrosse players could have been identified as the assailants because this flawed identification procedure was like a "multiple-choice test with no wrong answer."[10]

In other respects, however, Finnerty, Seligmann, and Evans were extremely lucky. They were lucky that their parents had the financial means to retain private counsel to represent them. They were even more fortunate that their parents chose excellent lawyers with the talent, experience, and commitment that ultimately would enable them to get all of the charges lodged against their clients dismissed.

This chapter examines the superb work of the legal teams that defended Finnerty, Seligmann, and Evans. Unquestionably, the defense of this case was enormously expensive and involved thousands of hours of legal work.[11] Equally important to this successful defense was the excellent investigative and expert assistance provided to the defense lawyers. Given the manner in which this case unfolded, there is little doubt that but for the Herculean efforts of the defense teams, this case would have likely gone to trial. Although that trial may not have resulted in criminal convictions, certainly it would have inflicted more

---

9. Taylor & Johnson, *supra* note 2, at 154, 168–71.

10. *See* Gary L. Wells, *Eyewitness Identification: Systemic Reforms*, 2006 Wis. L. Rev. 615, 623 (condemning lineups that use only suspects, no fillers, and comparing it to a flawed multiple-choice test). For a complete discussion of the outrageous identification procedures used in this case, see *infra* Chapter Thirteen (Wells, Cutler & Hasel).

11. Taylor & Johnson, *supra* note 2, at 189. Reade Seligmann's family, for example, paid about $90,000 a month in legal fees with a total bill of well over one-million dollars.

pain on all of those swept up in this tragedy and further traumatized an already divided community.

In the end, the Duke players were lucky because their parents were wealthy enough to retain excellent lawyers who could ensure that the adversarial system worked. The defendants had to endure a miserable and stressful ordeal, but the story ended happily for them. Reade Seligmann was right, though. Had he and his teammates been indigent or even middle class, this case may well have come out quite differently. As the Duke lacrosse case dramatically illustrates, justice in America does not come cheap. And, sadly, for too many poor defendants, it never comes at all.

The Defense Lawyers: The Early Stages

Initially, the players were advised by Duke's Dean of Students, Sue Wasiolek, that they did not need lawyers because the rape claim was not credible and if they just cooperated with the police, it would "go away."[12] After their house was searched, however, Finnerty, Evans, and Zash met with their coach, Mike Pressler and Assistant Athletic Director Chris Kennedy, who told them that even though the rape allegations were not viewed as credible, they would need representation. Kennedy recommended that they contact Attorney Wes Covington, a Durham lawyer who had handled some legal problems for the athletic department in the past.[13] On March 18, Covington met with the team's cocaptains and assured them that he could make the "problem go away."[14]

Covington spoke later that morning by phone to David Evans's parents and reiterated that the players did not need lawyers at this point because that would signal guilt to the police. His friends in the Durham Police Department assured him that if the players cooperated fully with the police everything would be fine. Covington delivered the same message to another player's father, Bruce Thompson, explaining that he was serving as the unofficial legal advisor to all the players. According to Covington, the accuser's story was not credible and his friend in the department would be able to "get this swept under the rug."[15]

---

12. *Id.* at 37.
13. *Id.* at 45.
14. *Id.* at 45–46.
15. *Id.* at 46.

Of course, Covington was wrong. Although the police at Duke Hospital may not have believed Mangum's story, Sergeant Gottlieb apparently did. Undeterred by the numerous inconsistencies in Mangum's story, by Kim Roberts's statement that the rape allegation was a "crock," or by Mangum's inability to identify her attackers, Gottlieb pressed forward. On March 21, Gottlieb met with SANE nurse Levicy, who advised him that Mangum had been raped and that her injuries were consistent with a sexual assault.[16] At that point, presumably satisfied that something had happened at the party and that DNA would supply the critical evidence, Gottlieb and Detective Benjamin Himan arranged to have all forty-six of the white lacrosse players come to the police station. Their plan was to get detailed statements from the players and pressure them into providing photos and DNA samples.[17]

Unimpressed by Wes Covington and his strategy to have all of the forty-six players freely submit to police interviews, the father of one of the players contacted Bill Thomas, one of Durham's leading criminal-defense lawyers.[18] Shortly thereafter, Dan Flannery contacted Attorney Bob Ekstrand who, with his wife and law partner Samantha, took steps to alert all of the players to the danger of cooperating with the police before taking the time to talk with their parents and consult with counsel. Ekstrand sensed — accurately, as it turned out — that given Gottlieb's involvement in the case, the tenor of the first news story about a gang-rape involving Duke players, and the seriousness of the allegations, Covington's strategy was fraught with danger for the players.[19] At the urging of another player's father, Washington, D.C., attorney Larry Lamade, Covington reluctantly had his assistant call the Durham police asking that the scheduled interviews be postponed for eight days.

The police and the prosecution reacted swiftly and aggressively to the requested delay. They drafted an application for a Nontestimonial Identification Order (NTO) that would require all forty-six white lacrosse players to provide DNA swabs and photos.[20] Once the sensational NTO application was released on March 23 and the media focused on the gang-rape allegations, the case could no longer quietly disappear. Indeed, the ensuing onslaught of publicity, much of it fueled by Mike Nifong, guaranteed that all subsequent decisions regarding the case would be subject to extensive publicity and heightened pub-

---

16. *Id.* at 47.

17. *Id.*

18. *Id.* at 48.

19. *Id.* at 50–56.

20. *See* N.C. Gen. Stat §§ 15A-271 to -282 (2007) (setting forth the procedures and limits of such an order).

lic scrutiny.[21] Moreover, the racial and class aspects of the case multiplied the media's interest in it exponentially. Wisely, the players and their families recognized that they would need the assistance of highly skilled counsel.

Amazingly, the players were criticized publicly and privately for retaining counsel. Duke Vice President Tallman Trask III told the lacrosse players' parents when he met with them on March 25 that everything would have worked out had the players not consulted with attorneys and simply cooperated with the police.[22] Additionally, some members of the Duke faculty denounced the players and demanded that they be ordered to speak with the police.[23] The press joined in on the attack, claiming that the players' silence was "sickening."[24]

Mike Nifong enthusiastically led the charge. In blatant violation of professional rules governing pretrial publicity,[25] Nifong blasted team members for refusing to cooperate or make statements to the police.[26] Additionally, he ridiculed the players for consulting with counsel, complaining that "one would wonder why one needs an attorney if one was not charged and had not done anything wrong."[27] And he improperly criticized players for a "stonewall of silence" that he speculated was "as a result of advice with counsel."[28] Finally, he mocked the players by saying that their "daddies" would buy them expensive lawyers.[29]

Although the players were savaged in the press and subjected to a barrage of criticism on campus, including noisy protests that drove the captains from their house at 610 N. Buchanan, the Ekstrands' strategy at the beginning was absolutely sound. In contrast to Covington, the Ekstrands recognized the folly of allowing the players to submit to potentially damaging police interrogations—regardless of their innocence—without first being thoroughly interviewed

---

21. For a critical assessment of Nifong's public comments, see Amended Bar Complaint, N.C. State Bar v. Michael B. Nifong, No. 06 DHC 35, Jan. 24, 2007 [hereinafter Amended Nifong Bar Complaint].

22. Taylor & Johnson, *supra* note 2, at 69.

23. *Id.* at 63.

24. *See, e.g.*, Ruth Sheehan, *Team's Silence Is Sickening*, News & Observer (Raleigh, N.C.), Mar. 27, 2006, at B1.

25. *See* N.C. State Bar Revised Rules of Professional Conduct 3.6(a) & 3.8(f) (2003). For a full discussion of the ethical issues in the case, *see infra* Chapter Eleven (Williams).

26. Amended Order of Discipline, *supra* note 7, at paras. 18–24.

27. *Id.* at para. 24.

28. *Id.* at paras. 18, 22.

29. Sal Ruibal, *Assault Scandal Highlights Divide for Durham, Duke*, USA Today, Mar. 30, 2006, at 9C.

by counsel. They began to question the players in an effort to get a complete and accurate picture of what had occurred that night. As they learned more about the party and its aftermath, especially in light of allegations set forth in the NTO application, they recognized that some players were at greater risk than others and would need separate counsel.[30] Wisely—and again in contrast to Covington—they quickly began to gather evidence that would support the players' recollections of the critical events. Defense lawyers often are not involved in a case until months or even years after the alleged crime, greatly complicating efforts to reconstruct what actually occurred. Here, with memories relatively fresh, the Ekstrands wisely got a jump-start on building alibis and uncovering evidence that would ultimately contradict Mangum's claims.

On the other hand, Bob Ekstrand was not in a very good position to respond to the media's intense criticism of the players. Not only was he trying to gather evidence to support the players' story of innocence, but he was also dealing with a large number of players—all of whom were potential defendants—and their concerned parents. As a result, he attempted to enlist the support of the Duke administration on behalf its embattled students. On March 27, convinced of the players' innocence, Ekstrand offered to meet with Duke President Richard Brodhead or his designee to present the evidence that he had already accumulated pointing to the players' innocence. Brodhead, however, declined the invitation.[31]

Perhaps even more importantly, Bob Ekstrand met with Mike Nifong on March 27 to urge him to wait for the results of the DNA tests before taking action. This was the first of a series of meetings defense lawyers would have—or seek to have—with Nifong in an effort to convince him that no sexual assault of any kind had occurred at 610 N. Buchanan. Nifong rebuffed Ekstrand, saying they had nothing to talk about unless Ekstrand was prepared to say who committed the rape. Nifong ended the meeting threatening to prosecute anyone who was at the party as an aider and abettor.[32]

Trying to Stop a Train Wreck

It was not Bob Ekstrand but Coach Mike Pressler who was able to arrange a meeting between President Brodhead and the four captains in order to give

---

30. Taylor & Johnson, *supra* note 2, at 61.

31. *Id.* at 85–86.

32. *Id.*

the players a chance to convince Brodhead of their innocence. At that March 28 meeting, Brodhead urged the players to issue a public statement professing their innocence. In view of the unrelenting media attack on the players, perhaps Bob Ekstrand should have had the players issue such a statement sooner. Nonetheless, he helped draft a statement issued later that day by Duke, which represented the players' first public denial of the rape allegations.[33]

Later on March 28, Dave Evans would meet with Attorney Joe Cheshire and his partner, Brad Bannon, who would become Evans's lawyers. Cheshire, the founding partner of the Raleigh firm of Cheshire, Parker, Schneider, Bryan, and Vitale, was one of the most prominent lawyers in North Carolina and a member of the American College of Trial Lawyers. He also had been President of the North Carolina Academy of Trial Lawyers and had founded that organization's Criminal Law Section. Additionally, Cheshire was the Chair of the North Carolina Indigent Defense Services Committee.

After a lengthy interview, Cheshire and Bannon were completely convinced that Evans was telling the truth.[34] The next day, Cheshire sought to meet with Nifong to show him evidence of his client's innocence. Nifong refused to meet unless, he said, Cheshire's client wished to be charged.[35] Remarkably, Nifong declined to meet even though at this point he had neither DNA results nor any other scientific evidence that supported Mangum's rape allegation.

At that point, Cheshire and Bannon sent a letter to the North Carolina Bar complaining of Nifong's improper media attacks on the Duke players. Albeit unusual, it was a masterful tactical move on their part. It was unusual because defense lawyers rarely risk the wrath of a prosecutor by filing such a grievance.[36] Defense lawyers also are reluctant to file grievances because state bars are generally unwilling to get involved in a pending case.[37] In the end, because state bars rarely discipline prosecutors, the cost to defense counsel of filing a

---

33. *Id.* at 93.

34. *Id.* at 94–95.

35. *Id.* at 97.

36. Numerous commentators have observed that defense lawyers seldom file such complaints for fear of hurting their client or negatively affecting their ability to defend other clients. *See, e.g.,* Fred C. Zacharias, *The Professional Discipline of Prosecutors*, 79 N.C. L. Rev. 722, 749, 758 (2001); Richard A. Rosen, *Disciplinary Sanctions Against Prosecutors for Brady Violations: A Paper Tiger*, 65 N.C. L. Rev. 693, 735 (1987); Robert P. Mosteller, *Exculpatory Evidence, Ethics, and the Road to the Disbarment of Mike Nifong: The Critical Importance of Full Open-File Discovery*, 15 Geo. Mason L. Rev. 257, 259 (2008).

37. Zacharias, *supra* note 37, at 749 n.100, 758–79; *see also* Transcript of the Disciplinary Hearing Committee at 21, N.C. State Bar v. Nifong, No. 06 DHC 35 (June 16, 2007) (statement of F. Lane Williamson) (describing how the Hearing Committee Panel Chair

bar complaint is usually prohibitive.[38] In this instance, however, Cheshire's stature and the flagrancy of Nifong's comments prompted Cheshire to go forward. Ultimately, the intervention of the State Bar proved critical to the defense's success.

The defense lawyers also went on the offensive in the press. Cheshire called a press conference on March 30, boldly announcing that DNA would show that the rape allegations were false. Defense lawyers representing Bret Thompson, Matt Zash, and Dan Flannery made similar public pronouncements.[39]

For the next two weeks, the defense lawyers released photos and other information casting doubt on the accuser's story and demonstrating their clients' innocence. Behind the scenes, they repeatedly tried to dissuade Nifong from charging any of the players. Once again, they offered to meet with him to present evidence that demonstrated their clients' innocence, but Nifong inexplicably turned them down. On April 4, Nifong did meet with Bill Thomas, who warned him to slow down and investigate the case more thoroughly. Nifong assured Thomas that he had interviewed the victim and found her convincing.[40] Similarly, on April 14, Thomas, Butch Williams (who represented Dan Flannery), and Wade Smith went to see Nifong.

Wade Smith, who subsequently would become Collin Finnerty's lawyer, did not represent anyone at the time of this meeting. The other defense lawyers hoped that Smith, given his stellar reputation, might be able to get through to Nifong, who appeared hell-bent on charging some players despite the lack of DNA evidence and the other problems with his case. Once again, the three lawyers urged Nifong not to rush to an indictment on April 17 in order to allow them time to present him with all of the evidence they had gathered to corroborate what the DNA showed—that no rape had occurred. Nifong's curt response was astonishing: "I know a lot more about this case than you do. Thank you for coming down."[41]

---

noted the controversial and unprecedented nature of the decision of the Bar Grievance Committee to file disciplinary charges during the pendency of a case).

38. *See* Rosen, *supra* note 36, at 735. In North Carolina, for example, "[i]n four decades of disciplining lawyers, the State Bar has punished only two prosecutors for withholding evidence. Both were put on a form of probation in which they could continue to practice law as long as they broke no more laws and consulted with a mentor." Joseph Neff, *False Actions Charged in Trial*, NEWS & OBSERVER (Raleigh, N.C.), Apr. 9, 2004, at A1.

39. TAYLOR & JOHNSON, *supra* note 2, at 98.

40. *Id.* at 159. Nifong had not, however, interviewed Mangum at this point. Amended Order of Discipline, *supra* note 7, at para. 14.

41. TAYLOR & JOHNSON, *supra* note 2, at 175.

The Players Are Indicted and the Defense Does Not Rest

Unable to dissuade Nifong from proceeding, the Duke players and their families had to wait until April 17 to see who would actually be charged. When Reade Seligmann was indicted, his family retained Kirk Osborn, a well-regarded Chapel Hill lawyer who had formerly worked as a public defender. As soon as they were able to arrange their client's bail, Osborn and Seligmann's first lawyer, Julian Mack, went to Nifong's office to show him their strong alibi evidence; Nifong refused to see them.[42]

Collin Finnerty also was indicted on April 17. Finnerty's family chose Wade Smith to represent them. Smith, a fellow of the American College of Trial Lawyers, had been selected as the top criminal litigator in North Carolina in 2004.[43] Senior partner in the Raleigh firm of Tharrington Smith, LLP, Smith is so highly regarded in North Carolina that in November 2006—in the midst of his involvement in this controversial case—the North Carolina Supreme Court appointed him to the North Carolina Innocence Commission.

Not surprisingly, as this was a case involving multiple experienced and outstanding defense lawyers, not all of them agreed with one another on the optimum tactics to pursue as events unfolded. For example, on May 1, Kirk Osborn and co-counsel Buddy Connor filed six motions on behalf of Seligmann, including a motion to recuse Nifong.[44] In that motion, Osborn accused Nifong of prosecutorial misconduct so egregious that it warranted Nifong's removal from the case. Additionally, Osborn attached detailed material supporting Seligmann's alibi, claiming that it showed Nifong's willingness to prosecute the innocent to further his "personal vested interest in getting elected."[45]

Wade Smith took a different approach. Although Finnerty also had a very compelling alibi supported by solid documentary evidence and the testimony of all of the players at the party, Smith elected not to make this evidence public. He reasoned that Nifong's refusal even to consider Seligmann's alibi strongly suggested that Nifong intended to push ahead regardless of what any of the

---

42. *See* Benjamin Niolet & Michael Biesecker, *D.A.: I Haven't Heard Accuser's Account*, News & Observer (Raleigh, N.C.), Oct. 28, 2006, at 12A.

43. *Business North Carolina "Legal Elite" Winners Directed Duke Lacrosse Defense*, Carolina Newswire, Jan. 2, 2008.

44. Taylor & Johnson, *supra* note 2, at 199.

45. *Id.*

defense lawyers showed him.[46] More importantly, Smith feared that if he revealed Finnerty's alibi prematurely, Nifong and his officers would modify Mangum's story in order to circumvent it.[47] As it turned out, Smith's fears were well grounded. Both Gottlieb's thirty-three-page memorandum, *Supplemental Case Notes for Sergeant M.D. Gottlieb*, and Nifong's investigator Linwood Wilson's December 21, 2006, interview with Mangum, represented flagrant attempts to revise Mangum's story to account for both the defense's evidence and the lack of incriminating DNA evidence.[48]

Nonetheless, all of the defense lawyers were unwavering in their belief that no rape had occurred and that the allegations against the players were totally unfounded. Moreover, despite differences in style, the defense teams cooperated fully and enthusiastically. United in their resolve to vindicate the players, they divided up certain tasks so as to allow specific lawyers to concentrate on areas that required particular attention.[49]

All of the defense teams continued to approach Nifong at different times in an effort to persuade him to consider the evidence they had marshaled pointing to the players' innocence. Fearing that his client, Dave Evans, was about to be indicted, Cheshire contacted Nifong on the weekend of May 7 and 8, offering to present Nifong evidence exonerating Evans.[50] Mangum had picked Evans out on April 4 "with about 90 percent certainty," but qualified her identification by saying "he looks just like him without a moustache."[51] Cheshire offered to prove to Nifong that Evans never had a moustache and to allow Nifong to interview him. Finally, he advised Nifong that he would show him the results of a polygraph test that Evans had passed. Nifong once again refused Cheshire's offer to meet.[52]

The magnitude of the case dictated that a multiple-lawyer defense team represent each of the indicted lacrosse players. Wade Smith was joined by firm members Bill Cotter, Doug Kingsbury, and Melissa Hill. Joe Cheshire and partner Brad Bannon defended Dave Evans. Kirk Osborn and Buddy Conners rep-

---

46. Telephone Interview with Wade Smith, cofounder of Tharrington Smith Law Firm, in Columbia, Miss. (Jan. 11, 2008) [hereinafter *Smith Interview*].

47. *Id.*

48. For a detailed analysis of the extent to which these belated attempts to fix Mangum's story differs from her early accounts, see TAYLOR & JOHNSON, *supra* note 2, at 260–63, 313–16.

49. *Smith Interview*, *supra* note 46.

50. TAYLOR & JOHNSON, *supra* note 2, at 219.

51. *Id.*

52. *Id.*

resented Reade Seligmann at first, and later Jim Cooney III a senior partner in North Carolina's largest law firm, took over as his lead counsel.[53]

Reade Seligmann's parents added Cooney to their son's defense team in part because they thought that Nifong might respond more favorably to a new defense voice.[54] In some cases, certainly, a prosecutor can be persuaded to back away from an entrenched position and take a fresh look at a case simply by hearing from a new advocate.[55] Prior to meeting with Nifong on December 5, Cooney made the conciliatory gesture of withdrawing Osborn's contentious motion to recuse Nifong. Despite this, Nifong would not budge. Rejecting Cooney's offer to open his entire file to Nifong and allow Nifong to interview Seligmann himself, Nifong responded that there was "nothing you could show me that will change my mind."[56] Nifong vowed to go forward as long as Mangum wanted to proceed.[57]

The case, ultimately, would not go forward as Nifong planned. In large part, the prosecution's case was derailed as a result of effective lawyering by the defense. From the outset, the defense lawyers had filed numerous motions demanding that Nifong provide them with evidence required to be disclosed under North Carolina's relatively new discovery provisions.[58] Despite the statutory mandate, Nifong did not readily provide the defense all of the information to which they were entitled. Rather, Nifong consistently released incomplete information to the defense and only did so at scheduled court appearances. Upon reviewing each installment of new material, the defense would discover that relevant information was still missing. For example, the documents would show that a meeting occurred between Sergeant Gottlieb and Mangum, but no report reflected what occurred at the meeting. The defense would then have to file a motion detailing the additional information they were seeking. According to Smith, the defense spent considerable time and energy trying to get Nifong to disgorge relevant information.[59]

---

53. Cooney's firm, Womble, Carlyle, Sandridge & Rice is based in Charlotte and has 530 lawyers in eleven offices. Cooney also was a fellow in the American College of Trial Lawyers.

54. TAYLOR & JOHNSON, *supra* note 2, at 285–86.

55. For a look at the many variables that affect the plea-bargaining process and influence defense counsel's negotiation strategy in a particular case, see Rodney J. Uphoff, *The Criminal Defense Lawyer as Effective Negotiator: A Systemic Approach*, 2 CLINICAL L. REV. 73 (1995).

56. TAYLOR & JOHNSON, *supra* note 2, at 301.

57. *Id.*

58. For an excellent discussion of discovery reform in criminal cases in North Carolina and the importance of the defense lawyer's effective use of those discovery provisions in the Duke case, *see* Mosteller, *supra* note 36.

59. *Smith Interview*, *supra* note 46.

The most dramatic example of Nifong's attempt to prevent the defense from gaining access to relevant information was his blatant attempt to suppress the exculpatory DNA results. First, he and Dr. Brian Meehan agreed that Meehan would prepare a report that only included certain "positive results" but would not include other test results that were potentially exculpatory.[60] Second, although Dr. Meehan's May 12 report intentionally omitted the potentially exculpatory material, Nifong represented to the court and to counsel that he was "not aware of any additional material or information which may be exculpatory in nature with respect to the defendant."[61] Third, Nifong aggressively resisted defense efforts to require him to turn over all of the underlying data and information on which Meehan relied, and he continued to make misrepresentations to cover up his efforts to hide exculpatory material.[62]

Nifong may well have been successful had it not been for the defense lawyers' persistence. As the North Carolina Bar's Amended Order of Discipline details, the defense filed a series of discovery requests followed up by motions to compel when Nifong would falsely state he had already turned over everything he had.[63] Ultimately, Judge Osmund Smith ordered that the complete file and all underlying data regarding the case from the two DNA labs be turned over to the defense. On October 27, 2006, Nifong provided the defense with 1,844 pages of data and documents. At no point, however, did Nifong ever provide the defense with a complete report of all examinations and tests Meehan had performed or any report memorializing Meehan's oral statements to him about the exculpatory results.[64]

Nifong undoubtedly hoped that the defense would not find the proverbial smoking gun in the mass of complicated scientific material he turned over. In most cases, Nifong's scheme would have worked. Most lawyers would have taken at face value the prosecutor's unequivocal representations that the testing yielded nothing exculpatory. Few lawyers would have been able to devote the time—or would have had the background—to digest nearly two-thou-

---

60. Amended Order of Discipline, *supra* note 7, at paras. 61–70. Although Meehan testified at the December 15, 2006, hearing on the defendants' motion regarding exculpatory evidence that he and Nifong had agreed not to report all the results, he would later claim that he omitted the exculpatory results because his May 12 report was only an interim report. *See* Mosteller, *supra* note 36, at 301 n.250.

61. Amended Order of Discipline, *supra* note 7, at para. 70.

62. *Id.* ¶¶ 71–75. For a detailed look at the DNA issues, see *infra* Chapter Fourteen (Gianelli).

63. Amended Order of Discipline, *supra* note 7, at paras. 77–80.

64. *Id.* at para. 104.

sand pages of complex material.[65] Moreover, few lawyers would have access to experts to help them craft their discovery requests[66] and to confirm their analysis of the DNA documents.[67]

Thus, it was a combination of North Carolina's open-discovery provisions, the assistance of experts, the defense lawyers' excellent motion practice, and the lawyers' sheer persistence that enabled the defendants to uncover powerful exculpatory evidence that eventually forced Nifong to resign from the case and led the Attorney General to dismiss the rape charges. The defense also used their motion to suppress Mangum's identifications of the defendants as a vehicle to lay out for the judge—and the public—the contradictions in Mangum's statements and the flawed process used to secure the identifications. The use of pretrial motions to educate the judge and the community at large, including prospective jurors, is a commonly employed tactic. All of the defense teams in the case effectively used their motions to widely disseminate information that demonstrated problems with the prosecution's case and supported their clients' innocence.[68]

The defense lawyers put a staggering amount of time into the case. Wade Smith said that the case "consumed him" and his team.[69] Smith essentially did not work on anything except this case from April 2006 until April 2007.[70] The other defense lawyers representing the other two defendants also worked exclusively, or almost exclusively, on the case. Not surprisingly, the defendants' legal bills were astronomical; estimates of the total legal fees range from $3 million to over $5 million.[71]

For the lay public, and for many lawyers as well, it is difficult to imagine that a relatively simple rape prosecution could be so costly and labor-inten-

---

65. Brad Bannon testified that he spent sixty to one-hundred hours just learning the basics of DNA analysis so that he could understand the significance of the fact that Evans's DNA was found on one of Mangum's fake fingernails. *See* Amended Order of Discipline, *supra* note 7, at para. 93. Additionally, Bannon then spent many hours analyzing the almost 2,000 pages of data before stumbling across the exculpatory material. Mosteller, *supra* note 6, at 37.

66. TAYLOR & JOHNSON, *supra* note 2, at 279–80.

67. *Id.* at 302 (describing Bannon's meeting with lawyers at Williams & Connolly and a top DNA expert Hal Deadman).

68. *Id.* at 269–70.

69. *Smith Interview, supra* note 46.

70. *Id.*

71. *See* TAYLOR & JOHNSON, *supra* note 2 (suggesting legal fees in excess of five-million dollars); Jeff Barker, *"Players" Parents Ask Duke to Pay Legal Fees,* THE BALTIMORE SUN, Apr. 11, 2007, at 1E (reporting that the legal fees were "as high as $3 million").

sive. This case, however, was no ordinary rape case. It was a media spectacle that imposed incredible demands on the lawyers caught up in the frenzy. Once Nifong opened the media floodgates, the defense could not afford to just sit back and watch their clients be castigated. They fought back in the press and attempted, as best they could, to counter the negative image of the players and presumption of guilt that permeated most of the news stories.[72]

Simply coping with the media, especially in a case that captured national—and even international—attention, imposed considerable time demands on each defense team. Wade Smith was "bombarded" by the press and devoted an enormous amount of time to interacting with the media.[73] The extraordinary media coverage also required the defense to spend many hours with the clients and their families formulating responses to the latest developments and trying to keep them, if not out of the spotlight, at least on message. Once again, differences in lawyering styles translated into slightly different approaches to dealing with the press. Joe Cheshire, for instance, held a number of press conferences; Smith did not. The defense lawyers also clashed on the wisdom of Dave Evans speaking to the press following his indictment.[74] Cheshire felt strongly that if Evans made a personal statement it would have a "real impact," so he encouraged Evans to speak to the media.[75] Evans did so, and his eloquent, moving statement may indeed have persuaded some that he and his teammates were innocent.[76]

Unquestionably, all of the defense lawyers recognized that the massive publicity engulfing the case would make picking a fair, unbiased jury in Durham exceptionally difficult, if not impossible. Thus, the defense teams spent hundreds of hours monitoring media accounts and collecting news stories in anticipation of a possible change-of-venue motion, as well as in preparation for an effective voir dire regardless of where the trial was held. Moreover, the case generated widespread attention on the internet. Because blogs and internet stories increasingly shape public opinion and potentially affect the attitudes of prospective jurors, defense lawyers also had to monitor—and attempt to turn to their clients' advantage—this relatively new medium.[77]

---

72. For a look at the appropriateness of the defense lawyer's use of the press to reply to prejudicial pretrial publicity, see James R. Devine, *The Duke Lacrosse Matter as Case Study of Rule 3.6(c)'s Right to Reply to Prejudicial Pretrial Extrajudicial Publicity*, 15 VILL. SPORTS & ENT. L.J. (forthcoming 2008).

73. *Smith Interview, supra* note 46.

74. TAYLOR & JOHNSON, *supra* note 2, at 227.

75. *Id.* at 223.

76. *Id.* at 226–27.

77. For a look at the influence of blogs, including comments by Joe Cheshire related to the Duke case, see ABA J., Jan. 2008, at 35–39.

The Pivotal Role of Defense Experts and Investigators

Notwithstanding the fact that the defendants assembled an excellent group of lawyers, they may not have been successful but for their additional ability to retain superb experts and investigators. Each of the defense teams employed a set of investigators focused on gathering facts that would cast doubt on the veracity of Mangum's claim as well as support the players' versions of the events that night. Wade Smith, for example, had three investigators who worked hundreds of hours on the case.[78] Tracking down witnesses and getting them to agree to be interviewed is often challenging for the defense — even more so when the defendants have been vilified as racist hooligans. Yet, investigators were able to locate witnesses to provide information about Mangum's promiscuous activities in the days before March 14, her dancing at a strip club days after the alleged rape, her prior gang-rape accusations, and her high-speed escape from the police in 2002. Clearly, good investigative work put the defense in an excellent position to challenge Mangum's credibility.[79]

Given the importance of DNA evidence in this case, employing DNA experts to advise the defense was also critical. Not only did the defense experts help lawyers better understand the significance of the DNA test results, but they aided the defense in highlighting the exculpatory nature of the absence of the players' DNA in the testing done by the State's experts. Moreover, because of its experts, the defense was well-positioned to blunt any incriminating inference from the fact that David Evans could have been a contributor to the DNA recovered from Mangum's fake fingernail found in a trashcan at 610 N. Buchanan.[80]

Additionally, experts helped the defense lawyers craft discovery requests that identified the data that the defense would need in order to scrutinize the testing done by the prosecution's outside laboratory. Admittedly, once the defense obtained the nearly two-thousand pages of material from the State, Brad Bannon invested an enormous amount of time and energy learning the principles of DNA analysis and studying the data on his own.[81] Nonetheless, Bannon confirmed the validity of his analysis by consulting with Hal Deadman, the former director of the FBI DNA lab.[82] Bannon was then able to produce a pow-

---

78. *Smith Interview*, *supra* note 46.
79. TAYLOR & JOHNSON, *supra* note 2, at 19–20, 35, 153, 166–67.
80. *Id.* at 220–23.
81. *See* Mosteller, *supra* note 6, at 1363–64.
82. TAYLOR & JOHNSON, *supra* note 2, at 302.

erful motion to compel that revealed to the court and the public the extraordinary exculpatory material that Nifong had sought to hide. Unquestionably, had this case gone to trial, the defense would have been able to present devastating expert testimony debunking Mangum's allegations.[83]

Moreover, experts retained by the defense were essential in solidifying the players' alibis. For example, Smith had the bathroom at 610 N. Buchanan thoroughly fingerprinted to support Collin Finnerty's claim that he never had been in there.[84] Smith also had an expert prepared to prove that cell-phone calls Finnerty made during the critical time period took place while he was "on the move" and not at 610 N. Buchanan, further buttressing his alibi.[85] Similarly, other defense experts were prepared to testify to the authenticity of the time-stamping on various digital photos to rebut any claim that the defense had tampered with them.[86]

In preparing their well-crafted motion to suppress Mangum's identifications,[87] the defense drew upon the expertise of two of the nation's most prominent eyewitness-identification researchers: Gary Wells and Elizabeth Loftus.[88] Admittedly, Nifong and Gottlieb sowed the seeds of their own demise by using flawed procedures. Nevertheless, because of their access to top notch experts, the defense lawyers were able to expose the unreliability of Mangum's identifications.[89]

The defense lawyers also retained experts to conduct a phone survey of prospective jurors and to analyze the results in support of their motion for a change of venue. This too was expensive. For the defense lawyers and their clients, however, the expense was worthwhile because they needed to substantiate what they feared—that they would not be able to pick a fair, unbiased jury in Durham. In fact, the survey showed that the enormous publicity surrounding the case had hardened attitudes along racial lines.[90] Thus, it confirmed that some potential jurors were likely to vote guilty no matter what the evidence showed. It is probable, therefore, that if a trial had taken place in Durham, it would have ended in a hung jury.[91]

---

83. For an exhaustive look at the DNA evidence, see *infra* Chapter Fourteen (Gianelli).

84. Taylor & Johnson, *supra* note 2, at 182.

85. *Id.*

86. *Id.*

87. *Smith Interview, supra* note 46.

88. For an article by Wells on this case, see *infra* Chapter Thirteen (Wells, Cutler & Hasel).

89. For an insightful assessment of the "outrageous" identification procedures used by the State on April 4, and a detailed discussion of the defendant's motion to suppress Mangum's identification, see Mosteller, *supra* note 6, at 1376–1403.

90. *Smith Interview, supra* note 46.

91. *Id.* The defense lawyers were convinced that no objective jury in Durham or elsewhere would convict after hearing all of the evidence in the case. They worried, however, that

Fortunately for the defendants—and the badly divided community as well—the case never went to trial. In the end, it was the decision of the North Carolina State Bar to file disciplinary charges against Nifong that made it impossible for him to proceed.[92] By publicly filing the complaint against Nifong, the Bar essentially forced him to withdraw from the case, which he did on January 12, 2007. North Carolina Attorney General Roy Cooper took over the matter and, following a thorough investigation by his office, eventually dismissed all charges against the defendants. That he did so is attributable in large part to the tremendous efforts of the defense in gathering, documenting, and presenting evidence that showed that Seligmann, Finnerty, and Evans were, in fact, innocent.

The Struggle for Justice for Those without Money

Although they had to endure a horrific ordeal, the three Duke lacrosse players were finally vindicated. They were able to establish their innocence primarily because they had outstanding lawyers aided by multiple investigators and experts—at an incredible cost to their parents.[93] Undoubtedly, only a handful of Americans could have afforded to mount such a defense. So where does that leave the vast majority of defendants in the United States who face similarly grave charges?

The answer depends, in short, on the defendant's economic status and the jurisdiction in which he is charged. Indeed, the quality of representation that a defendant will receive in this country varies markedly from jurisdiction to jurisdiction.[94] Most defendants, of course, are indigent.[95] An indigent defendant will be represented by a salaried public defender, a private lawyer under contract to the jurisdiction, or a private lawyer appointed by

---

some in Durham would never vote to acquit, no matter what the evidence showed. *Cf.* TAYLOR & JOHNSON, *supra* note 2, at 98 (noting that Cheshire never thought that a conviction was possible, but did worry about a hung jury).

92. TAYLOR & JOHNSON, *supra* note 2, at 320–21 (noting that the public filing presented Nifong with an unavoidable conflict of interest).

93. *See supra* notes 11, 68–71 and accompanying text.

94. For a detailed look at the uneven defense representation in this country, see Rodney J. Uphoff, *Convicting the Innocent: Aberration or Systemic Problem*, 2006 WIS. L. REV. 739, 744–67, 779–82.

95. Over 80 percent of those accused of a felony in state court are indigent and qualify for counsel at public expense. CAROLINE WOLF HARLOW, U.S. DEP'T OF JUSTICE, BUREAU OF JUSTICE STATISTICS, DEFENSE COUNSEL IN CRIMINAL CASES 1, 5 (2000).

the court, depending on the delivery system used by the charging jurisdiction. Some indigent defendants receive superb representation because their jurisdiction provides adequate defense funding, thereby ensuring that caseloads are not unduly burdensome and that counsel receives the assistance of experts and investigators.[96] In rare cases—for example, attorney Michael Tigar and his team's defense of Terry Nichols in the federal Oklahoma City-bombing case—an indigent defendant may be afforded representation equal to that in the Duke case. For indigent defendants in some jurisdictions, therefore, quality defense work ensures that the adversarial system works as intended and defendants receive the justice to which they are entitled under the Constitution.

In many other jurisdictions, however, the indigent defendant receives a defense lawyer who has neither the time nor the resources to raise any challenge whatsoever to the state's case.[97] This can be the case regardless of which delivery system (or combination of systems) the jurisdiction uses: public defenders, court-appointed lawyers, or contract attorneys. The problem stems from the fundamental fact that a significant number of states provide woefully inadequate funding for indigent-defense services, resulting in crushing caseloads or absurdly inadequate compensation.[98]

Imagine a defendant charged with rape whose contract lawyer is being paid an average of less than $100 per case.[99] Or take, for example, that same defendant represented by an appointed defense lawyer with a cap of $395 to de-

---

96. *See, e.g.*, Terry Brooks & Shubhangi Deoras, *New Frontiers in Public Defense*, 17 CRIM. JUST. 51 (2002) (touting the Bronx defenders, the Georgia Justice Project, and the Neighborhood Defender Services of Harlem as model programs); ABA COMMISSION ON LEGAL AID & INDIGENT DEFENDANTS, GIDEON'S BROKEN PROMISE 37 (2004), http://www.abanct.org/legalservices/selaid/defender/brokenpromises/fullreport.pdf (identifying the Defender Association of Seattle-King County as a program providing quality representation) [hereinafter GIDEON'S BROKEN PROMISE]; Laura Parker, *8 Years in a Louisiana Jail, but He Never Went to Trial*, USA TODAY, Aug. 29, 2005, at A1 (listing Colorado, Massachusetts, Minnesota and Oregon as states with quality defender programs).

97. For a sampling of the many reports, books, and articles decrying the dismal representation afforded defendants in underfunded jurisdictions, see, for example, GIDEON'S BROKEN PROMISE, *supra* note 96; DAVID COLE, NO EQUAL JUSTICE (1998); Norman Lefstein, *In Search of Gideon's Promise: Lessons from England and the Need for Federal Help*, 55 HASTINGS L.J. 835 (2004).

98. For a detailed critique of the extent to which underfunding adversely affects the quality of defense representation regardless of the delivery system employed, see Uphoff, *supra* note 94, at 754–64.

99. In two Oklahoma counties, Woods and Cherokee, contract lawyers were paid a per-case average in fiscal year 2005 of $79.41 and $93.46, respectively. E-mail from Terry Her-

fend the felony.[100] Or envision that defendant represented by a public defender who has at least one serious case set for trial on every trial date from January through August.[101] In each of these instances, the defendant is saddled with counsel who lacks the time or the economic incentive to conduct any factual investigation, much less carefully review the discovery material as Bannon did in the Duke case. Nor is such a defendant likely to benefit from any legal research or motion practice—so pivotal to the success of the Duke defendants. Moreover, counsel rarely will have access to investigators or expert witnesses.[102] Although *Ake v. Oklahoma*[103] recognizes that an indigent defendant is entitled to expert assistance, few defendants actually receive such assistance.[104] In sum, in the many underfunded jurisdictions in this country, most defense lawyers representing most indigent defendants would have been wholly incapable of applying the pressure on Nifong that was needed to uncover the exculpatory material he was hiding.

The vast majority of non-indigent defendants facing rape charges would fare just as badly as, or worse than, their indigent counterparts. Hiring competent defense counsel to handle a rape case generally costs tens of thousands of dollars, and all or most of the fee must be paid up front. On top of this, to retain qualified investigators and experts, lower- and middle-class defendants must pay sizable sums of money out of pocket; few defendants can raise the money needed to hire decent counsel, much less pay for other assistance. Consequently, most defendants who do not qualify for indigent representation are either forced to represent themselves or make do with a lawyer paid a wholly inadequate fee. Unfortunately, defendants who pay an inadequate fee usually get what they have paid for: inadequate representation. In many cases, this means a glorified plea facilitator.[105] Sadly, this leaves an innocent defendant, who desperately needs a good lawyer to establish this fact, totally dependent on the money he or she can raise, or the generosity of a lawyer willing to defend a

---

vey, Non-Capital Trial Division, Okla. Indigent Defendant System (Dec. 28, 2005, 10:50 CST) (on file with author).

100. *See* Spangenberg Group, A Comprehensive Review of Indigent Defense in Virginia 46–47 (2004), http://www.abanet.org/legalservices/downloads/sclaid/ indigent-defense/vareport2004.pdf.

101. *See* State v. Peart, 621 So. 2d 780 (La. 1993) (describing such a horrific schedule).

102. *See, e.g.*, Gideon's broken promise, *supra* note 96, at 10–11, 19.

103. 470 U.S. 68 (1985).

104. *See, e.g.*, The Spangenberg Group, *supra* note 100, at 59–66 (reporting that a lack of experts for indigent defendants is "pervasive and long-standing" in Virginia, and noting that expenditures for experts were made in less than 1 percent of all cases).

105. Uphoff, *supra* note 94, at 763.

client without adequate compensation. Ironically, then, low- and middle-income defendants often receive even worse representation than indigent ones, at least in those jurisdictions that have a good public-defender program or an adequately funded court-appointed-counsel system.[106]

Unlike Reade Seligmann, Collin Finnerty, and David Evans, therefore, the vast majority of non-indigent defendants facing a serious charge—and many indigent ones as well—do not receive the services of a zealous advocate with the time, experience, and resources to mount a vigorous defense. Instead, they are at the mercy of a plea-bargain-driven system of justice that tends to presume those ensnared in the system are guilty, not innocent.[107] Moreover, unlike the Duke players, the vast majority of defendants accused of a serious crime like rape are unable to post bail. Consequently, most such defendants languish in jail until their case is plea bargained or tried—unless of course, the police or the prosecutor come to realize that the defendant was wrongly charged.[108] But, as the Duke lacrosse case dramatically demonstrates, we cannot simply rely on the good faith, professionalism, and investigative efforts of the police and prosecution to ensure that the innocent are filtered out of the system.

Sergeant Mark Gottlieb was not the first law-enforcement officer whose personal animosity toward defendants colored an investigation, nor will he be the last. A significant majority of law-enforcement officers are dedicated to solving crimes and putting the guilty, not the innocent, behind bars. Yet, there are too many instances of police corruption, overreaching, and simply shoddy work to assume wistfully that the police always—or even usually—arrest the right person. Poor pay, too little training, inadequate supervision, and too many cases contribute to police shortcutting. Additionally, too often the police fall prey to the phenomenon of "tunnel vision," which causes them to lock onto a particular suspect or suspects and ignore relevant information that points to their innocence.[109]

Prosecutors can also suffer from tunnel vision. This is not surprising; they rely heavily on the evidence and witnesses brought to them by the police and, thus, may be completely unaware of exculpatory evidence in the police's possession. Of course, prosecutors are supposed to set up procedures to ensure that investigators provide them with all relevant exculpatory material related

---

106. *See id.* at 748–54.

107. *Id.* at 808–09.

108. *Id.*

109. For an excellent discussion of tunnel vision, see Keith A. Findley & Michael S. Scott, *The Multiple Dimensions of Tunnel Vision in Criminal Cases*, 2006 WIS. L. REV. 291.

to a case.[110] Too many of them, however, either ignore or downplay their obligation to uncover and then disclose exculpatory material.[111] Some attempt to bury such evidence in a mass of other material hoping that overworked or inattentive defense counsel will not find it. Even worse, all too often the police or the prosecutors—or both—deliberately withhold important evidence.[112]

Certainly, there are many excellent prosecutors who strive to be the ministers of justice called for by the *ABA Standards*[113] and *Model Rules of Professional Conduct*.[114] Nevertheless, although few prosecutors go to such unethical extremes as Mike Nifong in the Duke lacrosse case, he is not an aberration. A significant number of prosecutors fail to disclose exculpatory evidence, knowingly use highly questionable informant testimony, or grossly exaggerate dubious scientific evidence, all in the name of convicting a defendant whom they believe is guilty.

In the end, police and prosecutors tend to get caught up in the competitive enterprise of ferreting out crime. Given the nature of the competition, it is unrealistic to expect that they will consistently provide a check on themselves. Our adversarial criminal-justice system recognizes this fact and provides defendants a host of rights designed to safeguard the innocent, even at the expense of letting some of the guilty go free.[115] Yet, a defendant's constitutional rights—to the presumption of innocence, to cross-examine the prosecution's witnesses, to call his own witnesses, to benefit from reasonable doubt and, ultimately, to a fair trial—are virtually meaningless without the effective assistance of counsel. For it is defense counsel—through fact investigation, sound motion practice, and adequate trial preparation—who challenges the prosecution's case, thereby exposing its sometimes fatal weaknesses. Without such an advocate, the

---

110. *See* Kyles v. Whitley, 514 U.S. 419, 437 (1995).

111. *See, e.g.,* Ken Armstrong & Steve Mills, *Death Row Justice Derailed*, CHI. TRIB., Nov. 14, 1999, § 1, at 1 (reporting that Illinois prosecutors routinely fail to disclose exculpatory evidence); Mosteller, *supra* note 37, at 14–17 (describing the reasons for prosecution failure to turn over *Brady* material and arguing for the importance of full open discovery).

112. *See, e.g.,* Richard Moran, *The Presence of Malice*, N.Y. TIMES, Aug. 2, 2007, at A17 (indicating that in his study of 124 exonerations, 80 percent of the wrongful convictions resulted from intentional actions by criminal-justice officials, not good-faith mistakes); JAMES S. LIEBMAN ET AL., *A BROKEN SYSTEM: ERROR RATES IN CAPITAL CASES, 1973–1995* (2000) (noting that 17 percent of the reversed cases in their study involved the suppression of exculpatory evidence).

113. *See* ABA STANDARDS FOR CRIMINAL JUSTICE, Pt. 1, § 3-1.1(c) (1993) ("[The] duty of the prosecutor is to seek justice, not merely to convict.")

114. *See* MODEL RULES OF PROF'L CONDUCT R. 3.8 ("The responsibility of the public prosecutor differs from that of the usual advocate; his duty is to seek justice, not merely to convict.").

115. *In re Winship*, 397 U.S. 358, 372 (1970) (Harlan, J., concurring).

adversarial system grinds on largely unchecked and defendants, including those who are innocent, too often are steamrolled in the process.

Conclusion

In dismissing the charges against the Duke lacrosse players, Attorney General Roy Cooper spoke of "the enormous consequences of overreaching by a prosecutor" who had "pushed forward unchecked."[116] He concluded that "[w]hat has been learned here is that the internal checks on a criminal charge—sworn statements, reasonable grounds, proper suspect photo lineups, accurate and fair discovery—are all critically important."[117] Cooper was right; these internal checks are of fundamental importance to our criminal-justice system. But, without a good lawyer who has the time, incentive, and expert and investigative assistance to mount a robust defense, these internal checks provide only limited protection.

Justice was served in the Duke case largely because of the efforts of some outstanding defense lawyers. This is not to say that it is only the rich in this country who receive the benefit of good lawyering. Money does matter but it is not wholly determinative of whether a defendant will receive quality representation. A significant number of indigent defendants who find themselves charged with a serious felony like rape are, in fact, defended by competent lawyers with the time and resources to mount a vigorous defense. Unfortunately, however, a majority of defendants, especially members of the middle class and those charged in underfunded jurisdictions, are not. Unless and until we provide more of our citizens with better access to good lawyers, the promise of equal justice remains only an illusion. For the sake of other innocent defendants, we can and should do better.

---

116. TAYLOR & JOHNSON, *supra* note 2, at 352.
117. *Id.*

CHAPTER ELEVEN

An Examination of the District Attorney's Alleged Unethical Conduct

Kenneth Williams

Introduction

Prosecutors are the most important actors in the criminal-justice system. Their power is awesome. They decide whether to prosecute, whom to prosecute, which crimes to charge, and the number of charges to be brought. Although the grand jury is supposed to be a check on prosecutorial power and discretion, prosecutors tend to control the grand-jury process; the fox is guarding the henhouse.[1] Prosecutors also decide whether to plea-bargain with a defendant, allowing them to have a tremendous influence over the sentences meted out. Indeed, in most states, prosecutors alone have the power to request the death penalty in murder cases. Despite the fact that prosecutorial decisions are sometimes affected by political and other extralegal considerations, the Supreme Court's jurisprudence has rendered much of this decision-making virtually unreviewable.[2] Moreover, although prosecutors are elected officials in most jurisdictions, the public rarely holds them accountable for their decisions. To counterbalance their power, however, prosecutors do face significant ethical and legal constraints. This chapter will explore these responsibilities in the context of the Duke rape case.

The coverage of the Duke case left many with the impression that District Attorney Mike Nifong's actions were an aberration. This impression is not

---

1. *See* William J. Campbell, *Eliminate the Grand Jury*, 64 J. Crim. L. & Criminology 174, 174 (1973).
2. *See* Ashe v. Swenson, 397 U.S. 435, 452 (1970).

borne out by the facts. Although Nifong's behavior was extreme, prosecutor-ial misconduct of the type in which he engaged has become far too common around the country. This chapter will also discuss the systemic problem of prosecutorial misconduct and suggest several solutions on how to alleviate it.

The Ethical and Legal Obligations of Prosecutors

The prosecutor has a unique role in the American criminal-justice system: "The prosecutor is an administrator of justice, an advocate, and an officer of the court.... The duty of the prosecutor is to seek justice, not merely to con-vict."[3] As the Supreme Court put it in *Brady v. Maryland,*

> Society wins not only when the guilty are convicted but when crimi-nal trials are fair: our system of the administration of justice suffers when any accused is treated unfairly. An inscription on the walls of the Department of Justice states the proposition candidly for the fed-eral domain: "The United States wins its point whenever justice is done its citizens in courts."[4]

As a result, the Supreme Court has imposed certain disclosure duties on pros-ecutors.[5] In *Brady*[6] the Court held that the prosecution violates a criminal de-fendant's constitutional rights by failing to disclose exculpatory evidence. Exculpatory evidence is any evidence that is favorable to the defendant, includ-ing that which could be used to impeach government witnesses. The Court has also held that prosecutors have an affirmative obligation to turn over exculpa-tory evidence, even in the absence of a request from the defendant, if it clearly supports a claim of innocence.[7] The Court recently reiterated this duty as follows:

> The State here nevertheless urges, in effect, that "the prosecution can lie and conceal and the prisoner still has the burden to ... discover the evidence." ... A rule thus declaring "prosecutor may hide, defendant

---

3. AM. BAR ASSN'N, STANDARDS RELATING TO THE ADMINISTRATION OF CRIMINAL JUSTICE, PROSECUTION STANDARD §3.1.2(b)–(c) [hereinafter, ABA STANDARDS OF CRIMINAL JUSTICE].

4. Brady v. Maryland, 373 U.S. 83, 87 & n. 2 (1963).

5. No similar disclosure duties have been imposed under the Constitution on defense attorneys. An increasing number of states, however, provide for mutual discovery in crim-inal cases. Gordon Van Kessel, *Adversary Excesses in the American Criminal Trial*, 67 NOTRE DAME L. REV. 403, 485 (1982).

6. *Brady*, 373 U.S. at 87.

7. *See* United States v. Agurs, 427 U.S. 97, 107 (1976).

must seek," is not tenable in a system constitutionally bound to accord defendants due process.[8]

In addition to the constitutional duty to disclose evidence prosecutors, like all lawyers, are governed by the codes of ethical conduct. In North Carolina, for example, lawyers must comply with the North Carolina Rules of Professional Conduct. Prosecutors are subject to discipline for failing to abide by these codes of conduct, including Rules 3.3(a)(1), 3.6, and 3.8. Rule 3.3 states: "A lawyer shall not knowingly ... make a false statement of material fact or law to a tribunal or fail to correct a false statement of material fact or law previously made to the tribunal by the lawyer...."[9]

Rule 3.6 states:

> A lawyer who is participating or has participated in the investigation or litigation of a matter shall not make an extrajudicial statement that the lawyer knows or reasonably should know will be disseminated by means of public communication and will have a substantial likelihood of materially prejudicing an adjudicative proceeding in the matter.[10]

Rule 3.8 is the only rule that applies specifically to prosecutors and provides, in pertinent part:

The prosecutor in a criminal case shall:

   a. refrain from prosecuting a charge that the prosecutor knows is not supported by probable cause;

   b. make reasonable efforts to assure that the accused has been advised of the right to, and the procedure for obtaining, counsel and has been given reasonable opportunity to obtain counsel;

   c. not seek to obtain from an unrepresented accused a waiver of important pretrial rights, such as the right to a preliminary hearing;

   d. after reasonably diligent inquiry, make timely disclosure to the defense of all evidence or information required to be disclosed by applicable law, rules of procedure, or court opinions including all evidence or information known to the prosecutor that tends to negate the guilt of the accused or mitigates the offense, and, in connection with sentencing, disclose to the defense and to the tribunal all unprivileged mitigating information known to the prosecutor, except when the prosecutor is relieved of this responsibility by a protective order of the tribunal;

---

8. Banks v. Dretke, 540 U.S. 668, 696 (2004).
9. N.C. Rules of Prof'l Conduct R. 3.3(a)(1) (2007).
10. *Id.* R. 3.6.

....

g. except for statements that are necessary to inform the public of the nature and extent of the prosecutor's action and that serve a legitimate law enforcement purpose, refrain from making extrajudicial comments that have a substantial likelihood of heightening public condemnation of the accused and exercise reasonable care to prevent investigators, law enforcement personnel, employees or other persons assisting or associated with the prosecutor in a criminal case from making an extrajudicial statement that the prosecutor would be prohibited from making under Rule 3.6 or this Rule.[11]

Unfortunately, despite these clear standards, prosecutorial misconduct is not uncommon. As will be discussed later in this chapter, it occurs with some frequency, for two reasons. First, to prevail in court on a claim of prosecutorial misconduct, a defendant must prove that he was prejudiced by the offensive behavior. That is, he must demonstrate that proper conduct would have produced a different outcome in his case. This is a high burden. The Center for Public Integrity analyzed 11,452 cases in which appellate courts reviewed charges of prosecutorial misconduct.[12] The study revealed that the courts rejected the vast majority of these claims (8,709) on harmless-error grounds, holding that the alleged misconduct did not affect the defendant's substantial rights. Thus, prosecutors know that even if they engage in misconduct in a case, there is minimal likelihood that the conviction will be reversed on such grounds. Second, even though the professional consequences of prosecutorial misconduct are theoretically very serious, the Bar rarely imposes discipline for it. The Center found only forty-four cases since 1970 in which prosecutors faced disciplinary action for engaging in misconduct.[13]

The Unethical and Illegal Conduct of Mike Nifong

In this section, I will apply the legal and ethical standards set forth in the previous section to the behavior of Mike Nifong in the Duke lacrosse rape case.

---

11. *Id.* R. 3.8.

12. *See* Steve Weinberg, Ctr. for Pub. Integrity, Breaking the Rules: Who Suffers When a Prosecutor Is Cited for Misconduct? (2003), http://www.publicintegrity. org/pm/default.aspx?act=main.

13. *Id.*

Clear Violations

Failure to Disclose

Nifong's most egregious ethical lapse was his repeated failure to disclose exculpatory test results to the defendants, as both the U.S. Constitution and the North Carolina Rules of Professional Conduct require.[14] Before indicting the three lacrosse players, Nifong learned that preliminary testing of items from the accuser's rape kit failed to disclose the presence of any semen, blood, or saliva.[15] The accuser had claimed that the players did not wear condoms and that one of them had ejaculated during the encounter.[16] Additional testing of the rape kit was performed. This testing revealed that DNA from up to four different males was present on several items, but that the DNA on these items was inconsistent with the profiles of all the lacrosse players.[17]

Shortly after Nifong learned of the test results favorable to the three players, he received discovery requests asking for witness statements, results of any tests, all DNA analyses, and any other exculpatory information.[18] In response, he asked the director of the DNA lab to prepare a report omitting the test results that revealed the presence of DNA from unidentified males.[19] Nifong provided this falsified report to counsel for the defendants.[20] He was later served with a discovery request specifically asking that any expert witness "prepare, and furnish to the defendant, a report of the results of any (not only the ones about which the expert expects to testify) examinations or tests conducted by the expert."[21] Nifong continued to provide reports excluding the exculpatory test results.[22] In addition, Nifong failed to disclose prior inconsistent statements that the accuser had made to the police.[23]

By withholding exculpatory evidence from the defense, Nifong violated the U.S. Constitution, the laws of North Carolina, and Rule 3.8(d) of the North Carolina Rules of Professional Conduct. Specifically, the State Bar found that

---

14. Amended Findings of Fact, Conclusions of Law, and Order of Discipline paras. (c)(i)–(ii), at 20–21, North Carolina State Bar v. Nifong, No. 06 DHC 35 (Disciplinary Hearing Comm'n Jul. 11, 2007) [hereinafter Amended Nifong Bar Order].

15. *Id.* at para. 36.

16. *Id.* at para. 5.

17. *Id.* at para. 46.

18. *Id.* at para. 53.

19. *Id.* at para. 60.

20. *Id.* at para. 65.

21. *Id.* at para. 67.

22. *Id.* at para. 68.

23. *Id.* at para. 82.

"Nifong did not make timely disclosure to the defense of all evidence or information known to him that tended to negate the guilt of the accused" and that he "failed to make a reasonably diligent effort to comply with a legally proper discovery request."[24]

False Statements to the Court

A lawyer has a duty to be truthful with the court, both when appearing before it and in the documents he files with it. Nifong failed to be truthful on multiple occasions.

The Duke defendants made numerous discovery requests. On one occasion, they requested a report or written statement of the meeting Nifong had with Dr. Brian Meehan of the privately hired DNA-testing lab to discuss the test results.[25] Nifong said in court that, other than what was contained in the written report, all of the communications with Meehan were privileged "work product."[26] When Nifong made these representations to the court, he knew that he had discussed the existence of DNA from multiple unidentified males on the rape-kit items with Meehan on three occasions, and that those conversations were not privileged work product.[27] These were "intentional misrepresentations and intentional false statements of material fact to the court and to opposing counsel"[28] in violation of Rule 3.3. Nifong was ordered at the same hearing to provide the Duke defendants with "results of tests and examinations, or any other matter or evidence obtained during the investigation of the offenses alleged to have been committed by the defendant."[29] At a later hearing following up on this order, the following exchange occurred:

> Judge Smith: So you represent there are no other statements from Dr. Meehan?
>
> Nifong: No other statements. No other statements made to me.[30]

This, of course, was yet another bald-faced lie and an independent Rule 3.3 violation.

The defendants subsequently filed a Motion to Compel Discovery, detailing how they uncovered the existence of DNA from multiple, unidentified males

---

24. *Id.* at paras. (c)(i)–(ii), at 21.
25. *Id.* at para. 77.
26. *Id.* at para. 78.
27. *Id.* at para. 79.
28. *Id.* at para. 80.
29. *Id.* at para. 81.
30. *Id.* at para. 86.

on the rape-kit items and explaining that the prosecution had not previously provided this evidence to them;[31] the motion did not allege any attempt to conceal this evidence.[32] At a hearing in response to the motion, Nifong stated to the court that he was unaware of the existence of DNA from multiple unidentified males on the rape kit items until he received the motion to compel. His exact words were: "The first I heard of this particular situation was when I was served with these reports—this motion on Wednesday of this week."[33] But Meehan had finally had enough. He testified at this hearing that he had informed Nifong of all test results, including those from the rape kit, and that the pair had agreed "not to report on the results of all examinations and tests" that the lab had performed.[34] He proffered his understanding that the results indicating the presence of DNA from multiple unidentified males were not reported because of "privacy concerns."[35] Immediately after the hearing, Nifong fundamentally contradicted the representations he had just made to the court, stating, "[a]nd we were trying to, just as Meehan said, trying to avoid dragging any names through the mud but at the same time his report made it clear that all the information was available if they wanted it and they have every word of it."[36] This was effectively a confession of yet another breach of Rule 3.3.

Because he was not under oath, Nifong cannot be prosecuted for perjury as a result of the intentional misrepresentations that he made to the court and opposing counsel.[37] These misrepresentations, however, were flagrant violations of his ethical duty as a member of the North Carolina Bar.

Prejudicing the Proceeding and Disparaging the Accused

A lawyer participating in the investigation or litigation of a matter must refrain from making public statements that the lawyer has reason to know will have a "substantial likelihood of materially prejudicing an adjudicative proceeding."[38] The commentary to the parallel ABA Model Rule lists topics that or-

---

31. *Id.* at para. 94.
32. *Id.*
33. *Id.* at para. 95.
34. *Id.* at para. 97.
35. *Id.*
36. *Id.* at para. 98.
37. North Carolina defines perjury as "a false statement *under oath*, knowingly, willfully and designedly made in a proceeding, in a court of competent jurisdiction or concerning a matter wherein the affiant is required by law to be sworn as to some matter material to the issue or point in question." State v. Denny, 652 S.E.2d 212, 214 (N.C. 2007) (emphasis added).
38. N.C. RULES OF PROF'L CONDUCT R. 3.6(a).

dinarily will be considered "more likely than not to have a material prejudicial effect on a proceeding."[39] One such topic is "the character, credibility, reputation, or criminal record of a party, suspect in a criminal investigation or witness."[40] In addition, a lawyer may not make any public statements regarding any evidence "that the lawyer knows or reasonably should know is likely to be inadmissible as evidence in a trial."[41]

The rules also prohibit prosecutors from making any public communications that unnecessarily disparage the accused.[42] According to the ABA Report recommending the relevant amendment, it was designed to prohibit "gratuitous comments" by a prosecutor serving only to increase "public opprobrium" toward the accused.[43] The ethical rules, however, do permit a prosecutor to comment about information contained in a public record, such as an indictment.[44]

The rules prohibiting a lawyer from making disparaging, prejudicial public comments aim to preserve the accused's constitutional right to a fair trial. Because the rules limit attorney speech, they have been challenged on First Amendment grounds. The Supreme Court, however, has found these limits constitutional, reasoning that attorneys are officers of the court and as such have an obligation to safeguard the integrity of judicial proceedings.[45]

Instead of following the usual protocol by allowing an assistant district attorney to litigate the case, Nifong decided to handle it personally.[46] He quickly made all manner of public statements that went well outside the public record. For example, the indictments charged the defendants with rape, kidnapping, and committing a sexual offense against the accuser. They were relatively skeletal, containing little besides conclusory statements to that effect. Significantly, nowhere did they claim that the defendants acted out of racial animus.[47]

---

39. MODEL RULES OF PROF'L CONDUCT R. 3.6 cmt. 5.

40. *Id.*

41. *Id.*

42. N.C. RULES OF PROF'L CONDUCT R. 3.8(f).

43. *See* STEPHEN GILLERS & ROY SIMON, REGULATION OF LAWYERS: STATUTES AND STANDARDS 250 (2004).

44. MODEL RULES OF PROF'L CONDUCT R. 3.8 cmt. 5.

45. *See* Gentile v. State Bar of Nev., 501 U.S. 1030, 1075 (1991).

46. Amended Nifong Bar Order, *supra* note 14, at para. 11.

47. In fact, in North Carolina, a stiffer sentence may be imposed for any crime committed because of a victim's race. N.C. GEN. STAT. § 15A-1340.16(d)(17) (2007). Therefore, in the event that Nifong intended to argue that the crimes were motivated by racial hatred, the indictments should have contained such an allegation.

Despite this, Nifong made numerous public statements claiming that the alleged rape was racially motivated. For instance, at various times, Nifong made all of the following comments to television reporters:

> "The circumstances of the rape indicated a deep racial motivation for some of the things that were done. It makes a crime that is by nature one of the most offensive and invasive even more so.... This is not a case of people drinking and it getting out of hand from that. This is something much, much beyond that."[48]
>
> "I don't think you can classify anything about what went on as a prank that got out of hand or drinking that took place by people who are underage.... In this case, where you have the act of rape—essentially a gang rape—is bad enough in and of itself, but when it's made with racial epithets against the victim, I mean, it's just absolutely unconscionable.... The contempt that was shown for the victim, based on her race was totally abhorrent. It adds another layer of reprehensibleness, to a crime that is already reprehensible."[49]
>
> "It is a case that talks about what the community stands for."[50]
>
> "The thing that most of us found so abhorrent, and the reason I decided to take it over myself, was the combination gang-like rape activity accompanied by the racial slurs and general hostility."[51]
>
> "The racial slurs involved are relevant to show the mindset ... involved in this particular attack and obviously, it made what is already an extremely reprehensible act even more reprehensible."[52]

Although Nifong publicly claimed that the rape was motivated by racial hatred, he never sought to have it prosecuted as a hate crime. His public statements were clearly designed, therefore, to prejudice the community against the defendants. He knew that by making the case a referendum on the community's racial sensibilities, most juries in racially diverse Durham would have been inclined to return a guilty verdict—regardless of the facts. Because Nifong's public statements went well beyond what was alleged in the indictment and were designed to deny the defendants a fair trial, he clearly violated his ethical duty under Rule 3.6.[53]

---

48. Amended Nifong Bar Order, *supra* note 14, at para. 23.
49. *Id.* at para. 29.
50. *Id.* at para. 30.
51. *Id.* at para. 31.
52. *Id.* at para. 32.
53. *Id.* at para. (a), at 20.

Possible Violations

Pursuing Charges Not Supported by Probable Cause

The accuser told the police that she had been vaginally, rectally, and orally raped with no condom, with at least some of the alleged perpetrators ejaculating during the assault.[54] Before Nifong sought an indictment he discussed a number of weaknesses in the case with the Durham police officers who had investigated it.[55] They told Nifong that the accuser had made inconsistent statements to the police and changed her story several times, that the other dancer at the party during the alleged attack disputed the accuser's story, that the accuser had already viewed two photo arrays and had not identified any alleged attackers, that the three cocaptains had voluntarily cooperated with police, and that they all denied that the alleged attack had occurred.[56] Nifong also learned that the items from the rape kit contained no semen, blood, or saliva.[57] After being apprised of these serious weaknesses in the case he remarked, "you know, we're f***ed."[58] Nevertheless, he sought and obtained an indictment.

After the indictment, Nifong learned of other huge problems with the case; the lack of DNA evidence being the largest flaw.[59] Nearly as bad, the accuser kept changing her story.[60] Despite all this, Nifong continued to pursue the charges.

Ideally, prosecutors should only bring cases that they can prove beyond a reasonable doubt.[61] Otherwise, they waste resources and unfairly stigmatize defendants who are later acquitted. Rape cases are notoriously difficult to prove, as they rely so heavily on the accuser's credibility. Nifong's remark to the investigators in the case, quoted above, leaves little doubt that he was aware early on that the probability of obtaining a conviction was close to zero. The pertinent ethical rule, however, North Carolina Rule of Professional Conduct 3.8(a), only prohibits prosecutors from pursuing charges that are "not supported by probable cause." Unlike "beyond a reasonable doubt," probable cause is a very low evidentiary standard. It exists as long as there is evidence "sufficient to

---

54. *Id.* at para. 5.

55. *Id.* at para. 14.

56. *Id.*

57. *Id.* at para. 36.

58. *Id.* at para. 15.

59. *Id.* at para. 46.

60. *See* Joseph Neff, *To The End, The Account Continues To Change*, News & Observer (Raleigh, N.C.), Apr. 18, 2007, at A1.

61. *See* John Wesley Hall, Jr., Professional Responsibility of the Criminal Lawyer § 11:12 (2d ed. 1996).

warrant a prudent man in believing that the [suspect] had committed or was committing an offense."[62] The standard does not take into account the relative credibility of witnesses or any defenses that may be raised.[63] Despite the enormous holes in the prosecution's case, there may have been probable cause to pursue the charges—though just barely. Although Crystal Mangum's story vacillated wildly, she steadfastly maintained that she had been raped, and psychological experts report that it is not unusual for the trauma to make a rape victim confused about the details of the experience.[64] In addition, there was some evidence of what might have been an injury to Mangum's vaginal area, and she claimed that she had told her father that she had been raped shortly after the party. As a result, although one can debate whether a prudent prosecutor would truly have pursued this case, it is difficult to claim categorically that Nifong violated this ethical standard.

Intimidating Players Who Remained Silent

The ethical rules prohibit prosecutors from seeking "to obtain from an unrepresented accused a waiver of important pretrial rights." One of the most important pretrial rights is the right to remain silent,[65] and Nifong made numerous public statements criticizing the lacrosse players for not coming forward and speaking to law-enforcement authorities. He even went so far as to threaten to charge some of the other players, who had not come forward with information, with aiding and abetting the alleged crime, stating "[m]y guess is that some of this stonewall of silence that we have seen may tend to crumble once charges start to come out."[66] He told a reporter for the *New York Times*,

> There are three people who went into the bathroom with the young lady, and whether the other people there knew what was going on at the time, they do now and have not come forward. I'm disappointed that no one has been enough of a man to come forward. And if they would have spoken up at the time, this may never have happened.[67]

He told a reporter for CBS News,

---

62. Gerstein v. Pugh, 420 U.S. 103, 111 (1975).

63. *See* H. Richard Uviller, *The Virtuous Prosecutor in Quest of an Ethical Standard: Guidance from the ABA*, 71 MICH. L. REV. 1145, 1156 (1973).

64. *See* Arthur Garrison, *Rape Trauma Syndrome: A Review of a Behavioral Science Theory and Its Admissibility in Criminal Trials*, 23 AM. J. TRIAL ADVOC. 591, 636 (2000).

65. U.S. CONST. amend. V.

66. Amended Nifong Bar Order, *supra* note 14, at paras. 18, 20.

67. *Id.* at para. 19.

The lacrosse team, clearly, has not been fully cooperative [in the investigation].... The university, I believe, has done pretty much everything that they can under the circumstances. They, obviously, don't have a lot of control over whether or not the lacrosse team members actually speak to the police. I think their silence is as a result of advice with counsel; If it's not the way it's been reported, then why are they so unwilling to tell us what, in their words, did take place that night?[68]

He later told a CNN reporter that "[I]t just seems like a shame that they are not willing to violate this seeming sacred sense of loyalty to community."[69] In one of his strongest statements, he said, "I would like to think that somebody [not involved in the attack] has the human decency to call up and say, 'What am I doing covering up for a bunch of hooligans?'"[70]

One can hardly dispute that, through these comments, Nifong was attempting to intimidate the lacrosse players into waiving their constitutional right to remain silent. Under North Carolina Rule of Professional Conduct 3.8(c), however, a prosecutor is only prohibited from seeking waivers from unrepresented individuals. By the time Nifong made these statements, most of the players were either individually or collectively represented by counsel.[71] Moreover, it is unlikely that third-party statements can violate the rule—particularly statements to the general public. Thus, although his behavior was reprehensible, it does not appear that Nifong committed this ethical transgression.

Pursuing Cases for Political Gain

Nifong had recently been appointed as the District Attorney for Durham and was running for reelection when the rape case unfolded; he was involved in a competitive race to retain his job. Durham has a substantial African-American population, and his decision to pursue the case and take the lead role was certainly designed to appeal to the African-American community. This was a case "in which [Nifong's] self-interest collided with a very volatile mix of race, sex and class, a situation that if it were applied in a John Grisham novel would be considered to be perhaps too contrived."[72] The ethical rules do not specifically prohibit a prosecutor from pursuing a case for political gain if—once

---

68. *Id.* at para. 22.
69. *Id.* at para. 35.
70. *Id.* at para. 40.
71. *See generally supra* Chapter Ten (Uphoff).
72. North Carolina State Bar v. Nifong, No. 06 DHC 35, Transcript at 16 (Disciplinary Hearing Comm'n Jul. 16, 2007) (statement of F. Lane Williamson).

again—probable cause exists. Pursuing cases based on political calculations, however, certainly appears to conflict with the prosecutor's overall duty to see that justice is done. Furthermore, it could be in violation of North Carolina Rule of Professional Conduct 8.4(d), which prohibits any lawyer from "engag[ing] in conduct that is prejudicial to the administration of justice." Finally, under some circumstances, blatantly using prosecutorial power for political reasons might amount to selective prosecution, which would be cause for the case to be dismissed.[73]

Employing an Unconstitutional Lineup

Mangum was initially shown two photo arrays that included only Duke lacrosse-team members and was unable to identify any player as her attacker. Under Nifong's direction, she was shown a third photo array.[74] The photographs were shown to her through a PowerPoint presentation,[75] with each projected individually rather than simultaneously.[76] She was shown only the photographs of lacrosse players; the police did not use fillers, that is, photographs of individuals not regarded as suspects.[77] She had been advised that she would be viewing photos of individuals believed to have attended the party.[78] It was only after being shown this suggestive lineup that she identified the three team members as her attackers. The lineup was so suggestive and unreliable that it likely violated the constitutional rights of the accused team members and any conviction would, therefore, likely have been overturned on appeal.[79]

Two ethical rules appear to be on point. The first is Rule 4.4(a),[80] which states, in pertinent part: "In representing a client, a lawyer shall not ... use methods of obtaining evidence that violate the legal rights of [a third] person." If Nifong knew of the lineup techniques being employed by investigators—and there is strong evidence that he not only knew about it, but that he had personally directed them to be employed[81]—he surely was aware that "ev-

---

73. *Cf.* Reno v. Am.-Arab Anti-Discrimination Comm., 525 U.S. 471 (1999) (recognizing the possibility that selective enforcement due to political considerations could render governmental action inappropriate but finding no such problem in this case).

74. *See* Motion to Suppress the Alleged "Identification" of the Defendants by the Accuser, at 9–10, State v. Seligmann, Nos. 06 CRS 4331-36, 5581-83 (N.C. Super. Ct. Dec. 14, 2006).

75. *Id.*

76. *Id.*

77. *Id.*

78. *Id.*

79. *See* Simmons v. United States, 390 U.S. 377, 384 (1968).

80. N.C. Rules of Prof'l Conduct R. 4.4(a) (2007).

81. *See supra* Chapter One (Luck & Seigel), at 11–12.

idence" was being obtained against the Duke defendants in a manner violative of the U.S. Constitution. The second potentially applicable rule is 8.4. A good argument can certainly be made that Nifong's conduct was prejudicial to the "due administration of justice."

No Violations

Failure to Speak to the Accuser

Given the importance of a rape accuser's credibility in obtaining a conviction, one would have expected Nifong to speak with Mangum prior to seeking an indictment. An interview would have allowed him to assess her credibility, evaluate the strengths and weaknesses of the case, and fill any evidentiary gaps in preparation for trial. But Nifong did not interview her. The explanation he put forward was that doing so might have made him a witness in the case.[82] This was a ludicrous claim, and a prosecutor as experienced as Nifong most assuredly knew it. The *ABA Criminal Justice Standards* anticipated this issue by providing that a prosecutor should "avoid interviewing a prospective witness except in the presence of a third person."[83] Thus, although it is true that Nifong should not have interviewed the accuser alone, he could have remedied the problem by bringing a third person, such as a police officer, along with him. Nonetheless, Nifong's failure to interview Mangum did not violate any ethical standard. This general rule makes sense given a typical prosecutor's heavy caseload. It is simply unrealistic to expect a prosecutor to interview every accuser prior to filing charges. In addition, sometimes the physical evidence is so strong that an interview is unnecessary, or the accuser simply refuses to cooperate—which happens most often in the domestic-violence setting.

Failure to Present Exculpatory Evidence to the Grand Jury

Nifong failed to present any of the exculpatory evidence that he had discovered—including Mangum's prior inconsistent statements; the absence of blood, saliva or semen on the rape-kit items; and the other dancer's statement disputing that an assault had occurred at the party—to the grand jury when he sought indictments. Given that a prosecutor's overriding duty is to ensure that

---

82. Benjamin Niolet & Michael Biesecker, *DA: I Haven't Heard Accuser's Account*, News & Observer (Raleigh, N.C.), Oct. 28, 2006, at A12.

83. ABA Standards of Criminal Justice, Prosecution Standard § 3.3.1(g) (2008).

justice is done, it would seem reasonable to impose a corollary duty to present exculpatory evidence so that a grand jury is fully informed before issuing an indictment. The Supreme Court, however, has held that federal prosecutors have no constitutional or common-law duty to present exculpatory evidence to the grand jury.[84] Nor does such a duty exist under North Carolina's law or rules of ethics.[85] The only guidance that the rules provide is to require probable cause, as discussed above.

Prosecutorial Misconduct in the United States

> In my experience, misconduct of the sort Mr. Nifong engaged in is very rare and not at all typical of prosecutors in our state.[86]

There is substantial evidence that, contrary to this assertion by the President of the North Carolina Bar, Nifong's conduct in the Duke case was not an aberration and that prosecutorial misconduct has become a systemic problem, both in North Carolina and nationally.

In North Carolina alone, in less than a ten-year period, courts of appeals have reversed nine death sentences because of the prosecution's failure to disclose exculpatory evidence to the accused. The case of Alan Gell provides an excellent illustration.[87] In 1998, Gell, a high-school dropout, was convicted and sentenced to death for the murder of a retired truck driver. The State had no physical evidence connecting Gell to the murder, but its star witness testified that she saw Gell shoot the victim with a shotgun. The prosecution, however, failed to turn over the tape of a telephone conversation in which this witness said that she "had to make up a story" about the victim's death. The prosecution also contended that Gell killed the victim on April 3, 1995, despite possessing statements from several witnesses indicating that they saw the victim alive after that date. These statements were crucial because Gell had an alibi after

---

84. *See* United States v. Williams, 504 U.S. 36, 54 (1992).

85. *Cf. infra* Chapter Twelve (Seigel) (discussing the North Carolina grand jury procedure).

86. Steven D. Michael, President of the N.C. State Bar, N.C. State Bar Statement on Disciplinary Action Against Michael Nifong (June 16, 2007).

87. The facts that follow are reported in Christina Headrick & Joseph Neff, *Death Row Inmate Granted New Trial*, NEWS & OBSERVER (Raleigh, N.C.), Dec. 10, 2002, at A1.

April 3: he was either in jail for car theft or out of state from April 4 until after April 14, when the victim's body was discovered. Again, the prosecution failed to turn these statements over to the defense; Gell's conviction was overturned because of the prosecution's failure to disclose these pieces of evidence. He was subsequently retried and acquitted.[88]

The case of Jerry Lee Hamilton provides another example of prosecutorial misconduct. Hamilton was sent to death row based on the testimony of his nephew, who claimed that he and Hamilton had taken turns having sex with their victim before stabbing her to death.[89] No physical evidence connected Hamilton to the crime. Before his confession, Hamilton's nephew had written a letter to the prosecution seeking a deal; he was also facing unrelated charges and probation violations at the time. The prosecution failed to turn the letter over to the defense. Hamilton's conviction was overturned because "[Hamilton's nephew's] credibility was not just a major issue in this case, it was essentially the only issue."[90]

Another convicted murderer, Charles Munsey, was released from death row because the prosecutor in his case withheld evidence that the state's main witness, a jailhouse informant, was never an inmate in the prison in which he claimed Munsey confessed to him.[91] And death-row inmate Glenn Edward Chapman had his conviction overturned because the prosecution failed to provide the defense with the statement of a jail inmate who confessed to the crime and the statement of a witness who said he saw another man with the victim on the night of the murder.[92] Lest one think that these cases involved rogue actors, a prosecutor in the attorney general's office testified before the North Carolina Bar under oath that the North Carolina attorney general's office had a policy of withholding from the defense evidence that could impeach a prosecution witness' credibility.[93]

There is every reason to believe that these cases are just the tip of the iceberg. If prosecutorial misconduct occurs with such frequency in high-profile and closely scrutinized death-penalty cases, it is likely occurring even more

---

88. *See* Joseph Neff, *Gell Files Suit Over Prosecution*, NEWS & OBSERVER (Raleigh, N.C.), May 3, 2005, at B1.

89. *See* Alan Gell, *Death Row Doubts*, NEWS & OBSERVER (Raleigh, N.C.), Apr. 27, 2003, at A28.

90. *Id.*

91. *See* Jeff Neff, *N.C. Prosecutors Stifled Evidence*, NEWS & OBSERVER (Raleigh, N.C.), Dec. 19, 2004, at A1.

92. *Id.*

93. *Id.*

frequently in non-death penalty cases. Indeed, it is such a problem in North Carolina that it led the North Carolina State Senate to impose a two-year moratorium on executions while the state's death penalty is examined.[94] The American Bar Association supported this moratorium effort.[95] The issue has also led to other reforms. For instance, North Carolina's legislature created the first innocence commission in the nation[96] to examine claims of actual innocence by individuals alleging that they were wrongfully convicted.[97] North Carolina also enacted a law giving death-row inmates access to the complete case files of prosecutors and police.[98]

The situation is just as grave nationally. The *Chicago Tribune* conducted a nationwide study of prosecutorial misconduct and found that,

> With impunity, prosecutors have violated their oaths and the law, committing the worst kinds of deception in the most serious of cases. They have prosecuted black men, hiding evidence that the real killers were white. They have prosecuted a wife, hiding evidence her husband committed suicide. They have prosecuted parents, hiding evidence their daughter was killed by wild dogs.[99]

The *Tribune* found that at least 381 defendants nationwide have had their homicide convictions thrown out because the prosecutors either concealed evidence suggesting innocence or presented evidence that they knew to be false. Of these 381, sixty-seven had been sentenced to death. The newspaper concluded that these numbers "represent[] only a fraction of how often such cheating occurs."[100] Other studies have confirmed the *Tribune*'s conclusions. For instance, the *Pittsburgh Post-Gazette* conducted a two-year investigation and found that federal prosecutors "lied, hid evidence, distorted facts, engaged in cover-ups, paid for perjury and set up innocent people in a relentless effort to win indictments, guilty pleas and convictions."[101]

---

94. *See* Death Penalty Info. Ctr., *Legislative Activity—North Carolina*, http://www.death-penaltyinfo.org/article.php?did=2217.

95. *Id.*

96. *Id.*

97. *Id.*

98. *Id.*

99. Ken Armstrong & Maurice Possley, *Verdict: Dishonor*, Chi. Trib., Jan. 10, 1999, at 1.

100. *Id.*

101. Bill Moushey, *Win at All Costs*, Pittsburgh Post-Gazette, http://www.post-gazette.com/win/ (last visited Oct. 29, 2008).

The Center for Public Integrity, a nonpartisan organization that conducts investigative research on public-policy issues, analyzed 11,452 cases in which appellate-court judges had reviewed charges of prosecutorial misconduct.[102] The Center found that in 2,012 of these cases individual judges and appellate-court panels cited prosecutorial misconduct as a factor when dismissing charges at trial, reversing convictions, or reducing sentences. In 513 additional cases, an appellate judge, in either a concurring or dissenting opinion, contended that prosecutorial misconduct had occurred. The study also found that "in thousands more cases, judges labeled prosecutorial behavior inappropriate, but allowed the trial to continue or upheld convictions using a doctrine called 'harmless error.'"[103] The Center further reported that some prosecutors had convicted innocent defendants in more than one case over the course of their careers and that some of these prosecutors were cited multiple times for misconduct in other cases as well. It noted that "misconduct often occurs out of sight, especially in cases that never go to trial. Those cases by definition do not generate appellate opinions."[104] Although 90 percent of criminal cases are plea-bargained, one should not assume that those cases were devoid of prosecutorial misconduct.[105]

Furthermore, a study of capital cases nationwide between 1973 and 1995 found that state or federal courts overturned 68 percent of death sentences due to "serious error."[106] The two most common errors found were (1) egregiously incompetent defense lawyering, and (2) prosecutorial suppression of evidence that the defendant is innocent or does not deserve the death penalty.

The ABA has also studied the death-penalty systems of eight states. One of its key findings was that "most states have [capital] cases in which courts have found serious misconduct by prosecutors ... yet the prosecutors are not disciplined by the State disciplinary organization or by the prosecutor's office."[107]

---

102. *See* WEINBERG, *supra* note 12.

103. *Id.*

104. *Id.*

105. *See id.*

106. *See* James S. Liebman et al., *Capital Attrition: Error Rates in Capital Cases 1973–1995*, 78 TEX. L. REV. 1839, 1850 (2000).

107. ABA Death Penalty Moratorium Implementation Project, State Death Penalty Assessments: Key Findings, at 2 (Oct. 29, 2007), http://www.abanet.org/moratorium/assessmentproject/keyfindings.doc. The eight states studied were Alabama, Arizona, Florida, Georgia, Indiana, Ohio, Pennsylvania, and Tennessee.

Why Prosecutorial Misconduct Occurs and What Can Be Done about It

Prosecutors engage in misconduct for two reasons: (1) because they want to win, and (2) because they are not held accountable for misbehavior. Even though prosecutors are ethically required to seek justice, the voting public rewards them for obtaining convictions. In addition, they rarely have to answer for their actions. Theoretically, prosecutors should be accountable to the public, the courts, and the bar. In reality, though, the public rarely becomes aware of prosecutorial misconduct to the extent that it did in the Duke case and, when it does, it does not react so strongly against the prosecution. For instance, after the *Chicago Tribune* and the *Pittsburgh Post-Gazette* published the results of their investigations, there was no public outcry for reform.[108] It appears that the public is primarily concerned with its safety, and is therefore satisfied as long as convictions are obtained in high numbers.

Prosecutors are fully aware that, once they obtain a conviction, the heavy burden placed on the defense makes it unlikely to be overturned because of prosecutorial misconduct. Take, for example, a discovery violation. First, the defense must uncover the exculpatory evidence that should have been disclosed; this means finding something that one does not know exists. Second, defense counsel must demonstrate that the exculpatory evidence was in the possession of the prosecutor or his agent. Third, the defense must convince the court that the outcome of the proceeding would have been different had the evidence been disclosed.[109]

Even if the defense can satisfy this burden, courts rarely refer instances of prosecutorial misconduct to the bar for investigation. Likewise, defense counsel usually do not report instances of prosecutorial misconduct to the bar because they are likely to be disadvantaged by doing so.[110] For instance, if counsel reports a prosecutor to the bar, he can be sure that the prosecutor's office will be more adversarial toward him in future cases, making it harder for him to obtain things like continuances and stipulations. Finally, in the rare instances in which prosecutors are referred to the bar for alleged misconduct, it is un-

---

108. *See* ANGELA J. DAVIS, ARBITRARY JUSTICE: THE POWER OF THE AMERICAN PROSE-CUTOR 139 (2007).

109. United States v. Bagley, 473 U.S. 667, 682 (1985).

110. DAVIS, *supra* note 108, at 139.

likely to impose any discipline. The ABA, the Center for Public Integrity, the *Chicago Tribune* and the *Pittsburgh Post-Gazette* documented this in their studies.

Reform efforts have been made at the federal level. For instance, the so-called Hyde Amendment provides that a criminal defendant with private counsel who prevails may be awarded reasonable attorneys' fees and other litigation expenses "where the court finds that the position of the United States was vexatious, frivolous, or in bad faith, unless the court finds that special circumstances make such an award unjust."[111] There are two caveats, however, that make the Hyde Amendment an ineffective deterrent to federal prosecutorial misconduct. First, it does not apply to defendants who have to rely on government-provided counsel, which many if not most criminal defendants do. Second, the court can refuse to award fees if "special circumstances" exist. On a separate front, the McDade Amendment subjects federal prosecutors to state ethical laws and rules as if they were local attorneys practicing in that jurisdiction.[112] As has been pointed out, however, these laws have not effectively deterred local prosecutors from engaging in misconduct; it is unrealistic to believe that they will play a significant role in regulating their federal counterparts.

Very little has been done at the state level to alleviate the problem of prosecutorial misconduct.[113] Simply relying on defendants to seek redress in court will not reform the system. As mentioned earlier, most defendants are unsuccessful on appeal because of the requirement that they prove that they were harmed by the prosecution's malfeasance. The Supreme Court has failed to modify this onerous standard. Prosecutors, therefore, have little incentive to comply with ethical and constitutional requirements.

Mike Nifong was justifiably condemned for his actions in the Duke rape case. Few cases, however, receive a comparable level of scrutiny. Stronger measures must therefore be put in place to maximize deterrence of prosecutorial misconduct. First, because judges and defense attorneys are reluctant to report instances of prosecutorial misconduct, state bars should set up independent monitoring bodies that automatically commence an investigation whenever there is a judicial finding of prosecutorial misconduct. Second, the defense should not have to rely on the prosecutor to disclose evidence but should instead have full access to police and prosecution case files. Indeed, open discovery was adopted by North Carolina prior to the Duke lacrosse case

---

111. 18 U.S.C. § 3006A (2006).
112. 28 U.S.C. § 530B (2006).
113. *See generally* DAVIS, *supra* note 108.

and has generally been a success.[114] If a prosecutor is determined to be dishonest, however, even this will not remedy the situation—as the Duke case makes clear.

Thus, a third reform should be enacted: eliminating the doctrine of absolute prosecutorial immunity that is now uniformly in place nationwide.[115] The theory behind absolute immunity is twofold: First, that permitting civil suits against prosecutors would deter them from bringing difficult, but legitimate, prosecutions; and second, that it would cause prosecutors to spend too much time having to defend their in-court actions. These concerns could be addressed without absolute immunity by providing prosecutors with qualified immunity—the same level of protection that most public officials receive in carrying out their duties.[116] Under the doctrine of qualified immunity, if a public official's conduct is clearly illegal, that official can be held civilly liable. If the legality of the action is debatable, the official is not civilly liable and the case is readily dismissed.

Finally, convictions obtained through prosecutorial misconduct should not stand; that is, there should be an exclusionary rule for a prosecutor's failure to turn over exculpatory evidence and other serious acts of misconduct, even when it does not result in a harmful error. A good analogy is the rule that prohibits prosecutors from commenting on a defendant's exercise of his Fifth Amendment right to refuse to testify.[117] Prosecutors almost never comment on the defendant's failure to take the stand; they know that doing so would result in an automatic reversal. Likewise, prosecutors would be far more inclined to avoid misconduct if they knew that the failure to do so would automatically result in reversal of hard-won convictions.

Conclusion

Mike Nifong's conduct in the Duke case was egregious. He blatantly violated the laws and ethical standards that he swore to uphold. His dismissal, imprisonment, and humiliation were all justified—but it all occurred because of the national attention that the case received. Prosecutorial misconduct, how-

---

114. *See* Robert P. Mosteller, *Exculpatory Evidence, Ethics, and the Road to Disbarment of Mike Nifong: The Critical Importance of Full Open-File Discovery*, 15 Geo. Mason L. Rev. 257, 273–75 (2008).

115. *See* Imbler v. Pachtman, 424 U.S. 409, 434–35 (1976).

116. *See* Mitchell v. Forsyth, 472 U.S. 511, 524 (1985).

117. *See* Griffin v. California, 380 U.S. 609, 615 (1965).

ever, is not an uncommon occurrence, and often lurks behind the scenes. Now that the public is engaged, we should seize this rare opportunity to enact some much-needed reforms.

CHAPTER TWELVE

The Moment of Truth: The Decision to Institute Charges in a Rape Case

Michael L. Seigel

Introduction

One thing is clear from the facts of the Duke lacrosse rape case: for whatever reason, shortly after he learned of the allegations, Durham District Attorney Mike Nifong was hell-bent on indicting some of the lacrosse players for an alleged gang-rape of Crystal Mangum. Nothing was going to stop him—neither adverse facts (a confused accuser, no significant DNA matches to lacrosse players, DNA evidence indicating that Mangum had engaged in sex with other males, Kim Roberts's characterization of the allegations as a "crock," and so on), nor legal constraints (such as the law governing line-up procedures or North Carolina's open-discovery requirements), nor even the most obvious boundaries of ethical behavior. Nifong was on a demented drive to destruction.

Nifong was crazy, perhaps, but he was not stupid; even he realized at some point that the case was unwinnable. Accordingly, as the case began to unravel, he made a subtle switch from talking about victory and vindication and began, instead, to talk about taking the case to a jury and letting it make the ultimate decision.[1] But by this time the damage had already been done. Simply because

---

1. Shortly after learning the news about there being no DNA match with the lacrosse players, for example, Nifong stated at a forum held at North Carolina Central University, "Anytime you have a victim who can identify her assailant, then what you have is a case that must go to the jury." STUART TAYLOR & KC JOHNSON, UNTIL PROVEN INNOCENT: POLITI-

they were indicted, the lives of the three accused players—Reade Seligmann, Collin Finnerty, and Dave Evans—were forever altered. They and their family and friends endured a year of unbearable uncertainty, stress, vilification, and fear. Their reputations were forever tainted; ruined, even, in some quarters to this day. Duke suffered as well, with the case exacerbating pre-existing racial tensions both on campus and between town and gown. It also had its reputation, and that of its student body, called into question and dissected nationally. The Durham community was at first stunned by the allegations, then harmed by its false belief that the system was finally working on behalf of the underclass, then humiliated by having been misled by a public official. And Crystal Mangum suffered, too; yes, her false claims started it all, but a professional job by the prosecution would have saved her from the harm and ultimate disgrace caused by her own inner demons.[2]

All of the procedures designed to protect individuals suspected of committing a crime in North Carolina failed to prevent this travesty of justice. This is because, for the most part, limits on prosecutorial power and discretion rely on the good faith of prosecutors themselves. A jurisdiction can have all of the discovery rules, ethical obligations, line-up procedures, evidentiary regulations, and constitutional provisions it likes, but none of these will stop a prosecutor who, for whatever reason, is not bothered by the prospect of breaking the law and covering up his breach. Nifong was one of these prosecutors; he committed egregious illegal and unethical acts for apparent political (and pecuniary) gain.[3] Other prosecutors do terrible things because they believe the ends justify the means, or because they see others doing it, or because they get caught up in the competitive nature of the adversarial system and would rather win than see that justice is done.[4]

CAL CORRECTNESS AND THE SHAMEFUL INJUSTICES OF THE DUKE LACROSSE CASE 168–69 (2007).

2. To her credit, Mangum has reportedly graduated from college, although even this ostensibly positive development has been viewed in some circles with disdain. *See* Kristin Butler, *Summa Cum Looney*, CHRONICLE (Duke University), May 15, 2008, http://www.duke chronicle.com/home/index.cfm?event=displayArticle&uStory_id=19967edf-c28d-4602-9d73-54f7c8f5e8e0.

3. *See* TAYLOR & JOHNSON, *supra* note 1, at 79–85.

4. I think it is important to point out here that I was a federal prosecutor for about ten years of my legal career, first as an organized-crime specialist in the Eastern District of Pennsylvania, then as First Assistant United States Attorney for the Middle District of Florida. In my personal experience, I saw extremely little prosecutorial misconduct. Out of the roughly one-hundred prosecutors whose behavior I came to know well, I'd estimate only two of them were prone to crossing the line into unethical conduct under the right—or, if

There was, however, one critical moment when Nifong's train wreck could have been averted: when he was required to present the prosecution's evidence to a grand jury and ask it to return indictments against the players. If the grand jury had declined to indict, Nifong would have been derailed. The media attention likely would have focused on the grand jury's decision and the lack of solid evidence, the tide would have shifted, and the incident would have ended before it had a chance to pick up much steam.

This, of course, did not happen. Instead, the grand jury rubber-stamped the prosecution's case and returned the three true bills presented to it. The reason is simple: North Carolina has a laughably low bar for indictment. It is worthless. In fact, it's less than worthless: it is affirmatively harmful to defendants because it allows prosecutors to bypass a preliminary hearing, which at least requires a public airing of the State's case in front of a magistrate with defense participation.

The efficacy of the grand jury as an institution is a topic that has occupied criminal proceduralists for many years. They have staked out a variety of positions, from "leaving well enough alone" to "abolishing the institution altogether." The purpose of this chapter is to take up this topic once again, this time in the very specific context of the Duke lacrosse case. Is there a procedure that might have nipped in the bud Nifong's ill-advised, if not evil, pursuit of the lacrosse players? If so, would this inherently prodefendant reform make legitimate charges too difficult to pursue?

The chapter begins with a review of the grand-jury system as it exists today in North Carolina. It then looks at reforms traditionally put forward to strengthen the role of the grand jury as the protector of citizens from undue prosecutorial power. Concluding that these reforms miss the mark, the chapter wraps up by advocating the abolition of the grand jury for most cases and the reform of grand-jury procedures for cases involving sex crimes.

---

you will, wrong—circumstances. Moreover, it was the job of supervisors like me to see that they did not, in fact, cross that line. Therefore, I disagree with the contributors to this volume who contend or imply that prosecutorial misconduct is widespread. Nevertheless, I recognize that the circumstances in state courts are probably worse than what I saw, and I strongly believe that any misconduct—even if it occurs in less than 2 percent of cases— is too much.

North Carolina Grand Jury Procedure

The grand jury as an accusatorial body goes back many centuries.[5] Its incarnation as a source of protection for individuals suspected by the government of committing a crime, however, is a more recent development. Most scholars trace it to the 1681 English case involving the Earl of Shaftesbury. The Crown charged the Earl with treason and demanded that the grand jury hear the evidence against him in open court, but the grand jury insisted on secrecy and ultimately refused to do the King's bidding. As a result, our modern-day notion of the grand jury—one that investigates, accuses, and *protects against governmental overreaching*—was born.[6]

The American colonists had this modern view of the grand jury in mind when they guaranteed the right to indictment by grand jury in many state constitutions and later in the federal Bill of Rights.[7] North Carolina was one of the states that incorporated this protection in its constitution; the modern day version of the provision reads,

> Except in misdemeanor cases initiated in the District Court Division, no person shall be put to answer any criminal charge but by indictment, presentment or impeachment. But any person, when represented by counsel, may, under such regulations as the General Assembly shall prescribe, waive indictment in noncapital cases.[8]

North Carolina courts have interpreted this constitutional provision quite literally. "It is hornbook law that a valid indictment is a condition precedent to the jurisdiction of the Superior Court to determine the guilt or innocence of the defendant, and to give authority to the court to render a valid judg-

---

5. *See* John F. Decker, *Legislating New Federalism: The Call for Grand Jury Reform in the States*, 58 Okla. L. Rev. 341, 344 (2005) ("The grand jury can be traced back to twelfth-century England during the Reign of King Henry II.")

6. William J. Campbell, *Eliminate the Grand Jury*, 64 J. Crim. & Criminology 174, 175 (1973). For an extensive look at the history of the Anglo-American grand jury, see Mark Kadish, *Behind the Locked Door of an American Grand Jury: Its Secrecy, and Its Process*, 24 Fla. St. L. Rev. 1 (1996); Helene E. Schwartz, *Demythologizing the Historic Role of the Grand Jury*, 10 Am. Crim. L. Rev. 701 (1971–72).

7. U.S. Const. amend. V ("No person shall be held to answer for a capital, or otherwise infamous crime, unless on a presentment or indictment of a Grand Jury...."); *see* Decker, *supra* note 5, at 345–46. The Supreme Court has held that the grand-jury clause of the Fifth Amendment does not apply to the states, leaving them free to do as they see fit regarding this matter of criminal procedure. Hurtado v. California, 110 U.S. 516, 535 (1884).

8. N.C. Const. art. I, §22.

ment."[9] In light of this requirement, the state appears—on the surface, at least—to have a strong tradition of grand-jury protection for its citizens. But, as we shall see, nothing could be further from the truth.

In North Carolina, a grand jury is a "body consisting of not less than 12 nor more than 18 persons, impaneled by a superior court and constituting a part of such court."[10] The empanelment process is random: the clerk of the court places the names of everyone in a particular jury pool into a container and then blindly selects nine or eighteen persons to serve as grand jurors. Each grand juror serves for a one-year term, but the selection process is staggered so that nine members rotate on and off every six months. If a vacancy develops, the next superior court judge to convene a petit jury or hold a session of criminal court in the county may fill it. The "senior resident superior court judge" of the district may empanel a second grand jury if he determines that service is placing a "disproportionate burden" on the existing grand-jury members or their employers.[11]

The qualifications to serve on a grand jury are far from rigorous. In fact, no one—not even the prosecutor who will work with the grand jury—has the power to challenge a grand juror for cause or otherwise. A superior-court judge may, however, discharge an entire grand jury if its members have not been selected in accordance with the law or the grand jury is illegally constituted. Likewise, the judge may refuse to swear a particular grand juror, or discharge him after he has been sworn, "upon a finding that he is disqualified from service, incapable of performing his duties, or guilty of misconduct in the performance of his duties so as to impair the proper functioning of the grand jury."[12] The judge may also excuse a grand juror from service at the juror's request for good cause shown, and the foreperson of the grand jury—selected by the judge[13]—has the authority to excuse no more than two grand jurors from attendance at any particular session.[14]

Only a small fraction of grand juries in North Carolina are truly investigative in nature. These may be convened only in cases involving drug and other kinds of complex conspiracies (like continuing criminal enterprises).[15] The procedural requirements that the prosecution must meet before convening

---

9. State v. Ray, 164 S.E.2d 457, 461 (N.C. 1968).
10. N.C. GEN. STAT. § 15A-621 (2007).
11. *Id.* § 15A-622(b).
12. *Id.* § 15A-622(c).
13. *Id.* § 15A-622(e).
14. *Id.* § 15A-622(d).
15. *Id.*

such a grand jury are extensive. The district attorney or special prosecutor seeking the empanelment of an investigative grand jury must file a written petition with the Clerk of the North Carolina Supreme Court after obtaining the approval of a committee of at least three members of the North Carolina Conference of District Attorneys, as well as the concurrence of the State Attorney General. The Chief Justice then appoints a three-judge panel to review the petition, which must specify the individuals who might have knowledge regarding the perpetrators of the crime(s) alleged. The petition must be supported by an affidavit setting forth probable cause.[16]

In this small subset of cases, if all of these requirements are met, the grand jury that is convened operates much like a federal grand jury.[17] A prosecutor is present in the grand jury room to examine each witness and a court reporter is present to transcribe the proceedings. The prosecutor has the power to immunize witnesses and compel testimony. A witness may not have counsel in the grand jury room, but may have counsel present outside, and may consult with counsel at reasonable intervals for reasonable lengths of time. The record of the grand-jury proceedings is secret, except that the prosecutor may disclose it to the witness or his attorney and to law-enforcement personnel. Witness statements are discoverable,[18] however, and either party may use them at trial.[19]

For the vast majority of crimes, however—including the most serious, such as homicide, rape, sexual molestation, and aggravated assault—North Carolina does not have even these minimal grand-jury procedures in place. For these crimes, witnesses meet with the grand jury in complete secrecy. *Not even the prosecutor may be present*—only an interpreter, if needed, and a guard if a witness is in custody. What the witness says to the grand jury, and vice versa, is never known; no court stenographer is present and the proceedings are not recorded in any way. No one may refer to an occurrence before the grand jury after the fact. As a result, after the foreperson swears the witness in, anything goes. Hearsay is, of course, permitted, so the grand jurors will likely hear only from one or two police officers summing up the case. Worse yet, though he's under oath, given the cloak of secrecy and the lack of a record, there's no effective check on a witness' truthfulness.[20]

---

16. *Id.* §15A-622(h).

17. *See* Fed. R. Crim. P. 6.

18. *See* N.C. Gen. Stat. §15A-903 (2007).

19. *Id.* §15A-622(h).

20. *Id.* §15A-623(b)-(e); *see also* Robert P. Mosteller, *The Duke Lacrosse Case, Innocence, and False Identifications: A Fundamental Failure to "Do Justice,"* 76 Fordham L. Rev. 1337, 1374 (2007).

In most cases, one of the testifying police officers brings the proposed indictment with her into the grand-jury room and hands it to the foreperson. The foreperson must record on the indictment the names of all witnesses who testify in connection with the case. When the testimony is complete, the grand jury deliberates alone in absolute secrecy. It takes twelve votes, two-thirds of the entire grand jury, to return a true bill.[21]

The end result of this process is that the grand jury in North Carolina is nothing more than an indictment mill.[22] Grand jurors practically never see non-law-enforcement witnesses. They are rarely called upon to examine anything beyond the bare bones of the physical evidence related to the case. They hear a few minutes of one-sided summary testimony and then consider an indictment that has been shoved under their noses. If, for some reason, they return a "no true bill," the prosecution can simply find out what was bothering them and re-present the indictment at any time.[23]

The Duke lacrosse case makes this reality clear. Only two witnesses appeared before the grand jury before it returned one of the most important indictments in Durham history. They were the police officers most involved in investigating the case: Gottlieb and Himan.[24] These officers were far from unbiased; Gottlieb, in particular, had a history of being extremely tough on Duke students.[25] On April 17, 2006, the day that the Durham grand jury handed down the indictments of Seligmann and Finnerty, it heard evidence and returned true bills for *seventy-nine* other defendants. That's eighty-one indictments in all.[26] Assuming the grand jury worked an eight-hour day with an hour for lunch (probably a charitable assumption given the way courts tend to operate), it devoted an average of just over five minutes to each case. That's five minutes to swear the witnesses in, note their names on the proposed indictment, hear their testimony, excuse them from the room, deliberate, and con-

---

21. N.C. Gen. Stat. § 15A-623(a), (c), (d) (2007).

22. Even with their additional procedural protections, the same could be said for federal grand juries. In 1991, for example, grand jurors voted "no true bill" in only sixteen of the 25,943 matters presented to them, an indictment return-rate of 99.9 percent. *See* Roger Roots, *If It's Not a Runaway, It's Not a Real Grand Jury*, 33 Creighton L. Rev. 821, 827 (2000). In my ten years working as a federal prosecutor in two different jurisdictions, I am aware of only one instance in which a colleague had an indictment rejected by a grand jury. The event was so rare that everyone in the office teased the prosecutor about it for days. Eventually, he re-presented the indictment and the grand jury reversed its position.

23. State v. Lewis, 37 S.E.2d 691, 692–93 (N.C. 1946).

24. Taylor & Johnson, *supra* note 1, at 178.

25. *Id.* at 52–55.

26. *Id.* at 178.

duct and record its vote. To anyone who cares about justice, this process—or, more accurately, this lack of process—should be shocking.

It has not, apparently, shocked the North Carolina courts. Indeed, in *State v. Jones*,[27] the defendant argued on appeal that the trial court's denial of his motion for a transcript of the testimony presented to the indicting grand jury constituted reversible error. The appellate court called this argument "feckless," pointing out, of course, that "[i]t is not the custom in this State to record evidentiary proceedings before the grand jury. The witnesses examined by the grand jury are marked on the bill of indictment, but their testimony is not recorded."[28] Never did it occur to the reviewing court that grand-jury proceedings *should* be recorded.

Does It Really Matter?

The usual response to these lamentations is "Who cares?" The job of the grand jury, the argument goes, is merely to find probable cause—the lowest burden of proof in the criminal arena.[29] In the vast majority of cases, police and prosecutors are not going to waste their time pursuing innocent people; if they present an indictment, it is highly likely that the defendant is guilty. Furthermore, in those rare instances when the grand jury makes a mistake, or is fooled into action by an unethical prosecution team, it's no big deal: the defendant will either get the indictment dismissed or, at worst, be acquitted at trial. This is unfortunate, according to advocates of the status quo, but at least the grand jury is there as a bulwark against the most extreme governmental excesses.[30]

There is one huge flaw in this argument: unwarranted charges are, in fact, a big deal. For starters, as the Duke case demonstrates, they cause immeasurable turmoil in the defendant's life. He may be suspended or expelled from school, like the Duke defendants, or lose his job, or find himself facing a divorce. If he has any money or equity in his home, attorneys' fees will eat most

---

27. 210 S.E.2d 454 (N.C. Ct. App. 1974).

28. *Id.* at 456.

29. *See* Michigan v. DeFillippo, 443 U.S. 31, 37 (1979) ("'[P]robable cause' to justify an arrest means facts and circumstances within the officer's knowledge that are sufficient to warrant a prudent person, or one of reasonable caution, in believing, in circumstances shown, that the suspect has committed, is committing, or is about to commit an offense." (citations omitted)).

30. *See* Thomas P. Sullivan & Robert B. Nachman, *If It Ain't Broke, Don't Fix It: Why The Grand Jury's Accusatory Function Should Not Be Changed*, 75 J. Crim. L. & Criminology 1047, 1053 (1984); W. Wilson White, *In Defense of the Grand Jury*, Pa. Bar Assoc. Q. 260, 261 (1954).

it up. In many instances, the harm to his reputation will be irreparable. This is true even if his case garners no publicity, for surely his reputation among friends, family, and business associates will suffer.[31] If his case does get media attention, like the Duke case, he may become infamous overnight. If he's accused of doing something heinous and, unlike the Duke defendants, he does not have access to the hefty resources needed to post bail, or he is denied bail altogether, his initial fate will be worse than all this: he will be detained in jail for months pending trial.

These harmful effects counsel against writing off the charging decision as a minor step in the criminal-justice process. They call for the imposition of at least minimal procedural protections during the grand-jury phase of a case. Another alternative might be the elimination and replacement of the grand jury altogether. A third possibility, and perhaps the best solution for cases like the Duke affair, might be to truly transform the grand-jury proceeding.

Basic Grand Jury Procedures

At a bare minimum, a grand-jury system ought to be patterned after the federal model or the one that North Carolina uses when investigating complex conspiracy cases. In these contexts, as noted above, the prosecutor presents the evidence to the grand jury, and everything—not only witness testimony but any and all remarks the prosecutor makes to the grand jury even when no witness is present—is recorded stenographically. The witness may have counsel standing by and may interrupt the proceedings at reasonable intervals for attorney-client consultations. Hearsay testimony is accepted but the grand jurors are free to request that a particular witness or group of witnesses be brought in before it deliberates on a proposed indictment.

Under this basic approach, if the grand jury indicts a defendant, he has a limited right to review transcripts of the proceeding. North Carolina law on this point is actually more defendant-friendly than its federal counterpart. Under North Carolina's open-discovery statute, the defendant is entitled to see the testimony of all grand-jury witnesses; under federal law, he is only provided with a copy of the grand-jury testimony of witnesses who eventually testify at trial (unless other testimony constitutes exculpatory, or *Brady*, material).[32] In neither case, however, will the defendant routinely get to see the nontestimo-

---

31. For an extensive discussion of the reputational harm that comes from being indicted, see *supra* Chapter Eight (Taslitz).

32. *See* Jencks Act, 18 U.S.C. §3500 (1970); Brady v. Maryland, 373 U.S. 83 (1963).

nial portions of the record. The pertinent rule in North Carolina provides a judge with the discretion to order disclosure of any portion of investigative grand jury proceedings "[t]o protect a defendant's constitutional rights."[33] But courts have interpreted their discretion under this provision as quite circumscribed. In *State v. Crummy*,[34] for instance, the defendants requested disclosure on the grounds that the grand jury had violated their rights to due process and confrontation because it had "operated outside of its scope and indicted defendants without hearing all the evidence, and the prosecutor was guilty of misconduct."[35] After holding a hearing, the trial court ruled that "the Defendants offered no evidence or legal arguments to support their demand for Investigative Grand Jury Petitions, Affidavits, Transcripts, Subpoenas and other documents"[36] and thus denied their petition. The appellate court deferred to the trial court's exercise of its discretion.[37] Rulings like the one in *Crummy* present a Catch-22 for defendants: they need specific facts to convince a court to provide them with nontestimonial grand-jury materials, but those facts are most likely contained in the forbidden materials themselves, meaning that defendants can almost never meet their burden to see them.[38]

As a former federal prosecutor, I used to believe that this basic grand-jury procedure was sufficient to protect against abuse of the grand-jury process and the indictment of innocents. I would tell my classes that, yes, grand juries routinely return the indictments put before them, but that is because these indictments have merit. I contended that, if a rogue prosecutor attempted to use the power of the grand jury merely to harass individuals, the grand jurors would indeed take notice and bring this unethical behavior to the attention of the presiding judge. I referenced occasions in my practice when grand jurors asked witnesses questions, or asked to meet with and question a particular witness prior to considering a proposed indictment. I explained how, if at all possible, I would accommodate these requests; I always wanted to maintain the grand jury's trust and confidence.[39]

---

33. N.C. Gen. Stat. § 15A-622(h)(2) (2007).

34. 420 S.E.2d 448 (N.C. Ct. App. 1992).

35. *Id.* at 325.

36. *Id.*

37. *Id.* at 325–26.

38. *Cf.* State v. Rankins, 515 S.E.2d 748, 752 (N.C. Ct. App. 1999) ("An accused in this jurisdiction has no right to obtain a transcript of the grand jury proceedings against him.... Defendant is adequately protected by his right to object to improper evidence and cross-examine the witnesses presented against him at trial.").

39. Others have proffered a similar defense of the federal grand-jury system. *See* Sullivan & Nachman, *supra* note 30, at 1053.

The Duke case, however, has altered my perspective. The critical question is this: If these bare-bones procedures had been in place, would the Durham grand jury have prevented Nifong from obtaining an indictment against Seligmann, Finnerty, and Evans? The clear answer is no. Nifong would have been in the grand-jury room, giving him even more control over the proceedings. He still would have put on the summary testimony of Officers Himan and Gottlieb. Staying well within the bounds of the law, they would have provided only a partial picture of the evidence, piecing together those elements that supported the players' guilt and ignoring the rest. In their demeanor and choice of words, the three men would have inflamed the passions of the grand jury until it was anxious to indict. If, by chance, they faced a "difficult" grand juror or two who wanted to hear from the complainant, Nifong could have handled them deftly by "explaining" how traumatized she was and urging them not to burden her further by requiring live testimony. Assuming the worst case for Nifong, he could have produced Mangum if necessary and limited her testimony to a very brief set of leading questions.

What I failed to realize when I was a prosecutor, but what the Duke case has made crystal-clear, is that a grand jury with traditional safeguards will rarely be in a position to second-guess a prosecutor who is acting with ill motives. If the prosecutor's goal is simply to bring charges against the defendant, it is not hard for him, under almost all circumstances, to tailor the grand-jury presentation to convince the grand jury to indict. If he's desperate enough, the prosecutor could even make remarks to the grand jurors (when witnesses were not present) designed to cajole, prejudice, or even intimidate them into returning a true bill. Given the nearly impenetrable shield of secrecy, it is nigh impossible for a defendant to learn of, let alone challenge, such conduct.

In other words, as it is presently constituted in most states and at the federal level, the grand jury does not serve as a particularly staunch check on a prosecutor's abuse of power. That must come from the good conscience of the prosecutor herself—and, in most cases, it will. But if the grand jury is to significantly benefit the falsely accused, it requires serious reform.

Select Grand Jury Reforms

Much has already been written about reforming the grand jury that I will not repeat here. Instead, I will delineate the most commonly proposed reforms and analyze their usefulness. A great deal of this information comes from the *Federal Grand Jury Bill of Rights*, drafted by the Commission to Reform the Federal Grand Jury, a group convened in May 2000 by the National Association of Criminal Defense Attorneys.[40] The Commission based the Bill of Rights on a set of principles adopted by the ABA in 1981 and a Model Grand Jury Act proposed by the ABA's Grand Jury Committee that same year.[41]

Permitting Counsel in the Grand Jury Room

A common reform proposal would allow a witness's own counsel to be present in the room when the witness testifies. Counsel would be there solely in an advisory capacity; she would not be able to speak to the grand jurors, object to questions, or stop the proceeding. The upside of this reform, of course, is the protection it would provide to a witness who might be in danger of self-incrimination.[42] Also, with counsel present, the prosecutor would likely be on his best behavior. The downside is that the witness might be inclined to say less based on the advice of counsel, thereby slowing down the investigation. More importantly, defense counsel may share what he learned in the grand jury room with attorneys for other potential defendants.

Requiring Prosecutors to Present Exculpatory Evidence

The principle motivating this reform is to ensure that grand jurors hear all of the important evidence in a case before making any decisions. The goal is laudable in theory. In practice, however, it would be difficult to define the parameters of "exculpatory evidence," which would make this a very complicated rule to enforce.[43]

---

40. *See* NAT'L ASS'N OF CRIMINAL DEFENSE LAWYERS, REPORT OF THE COMMISSION TO REFORM THE FEDERAL GRAND JURY (2005), http://www.nacdl.org/public.nsf/Printer-Friendly/GrandJuryReform [hereinafter "NACDL"].

41. For the complete text of the ABA Model Act, and a comprehensive discussion thereof, see Peter Arenella, *Reforming the State Grand Jury System: A Model Grand Jury Act*, 13 RUTGERS L.J. 1 (1981). Professor Decker has also exhaustively examined various reforms, and reports on the number of states that have adopted each. *See* Decker, *supra* note 5, at 367–85.

42. *See generally* Kathryn E. White, *What Have You Done with My Lawyer?: The Grand Jury Witness's Right to Consult with Counsel*, 32 LOY. L.A. L.R. 907 (1999).

43. In *United States v. Williams*, 504 U.S. 36 (1972), the Court held that federal courts could not use their supervisory powers to require the disclosure of exculpatory material to the grand jury. *See* Susan M. Schiappa, *Preserving the Autonomy and Function of the Grand Jury: United States v. Williams*, 43 CATH. U. L. REV. 311 (1993).

Prohibiting Prosecutors from Knowingly Presenting Constitutionally Inadmissible Evidence

Reformers have specifically tailored this proposal to reverse the Supreme Court's holding in *United States v. Calandra*[44] that the exclusionary rule does not apply to grand-jury proceedings. Its goal is to ensure that a prosecutor will not be able to proceed with a case unless she has sufficient admissible evidence to convict. Although this goal is valuable, the rule would be of limited use in achieving it. In most cases, the prosecutor does not "know" evidence is excludable until a court so rules—and this takes place, by definition, postindictment. Furthermore, the rule would require courts to dismiss indictments obtained through the use of inadmissible evidence even if the prosecution had subsequently developed admissible evidence sufficient to sustain the indictment and obtain a conviction—an outcome that, to many, seems perverse.

Providing Targets or Subjects with an Opportunity to Be Heard

This is perhaps the most significant of the reform proposals. As described in the *Federal Grand Jury Bill of Rights*:

> A target or subject of a grand jury investigation shall have the right to testify before the grand jury. Prosecutors shall notify such targets or subjects of their opportunity to testify, unless notification may result in flight, endanger other persons or obstruct justice, or unless the prosecution is unable to notify said persons with reasonable diligence. A target or subject of the grand jury may also submit to the court, to be made available to the foreperson, an offer, in writing, to provide information or evidence to the grand jury.[45]

This requirement would ensure that suspects (called subjects in federal parlance) and putative defendants (called targets) who wanted to get their story before the grand jury prior to its deliberations could do so. It appears that this procedure would add a significant level of protection for innocent persons in danger of being charged. Of course, the decision to testify, even if one is wholly innocent, is a difficult strategic choice. Thus, providing a subject or target with the ability to present information in an alternative form makes this proposal

---

44. 414 U.S. 613 (1974).
45. NACDL, *supra* note 40, at 8.

even more powerful. The critique of this reform, and one that is not trivial, is that it would convert the grand process into a "mini-trial," causing unnecessary confusion and delay, especially when considering that all the grand jury must find is probable cause.

Prohibiting Hearsay in the Grand Jury

This is probably the most pie-in-the-sky proposal put forth by the ABA's Grand Jury Committee in its 1981 Model Act. Prohibiting hearsay in the grand jury (unless there were no alternative) would certainly help to enlighten grand jurors about the strengths and weaknesses of a case. It would eliminate the common practice of using law-enforcement witnesses to summarize entire investigations. But it is simply not practical. Who would decide whether hearsay evidence was the only alternative under a specific set of circumstances? What would the exceptions look like? Would the prosecution be required to call entire categories of witness, or could she end her presentation when the probable-cause threshold was met? This reform, especially when coupled with some of the others, would transform the grand-jury process into an odd, cumbersome, one-sided pseudo-trial, with rules enforced after the fact.

Requiring Prosecutors to Instruct the Jurors on the Law

In and of itself, it appears to be a benign exercise in common sense to require prosecutors to instruct the grand jury on the law and remind it that, to indict, probable cause must exist for each and every element of the crime. How could grand jurors do their job intelligently without some knowledge of the law? This reform, however, is usually coupled with a second proposal allowing defendants access to these instructions so that they can attack them as erroneous. Fearing the dismissal of their indictments on such grounds, prosecutors would feel obliged to parse every word of their guidance to the grand jury with the greatest of care, making the process more unwieldy. Moreover, because of the law's nature and complexity, prosecutors would inevitably make (at least arguable) mistakes. The result would be endless debate in the trial court over the prosecutor's grand-jury instructions and potential interlocutory appeals if the presiding judge sided with the defendant.

Application of These Reforms to the Duke Case

Would one or more of these reforms have prevented the three indictments in the Duke lacrosse rape case? Are they worth pursuing in North Carolina and beyond?

Two of the reforms, although perhaps laudable in their own right, would have had zero effect on the Duke prosecution: that counsel be permitted in the grand-jury room and that the prosecutor instruct the jury on the law. In the Duke case, the only grand-jury witnesses were the two police officers, Himan and Gottlieb; they certainly did not need advice during their testimony. As to the latter requirement, there is no indication that, had the grand jury been fully instructed on the crime of sexual assault in North Carolina, they would have voted any differently.

In all likelihood, several of the other reforms also would have failed in the Duke case because they rely on the good faith of the prosecutor for their execution. Even if Nifong had been required to present exculpatory evidence, he probably would not have done so. After all, he was willing to hide exculpatory DNA evidence from the defense; why act differently with respect to the grand jury? As to other exculpatory evidence, some of it—such as Mangum's inconsistent stories—Nifong would have papered over or explained away (for example, he could have noted that victims of rape are often confused due to the trauma). Additionally, the defense, rather than the police, uncovered much of the exculpatory evidence; Nifong could not have presented to the grand jury that which he did not know. As to evidence knowingly obtained in violation of the defendants' constitutional rights, such as the identifications obtained from the horribly flawed lineup procedures, Nifong's position surely would have been that the irregularities did not rise to constitutional dimensions.

Adding procedural requirements at the grand-jury stage that depend on the prosecutor's judgment and conscience for their efficacy may help in the majority of cases. They are demonstrably ineffective, however, when a prosecutor is determined to circumvent them to get what he wants—an indictment at any cost. True, the charges might later be dismissed by a judge reviewing the grand-jury record, but—as we've already seen in the Duke lacrosse case—this is too late to prevent a significant amount of harm to those falsely accused.

The remaining two reforms, though, are of a different type. Prohibiting hearsay in the grand jury would force even a dishonest prosecutor to present more than summary law-enforcement testimony before requesting an indictment. Whatever its specific contours, in the Duke rape case, such a rule undoubtedly would have forced Nifong to bring Mangum before the grand jury to testify. That might have been outcome-determinative in and of itself; even an experienced prosecutor like Nifong would have had difficulty presenting her as credible witness on the stand. This reform, combined with the requirement that putative defendants be given the opportunity to testify and present exculpatory evidence before the grand jury, might have altered the outcome of the Duke case dramatically. If the grand jury had heard from Mangum, compared her story to those of Seligmann, Finnerty, and Evans, and reviewed a written defense submission outlining the lack of DNA evidence and Seligmann's alibi, it probably would have declined to indict.[46] After all, the three lacrosse players were telling the truth, and most of those who took the time to listen to them seem to have been persuaded of their innocence.

This conclusion, however, leads to a serious dilemma. These procedures might have saved the players from indictment, and would likely prevent the indictment of many innocent persons in the future but, as noted above, they would also be extremely cumbersome. Consider that a small jurisdiction like Durham asked its biweekly grand jury to review roughly eighty cases a session at the time of the Duke case. If prosecutors were required to present first-hand testimony and give the defense a chance to make a presentation in all eighty-or-so cases each and every session, the Durham criminal-justice system would grind to a halt. The extra time necessary to accommodate the additional evidence would be a huge burden all by itself. On top of this, skilled defense attorneys would learn how to further delay proceedings by manipulating their right to present evidence. For example, defense presentations might be intentionally confusing, requiring prosecutors and witnesses to spend even more time trying to help the grand jury sort things out. Moreover, many of the problems faced by prosecutors at the trial stage—obtaining the testimony of recalcitrant witnesses, for instance—would be duplicated at the grand-jury stage, all in the name of demonstrating mere probable cause. True, innocent persons would be more likely to avoid indictment, but the cost would be the failure to pursue many meritorious cases for logistical reasons, if not the total collapse of the system under its own weight.[47]

---

46. Supporting this prediction is that fact that at least some of the grand jurors who had voted to indict said in interviews after much of the exculpatory evidence came to light that, had they known of it at the time, they would probably have come to a different conclusion. Chris Cuomo & Laura Setrakian, *Exclusive: Duke Lacrosse Grand Jurors Speak Out*, ABC News, Feb. 6, 2007, http://abcnews.go.com/GMA/Story?id=2852337.

47. *See* Andrew D. Leipold, *Why Grand Juries Do Not (and Cannot) Protect the Accused*, 80 Cornell L. Rev. 260, 289 (noting the "steep administrative costs associated with" procedural grand jury reforms); *cf.* Sullivan & Nachman, *supra* note 30, at 1056 (noting that prevailing reforms would place additional burdens on the judiciary and "add substantial time and expense to what is already a slow, cumbersome, and costly process"). Leipold goes

The Preliminary Hearing as an Alternative?

Faced with this dilemma—either an ineffective grand jury or a cumbersome one—some commentators have argued for abolishing the institution outright and replacing it with a preliminary hearing.[48] Many states have followed this path, at least in part, in light of the U.S. Supreme Court's 1886 ruling that the grand-jury requirement set forth in the U.S. Constitution does not apply to the states.[49] Florida, for example, permits prosecution on the basis of an information, followed by a preliminary hearing, for all crimes.[50] North Carolina, on the other hand, permits the use of an information only in misdemeanor cases or in felony cases when the defendant waives indictment.[51] In these situations, the filing of the information is also followed by a preliminary hearing.

The procedures for North Carolina's preliminary hearings are comparable to those in other states. The hearing is held in open court, the defendant is represented by counsel, and

> The State must by nonhearsay evidence, or by evidence that satisfies an exception to the hearsay rule, show that there is probable cause to believe that the offense charged has been committed and that there is probable cause to believe that the defendant committed it.[52]

---

on to make a much more profound argument, which is that even with substantial procedural adjustments, grand juries still could not carry out their screening function successfully because laypeople reviewing a one-sided presentation are ill-equipped to determine probable cause. *See* Leipold, *supra* note 47, at 294–310.

48. Probably the most famous of these commentators was William Campbell, Senior Judge, United States District Court for the Northern District of Illinois. William J. Campbell, *Eliminate the Grand Jury*, 64 J. Crim. & Criminology 174, 174 (1973) ("My thesis is simple.... The grand jury should be abolished; prosecution should be commenced upon an information filed by the prosecuting official and followed by a probable cause hearing before a judicial officer, such as a magistrate, who would determine whether there is sufficient evidence to permit the prosecution to continue.").

49. Hurtado v. California, 110 U.S. 535 (1884). According to Decker, no state has completely abolished the grand jury for all circumstances, but "many have eliminated the obligation that prosecutors secure indictments...." Decker, *supra* note 5, at 367.

50. Fla. R. Crim. P. 3.133.

51. N.C. Const. art. I, §22.

52. N.C. Gen. Stat. §15A-611(b) (2007).

Each witness must testify under oath and is subject to cross-examination,[53] and "[t]he defendant may testify as a witness in his own behalf and call and examine other witnesses, and produce other evidence in his behalf."[54]

A preliminary hearing, then, *is* a mini-trial of sorts. Because the burden of persuasion is so low, a judge presiding over a preliminary hearing often truncates the defense's cross-examination of the prosecution's witnesses and the defense's own presentation of evidence. At the same time, the prosecution tries to make its case with the least possible amount of evidence in order to avoid prematurely showing its hand. But at least the defense gets to confront the main accuser(s) in the case, and obviously unsupportable charges are thrown out at this early stage in the process.

Some argue, nonetheless, that grand-jury indictments are superior to informations followed by probable-cause hearings. They advance several arguments in support of this position: First, that grand jurors are better equipped to measure the intangibles in a case, such as the defendant's "intent, motive or other state of mind bearing on criminal responsibility for his acts."[55] While a magistrate judge would feel compelled to find probable cause and pass on such matters to the petit jury, the argument goes, grand jurors will refuse to return a true bill unless they determine that the defendant is actually guilty. Indeed, one commentator has gone so far as to argue that the real purpose of the grand jury is not to find probable cause but to act as a constraint on governmental power by refusing to indict unpopular or immoral cases even when the evidence is strong.[56] In other words, the grand jury has the power to nullify. Obviously, a magistrate or judge will rarely—if ever—serve in this capacity.

A second defense of the grand jury is based on the aid that it provides prosecutors in ferreting out crime and indicting the right individuals. This assistance is tied not only to the power conferred upon grand juries to compel testimony and documentary disclosure—which is typically transferred directly to the prosecutor in jurisdictions not employing a grand-jury system—but also to the "feel" for a case that grand jurors can offer. For example, a prosecutor will sometimes bring a witness before the grand jury to see how credible it finds him, which will give the prosecutor a measure of the strength of his case. The prosecutor might also use the grand jury as a more general

---

53. *Id.* §15A-611(a)(4).

54. *Id.* §15A-611(a)(3).

55. White, *supra* note 30, at 261.

56. Ric Simmons, *Re-Examining the Grand Jury: Is There Room for Democracy in the Criminal Justice System?* 82 B.U. L. Rev. 1 (2002).

sounding board, asking it to provide feedback on various aspects of the investigation.[57]

Yet a third argument in favor of retaining a grand-jury system is grounded in democracy. Many commentators believe that maximizing participation by the citizenry in the functioning of government is critical to a successful democratic society. Taking the public out of the investigative and charging phases of the criminal-justice system would, these commentators argue, give citizens a sense of distance from and even distrust of the system's outcomes. Even if it is imperfect, only the grand jury can serve the important function of connecting the people to the process.

Finally, a fourth argument against abolishing the grand jury involves secrecy and timing. Because of secrecy rules, if a grand jury declines to indict a defendant, the fact that he was even investigated may never become public. As a result, the defendant is spared any reputational harm. On the other hand, preliminary hearings occur only after an information has been filed and the charges are public record. In addition, the hearing itself takes place in open court. Even if the magistrate judge dismisses the indictment for lack of probable cause, the cat, as it were, is already out of the bag.[58]

Whither the Balance?

So, which is preferable: an inevitably flawed grand jury process (due to logistical limitations), or none at all? For the vast majority of cases, the answer appears to be the latter. A grand jury operating as an indictment mill is simply no use to a defendant. He would be much better off being accused by the prosecutor and then getting his chance to challenge the charges in open court at a preliminary hearing. Indeed, prosecutors implicitly recognize this fact: when given the choice, they usually avoid a preliminary hearing by bringing the case to the grand jury first. Nifong did just that in the Duke lacrosse case because he did not want Mangum exposed to cross-examination;[59] similarly (although unlike Nifong, not nefariously), my fellow federal prosecutors and

---

57. *See* White, *supra* note 30, at 263.

58. These are not, of course, the only arguments made to defend the grand jury. Sullivan and Nachman contend, for example, that there simply is insufficient proof of widespread grand-jury abuse to justify tinkering with the system. Sullivan & Nachman, *supra* note 30, at 158–61.

59. Taylor & Johnson, *supra* note 1, at 173.

I routinely avoided preliminary hearings by indicting defendants either prior to or within thirty days of their arrest. The bottom line is this: dismissal of unfounded charges at a preliminary hearing is probably the best outcome an overloaded criminal-justice system can realistically provide in the run-of-the-mill case.

Is the Duke Case Special?

Would a preliminary hearing-based process have helped the Duke defendants? In one sense, the answer must be "of course." At a preliminary hearing, Nifong would have been forced to put Crystal Mangum on the witness stand to testify about the events of March 18. Given her many conflicting statements, one can only imagine how poorly she would have fared against skilled cross-examination. In addition, the defense could have offered evidence consistent with innocence. Because probable cause is such a low threshold, it is difficult to be certain what the outcome would have been. But the odds are high that a judge would have dismissed the case for lack of probable cause;[60] on the other hand, we know from the actual case that the odds of a North Carolina grand jury refusing to indict the defendants were nil.

However, vindication through a preliminary hearing would not have prevented Evans, Finnerty, and Seligmann from experiencing the public ridicule, pain, and suffering caused by the public filing of the false charges in the first place. They would have operated under a black cloud of suspicion for weeks or months until they finally got the chance to clear themselves at the preliminary hearing. This is not an inconsequential matter. Without doubt, the worst accusation that an individual can face today is that he is a child molester or rapist. In most instances, even murderers—except, perhaps, serial killers—are held in higher regard. Many of them have understandable, if not acceptable, reasons for their action (e.g., physical or emotional abuse); others, like mafia hitmen, reap the benefits of glamorous media portrayals. As a result, in cases involving allegations of child molestation or rape, a grand jury-based procedure—with beefed-up safeguards—might be superior to one based on prosecutorial charges and a preliminary hearing. A robust grand-jury inquiry could quickly and secretly

---

60. Taylor and Johnson disagree with this. They believe that the outcome would have been the same because the judge assigned to the case at the time was prosecution-friendly. *See* Taylor & Johnson, *supra* note 1, at 173.

weed out false allegations, thereby reaching the correct result while causing minimal harm to those falsely accused.

Proposal

Let's take a step back for a moment. Providing special treatment for cases involving alleged sex crimes is nothing new.[61] Most of the modern innovations, of course, have imposed additional burdens on the accused. For example, most states have enacted special evidentiary rules to make it easier to convict alleged sex offenders[62] and have enhanced the sentences imposed upon conviction. In addition, after their release from prison, sex offenders must register with state and federal authorities and comply with myriad restrictions on their residency and employment.[63] This treatment clearly indicates how much the public holds sex offenders in fear and disrepute.

The especially harsh treatment of alleged and convicted sex offenders supports the thesis that rape and child molestation are the most odious charges that an individual can face. Moreover, once these charges are brought, enlightened authorities will aggressively pursue them. Some observers are likely to believe the allegations regardless of the case's eventual disposition. Therefore, society has a special obligation to ensure that such charges are warranted in the first place, and to dispose of them in the manner least harmful to the accused if they are not.

These goals can be accomplished by requiring that child molestation and rape charges be instituted only by grand-jury indictment. Further, the process for such cases should include special safeguards for the accused. First, there should be a requirement that the complainant testify before the grand jury. This will prevent the prosecution from papering over weaknesses in the complainant's credibility by using a summary law-enforcement witness. (Child-witnesses should, of course, be permitted to be accompanied by a nontestifying adult of their choosing.) Second, the accused should be given the opportunity to testify before the grand jury to argue his innocence. Though probably not essential, this provision would be more effective if counsel, playing only an advisory role, could accompany the defendant into the grand jury room. This

---

61. This topic is discussed at length *infra* in Chapter Fifteen (Orenstein).

62. *See, e.g.*, FED. R. EVID. 413–15.

63. *See, e.g.*, Megan's Law of 1996, Pub. L. No. 104-145, 110 Stat. 1345 (1996) (amending 170101(d) of the Violent Crime Control and Law Enforcement Act of 1994) (codified as amended at 42 U.S.C. § 14071(2000)).

would encourage more defendants to testify by reducing the potential risk; if things started looking bad, defense counsel could advise his client to exercise his Fifth Amendment privilege against self-incrimination. Third, the defense should be permitted to provide to the grand jury, in written or recorded form, any and all exculpatory material of its choosing. If the prosecution objected to the defense material as confusing or unwieldy, the presiding judge would take up the matter.

The end result of this robust grand-jury process would be an informed decision by the grand jury on the issue of probable cause. A "no true bill" would end the investigation, causing minimal injury to the defendant. Had this process been in place in Durham during the spring of 2006, events might have played out very differently indeed.

PART FIVE

LESSONS LEARNED ABOUT CRIMINAL EVIDENCE

The Duke Lacrosse Rape Investigation: How Not to Do Eyewitness-Identification Procedures

Gary L. Wells, Brian L. Cutler, & Lisa E. Hasel

Introduction

There is no doubt about the power of eyewitness-identification evidence to obtain convictions in criminal cases. In some ways, the best evidence for this comes from the fact that approximately 75 percent of the 215 DNA-based exonerations were cases of mistaken identification that were accepted by juries as evidence that those innocent individuals were guilty.[1] But, well before the onset of forensic DNA testing in the 1990s, experiments by psychological scientists had demonstrated that mistaken identifications occur with surprising frequency and that mistaken identification testimony is difficult to distinguish from accurate identification testimony.[2] Hence, a central theme for psycho-

---

1. *See* Innocence Project, *Eyewitness Misidentification*, INNOCENCEPROJECT.ORG, http://www.innocenceproject.org/understand/Eyewitness-Misidentification.php.

2. *See* R.C.L. Lindsay, G.L. Wells & C. Rumpel, *Can People Detect Eyewitness Identification Accuracy Within and Between Situations?*, 66 J. APPLIED PSYCHOL. 79 (1981); G.L. Wells, T.J. Ferguson & R.C.L. Lindsay, *The Tractability of Eyewitness Confidence and Its Implication for Triers of Fact*, 66 J. APPLIED PSYCHOL. 688 (1981); G.L. Wells, R.C.L. Lindsay & T.J. Ferguson, *Accuracy, Confidence, and Juror Perceptions in Eyewitness Identification*, 64 J. APPLIED PSYCHOL. 440 (1979); G.L. Wells, R.C.L. Lindsay & J.P. Tousignant, *Effects of Expert Psychological Advice on Juror Judgments in Eyewitness Testimony*, 4 LAW & HUM. BEHAV. 275 (1980).

logical science has been the development of ways to prevent mistaken identifications from happening in the first place.[3] Broad treatments of the scientific literature on eyewitness identification are available in numerous books[4] and scholarly articles.[5]

The Duke lacrosse rape case represents an interesting problem that is, in some respects, different from the prototypical mistaken identification case. Usually, the concern is that an eyewitness will make a "genuine error" in the sense that the eyewitness is mistaken but honestly believes that the identified person is the perpetrator. If we accept the apparent consensus that a rape never even occurred in the Duke lacrosse case, then we must consider two possibilities. One is that the "victim-witness" was simply lying and never believed that the individuals she identified had raped her. The other possibility is that she had developed a false memory of being raped and somehow came to believe that these were the men who had committed the act. We have no way of knowing with certainty at this time which of these two possibilities, the assumption of lying or the assumption of genuine error, is closer to the truth. For our current purposes, however, the distinction matters little because, under either assumption, the identification procedures used in the Duke lacrosse case were profoundly flawed, dangerous, and nondiagnostic of the guilt or innocence of the accused individuals.

The principal thesis of this chapter is that the legal system had the opportunity, ability, and tools readily at its disposal to conduct a proper identification procedure. Furthermore, a proper identification procedure would have likely shown that the victim-witness was not credible and, therefore, absent other compelling evidence, charges would not have been filed. The Duke lacrosse case also holds a special irony for eyewitness scientists because the Durham Police Department had adopted new eyewitness identification procedures prior to these allegations of rape, procedures that were modeled on the best that eyewitness science had to offer.[6] Indeed, North Carolina had al-

---

3. G.L. Wells, *Applied Eyewitness Testimony Research: System Variables and Estimator Variables*, 36 J. Pers. & Soc. Psychol. 1546 (1978).

4. *See, e.g.,* Brian L. Cutler & Steven D. Penrod, Mistaken Identification: The Eyewitness, Psychology, and the Law (1995); 2 Handbook of Eyewitness Psychology: Memory for People (R.C.L. Lindsay et al. eds., 2007).

5. G.L. Wells & D.S. Quinlivan, *Suggestive Eyewitness Identification Procedures and the Supreme Court's Reliability Test in Light of Eyewitness Science: 30 Years Later*, 32 Law & Human Behav. (forthcoming 2008).

6. In the interests of full disclosure, readers should note that the first two authors of this chapter were expert eyewitness consultants for the defense in the Duke lacrosse case. In addition, they consulted for the North Carolina Actual Innocence Commission to help de-

ready become a model state in leading the reform of eyewitness-identification procedures, thanks largely to its North Carolina Actual Innocence Commission, chaired by then-Chief Justice of the North Carolina Supreme Court, Beverly Lake. In fact, critical public meetings of the North Carolina Innocence Commission that announced and described the recommendations for eyewitness identification procedures took place with great fanfare on June 10, 2004, in—of all places—Durham, North Carolina.

Although the Durham Police Department adopted the North Carolina Actual Innocence Commission's recommended eyewitness identification procedures as their policy prior to the Duke case, the procedures used in that case violated what can be considered "rule one" of those procedures, which we will describe later. Precisely why the Durham Police Department's own identification procedures were not followed in this case is not clear to us. It could be argued that proper identification procedures would have been followed if the Durham Police Department itself had total control of the investigation and that it was the Prosecutor Mike Nifong who directed an identification procedure that was flawed. Additional inquiries might sort out that particular puzzle. We take no position on who created the identification procedure in the Duke lacrosse case or why it was created; we only know that it was a very bad idea.

In the remainder of this chapter, we will describe some of the eyewitness science as it relates to the basic idea of eyewitness identification and discuss why procedural safeguards are so important. Then, we will analyze the procedures used in the Duke lacrosse rape case and the behaviors of the alleged victim-witness. Finally, we will examine how the identification procedures could have been improved and how this would likely have uncovered the witness' credibility problems early in the process.

The Logic and Science of Eyewitness Identification

The general idea of eyewitness identification is relatively straightforward: If an eyewitness, whether bystander or victim, observed the perpetrator committing the crime in question, then investigators can establish the identity of that perpetrator simply by asking the witness to identify him or her. The presumption is that, if the witness had a good view and was attending to the phys-

---

velop the eyewitness-identification-procedure recommendations that the Durham Police Department adopted before the Duke lacrosse case.

ical appearance of the perpetrator, the witness' memory could be a valid indicator of identity. Unless the witness is motivated to lie, there seems little reason not to trust the witness, especially if the witness is certain. After all, the visual recognition of people is something that humans do repeatedly, without apparent error, in their everyday encounters. No stranger could masquerade as one's spouse, child, or coworker. And people seen at one point in time, such as high-school classmates, are often readily recognized from their photos even thirty years later.[7]

Against this backdrop of reliable facial recognition, most people do understand that recognition is not foolproof. For example, many people have had the experience of looking for their waiter or waitress in a restaurant and being unable to pick him or her out from similarly dressed counterparts even though they do not look much alike. Moreover, many of us have been in the awkward situation when being introduced to a person and saying "nice to meet you" only to have him or her respond "we met last month" or, even worse, "we met earlier tonight." But these little events tend not to shake many people's faith in eyewitness identifications of perpetrators because witnessing a crime event (or being its victim) is a meaningful, powerful event that surely creates a deep memory of the perpetrator, whereas a mere casual encounter with a stranger does not. Despite this everyday logic, however, the scientific evidence indicates that stress, which commonly accompanies being a victim or witness to a crime, actually impairs memory rather than helps it.[8] Yes, people tend to pay more attention to serious events than to mundane ones, but attention does not guarantee an accurate memory.

It might be easy for people to understand how an eyewitness can look at a lineup and say "I don't know." That type of recognition failure is readily explained through people's common understanding of failures to pay attention when witnessing something, or the common concept of forgetting. What people understand far less is how an eyewitness can look at a lineup and identify the wrong person. People can probably grasp the idea of mistaken identification emanating from coincidental resemblance or lying but, short of the unlikely event of a defendant who bears an uncanny resemblance to the culprit or a deceptive eyewitness, why would a witness identify an innocent suspect as the culprit?

The question of why honest eyewitnesses mistakenly identify someone, rather than refuse to make an identification, is one of the most fundamental

---

7. H.P. Bahrick, P.O. Bahrick & R.P. Wittlinger, *Fifty Years of Memory for Names and Faces,* 104 J. EXPERIMENTAL PSYCHOL. 54 (1975).

8. C.A. Morgan et al., *Accuracy of Eyewitness Memory for Persons Encountered During Exposure to Highly Intense Stress,* 27 INT'L J.L. & PSYCHIATRY 265 (2004).

questions that eyewitness scientists have faced. One fairly simple psychological model is based on the notions of pressure and preference. When shown a lineup, eyewitnesses have a natural tendency to feel pressured to make positive identifications. Thoughts such as "I was there, I should be able to recognize him," "People are counting on me," "I don't want to let someone get away with this crime," and "If I can't pick him out, then I have failed" are understandable when presented with a lineup. In addition, almost any lineup will include someone who looks more like the witness' memory of the perpetrator than the remaining members of the lineup. Hence, even eyewitnesses with only vague memories of the perpetrator will often have a preference for one lineup-member over the others (this is called making a relative judgment).[9] Pressure and preference together can be a powerful force resulting in choice.

The pressure-and-preference notion, although simple, is actually quite rich in its implications for identification procedures. Pressure can be reduced by making it clear to the eyewitness that the actual perpetrator might not be in the lineup at all and, therefore, the accurate response might be "none of the above." Importantly, a pre-lineup instruction to the effect that the perpetrator might not be present in a lineup serves to make eyewitnesses much more likely to reject lineups in which the actual perpetrator is not present. However, this instruction has little effect on accurate identifications of the perpetrator when he is present in the lineup.[10] There is nothing highly unusual about witnesses confronting lineups in which the actual perpetrator is not present; it simply means that the police thought that a particular person might have committed the offense but in fact he did not. Virtually every DNA exoneration case involving mistaken eyewitness identification from a lineup presented exactly that type of situation; the lineup viewed by the eyewitness did not contain the actual perpetrator.

In many jurisdictions that have reformed their lineup procedures (including the Durham Police Department), the prelineup instructions go even further to include statements such as "Do not feel that you have to make an identification" and "It is just as important to clear the innocent from suspicion as it is to incriminate the guilty." Reducing pressure to make a positive identification is one key to preventing misidentifications of innocent people

---

9. G.L. Wells, *The Psychology of Lineup Identifications*, 14 J. APPLIED SOC. PSYCHOL. 89 (1984).

10. N.M. Steblay, *Social Influence in Eyewitness Recall: A Meta-analytic Review of Lineup Instruction Effects*, 21 LAW & HUMAN BEHAV. 283 (1997); S.E. Clark, *A Re-examination of the Effects of Biased Lineup Instructions in Eyewitness Identification*, 29 LAW & HUMAN BEHAV. 395 (2005).

and, hence, a core element of proper identification procedures. As we will note later, this pressure was not reduced in the critical (final) identification phase of the Duke lacrosse rape case—in fact, the procedures exacerbated it.

Preference is a somewhat more complex problem. Clearly, we want the eyewitness to prefer the perpetrator if he is in the lineup; indeed, research shows that the perpetrator naturally attracts such preferences.[11] The biggest problem occurs when the perpetrator is not in the lineup because there is usually someone else in it who looks more like the perpetrator than the others do, thereby resulting in the witness' preference for an innocent person. The removal-without-replacement effect, first demonstrated in an experiment fifteen years ago, illustrates the preference problem.[12] After staging a theft 200 times for 200 separate eyewitnesses, the researchers showed half of the eyewitnesses a six-person lineup that included the thief. All of these witnesses were warned that the thief might or might not be in the lineup; 54 percent correctly identified the thief, 21 percent identified no one, and the remaining 25 percent identified other lineup members. The other half of the witnesses were also warned that the thief might or might not be present and in fact viewed a lineup in which the thief was removed and not replaced with anyone (hence the term "removal without replacement"). The critical question for the study was: What will happen to the 54 percent who would have chosen the thief had he been present? Will they be added to the 21 percent who identified no one, thereby resulting in 75 percent making no identification? This turned out not to be the case. Only 11 percent of the people moved to the no-identification category, so only 32 percent of the eyewitnesses who saw the lineup without the thief did not make an identification. The remaining 43 percent simply shifted their choices to another lineup member. Hence, even though the real thief was not in the lineup and the witnesses were warned that he might not be in the lineup, preferences continued to exert an influence that resulted in mistaken identifications.

The simple notion that eyewitnesses will prefer a particular lineup member even if the perpetrator is not in the lineup is at the heart of perhaps the single most important procedural requirement: a lineup should contain only one suspect, and the remaining lineup members should be fillers.[13] By fillers, we mean people who are known-innocents who simply fit the perpetrator's general description. The identification of a filler does not, of course, result in charges

---

11. S.E. Clark, R.T. Howell & S.L. Davey, *Regularities in Eyewitness Identification*, 32 LAW & HUMAN BEHAV. 187 (2008).

12. G.L.Wells, *What Do We Know About Eyewitness Identification?*, 48 AM. PSYCHOL. 553 (1993).

13. G.L. Wells & J.W. Turtle, *Eyewitness Identification: The Importance of Lineup Models*, 99 PSYCHOL. BULL. 320 (1986).

against the identified person. Instead, it tells us that the suspect is not the perpetrator, that the eyewitness is not reliable, or both. This is a simple yet powerful principle because, if done correctly (meaning that each filler fits the general description of the perpetrator), an innocent suspect's chance of being the person who looks most like the perpetrator is far lower than the collective probability represented by the well-chosen fillers. Most proper identification procedures require at least five fillers for every suspect. Ideally, then, five out of every six witnesses who attempt an identification from a perpetrator-absent lineup will mistakenly identify a filler rather than an innocent suspect.

Primary Features of Good Eyewitness-Identification Procedures

No set of identification procedures can guarantee that mistaken eyewitness identifications will not occur. Nevertheless, some procedures are far less likely to yield mistaken identifications than others. Based on the science, a number of groups have articulated in recent years several sets of procedural recommendations for lineups and photospreads. These groups include the American Psychology-Law Society,[14] the National Institute of Justice,[15] and the North Carolina Innocence Commission. Although their procedural recommendations vary somewhat, they clearly have some common elements:

- A lineup should have only one suspect, with the other members being fillers.
- There should be at least five fillers for every suspect.
- Fillers should match the general description that the eyewitness gave of the culprit, and lineup administrators should take any other measures that will ensure the suspect does not stand out.
- Witnesses should be warned that the perpetrator might not be in the lineup, and told not to guess.
- Lineup administrators should take measures to avoid influencing the witness. (The American Psychology-Law Society recommendations and the North Carolina Innocence Commission recommendations explicitly state

---

14. G.L. Wells et al., *Eyewitness Identification Procedures: Recommendations for Lineups and Photospreads*, 22 Law & Human Behav. 603 (1998).

15. U.S. Dep't of Justice, Technical Working Group for Eyewitness Evidence, Eyewitness Evidence: A Guide for Law Enforcement (1999), http://www.ncjrs.gov/pdf files1/nij/178240.pdf.

that the lineup administrator should not know which lineup member is the suspect, a procedure known as a double-blind lineup.)
• The lineup administrator should record a clear statement of the witness' certainty at the time of the identification.

Clearly, no set of recommendations can detail every possible way that an identification procedure might bias an eyewitness. We note, for example, that none of the three sets of recommendations discussed here specifically say not to show a suspect's photo repeatedly. But, of course, doing so familiarizes the witness with that person's face and can lead to a memory-source error (that is, the witness remembers the face from prior photos rather than the crime scene). In the context of these clear and fairly well-defined procedural recommendations, we will now review the basic facts and procedures that the authorities used in the Duke lacrosse rape investigation.

The Duke Lacrosse Rape Investigation

At midnight on March 14, 2006, Crystal Mangum, the alleged victim-witness, and her fellow dancer began their routine. The events that occurred from that moment until the alleged rape was reported are beyond the scope of this chapter.[16] The mental state of the witness during the party, however, would affect her ability to identify her attackers later. Although she initially reported having only one drink at the party, she later said that she was drunk that evening and, therefore, did not feel any pain after the alleged attack. At another time, she reported having drunk very little alcohol that evening, but becoming "fuzzy" when she and the other dancer began to perform. However, partygoers reported that she appeared intoxicated and, multiple times throughout the routine, stumbled and fell to the floor.

Later, in the early morning of March 15, Durham police questioned Mangum about the alleged attack. She named her alleged attackers—Adam, Matt, and Brett—during these three separate discussions, but she did not once give a description of them. Detective Benjamin Himan reported, however, that two days later she described them to Sergeant Mark Gottlieb and him as follows:

Adam: White male, short, red cheeks, chubby face, brown fluffy hair.

---

16. For a thorough discussion of the underlying facts, see *supra* Chapter One (Luck & Seigel).

Matt: Heavyset with short haircut between 260 and 270 lbs.
Brett: Chubby.[17]

During the same discussion, Gottlieb took handwritten notes that he later typed into a report of all of his activities in the case. Although he did not include the names of the alleged attackers in his notes, we have attempted to match them with the names and descriptions reported by Himan:

Possibly Adam: [White male] medium height (5'8" + with Himan's build), dark hair, medium build, and had red (rose colored) cheeks
Possibly Matt: [White male], young, blonde hair, baby faced, tall and lean
Possibly Brett: [White male], 6+ feet tall, large build, with dark hair[18]

Two days later, the Durham police showed Mangum four separate photo lineups. The photo arrays contained only members of the lacrosse team, and each included a lacrosse player named Adam, Matt, or Brett. In accordance with the department's protocol, the person administering the test, Investigator Richard Clayton, was largely unfamiliar with the investigation and did not know which players—if any—were suspects. The witness was told that the "person who committed the crime may or may not be included. I do not know whether the person being investigated is included." Additionally, she was told to "[k]eep in mind that things like hair styles, beards, and mustaches can be easily changed and that complexion colors may look slightly different in the photographs. You should not feel like you have to make an identification." Clayton described the additional instructions he gave her about the first four lineups, stating:

I informed her that if she did recognize a person in the photo in the array to be as descriptive as possible regarding the details of that person. I then told her to use a scale from 1–10 if she was able to recognize the person. [One] being the least and 10 being the highest. I gave her an example as 10 being that she positively recognized the person on the photo 100%. Each photo was displayed for 30 seconds. I showed

17. *See* Motion to Suppress the Alleged "Identification" of the Defendants by the Accuser, at 9–10, State v. Seligmann, Nos. 06 CRS 4331-36, 5581-83 (N.C. Super. Ct. Dec. 14, 2006) [hereinafter Motion to Suppress].

18. *Id.* For a more detailed analysis of the witness's descriptions, see Table 1 at the end of this chapter.

her one photo at a time. After a photo was displayed I did not go back to any previous displayed photos in the array.[19]

While viewing the first lineup — Photo Array A — the witness stated that the lineup task was harder than she thought it would be and that all of the photos looked alike. Photo Array A included Reade Seligmann in position #5, and the witness said that she was 70 percent sure that she had seen him at the party but could not remember where.[20] In a later identification procedure, of course, she would identify Seligmann as one of her attackers. Mangum also said she was 100 percent confident that one person from Photo Array B, two from Photo Array C, and one from Photo Array D were at the party. It was eventually determined, however, that one of individuals she placed at the party with "100 percent certainty" spent that entire evening in nearby Raleigh, North Carolina, and could not have been in attendance. Clayton's report of these four lineups concluded that the witness did not identify any of the men in the photo arrays as her attacker.

On March 21, five days after examining Photo Arrays A–D, the witness viewed two more. Once again, they only included Duke lacrosse players, and the witness received the same warnings and instructions as before. Clayton went through Photo Arrays E and F with Mangum twice. She did not identify any of the people in the lineups as an assailant. Dave Evens, whom she later identified as one of her alleged attackers, was in Photo Array F.

After Mangum had viewed the initial seven lineups but made no identification, Nifong suggested to Himan and Gottlieb that they put the mug-shot-type photographs of the lacrosse players into a group and merely ask Mangum whether she recalled seeing the individuals at the party. A little over two weeks after viewing Photo Arrays E and F, the witness to come to the station for yet another identification attempt, this time conducted in the manner suggested by Nifong. On this occasion, instead of being in a private setting with Clayton, Gottlieb and two crime-scene investigators were also present. Additionally, the police video- and audiotaped the procedure using equipment placed in plain view of the witness, which they had not done during the previous identification attempts.

Using a PowerPoint presentation, the investigators presented photographs of all forty-six lacrosse players. Even though they knew that at least two non-lacrosse players were at the party, only team members were included . Gottlieb told the witness that "we are going to sit in the far side of the room at the

---

19. Motion to Suppress, *supra* note 17, at 16.
20. *Id.* at 17.

desk and look at people we had reason to believe attended the party."[21] He reported that he

> also told her it was important to tell us if she recalled seeing a particular individual at the party and to let us know how she recalled seeing them from that night, what they were doing, and any interactions she may have had or observed with a particular individual.[22]

While reviewing the pictures of the forty-six lacrosse team members, Mangum claimed to recognize seventeen of them. She stated that four of the players resembled her three alleged attackers. The first person she identified was Matthew Wilson (Image 4), saying "He looked like Brett but I'm not sure.... One of the guys that assaulted me."[23] The next person in the lineup (Image 5) was Dave Evans, and she also identified him as one of her attackers, stating "He looks like one of the guys who assaulted me sort [of].... He looks just like him without the mustache ... About 90%."[24] Two photographs later, the witness identified Reade Seligmann (Image 7) as one of her attackers, saying "He looks like one of the guys who assaulted me ... 100%.... He was the one that was standing in front of me ... um ... that made me perform oral sex on him."[25] Near the end of the presentation, she identified Collin Finnerty (Image 40) as one of her attackers as well, saying "He is the guy who assaulted me.... He put his penis in my anus and my vagina.... The second one ... 100%."[26]

During the procedure, she identified the individuals in Images 3, 4, 9, 11, 13, 15, 17, 20, 21, 26, 31, 34, 37, and 38 as being at the party. In fact, it was later determined that two of the players were not there. Eleven of them had appeared in previous lineups, but she had not identified them as having even been at the party. One individual was incorrectly identified as the person who had made an obscene comment about a broomstick. She did, ironically, identify the person who had made the obscene comment, but described him as "sitting in the kitchen ... um, making a drink." Additionally, even though Mangum had, in previous lineups, identified five individuals as being at the party, she did not recognize three of them in the PowerPoint lineup.[27]

---

21. *Id.* at 16.
22. *Id.*
23. *Id.* at 19.
24. *Id.*
25. *Id.*
26. *Id.*
27. *Id.* at 19–20.

After identifying Reade Seligmann, Dave Evans, and Collin Finnerty as her attackers, the witness made a few comments about them that deviated from her earlier descriptions. When viewing the photograph of Evans, she stated that he looked like her attacker, just without a mustache. Photographs taken of Evans in the days prior to and following the alleged attack, however, show that he did not have a mustache at that time.[28] Additionally, she said that she recognized Finnerty because of the freckles on his face. However, she had never mentioned freckles as a characteristic of any of her attackers before that moment. In fact, the witness was not shown a photograph of Finnerty before the PowerPoint identification procedure because he did not match any of the descriptions of her alleged attackers.

Analysis of the Identification Procedures in the Duke Case

It should be apparent to almost anyone that the identification procedures used by the investigators on the Duke case were terribly flawed. These flaws are apparent not only in contrast to the guidelines set out by the American Psychology-Law Society, the National Institute of Justice, and the North Carolina Innocence Commission, but also in contrast to the Durham Police Department's own procedures (because by this time the Durham Police Department had already adopted the North Carolina Innocence Commission's recommendations).

As an important aside, we should note that identification procedures matter the most when there are reasons to believe that the witness's memory is weak. The witness in this case was clearly drinking heavily and gave inconsistent descriptions of her attackers (see Table 1 for a summary). Hence, these were circumstances in which it was especially important to follow pristine identification procedures, which are designed to help protect innocent persons from mistaken identification.

In Table 2, found at the conclusion of this chapter, we summarize some of the important aspects of proper identification procedures and illustrate how the Duke procedures deviated from them. Perhaps the most important of these deviations was the failure to use fillers. In effect, the identification procedure, for Mangum, was like a multiple-choice question which had no wrong answer. The beauty of using fillers is that an eyewitness who is merely guessing or has

---

28. *Id.* at 36.

an unreliable memory is likely to err on a filler. These filler errors will call into question the credibility of the witness. Fillers in this case would have been easy to obtain. One might have contacted the University of Illinois lacrosse team, for example, and included their photos in the procedure, which would likely have revealed the witness to be picking people who clearly were not involved in the incident at all.

Clearly, the situation that was facing the investigators in this case was not a typical eyewitness identification situation in which there is a single *a priori* suspect. If all Duke lacrosse players (or, at least, those who were at the party) were considered suspects, then it would have taken roughly 230 filler photos to meet the five-filler-per-suspect requirement. One might argue that it would be unreasonable to have the witness go through about 286 photos to try to identify her attackers. But the proper alternative was not to abandon the concept of fillers altogether; instead, using a reduced number of fillers would have been acceptable. Assume, for a moment, the real possibility that the witness was randomly picking individuals from the photos during the third lineup procedure. If there had been even two true fillers for each of the forty-six suspects in that lineup, the chances that she could have avoided picking one of the known-innocent fillers in three picks is 1/33, or only one chance in twenty-seven—a .037 percent chance.

Interestingly, when the first identification procedures were used on March 16 and March 21, the administering officers were careful to instruct the witness that the persons who committed the crime might not be included. But this warning was completely dropped in the final identification procedure. Furthermore, in this last identification procedure, the witness was assured prior to viewing that the lineup contained only persons whom the police believed to be at the party. It should not go unnoticed that it was only in this last procedure, which in effect assured the witness that there were no filler photos, that the witness made identifications of her attackers.

In addition to the officers' failure to use fillers, Mangum had failed to identify two of the three individuals that she finally picked out as her attackers when shown their pictures in prior displays. This repeated presentation of certain suspects' photos is obviously egregious; ironically, existing recommendations for proper identification procedures have spent little time discussing this issue. Indeed, they have probably overlooked this problem precisely because it seems so obvious.

Final Remarks

By now, it is clear that the alleged rape at the lacrosse party that night never occurred. Hence, it might be argued that the identification procedures were irrelevant. We disagree. We contend that proper procedures, including the use of fillers, would likely have shown that the witness' account was fatally flawed.

The foregoing analysis shows that the identification procedures used in the Duke lacrosse case miserably failed to protect the interests of the accused. The explanation for these breaches of both common sense and the explicit policies already adopted by the Durham Police Department are open to debate and addressed in other chapters in this volume. As eyewitness-identification scientists, it is not our task to speculate on the motives or reasoning of the investigators in this case. But we think that it is important to note that guidelines and policies for conducting eyewitness-identification procedures exist for very good reasons, and we would urge police departments to adhere to these procedures and respect their underlying principles, regardless of underlying political or social currents that might surround a given case. We also encourage departments to resist the urgings of prosecutors to deviate from the department's identification procedures after they have been carefully developed and implemented for very good reason.

Table 1
Descriptions Given by the Witnesses Compared to Characteristics of the Identified Parties

Descriptions in Himan's Report	Descriptions in Clayton's Report	Descriptions of Persons Eventually Identified by Crystal Mangum
"Adam" White male, short, red cheeks, chubby face, brown fluffy hair.	Possibly "Adam" White male, medium height (5'8" or above, with Himan's build), dark hair, with red (rose colored) cheeks.	Reade Seligmann White male, 6'1", 215 pounds, black hair.
"Matt" Heavyset, between 260 and 270 pounds, short hair.	Possibly "Matt" White male, young, blonde hair, baby-faced, tall and lean.	Dave Evans White male, 5'9", 185 pounds, brown hair.
"Brett" Chubby.	Possibly "Brett" White male, over 6', large build, dark hair.	Collin Finnerty White male, 6'5", 215 pounds, reddish-brown hair, freckled face.

Table 2

Comparison between the Identification Procedures Used in the
Duke Lacrosse Rape Investigation and Three Sets of
Recommended Identification Procedures

Recommendations	Durham PD Rape Investigation	National Institute of Justice	American Psychology-Law Society	North Carolina Innocence Commission
Five fillers for each suspect	No fillers	Recommended	Recommended	Recommended
Select fillers who fit description	No	Recommended	Recommended	Recommended
Avoid showing the same faces multiple times	No; some faces were shown two or three times	Not addressed	Recommended, although not a "core" recommendation	Recommended
Secure confidence statement at the time of identification	Yes	Recommended	Recommended	Recommended
Present the photographs sequentially	Yes	Recommended; recommends simultaneous presentation as well.	Recommended; recommends simultaneous presentation as well.	Recommended
Double-blind procedure	No	Not addressed	Recommended	Recommended

CHAPTER FOURTEEN

DNA Profiling

Paul C. Giannelli

Introduction

DNA profiling was first reported in 1985 by Dr. Alec Jeffreys of the University of Leicester, England.[1] The initial reports on what was then called, somewhat misleadingly, "DNA fingerprinting" were dramatic. One judge wrote that DNA evidence was the "single greatest advance in the 'search for truth' ... since the advent of cross-examination."[2] A National Academy of Sciences report would later echo that sentiment: "DNA analysis is one of the greatest technical achievements for criminal investigation since the discovery of fingerprints."[3] This was not mere hyperbole. The advent of DNA profiling revolutionized forensic science. No other technique has been as complex or so subject to rapid change. New DNA technologies were introduced at the trial level, even as cases litigating the older procedures worked their way through the appellate-court system. As one prosecutor observed, DNA evidence "raised issues at the cutting edge of modern law and science."[4]

The first cases unquestioningly accepted DNA evidence; the defense did not call an expert in *Andrews v. State*,[5] which in 1988 became the first reported appellate case to uphold the admissibility of DNA evidence. Nor was a defense expert called the next year in *Spencer v. Commonwealth*,[6] the first DNA-based

---

1. *See generally* Joseph Wambaugh, The Blooding (1989).

2. People v. Wesley, 533 N.Y.S.2d 643, 644 (Sup. Ct. 1988).

3. Nat'l Research Council, The Evaluation of Forensic DNA Evidence 73 (1996) [hereinafter NRC 1996 Report].

4. Harlan Levy, And the Blood Cried Out: A Prosecutor's Spellbinding Account of the Power of DNA 21 (1996).

5. 533 So. 2d 841 (Fla. Dist. Ct. App. 1988).

6. 384 S.E.2d 785, 792, 797 (Va. 1989).

death-penalty execution case.[7] The prosecution's experts testified that " 'no dissent whatsoever [exists] in the scientific community' concerning the reliability of the DNA printing technique."[8] *People v. Castro*,[9] however, shattered this initial euphoria. The *Castro* court wrote: "In a piercing attack upon each molecule of evidence presented, the defense was successful in demonstrating to this court that the testing laboratory failed in its responsibility to perform the accepted scientific techniques and experiments."[10] The court did not, however, question the underlying science, only its application. As molecular biologist Eric Lander pointed out: "At present, forensic science is virtually unregulated — with the paradoxical result that clinical laboratories must meet higher standards to be allowed to diagnose strep throat than forensic labs must meet to put a defendant on death row."[11] Even the FBI's top DNA scientist, Dr. Bruce Budowle, would later acknowledge the shortfalls of DNA evidence when it was first introduced:

> The initial outcry over DNA typing standards concerned laboratory problems: poorly defined rules for declaring a match, experiments without controls, contaminated probes and samples, and sloppy interpretation of autoradiograms. Although there is no evidence that these technical failings resulted in any wrongful convictions, the lack of standards seemed to be a recipe for trouble.[12]

The *Castro* decision highlighted the need for a more rigorous approach to forensic DNA analysis and, by implication, to all forensic evidence. The National Academy of Sciences' 1992 report on the subject noted the importance of certain practices: "No laboratory should let its results with a new DNA typing method be used in court, unless it has undergone ... proficiency testing via blind trials."[13] The initial skirmishes over laboratory protocols quickly evolved into fights over statistical interpretation and population genetics. Nev-

---

7. See *Murderer Put to Death in Virginia: First U.S. Execution Based on DNA Tests*, N.Y. Times, Apr. 28, 1994, at A19 (reporting Spencer's execution).

8. 384 S.E.2d at 797 (quoting experts).

9. 545 N.Y.S.2d 985, 996 (Sup. Ct. 1989).

10. For a discussion of the importance of the *Castro* case, see Jennifer L. Mnookin, *People v. Castro: Challenging the Forensic Use of DNA Evidence, in* Evidence Stories 207 (Richard Lempert ed., 2006).

11. Eric S. Lander, *DNA Fingerprinting on Trial*, 339 Nature 501, 505 (1989).

12. Eric S. Lander & Bruce Budowle, *DNA Fingerprinting Dispute Laid to Rest*, 371 Nature 735, 735 (1994).

13. Nat'l Research Council, DNA Technology in Forensic Science 55 (1992).

ertheless, by the time the Academy published its second report in 1996,[14] courts had accepted the underlying science and basic protocols. Subsequent litigation would, instead, focus on new technologies and novel applications.[15]

Two critical developments made the impact of DNA profiling far greater than anyone could have predicted at the time of Jeffreys' 1985 discovery. One was the employment of DNA testing to exonerate hundreds of convicted prisoners. The other was the creation of a national database of DNA profiles, which permitted "cold hits" in cases without a suspect.

DNA Exonerations

Because of the capability to test decades-old evidence for DNA, news reports of the exoneration of the innocent became almost commonplace.[16] The Cardozo School of Law Innocence Project asserts that "[s]ince 1989, there have been tens of thousands of cases where prime suspects were arrested or indicted— until DNA evidence (prior to trial) proved that they were wrongly accused."[17] More dramatically, DNA has freed over 200 convicts, some of whom were on death row.[18] Indeed, John Grisham's only nonfiction work to date examines the case of one exoneree, Ron Williamson, who came within five days of execution.[19]

The impact of these exonerations has extended well beyond the lives of the wrongly incarcerated individuals. As the number of innocent inmates released from prison skyrocketed, reformers began to cast a critical eye on the causes of these miscarriages of justice. A recent study of 200 DNA exonerations found that mistaken eyewitness identifications were, by far, the most widespread cause for wrongful convictions; they were involved in 79 percent of the cases, followed by forensic (expert) evidence (57 percent), informant testimony (18 percent), and false confessions (16 percent).[20] As a result, several organiza-

---

14. *See* NRC 1996 REPORT, *supra* note 3.

15. *See* PAUL C. GIANNELLI & EDWARD J. IMWINKELRIED, 2 SCIENTIFIC EVIDENCE ch. 18 (4th ed. 2007) (discussing the case-law development).

16. *See, e.g.,* Barbara Novovitch, *Free After 17 Years for a Rape That He Did Not Commit,* N.Y. TIMES, Dec. 22, 2004, at A18 (discussing the case of Brandon Moon).

17. Innocence Project, Facts on Post Conviction DNA Exonerations, INNOCENCEPROJECT.ORG, http://www.innocenceproject.org/docs/DNAExonerationFacts_WEB. Pdf (last visited Oct. 29, 2008).

18. *See* TIM JUNKIN, BLOODSWORTH: THE TRUE STORY OF THE FIRST DEATH ROW INMATE EXONERATED BY DNA (2004).

19. JOHN GRISHAM, THE INNOCENT MAN: MURDER AND INJUSTICE IN A SMALL TOWN (2006).

20. Brandon L. Garrett, *Judging Innocence,* 108 COLUM. L. REV. 55 (2008).

tions, including the ABA,[21] advocated several reforms, including videotaping all interrogations, requiring the accreditation of crime laboratories, employing double-blind lineups and photographic displays,[22] and requiring corroboration of jailhouse-informant testimony. In addition to the evidentiary issues, commentators also scrutinized the roles of the various actors in the criminal justice system. Barry Scheck and his colleagues at the Innocence Project, examining sixty-two cases, identified police misbehavior in 50 percent of them,[23] prosecutorial misconduct in 42 percent, and ineffective assistance of defense counsel in 27 percent.

DNA Databases

DNA's discriminatory power, combined with computer technology, permits comparison of DNA profiles derived from crime scenes with profiles from convicted offenders. Since 1989, every state has enacted legislation authorizing the collection of samples from at least some convicted offenders for DNA databases, although the targeted offenses and procedural requirements differ widely. The initial wave of legislation focused on sex and violent offenders, but in most states the statutes gradually expanded to include all felons; several even include certain categories of arrestees. In 1994, Congress passed the DNA Identification Act,[24] which authorized the FBI to establish the Combined DNA Index System (CODIS), a national database of DNA profiles. This newfound ability to obtain a "cold hit" meant that DNA analysis could not only be used to construct a case against an identified suspect, but also to investigate a case by identifying a previously unknown suspect.[25] For example, by using DNA databases, law enforcement linked Fletcher Worrell to twenty-five rapes committed over a thirty-year period in three different states.[26]

---

21. *See* Am. Bar Ass'n, Criminal Justice Section, Achieving Justice: Freeing the Innocent, Convicting the Guilty (Paul C. Giannelli & Myrna Raeder eds., 2006).

22. For an in-depth discussion of the reforms advanced for eyewitness identifications, see *supra* Chapter Thirteen (Wells, Cutler & Hasel).

23. Barry Scheck et al., Actual Innocence: Five Days to Execution and Other Dispatches from the Wrongly Convicted 246 (2000) (examining sixty-two of the first sixty-seven exoneration cases).

24. 42 U.S.C. §14131(1)(a), (c) (2004).

25. *See* David Lazer, *Introduction* to DNA and the Criminal Justice System 7 (David Lazer ed., 2004) ("[T]hrough March 2004, 16,100 crime investigations in the United States had been aided through convict DNA databases.").

26. Julia Preston, *Rape Victims' Eyes Were Covered, but a Key Clue Survived*, N.Y. Times, Apr. 28, 2005, at A23.

Problems

Despite the power of DNA evidence, its proper use cannot be taken for granted. The U.S. Department of Justice Inspector General has released two reports relating to DNA, one involving misconduct by an FBI analyst in testing[27] and the other specifying shortcomings in CODIS procedures.[28] In addition, the Earl Washington case raised grave concerns with the State of Virginia's DNA laboratory.[29] In the most serious example to date, the Houston Police Department had to close its DNA-testing operations due to major deficiencies,[30] one of which had resulted in DNA evidence contributing to the wrongful conviction of Josiah Sutton.[31] The ensuing investigation stated that,

> the DNA Section was in shambles, plagued by a leaky roof, operating for years without a line supervisor, overseen by a technical leader who had no personal experience performing DNA analysis and who was lacking the qualifications required under the FBI standards, staffed by underpaid and under-trained analysts, and generating mistake-ridden and poorly documented casework.[32]

---

27. U.S. Dep't of Justice, Office of the Inspector Gen., The FBI Laboratory: A Review of Protocol and Practice Vulnerabilities (2004) (describing the investigation of FBI analyst Jacqueline Blake's failure to use negative controls in DNA testing).

28. U.S. Dep't of Justice, Office of the Inspector Gen., Audit Report: The Combined DNA Index System, at ii (2001) ("[T]he integrity of the data contained in CODIS is extremely important since the DNA matches provided by CODIS are frequently a key piece of evidence linking a suspect to a crime.").

29. The governor ordered an audit by ASCLD/LAB, which has released a report. ASCLD/LAB, Limited Scope Interim Inspection Report (2005).

30. *See* Quality Assurance Audit of Houston Police Department Crime Laboratory DNA/Serology Section (2002).

31. *See* Adam Liptak & Ralph Blumenthal, *New Doubt Cast on Crime Testing in Houston Cases*, N.Y. Times, Aug. 5, 2004, at A19 ("[P]rosecutors in Mr. Sutton's case had used [DNA] to convict him, submitting false scientific evidence asserting that there was a solid match between Mr. Sutton's DNA and that found at the crime scene. In fact, 1 of every 8 black people, including Mr. Sutton, shared the relevant DNA profile. More refined retesting cleared him.").

32. Michael R. Bromwich, Third Report of the Independent Investigator for the Houston Police Department Crime Laboratory and Property Room (June 30, 2005).

DNA Profiling

DNA (deoxyribonucleic acid) is a chemical messenger of genetic information, an inherited code that gives people both common and individual characteristics.[33] DNA is found in packages called chromosomes. Humans have twenty-three pairs of chromosomes, forty-six in all, half of which are inherited from each parent. Except for identical twins, no two individuals share the same nuclear DNA pattern. With few exceptions, DNA does not vary from cell to cell. Thus, blood obtained from a suspect can be compared with semen, sweat, saliva, hair, or even dandruff recovered from a crime scene. Some of the items from which DNA profiles have been gleaned include fingernail scrapings, hatbands, ski masks, shirt collars, cigarette butts, and postage stamps. Profiles may also be obtained from animals, plants, and viruses.[34]

The DNA molecule is composed of a chain of nucleotide bases twisted into a double-helix structure, resembling a twisted ladder. Each "rung" of the helix is known as a "base pair." The order of the base pairs on the ladder is known as the "DNA sequence;" it constitutes an individual's "genetic code." Approximately 99.5 percent of the base pairs found in humans are the same; this is why all humans have two arms, two legs, a heart, a liver, and so forth. It is the half-percent area of base-pair variation ("polymorphisms") that produce individual differences such as hair and eye color. These areas are also the focus in forensic DNA analysis.[35] Because examining every polymorphic site on the DNA molecule is not practical, the analysis focuses on a number of sites (loci) that are highly polymorphic. These loci are investigated to determine whether the evidence and suspect samples contain the same genetic variations (called alleles). Thus, DNA analysis does not examine an individual's entire genome, but rather a snapshot of a number of specific areas.

---

33. The description in the text is greatly simplified. A more thorough introductory discussion can be found in NORAH RUDIN & KEITH INMAN, AN INTRODUCTION TO FORENSIC DNA ANALYSIS (2d ed. 2002). For a more in-depth, technical treatment, see JOHN M. BUTLER, FORENSIC DNA TYPING (2d ed. 2005).

34. *See* United States v. Boswell, 270 F.3d 1200 (8th Cir. 2001) (comparing swine blood in a false-statement prosecution); State v. Bogan, 905 P.2d 515 (Ariz. Ct. App. 1995) (allowing the admission, in a murder case, of evidence from DNA testing of the seed pods from palo verde trees); State v. Schmidt, 699 So. 2d 448 (La. Ct. App. 1997) (involving an attempted murder through injecting HIV; an expert testified that the viruses from the two people involved were "closely related").

35. A single DNA molecule contains roughly three-billion base pairs, approximately three million of which are thought to be polymorphic.

DNA profiling involves two fields: (1) molecular biology and (2) population genetics, and the testing process involves two corresponding steps—first, determining whether the genetic characteristics (alleles) at various loci on the DNA strand match, and second, assuming a match at each locus examined, calculating the population frequency for these matches. The more matches, the more significant the test results.

Short Tandem Repeats (STR) Testing

There have been three generations of DNA-profiling procedures used in forensic cases. The initial technique, Restriction Fragment Length Polymorphism (RFLP) analysis by gel electrophoresis, was soon supplanted by Polymerase Chain Reaction (PCR)-based methods involving the DQ-alpha locus and later multiple loci.[36] These, in turn, were replaced by Short Tandem Repeats (STR), the current procedure, and the one used in the Duke lacrosse case.[37]

STR analysis identifies fragments of DNA from polymorphic loci (areas of the genome) and measures their length. The polymorphic areas examined by the test are typically made up of sequences of four base pairs that repeat themselves—thus the term "short tandem repeats." At a particular locus, one person may have six repeats and another may have ten repeats, and therefore the length of their DNA fragments will differ. A DNA fragment of a particular length is called an allele.

Typically, two alleles, one inherited from each parent, reside at each locus. For example, testing at one locus may be reported as "10, 13," representing the number of repeats for the respective alleles. (Only one allele will be developed at a locus if both parents pass down the same allele.) These repeats are not specific to only one person. The entire population may fall into fifteen or twenty different repeat categories (genotypes), depending on the locus. Consequently, multiple loci are tested. CODIS uses thirteen loci for the national database. In casework, more loci (often sixteen) may be used. Much of the testing is now

---

36. In many instances, the forensic sample was too small, or too damaged by environmental conditions, for RFLP testing. PCR is an amplification technique (essentially, molecular photocopying), which allows a scientist to amplify an insufficient sample until there is enough DNA for further analysis. PCR amplification, incidentally, is also a step in STR testing.

37. In addition to nuclear DNA analysis—genetic information extracted from the nucleus of a cell—courts have admitted evidence based on mitochondrial DNA testing, which obtains DNA from the mitochondria in our cells. This technique is used to test bone, teeth, and hair shafts without roots, items that often contain low concentrations of degraded DNA, making nuclear DNA-testing impractical.

automated; in the Duke lacrosse case, software and instrumentation supplied by Applied Biosystems, Inc., was employed.

Exclusions. Generally, a non-match at any locus means the suspect is excluded as the source of the evidence DNA, making it much easier to exclude a suspect than to include one. In this respect, DNA profiling is similar to the use of forensic blood-typing, which was used in the pre-DNA era. Approximately 45 percent of the population has type O blood, 42 percent type A, 10 percent type B, and 3 percent type AB. (Blood types, incidentally, are also alleles.) If the crime-scene blood's type is O and a suspect has type A, the suspect is excluded as the potential source of that blood.

Table 1 provides an example of suspect and evidence profiles at three loci:

Table 1
Example of Suspect and Evidence Profiles from Three Loci

Locus	Suspect	Evidence
D7S820	11, 12	11, 12
CSF1PO	10, 12	10, 12
D3S1358	14, 16	14, 15

There is concordance at the first two loci but not at the third. Therefore, the suspect is excluded as a DNA contributor. In the Duke case, testing excluded all but one of the forty-six players who submitted reference samples as potential contributors of the DNA found on the critical evidence samples.

Inclusions. If the developed alleles match at each locus, a random match probability is calculated—that is, what are the chances that a person with the same genetic characteristics as those found on the evidence sample would be randomly (coincidently) found in an unrelated individual in the population?[38] If the evidence sample is degraded, only a few loci may be developed (allowing only a partial profile of, say, six or eight loci), which reduces the discriminating power of the results.[39]

---

38. Because a number of people will have the same genetic markers at one locus, more than one locus is tested. The frequencies of the individual alleles are multiplied together (according to the "product rule"), to compute an aggregate-probability estimate. For the calculations to be reliable, all the loci tested must be independent. For this assumption to be true, individuals must reproduce randomly so that distinct subgroups (population substructure) are absent.

39. Assume STR testing is performed at thirteen loci. Assume further that each locus distinguishes one person in twenty. The probability of randomly finding a person with those genetic markers is 1/81,920,000,000,000,000, or 1 in 82 quadrillion. In sum, thirteen separate DNA tests, taken together, produce a rare event. The one-in-twenty figure is used only to simplify the hypothetical; the actual figure differs for each allele at each locus.

Mixtures. Sometimes more than one person may contribute DNA to an evidence item. This is quite common in rape cases, where the rapist's semen may be mixed with epithelial vaginal cells. A differential extraction technique is used to separate sperm from non-sperm fractions in these cases. Although non-sperm fractions have historically been assumed to be epithelial vaginal cells, some may also originate from the rapist.

Table 2 illustrates a four-locus mixture, with a victim who inherited the same allele from both parents at the second locus and an inconclusive result from the evidence sample at the third locus.

Table 2
Example of Combined Suspect, Evidence, and
Victim Profiles from Four Loci

Locus	Suspect	Evidence	Victim
D7S820	11, 12	8, 11, 12	8, 12
CSF1PO	10, 12	10, 12	10
D3S1358	14, 15	Inconclusive	15, 16
FGA	20, 23	20, 21, 23, 24	21, 24

Elimination samples from the victim are required to interpret the testing results. Similarly, elimination samples from other parties—the victim's husband or other consensual sex partner, for example—may also be sought to assist in the interpretation. In the Duke case, the victim's boyfriend provided a reference sample.

Y-Chromosome (Y-STR) Testing

Conventional STR analysis is also called autosomal testing because it focuses on non-sex chromosomes. A different procedure, Y-STR testing, can sometimes overcome the problems associated with interpreting mixtures because it focuses on cells containing the Y chromosome, which only males have. This can be significant if investigators recover a non-sperm evidence sample—for example, male saliva on a female victim. DNA laboratories performed both autosomal and Y-STR testing in the Duke case.

The Duke Lacrosse Case

Gathering the Forensic Evidence

In the Duke case, as is common in cases involving allegations of rape, a Sexual Assault Nurse Examiner (SANE nurse), Tara Levicy, used what is known as a "rape kit" to collect evidence. Nurses typically collect vaginal smears, fingernail scrapings, and trace evidence such as hairs and fibers. Because Crystal Mangum said that she had been vaginally, rectally, and orally penetrated without a condom and at least one of the perpetrators had ejaculated, Levicy obtained cheek scrapings, oral swabs, vaginal swabs, rectal swabs, and pubic-hair combings at Duke Hospital Emergency Room on March 14, 2006. Levicy, a trainee, also took a pair of white panties and other items of clothing from Mangum. In addition, Levicy noted that Mangum's conduct was consistent with sexual victimization. Dr. Julie Manly, the examining physician, found vaginal swelling ("diffuse edema of the vaginal walls"), an ambiguous discovery. Mangum also told authorities she last had sex a week before the incident.

On March 16, 2006, the Durham police executed a search warrant at 610 N. Buchanan Blvd., where the party had occurred. The three residents, Dan Flannery, Matt Zash, and David Evans, voluntarily assisted the police, providing statements and evidence for DNA testing. During this search, Scene Investigator Angela Ashby discovered (1) five false fingernails in a trash can in the bathroom where the rape allegedly occurred (three painted red and previously applied; and two unpainted and unapplied); and (2) an unpainted, unapplied false fingernail on a computer in one of the bedrooms.

Five days later, the prosecutors obtained a Nontestimonial Identification Order[40] to compel the players to be photographed and provide DNA reference samples. The next day, all forty-six Caucasian members of the team complied with the order by providing cheek swabs, known as "buccal samples."

The DNA Analysis

Ashby delivered the rape-kit items and buccal samples to Agent Rachel Winn at the Serology Section of North Carolina's State Bureau of Investigation (SBI) laboratory. Using presumptive tests, Winn found no semen, blood, or saliva on the rape-kit items. Consequently, they were not sent on to the DNA Section for further testing. After Ashby transported the fingernails to SBI the next day, Winn forwarded them, along with the players' buccal samples, to Jennifer Leyn in the DNA Section.

On March 30, SBI notified Michael Nifong, the district attorney, about the lack of semen, blood, and saliva on the rape-kit items. Given Mangum's gang-rape story, this information should have raised a red flag. During this time, Nifong was making sensational statements to the news media, and on April 4 the police conducted the flawed eyewitness-identification photographic display.

---

40. N.C. Gen. Stat. §§ 15A-271 to 15A-282 (2005) (authorizing such orders).

Subsequently, the prosecutors obtained an order transferring the forensic evidence to DNA Security, Inc. (DSI), a private firm located in Burlington, North Carolina, for more sensitive testing. The April 5 request for transfer noted that, "[i]n cases without semen present, it is sometimes possible to extract useful DNA samples for comparison purposes using a technique known as Y-STR. This technique isolates cells containing a Y chromosome from the entire sample, which must have been contributed by a male person. The SBI laboratory is not equipped to conduct Y-STR DNA analysis."[41] Elimination samples from several other persons, including the victim's boyfriend, Matthew Murchison, were also sent to DSI.

On April 10, after initial testing on some of the rape-kit items, Dr. Brian Meehan, the DSI laboratory director, met with Nifong, Investigator Benjamin Himan, and Sergeant Mark Gottlieb. After this meeting, Nifong told an ABC reporter that the DNA testing by DSI had not yet come back, and he later told a public forum that the lack of DNA "doesn't mean nothing happened. It just means nothing was left behind."[42] The state laboratory issued a report covering the autosomal DNA testing on April 10.[43]

Following the indictment of Reade Seligmann and Collin Finnerty on April 17, Seligmann's attorney filed a discovery motion, which included a request for all DNA test results and any exculpatory evidence.[44] A second meeting between Nifong, Meehan, and the police occurred on April 21. By this time, more testing had been completed. A third meeting took place on May 12. In the meantime, on May 2, Nifong had won the vigorously contested primary election.

---

41. Petition of David J. Saacks, N.C. State Bar v. Nifong, No. 60 DHC 35 (July 31, 2007) (No. 207).

42. Amended Findings of Fact, Conclusions of Law and Order of Disciple at para. 50, N.C. State Bar v. Nifong, No. 06 DHC 35 (July 31, 2007) [hereinafter Amended Order of Discipline].

43. The SBI lab had reported that a white towel, found outside the bathroom, contained a sperm-fraction and non-sperm fraction DNA mixture. David Evans was the dominant contributor, but a minor contributor did not match the profile of the accuser or any of the players. The lab also found that swabs from the bathroom floor contained semen, a sperm fraction, and a non-sperm fraction. Matt Zash, who shared the house and bathroom with Evans, was the dominant contributor. The lab also analyzed the fingernail extraction from the three painted nails found in the bathroom: "The DNA profile obtained from the false fingernails (Item 60) is consistent with a mixture: The predominant profile matched the DNA profile" of the accuser. "The weaker profile is consistent with a mixture from multiple contributors. No Conclusion can be rendered...." These items as well as others were transferred to SDI. N.C. SBI Lab Rep., No. R2006670, April 10, 2006, at 7.

44. N.C. Gen. Stat. § 15A-903 (2007) (laying out North Carolina's discovery statute).

The DSI Laboratory Report

DSI issued a ten-page laboratory report on May 12, 2006, which revealed that three evidence specimens contained DNA consistent with the profiles of several persons who had provided reference specimens.[45] As it turned out, two of the three findings would not be important. One involved an unapplied fingernail (DSI # 15901) containing an autosomal DNA mixture that matched the DNA profile of Kevin Coleman, a player, at fourteen of fifteen loci. Crystal Mangum, however, was excluded as a contributor. Moreover, this fingernail had been found in a bedroom, not in the bathroom where the crime allegedly occurred. The second analysis—of a sperm fraction from a vaginal swab (DSI # 15775)—revealed an autosomal DNA mixture consistent with Mangum's profile. The Y-STR analysis revealed a male profile consistent with that of her boyfriend.

Unlike the first two findings, the third proved consequential. It concerned the mixture developed from the three applied false fingernails found in the bathroom (DSI # 15823). This testing, which included both autosomal and Y-STR analyses, revealed the presence of more than two persons' DNA fragments along with Mangum's profile; David Evans could not be ruled out as a contributor. (For more details, see Appendices A & B.) The report read:

> The probability of excluding a randomly selected individual from the mixture autosomal DNA profile is greater than 98%. David Evans cannot be excluded as a contributor to this mixture profile.
>
> A search of all possible Y-chromosome profiles within the mixture Y-chromosome DNA profile in a database of 3,561 profiles found 14 matches. David Evans cannot be excluded as a contributor to the mixture Y-chromosome profile.[46]

These findings had some probative value—but not much. First, the testing was not conclusive; it merely placed Evans in a category of people who could have been the contributor. In a population of one-million people, for example, twenty thousand would fall within the 2 percent indicated in the autosomal results. Second, assuming Evans was the contributor, the possibility of an innocent transfer existed. There was never any question that Evans used that bathroom (it was in his house) or that Mangum had been in the bathroom on the night of the incident. The trash can apparently contained items, such as fa-

---

45. Report of DSI Security, Inc., N.C. State Bar v. Nifong, No. 06 DHC 35 (May 12, 2006) [hereinafter DSI May 12 Report].

46. *Id.* at 6.

cial tissues and Q-tips, that could have contained Evans's DNA.[47] Third, the presence of the pair's DNA did not establish sexual intercourse; the evidence had been obtained from fingernails, not the rape-kit items. Finally, the fingernails were found in a trash can, suggesting that they had been intentionally discarded, not lost during a struggle. Nevertheless, the results were the only forensic evidence that indicated that Evans and Mangum may have had physical contact in the bathroom and therefore buttressed her version of the events. These results apparently led to Evans's indictment on May 15, and thus would need to be closely scrutinized by his attorneys.

The following significant, albeit obscure, sentence also appeared in the report:

> Individual DNA profiles for non-probative evidence specimens and suspect reference specimens are being retained at DSI pending notification of the client [Nifong].[48]

This sentence masked the fact that the testing had yielded powerfully exculpatory results even before the first Meehan-Nifong meeting on April 10. Months later, after Nifong had recused himself from the case, DSI submitted an amended lab report on January 12, 2006 at the request of the Attorney General's office. The second report revised the above sentence:

> Individual DNA profiles for evidence specimens (item numbers 15772, 15776, 15785, 15816–15818) consistent with male profiles that did not match DNA profiles from any reference specimens and DNA profiles for reference specimens ... were being retained at DSI pending notification from the client....[49]

The items cited came from the rape kit. As Professor Robert Mosteller has noted, the difference between the two reports is "striking": the "language of the first report suggests inconsequential results; the revised report's language speaks of significant and exculpatory conclusions."[50]

---

47. STUART TAYLOR, JR. & KC JOHNSON, UNTIL PROVEN INNOCENT: POLITICAL CORRECTNESS AND THE SHAMEFUL INJUSTICES OF THE DUKE LACROSSE RAPE CASE 221 (2007).

48. DSI May 12 Report, *supra* note 45, at 5.

49. Amended Report of DSI Security, Inc. at 5, N.C. State Bar v. Nifong, No. 06 DHC 35 (Jan. 12, 2007).

50. Robert P. Mosteller, *Exculpatory Evidence, Ethics, and the Road to the Disbarment of Mike Nifong: The Critical Importance of Full Open-File Discovery*, 15 GEO. MASON L. REV. 257, 292 (2008).

More Discovery Requests

After Evans's indictment on May 15, Finnerty's attorneys requested discovery of "any" DNA results. The prosecution provided Meehan's original report to all defendants and filed the following statement with the court: "The State is not aware of any additional material or information which may be exculpatory in nature with respect to the Defendant."[51]

At a May 18 hearing, Judge Ronald Stephens asked if the prosecution had provided the defendants with all discovery material. Nifong replied: "I've turned over everything I have."[52] Another discovery request followed on May 19, asking for, among other things, a "written statement of the meetings between Nifong and Meehan." Judge Stephens entered an order requiring that all tests and oral statements of witnesses be reduced to written form.

On August 31, the three defendants filed an Omnibus Motion to Compel Discovery—seeking, among other things, the underlying data for all DSI testing and the substance of comments made by Meehan at his three meetings with Nifong and the police. The motion specifically asked for any test findings, even if those results did not match any of the defendants or other persons who had provided reference samples. Nifong told Judge W. Osmond Smith III who had been appointed on August 18 to preside over the case, that the report was complete:

> Judge Smith: So you represent there are no other statements from Dr.
>   Meehan?
> Nifong: No other statements. No other statements made to me.[53]

Judge Smith ordered disclosure of the complete files and underlying data from SBI and DSI by October 20. On October 19, Evans's counsel faxed Nifong a proposed order reflecting the ruling.

The Underlying Data

On October 27, 2006, Nifong provided 1,844 pages of DSI documents and materials, including tables of alleles and electropherograms, but did not include either a complete written report or a summary of his conversations with Meehan. In other words, these materials were turned over without any synopsis of their contents. Without a background in science or any previous ex-

---

51. Amended Order of Discipline, *supra* note 42, at para. 70.
52. *Id.* at para. 74.
53. *Id.* at para. 86.

perience with DNA analysis, Brad Bannon, one of Evans's attorneys, bought and immersed himself in a book on the subject. After spending between sixty and one-hundred hours reviewing the DSI data, Bannon made several discoveries. First, he realized that there might be a contamination problem: Meehan's DNA profile appeared in one of the tests. More importantly, Bannon found that the May 12 DSI report had omitted test results indicating the presence of at least four unidentified male DNA fragments on rape-kit items:

1. Panties, stain A, sperm fraction: DSI #15767 identified male alleles at eight of the sixteen Y-STR loci, with multiple alleles at three loci, indicating multiple male contributors. Handwritten notes stated that none of the profiles matched any of the reference samples, including those of the players.

2. Rectal swabs, sperm fraction: DSI #15776 identified male alleles at five of the sixteen Y-STR loci. Handwritten notes stated that none of the profiles matched any of the reference samples, including those of the players.

3. Panties, stain A, epithelial fraction: DSI #15777 identified male alleles at all sixteen Y-STR loci, with multiple alleles at eight loci, indicating multiple male contributors. Handwritten notes stated that none of the profiles match any reference samples, including those of the players. However, the notes further stated that there could be a match with the profile seen on DSI # 15778. (For the raw data, see Appendix C.)

4. Panties, stain B, epithelial fraction: DSI #15778 identified male alleles at nine of the sixteen Y-STR loci, with multiple alleles at two loci, indicating multiple male contributors. Handwritten notes stated that none of the profiles matched any of the reference samples, including those of the players. The notes further concluded that the profile did not match the profile seen on the sperm fraction of stain A of the panties (DSI #15767) but could match the profile seen on the epithelial fraction of stain A (DSI #15777).

5. Panties, stain D, epithelial fraction: DSI #15780 identified male alleles at twelve of the sixteen Y-STR loci tested, with multiple alleles at one locus, indicating multiple male contributors. Handwritten notes stated that none of the profiles matched any of the reference samples, including those of the players.[54]

---

54. Motion to Compel Discovery: Expert DNA Analysis, N.C. v. Evans, Super. Ct., filed Dec. 13, 2006, at 5–6; *see also* Appendix D, *supra*.

This information was exculpatory because it provided an alternate explanation for Mangum's physical condition (such as her vaginal swelling) on the night of the lacrosse party. Furthermore, testing sensitive enough to identify these alleles would have presumably identified semen supposedly ejaculated during the alleged gang-rape.

The December 15 Hearing

The defense attorneys filed another discovery motion on December 13, detailing this information. The next hearing was two days later, at which time Nifong stated: "The first I heard of this particular situation was when I was served with these reports—this motion Wednesday of this week."[55] Although the defense had not been notified in advance, Nifong called Meehan as a witness at the hearing. After a few perfunctory questions on direct examination, he turned Meehan over to the defense for cross-examination. Calling Meehan as a witness and then forgoing direct examination placed a tremendous burden on the defense attorneys, who had not prepared for a cross-examination. Nevertheless, they responded in exemplary fashion.

As the person who had waded through the 1,844 pages of lab data, Bannon, Evans's attorney, went first. Meehan proved to be an elusive witness. Although he admitted discussing all extant DNA results with Nifong at the April 10, April 21, and May 12 meetings, he also insisted that the May 10 report was not a "final" report, implying that a nonfinal report did not have to be complete. He also testified that Nifong had never asked him to exclude anything from the report.

During his investigation, however, Bannon had noted that DSI was accredited by the American Society of Crime Directors/Laboratory Accreditation (ASCLD/LAB), an organization that provides standards for laboratory reports, including requirements for (1) an "accurate summary of significant material contained in the case notes," and (2) "interpretive information as well as examination results wherever possible."[56] Bannon's cross-examination contained the following exchange:

Bannon: Do you rely on those protocols routinely to maintain your accreditation with ASCLD/LAB?

---

55. Amended Order of Discipline, *supra* note 42, at para. 95.

56. ASCLD Guidelines for Forensic Laboratory Management Practices, 14 Crime Lab. Dig. 39, 43 (1987).

Meehan:	Yes.
Bannon:	I'd like to direct your attention to standards for reports. It says, No. 4, item reports shall include....
Meehan:	I'm there.
Bannon:	Doesn't it say, Results for each DNA test?
Meehan:	Yes.
Bannon:	You didn't include the results for each DNA test in your report dated May 12; is that correct?
Meehan:	That's correct.
Bannon:	So you violated this protocol of your own lab?
Meehan:	That's correct.[57]

Meehan also attempted to cite privacy concerns to justify his failure to provide a full report; he claimed that the profiles of unindicted players should not be disclosed to the public. He testified: "[W]e were trying to do what we thought was the right thing to do was minimize the exposure of the rest of the players. It would have meant that we produced profiles and names of all of those people."[58] Bannon would have none of it:

> The issue about privacy, what I would like for you to explain to me is how it would violate anyone's privacy to report that your lab uncovered multiple male DNA characteristics on multiple rape kit items that did not match any of the people who are being prosecuted or any of the suspects that have been submitted in reference samples?[59]

The judge sustained an objection on the grounds that Meehan had previously answered that question. But, though Meehan had given a response, he never really *answered* the question. The May 12 lab report could have provided the critical information about multiple, unidentified male DNA fragments without providing the DNA profiles of all the reference samples.

Jim Cooney, Seligmann's lawyer, next questioned Meehan. He had the advantage of observing Meehan during Bannon's cross-examination and was able to bore in on the critical issue:

---

57. Transcript of December 15, 2006 Hearing at 65–66, State v. Finnerty, Nos. 06 CRS 4331-36, 5582-83 (N.C. Super. Ct. Dec. 15, 2006) [hereinafter Transcript of Dec. 15 Hearing].

58. *Id.* at 41.

59. *Id.* at 69–70.

Cooney: Did your report set forth the results of all of the tests and
           examinations that you conducted in this case?

Meehan: No. It was limited to only some results.

Cooney: Okay. And that was an intentional limitation arrived at
           between you and representatives of the State of North Car-
           olina not to report on the results of all examinations and
           tests that you did in this case?

Meehan: Yes.[60]

"Bingo" was the way one book described that answer.[61]

In addition to the omission from the May 12 Report, the conduct of Nifong and Meehan in distributing the underlying data on October 27 without
a synopsis raised further questions:

Cooney: And in order for Reade Seligmann or Collin Finnerty or Dave
           Evans to have found the results of the tests that excluded,
           they needed to go through those six inches of paper to find
           them: isn't that correct?

Meehan: That is correct.

Cooney: Because you hadn't put them in the report; is that fair?

Meehan: That is fair.[62]

The Aftermath

As it turned out, this hearing proved to be the pivotal event in the criminal
investigation. On December 22, Nifong dropped the forcible rape charge, but
not the sexual-assault or kidnapping offenses, after an investigator from his
office interviewed Mangum, who now could not recall being penetrated. Remarkably, this was the first time anyone in the prosecutor's office had interviewed
the alleged victim. The North Carolina Bar's Grievance Committee, which had
been considering the pretrial-publicity issues since October, filed its ethics
complaint against Nifong on December 28. Asking the state Attorney General,
Roy Cooper, to take over the prosecution of the case, Nifong recused himself
on January 12, 2007. Cooper would drop the charges on April 11 and declare
the defendants "innocent."

The Disciplinary Hearing Commission panel held its hearing on June 12
through June 16, eventually finding that Nifong had violated numerous stan-

---

60. *Id.* at 85.

61. TAYLOR & JOHNSON, *supra* note 47, at 311.

62. Transcript of Dec. 15 Hearing, *supra* note 57, at 86.

dards of professional conduct.[63] By instructing Meehan to write a report mentioning only positive matches, Nifong knowingly disobeyed an obligation under the rules of a tribunal—that is, discovery requirements.[64] The failure to provide a complete report also violated an ethical rule that requires prosecutors to disclose exculpatory evidence.[65] Other violations included (1) making false statements of material fact or law to a tribunal;[66] (2) making false statements of material fact to a third person (the defense attorneys) in the course of representing a client;[67] and (3) engaging in conduct involving dishonesty, fraud, deceit, or misrepresentations.[68] Finally, the Committee ruled that Nifong had lied to the Grievance Committee during its investigation, another violation.[69]

In addition to the disciplinary sanctions, Nifong was subsequently held in contempt by the trial judge in the case and spent a day in jail.[70]

An Explanation?

Nifong's motivations at different stages of the affair are sometimes difficult to fathom. Although his political agenda is apparent, it is not clear why he did not retreat at various points during the process. He won the critical primary election on May 2 and, as the Democratic candidate, was an overwhelming favorite in the general election. Mosteller speculates that Nifong might have believed that the critical information buried in the October 27 data either would not be discovered until after the general election, ten days away on November 7, or that it would never be discovered because the case would eventually be dismissed due to the suggestive and unreliable identification procedure.[71] F. Lane Williamson, chair of the Disciplinary Hearing Commission panel, thought it probable that the criminal case would eventually be dismissed: "And

---

63. In addition to his conduct involving the DNA, the Committee found that Nifong violated ethical rules concerning pretrial publicity. *See supra* Chapter Eleven (Williams).

64. N.C. RULES OF PROF'L CONDUCT R. 3.4(c). The discovery obligations were based on (1) the state nontestimonial identification statute, (2) the state discovery statute, and (3) the court's June 22 discovery order.

65. *Id.* R. 3.8(d).

66. *Id.* R. 3.3(a)(1).

67. *Id.* R. 4.1.

68. *Id.* R. 8.4(c).

69. *Id.* R. 3.4(d). For a comprehensive discussion of Nifong's ethical lapses, see *supra* Chapter Eleven (Williams).

70. *See Ex-Duke Prosecutor Held in Contempt*, N.Y. TIMES, Sept. 1, 2007, at A7.

71. Robert P. Mosteller, *The Duke Lacrosse Case, Innocence, and False Identifications: A Fundamental Failure to "Do Justice,"* 76 FORDHAM L. REV. 1337, 1364 (2007).

while we don't know, it seems reasonably clear that one would predict that at the suppression hearing in February the case would have been dismissed."[72]

Meehan's motivation is even more obscure. One of the investigator's notes recorded Meehan as stating that he could "possibly adjust prices because [his company] would really like to be involved in [the] case."[73] The lure of participating in a high-profile case, however, does not explain why he went along with omitting critical information from his report. Perhaps he wanted to establish his lab's credentials to other prosecutors. In any event, Williamson would label him "Dr. Obfuscation" for his testimony in the disciplinary hearings,[74] and he was removed from his company after the civil-rights suit was filed.

Lessons Learned

Pretrial Disclosure

In *Brady v. Maryland*,[75] the Supreme Court ruled that the prosecution must disclose exculpatory information, if material, to the defense. The Court, however, has given a stringent definition of "materiality": the evidence must be outcome-determinative.[76] As Mosteller has concluded, the *Brady* doctrine does not effectively accomplish its ostensible goal.[77] In response to the Grievance Committee's notification letter, Nifong argued that the omitted DNA analysis was "non-inculpatory" rather than "specifically exculpatory."[78] This is not an uncommon prosecutorial response.[79] Mosteller has argued persuasively that North Carolina's "open file" discovery statute is far more effective than *Brady* in ensuring a fair trial.[80]

---

72. Transcript of the Disciplinary Hearing Committee at 22, N.C. State Bar v. Nifong, No. 06 DHC 35 (June 16, 2007) (statement of F. Lane Williamson).

73. Motion to Compel Discovery, N.C. State Bar v. Nifong, No. 60 DHC 35 (July 31, 2007) (No. 229).

74. Benjamin Niolet & Joseph Neff, *Other Reputations Rose and Fell, Too*, News & Observer (Raleigh, N.C.), June 19, 2007.

75. 373 U.S. 83 (1963).

76. *See* United States v. Bagley, 473 U.S. 667, 682 (1985) ("[The suppressed evidence is "material"]only if there is a reasonable probability that, had the evidence been disclosed to the defense, the result of the proceeding would have been different.").

77. Mosteller, *supra* note 50, at 308.

78. *Amended Order of Discipline*, *supra* note 42, at para. 107.

79. *See* Paul C. Giannelli, *Criminal Discovery, Scientific Evidence, and DNA*, 44 Vand. L. Rev. 791, 801–02 (1991) (discussing unjustifiable limitations on discovery).

80. *See generally* Mosteller, *supra* note 50.

There is little question that comprehensive discovery is critical in cases relying on forensic evidence, and DNA is no exception.[81] In 1989, the *Journal of Forensic Sciences*, the official publication of the American Academy of Forensic Sciences, published a symposium on the ethical responsibilities of forensic scientists. One article discussed a number of questionable laboratory reporting practices, including (1) "preparation of reports containing minimal information in order not to give the 'other side' ammunition for cross-examination," (2) "reporting of findings without an interpretation on the assumption that if an interpretation is required it can be provided from the witness box," and (3) "[o]mitting some significant point from a report to trap an unsuspecting cross-examiner."[82] All of these practices undermine discovery.

In accord, the National Academy of Sciences recommended extensive discovery in DNA cases: "All data and laboratory records generated by analysis of DNA samples should be made freely available to all parties. Such access is essential for evaluating the analysis."[83] The recent *ABA Standards on DNA Evidence* also provide for full discovery.[84] Most attorneys have neither the time nor the expertise to challenge scientific evidence. Even Bannon's discovery was, in a sense, inadvertent. He was not looking for the exculpatory information. Instead, he was trying to understand the DNA technique used to separate the male and female DNA on the false fingernail found in the trash can as well as the significance of his client's partial match. A less determined attorney would not have devoted the sixty to one hundred hours to the effort that Bannon did. Many, such as overworked and underpaid public defenders, literally could not.[85] In any event, no attorney should have to search through the haystack for the exculpatory needle. A laboratory report should be comprehensive and include a section specifying the limitations of the technique used in the analysis. The report should also be comprehensible to laypersons.

---

81. *See* Fed. R. Crim. P. 16 adv. note (1975) ("[I]t is difficult to test expert testimony at trial without advance notice and preparation."), *reprinted in* 62 F.R.D. 271, 312 (1974).

82. Douglas M. Lucas, *The Ethical Responsibilities of the Forensic Scientist: Exploring the Limits*, 34 J. Forensic Sci. 719, 724 (1989). Lucas was the Director, Centre of Forensic Sciences, Ministry of the Solicitor General, Toronto, Ontario.

83. NRC I Report, *supra* note 13, at 146 ("The prosecutor has a strong responsibility to reveal fully to defense counsel and experts retained by the defendant all material that might be necessary in evaluating the evidence.").

84. ABA Standards for Criminal Justice, DNA Evidence 4-1 (2007).

85. *See supra* Chapter Ten (Uphoff) (discussing the disparity of criminal representation for rich versus poor defendants).

Defense Experts

If needed, the Duke defendants could have afforded to retain DNA experts. In fact, Bannon flew to Washington, D.C., to consult with a retired FBI examiner, Hal Deadman. Most criminal defendants, however, are indigent. In *Ake v. Oklahoma*,[86] the Supreme Court recognized a limited right to a defense expert for indigent defendants, yet studies suggest that implementation of this right has lagged.[87]

The National Academy of Sciences' 1992 report indicated that experts will be needed in most cases:

> Defense counsel must have access to adequate expert assistance, even when the admissibility of the results of analytical techniques is not in question because there is still a need to review the quality of the laboratory work and the interpretation of results.[88]

As other commentators have argued, "[a]lthough current DNA tests rely heavily on computer-automated equipment, the interpretation of the results often requires subjective judgment."[89] Mixtures, degradation, allelic dropout, spurious peaks, and false peaks must be considered in evaluating some DNA electropherograms. In short, adequate representation often requires expert assistance.

Nontestimonial Identification Orders

North Carolina's Nontestimonial Identification statute is an aspect of the case that most have overlooked. Only a handful of jurisdictions have comparable provisions.[90] The phrase "nontestimonial order" derives from Fifth Amendment jurisprudence; the privilege against self-incrimination is limited to testimonial statements and does not extend to physical evidence.[91] Thus, a sus-

---

86. 470 U.S. 68 (1985).

87. *See* Paul C. Giannelli, Ake v. Oklahoma: *The Right to Expert Assistance in a Post-Daubert, Post-DNA World*, 89 CORNELL L. REV. 1305 (2004) (discussing the need to bolster the right to defense experts).

88. NRC I REPORT, *supra* note 13, at 147, 149 ("Because of the potential power of DNA evidence, authorities must make funds available to pay for expert witnesses....").

89. *See* William Thompson et al., *Part I: Evaluating Forensic DNA Evidence*, in THE CHAMPION 16 (Apr. 2003).

90. PAUL C. GIANNELLI & EDWARD J. IMWINKELRIED, 1 SCIENTIFIC EVIDENCE §2.04(a)(2) (4th ed. 2007) (identifying nine states).

91. *See* Schmerber v. California, 384 U.S. 757, 764 (1966) ("The distinction which has emerged, often expressed in different ways, is that the privilege is a bar against compelling 'communications' or 'testimony,' but that compulsion which makes a suspect or accused the source of 'real or physical evidence' does not violate it.").

pect may be compelled to produce a blood or handwriting sample, even if incriminating, without violating the privilege.

Nevertheless, important Fourth Amendment search-and-seizure issues are involved. The legal basis for NTO statutes rests on dicta in *Davis v. Mississippi*[92] and *Hayes v. Florida*,[93] both of which involved fingerprints. Significantly, instead of the higher probable-cause standard required for a warrant, such orders require a lesser showing: "reasonable suspicion," a standard derived from stop-and-frisk law.[94] The recent ABA Standards on DNA Evidence sanction such statutes. Under Standard 2.2, DNA may be collected from a suspect in a noninvasive manner (such as saliva samples) if there is "reasonable suspicion" that the suspect committed the crime, and in an invasive manner (such as blood samples) if there is "probable cause" that the suspect did so.[95]

In the Duke case, there is no question that the state lacked probable cause to require forty-six players to provide buccal samples for DNA analysis. On the other hand, whether there was reasonable suspicion is an interesting issue. Unlike the North Carolina provision, statutes in other states permit use of a NTO only if the evidence "cannot be otherwise obtained,"[96] a requirement consistent with the Fourth Amendment's reasonableness prescription. For example, in the absence of a flight risk, the police should first seek to obtain the samples by consent. Robert Ekstrand, an attorney representing many of the players, appreciated that the order could be challenged on constitutional grounds.[97] He also recognized, however, that DNA testing would exonerate his clients. Indeed, all forty-six players believed the same thing. None objected to providing samples: "We have nothing to hide," was how Kyle Dowd, one of the players, summed it up.

---

92. 394 U.S. 721, 727–28 (1969).

93. 470 U.S. 811, 817 (1985) ("[The Court has] not abandon[ed] the suggestion in *Davis* ... that under circumscribed procedures, the Fourth Amendment might permit the judiciary to authorize the seizure of a person on less than probable cause and his removal to the police station for the purpose of fingerprinting."); *see also* Kaupp v. Texas, 538 U.S. 626, 630 n.2 (2003) ("We have ... left open the possibility that, 'under circumscribed procedures,' a court might validly authorize a seizure on less than probable cause when the object is fingerprinting.") (quoting *Hayes*, 470 U.S. at 817).

94. *See* Terry v. Ohio, 392 U.S. 1 (1968).

95. ABA Standards for Criminal Justice, DNA Evidence 2.2 (2007).

96. *See, e.g.*, Ariz. Rev. Stat. Ann. § 13-3905(A) (2006). On the other hand, the North Carolina statute contains discovery and right-to-counsel provisions that are absent from many of the other NTO statutes.

97. Taylor & Johnson, *supra* note 47, at 59.

Conclusion

The DNA evidence played a critical, perhaps determinative, role in the Duke lacrosse case. Without it, the case may have gone forward as a credibility contest—a "he said, she said." Pre-DNA serology, such as ABO typing and protein/enzyme analysis, would not have revealed the presence of multiple male DNA fragments on the rape kit items. In sum, DNA did its job. Unfortunately, Mike Nifong did not do his.

Appendix A
Autosomal STR Analysis on Specimens #15723, #15823, and #15765[*]

Locus	Specimen #15723 Reference specimen from David Evans	Specimen #15823 DNA from crime-scene fingernail (provided by NCSBI)	Specimen #15765 Reference specimen from Crystal Mangum
Amel	X, Y	X, Y	X, X
D8S1179	11, 13	10, 11, 12 13, 14, 15	13, 15
D21S11	30.2, 31.2	28, 29, 30, 30.2, [31.2], 32.2	28, 32.2
D7S820	11, 12	8, [11], 12	8, 12
CSF1PO	10, 12	INC	10, 11
D3S1358	14, 16	14, 15, 16	15, 16
THO1	6, 9.3	[6], 7, 8, 9, 9.3	7
D13S317	10, 11	[10], 11	11
D16S539	9, 11	9, 10, 11, 12	11, 12
D2S1338	23, 25	INC	19, 22
D19S433	13, 15.2	12.2, [13], 13.2, 14, 15, 15.2	13.2, 15
VWA	17, 18	15, 16, 17, 18	16, 17
TPOX	8	8, 9, 11	9, 11
D18S51	12, 14	INC	16, 18
D5S818	11, 13	10, 11, 12, 13	11, 12
FGA	20, 23	[20], 21, [23], 24	21, 24

[*] DSI May 12 Report, *supra* note 45, at 5. Numbers enclosed in brackets indicate a match coincident with a stutter fragment (artifact) or a fragment of low intensity. "INC" indicates an inconclusive result. More than four alleles at four of the sixteen loci analyzed indicate the presence of DNA from at least three persons: one was Mangum, another was possibly Evans, and the third was neither a player nor anyone else tested. "Amel" refers to the amelogenin locus, a site, analyzed with multiplex STR systems, that distinguishes sex—e.g., "X, X" for female and "X, Y" for male. The Y-STR testing of this specimen is found in Appendix B, *infra*.

Appendix B
Y-STR Analysis on Specimens #15723 and #15823*

Locus	Specimen #15723 Reference specimen from David Evans	Specimen #15823 DNA from crime-scene fingernail (provided by NCSBI)
DYS456	17	15, 16, 17
DYS389I	13	12, 13, 14
DYS390	24	21, 22, 24
DYS389II	29	28, 29, 31
DYS458	18	15, 17, 18
DYS19	14	13, 14
DYS385	12, 14	11, 12, 14
DYS393	13	13
DYS391	10	10, 11
DYS439	13	13
DYS635	23	22, 23, 25
DYS392	13	13, 15
YGATAH4	12	10, 11, 12
DYS437	15	14, 15, 16
DYS438	12	10, 11, 12
DYS448	19	19

---

* *Id.* Typically, there is only one marker at each locus in Y-STR (male) testing. A person, however, may have more than one allele at locus DYS385. In the Y-STR test, alleles at many of the loci indicate at least one, sometimes two, other males who were neither players nor anyone else tested. The autosomal testing of this specimen is found in Appendix A, *supra*.

Appendix C
Y-STR Analysis on Specimen #15777*

Locus	Specimen #15777 Epithelial fraction of Stain A from panties
DYS456	15
DYS389I	12, 14
DYS390	23
DYS389II	29, 32
DYS458	14, 17, 18
DYS19	13, 14
DYS385	14
DYS393	9, OL, 13, 14, 15
DYS391	11
DYS439	12, OL
DYS635	23
DYS392	11, 12, 13
YGATAH4	11, 12, 13
DYS437	14
DYS438	OL, 12
DYS448	19

---

* Amended Report of DSI Security, Inc., *supra* note 49, at 2. "OL" signifies the presence of DNA that is insufficient to characterize. This profile indicates a mixture; it identified male alleles at all sixteen Y-STR loci, with multiple alleles at several loci, indicating multiple male contributors. Handwritten notes stated that none of the profiles match any reference samples, including those of the players. The notes further stated that there could be a match with the profile seen on DSI #15778.

Appendix D
Y-STR Testing on Specimen #15780[*]

Locus	Specimen #15780 Epithelial fraction of Stain D from panties
DYS456	15
DYS389I	13
DYS390	21
DYS389I	INR
DYS458	17, 18
DYS19	NR
DYS385	14, 15
DYS393	13
DYS391	11
DYS439	12
DYS635	21
DYS392	NR
YGATAH4	NR
DYS437	15
DYS438	11
DYS448	21

[*] *Id.* at 5. Panties, stain D, epithelial fraction: DSI #15780 identified male alleles at twelve of the sixteen Y-STR loci tested, with multiple alleles at one locus, indicating multiple male contributors. Handwritten notes stated that none of the profiles matched any of the reference samples, including those of the players. Typically, there is only one marker at each locus in Y-STR (male) testing. A person, however, may have more than one allele at locus DYS385.

Presuming Guilt or Protecting Victims?: Analyzing the Special Treatment of Those Accused of Rape

Aviva Orenstein

Introduction

Using the events of the Duke rape case, this chapter explores how American law and society treat those accused of sex crimes differently from other defendants. It examines the underlying racial and gender stereotypes reflected in the Duke case, and questions how they interact with social and legal determinations of guilt. The egregious prosecutorial misconduct in the Duke case, however, complicates the inquiry into what it can teach us generally about rape-trial rules and the law's treatment of the accused. The primary problems in the case arose from unethical prosecution tactics, excessive and one-sided media publicity, and a rush to judgment—not from rules designed to protect rape victims. Nevertheless, the case at least provides a springboard into an examination of the special evidentiary rules for rape cases and the distinctive treatment—legal and extralegal—of those accused of rape, some of which undermines or conflicts with the presumption of innocence.

Some may conclude that the moral of the Duke case is that men are sitting targets for women whose false claims of rape are supported by a society and legal establishment that is quick to presume guilt. Certainly, we must confront the possibility of false accusations (deriving either from mistake or malice) and honestly examine how the system treats the accused. No one can or should claim that women never lie or are never mistaken about rape. Such categorical statements are demonstrably untrue and have the effect of presuming guilt based on an accusation alone. The Duke rape allegations remind us in vivid, human terms of the possibility of and damage from false allegations. The consequences of an accusation, let alone a conviction, can be devastating, transcending strictly legal matters and affecting privacy, opportunity, mental health, reputation, and even safety.

I am concerned about deriving the wrong lessons from the Duke case. In hindsight, knowing that these innocent young men were subjected to a false accusation, it is tempting to over-read the Duke case as a cautionary tale about the dangers of legal reforms in sex-crime prosecutions. Over the last thirty years, changes to evidentiary rules and other legal doctrines have enabled women to come forward and testify about sex crimes with less fear and humiliation than in times past. For all the hardship that a man accused of rape may face, there are still powerful stories drawing on gender, racial, and socioeconomic stereotypes that make it difficult to convict even those truly guilty of rape. Generally, the problem with rape prosecutions is not false reporting, but underreporting.[1] The laudable goal of many legal reforms has been to make victims' lives easier and encourage reporting of rape.

Therefore, the law must strike a delicate balance between the needs of victims and the rights of the accused. The rules and procedures must be formulated with both the sexually brutalized victim and the absolutely innocent accused in mind. In this chapter, after briefly analyzing the cultural sway of myths about rape victims and accused rapists, I catalog various differences in evidence law and legal culture between sex crimes and other types. This chapter also briefly considers how those convicted of sex crimes may be singled out for special treatment in regard both to prison violence and postsentence limitations on their privacy and mobility.

---

1. Available data indicate that rape is significantly underreported. The 2005 *National Crime Victimization Survey* results estimate that 38.3 percent of rapes are reported to police. The 2006 numbers show a reporting rate of 41.4 percent. This indicates a significant underreporting problem, especially when compared with other violent, and even property, crimes. *See* SHANNAN CATALANO, U.S. DEP'T OF JUSTICE, BUREAU OF JUSTICE STATISTICS, NATIONAL CRIME VICTIMIZATION SURVEY (2005), http://www.ojp.usdoj.gov/bjs/pub/ pdf/cv05. pdf; *see also* MICHAEL RAND & SHANNAN CATALANO, U.S. DEP'T OF JUSTICE, BUREAU OF JUSTICE STATISTICS, NATIONAL CRIME VICTIMIZATION SURVEY (2006), http://www.ojp.usdoj. gov/bjs/pub/pdf/cv06.pdf.

Competing Narratives

The tragedy at Duke is a rape "story." It is a story in the sense of providing a narrative, and a story in the sense of being a lie; the charges were not only impossible to prove (the accused were not guilty beyond a reasonable doubt) but actually false (the accused were innocent).[2]

The role of narrative in evidence law has been a subject of rich discussion. To prove a case to the jury, a lawyer must tell a plausible story that not only fits with the facts, but also resonates with the jurors' life experience.[3] In this respect, rape cases are merely subsets of a larger phenomenon concerning how the facts of a case are translated by the legal system into a decision about guilt (in the criminal context) or liability (in the civil context).

Stories are particularly powerful and evocative in rape cases. Issues of gender burden the rape narrative, and often those of race and class do as well.[4] The narrative involves sex, violence, and presumptions about human behavior. These presumptions permeate every part of the legal process, from initial reports of a sex crime to the final stages of punishment and beyond, including restrictions on the lives of convicted sexual predators after their sentences have been served. To understand the utility and importance of various evidence rules, we must first understand the narratives that they are designed to support or counteract.

A rape story often relies on "rape myths," empirically untrue but nevertheless firmly held notions about the incidence and nature of rape. These prejudicial false beliefs about rape, rapists, and rape victims rely on and perpetuate diverse and sometimes contradictory gender stereotypes and cultural archetypes. Competing, inconsistent narratives are particularly evident in the Duke case. Both prosecution and defense versions of what happened relied on deep cultural myths about rape and on gender and racial stereotypes. Why, besides

---

2. *See* Robert P. Mosteller, *The Duke Lacrosse Case, Innocence, and False Identifications: A Fundamental Failure to "Do Justice,"* 76 FORDHAM L. REV. 1337, 1341n.15 (2007) ("The historical record is clear that no sexual assault of any type occurred at 610 North Buchanan Street on the night of March 13 to 14, 2006, involving Crystal Mangum.").

3. *See* Nancy Pennington & Reid Hastie, *A Cognitive Theory of Juror Decision Making: The Story Model,* 13 CARDOZO L. REV. 519 (1991).

4. In addition, the terminology is controversial. Although men do get raped (particularly in prison) I will refer to the person claiming to have been raped as "she" because most rape victims are women. Furthermore, I will use the term "victim" for the woman (in addition to "accuser" or "complainant"), even in this case where the allegations turned out to be false. That these terms are fraught with uncertainty and political implication demonstrates the legal and cultural challenges posed by even talking about rape stories.

the fact that the prosecutor was an unethical media hound, did the case attract national attention? The answer lies, at least in part, in the fact that, at every stage, the story fit into neat gender, race, and socioeconomic stereotypes that provided stock figures at whom the public could take collective umbrage. As outlined below, the story morphed from a tale of boyish privilege and thuggery to one of female unreliability and perfidy aided by an unethical prosecutor. In both versions, stereotypes about "young men" play a prominent role.

Frat Boys Gone Wild

The story, as originally portrayed by the media and nurtured by Durham District Attorney Mike Nifong, emerged as a tale of privileged, callous, white boys who had been empowered by their elite status as almost-Ivy League students and jocks. According to this version, these young men, with gang-like camaraderie, sexually attacked a working-class black woman. Their sense of entitlement derived from the fact that they hired her to dance for them, and that they presumably believed they had purchased the rights to her body. Because Duke is a Southern institution, the story resonated richly with issues of race and class, with shades of Southern masters demanding sexual favors from their slaves. Furthermore, these privileged young men looked as if they would get away with their crimes by hiring fancy, high-priced counsel and maintaining a strict code of silence.

This story resonates with some stereotypes about young men in general and wealthy young men in particular. Like those accused (and later exonerated) in the Central Park jogger case, the young men were portrayed as out-of-control, dangerous marauders. Like Alex Kelly, the prep-school teen who raped two young women in his senior year of high school and then lived for a decade outside the reach of American authorities as a ski bum in Europe,[5] they were portrayed as privileged and coddled.

The Lying Ho

As more information emerged about the problems of proof in the case — the inconsistencies in the alleged victim's story, her prior identifications of others, the tainted photo lineup, the presence of DNA from other men, and the absence of DNA from the accused — the story changed. It still relied on cultural stereotypes, just different ones. It emerged as a tale of a drugged-out,

---

5. Max Haines, *Flight from Justice with His Parents' Help, Rapist Alex Kelly Evaded the Law for 8 Years*, THE TORONTO SUN, Nov. 9, 1997, at 44.

black exotic dancer with a criminal record, class envy, and a chip on her shoulder—one who was lying, delusional, or both. This image of the victim as a liar or someone cognitively incapable of reliably relaying facts can be traced back to the historical, generalized suspicion of women accusing someone of rape.[6] This characterization was particularly prevalent in the case of promiscuous women, who were suspect because of their sexual agency and because they flouted cultural norms. The substantive law of rape reflected this: it often required corroboration, prompt outcry, and evidence of physical struggle. It was also apparent in the process of rape trials, during which the victim was treated with humiliation and suspicion.

The fact that the alleged victim was an exotic dancer plays heavily into the tale. One strong theme in the rape literature is the defense that the so-called victim was not raped, but merely a prostitute cheated out of her fee and looking for revenge. North Carolina law, however, is clear that prostitutes and other women who trade in sexuality can be victims of rape. In fact, as far back as an 1885 rape case, the state's supreme court observed: "[The fact] that [the victim] was a lewd woman and placed so small an estimate upon her favors, can make no difference."[7] In 1996, the North Carolina Supreme Court held that "[a]lthough the victim was a prostitute and initially sought a sexual encounter for payment, consent to sexual intercourse can be withdrawn at any time prior to penetration."[8] These admirable legal statements do not, however, address the cultural values assigned to women deemed to be promiscuous, especially if they behave sexually for money, as do exotic dancers.

Also important are racial stereotypes and their intersection with those of gender. In the narrative I call "frat boys gone wild," the victim's identity as a black woman underscores the power differential between the accused lacrosse players and the victim, which adds a nasty racial element to the alleged crime. Race apparently played a role in Nifong's political calculations to pursue the case vigorously. But a counternarrative relies on negative stereotypes of black women as unreliable, untruthful, and indolent.[9] (After all, the accuser didn't finish the dance for which she was paid.) Black women are seen as "promiscuous by na-

---

6. *See Anne M. Coughlin, Sex and Guilt,* 84 VIRGINIA L. REV. 1, 8 (1998) (noting the "inclination of courts to approach rape complaints with deep suspicion"); *see generally* Morrison Torrey, *When Will We Be Believed? Rape Myths and the Idea of a Fair Trial in Rape Prosecutions,* 24 U.C. DAVIS L. REV. 1013 (1991).

7. State v. Long, 93 N.C. 542, 542 (1885).

8. State v. Penland, 472 S.E.2d 734, 742 (N.C. 1996).

9. *See generally Susan Hanley Kosse, Race Riches & Reporters—Do Race and Class Impact Media Rape Narrative? An Analysis of the Duke Lacrosse Case,* 31 S. ILL. U. L.J. 243 (2007) (documenting that media reports portrayed the victim as a stripper and exotic dancer who

ture and impervious to sexualized injury."[10] This image is arguably traceable to the legacy of slavery, in which African women were property without personal agency, sexual or otherwise. That image is further promoted by some contemporary rap music that portrays black women as sexually manipulative bitches or "hos." On March 31, 2006, when the investigation was still underway, Rush Limbaugh described the incident as one in which the Duke lacrosse team "raped some hos."[11]

A final important factor is the accuser's alleged drug use, which was significant not only in terms of her ability to perceive and recall events, but which also had the effect of evoking the gender and racial image of the crack whore, who "is in many ways the cousin of the 'welfare queen': both are, in the popular imagination, irresponsible, desperate, manipulative, female, and black."[12]

Put these negative images together—someone who is a liar, sexually out of control, addled by drugs, and manipulative of men through her sexuality—and you have the perfect candidate for the cultural image of the "type" of woman who would make a false rape claim. Indeed, empirical evidence from psychological studies and jury verdicts substantiates that black women are unfairly stereotyped as less credible than white women are when charging rape.[13]

---

had previously made allegations of sexual abuse, rather than as a mother, college student, or veteran).

10. Martha Chamallas, *Discrimination and Outrage: The Migration from Civil Rights to Tort Law*, 48 Wm. & Mary L.R. 2115, 2165 (2007).

11. Media Matters, *Limbaugh Called Alleged Duke Rape Victim a "ho[ ]"*, Apr. 3, 2006, http://mediamatters.org/items/200604030004. The article also reported that Limbaugh apologized the same day.

Generally, the skepticism about women's report of rape arises in consent cases. It is interesting that in a stranger-rape situation, in which the fact of sex is contested, the woman is sometimes disbelieved. Professor Andrew Taslitz has written about the distinction between mistrust of women's accounts in various types of rape cases; he argues that there are strong reasons to conclude that disbelief of women in stranger-rape cases is more prevalent when there is also a racial dynamic. *See* Andrew Taslitz, Rape and the Culture of the Courtroom (1999).

12. Muneer I. Ahmad, *The Ethics of Narrative*, 11 Am. U. J. Gender Soc. Pol'y & L. 117, 118 (2002).

13. Sarah Gill, *Dismantling Gender and Race Stereotypes: Using Education to Prevent Date Rape*, 7 U.C.L.A. Women's L.J. 27, 40 (1996).

Special Accommodations for Victims in Rape Trials, Special Burdens for the Accused

Legal rules, special statutory provisions, and legal culture all treat rape differently from other crimes. Indeed, the mere allegation of a sex crime brings with it special disabilities for both the accuser and the accused. This is a sobering thought as one examines the Duke case, in which innocent people faced a barrage of negative media, criticism, and shaming—for alleged sexual misconduct, racism, and lawyering up. Because of gross prosecutorial misconduct, these young men could have landed in jail on false charges. A recurrent theme in the postmortem on the case concerns the "rush to judgment" in which many engaged in before the facts were fully known. Besides the tendency to presume guilt, however, there are other factors at work that affect public and juror perception of guilt or innocence in rape cases. Consider the following thought experiment: What would have happened to the three accused Duke students had the charges not been dismissed? Are we comfortable with the legal system's treatment of men accused of rape, given the stark reminder, provided by the Duke case, that those accused could be innocent?

Naming Names

Usually, at the time of the victim's initial accusation, the name of the alleged rapist is known. Consequently, given rape's reputation as one of the most heinous crimes, the press coverage may permanently damage the alleged rapist's reputation even if no conviction is secured. In the Duke case, the pretrial statements by Nifong were entirely over the top, including his expression of his personal belief in the accuseds' guilt and his criticisms of them as racially motivated and hiding behind lawyers. These statements violated his ethical obligations and were elements in the case for his disbarment. Yet the mere fact of being accused, along with prosecutorial statements that are well within appropriate ethical boundaries, can brand an individual for a very long time. Here, I risk echoing the much-reviled dictum of Sir Matthew Hale, who famously cautioned jurors in rape cases: "It must be remembered that this is an accusation easily to be made and hard to be proved, and harder to be defended by the party accused, tho' never so innocent."[14] That is not my intention, but

---

14. MATTHEW HALE, 1 HISTORY OF THE PLEAS OF THE CROWN 634 (Philadelphia, R.H. Small 1847).

I do believe that the allegation of a sex crime, which by definition is personal and invasive, carries an extra degree of shame and disgust that does not attach as easily to other crimes.

Moreover, it is rare indeed that defendants are pronounced "innocent" by a state's attorney general after a full investigation, as happened in the Duke case. Therefore, in many cases, a stigma may remain for the named accused even after charges are dropped.

By contrast, the name of the victim often is not officially released. In the Duke case, the Attorney General did not refer to the complaining witness by name.[15] The prohibition on naming the victim typically stems from self-imposed limits by the media, but some states have legal prohibitions on disclosure. In many cases, judges will issue an order forbidding disclosure of the name, address, and likeness of the victim. As famously happened in the Kobe Bryant rape case, Bryant's defense attorney violated this norm: in contravention of a direct court order she "accidentally" named the accuser six separate times in a hearing, to the irritation of the judge and outrage of the public.[16]

Various arguments can be made about the utility, wisdom, and fairness of withholding the alleged victim's name. Elsewhere I have argued that the practical policies of encouraging women to report attacks and protecting the victim's privacy merit the practice.[17] Disclosing her identity could harm the victim, yet withholding it could be seen as stigmatizing her status as shameful or treating the victim as a weak person without full agency. Yet, from the defendant's perspective, withholding the name of his accuser, while simultaneously releasing his, seems grossly unfair. Arguably, this imbalance subverts the presumption of innocence. If the victim's name is withheld, then perhaps the accused's name should be as well. Another alternative was suggested by the public editor of the *New York Times*: the media should "adopt a policy of naming false accusers."[18] The public editor decided against

---

15. *See* Mosteller, *supra* note 2, at 1342 n.16.

16. Colleen Slevin, *Tactics of Kobe's Lawyer Testing Legal Boundaries*, THE STAR-LEDGER (Newark, N.J.), Oct. 13, 2003, at 10; Carol Slezak, *Unseemly Defense Tactics Part of the Legal Game*, CHICAGO SUN-TIMES, Oct. 14, 2003, at 100 ("Mackey called Bryant's alleged victim by her full name six times at the hearing, and I am to believe Mackey simply made a mistake. Six times. How did Mackey get away with this egregious behavior?").

17. *See* Aviva Orenstein, *Special Issues in Rape Trials*, 76 FORDHAM L. REV. 1485, 1593–97 (2007).

18. Byron Calame, *Revisiting the Times's Coverage of the Duke Rape Case*, N.Y. TIMES, Apr. 22, 2007, at 12.

advocating that position in the Duke case, however, because of the special circumstances of prosecutorial misconduct and the accuser's mental health.

Furthermore, although accusers enjoy more privacy protection than those accused in the mainstream media and formal court documents, this is not the case in other media such as internet news and blogs, which often reveal the identity of a rape victim. In any case, as we trace the experience from the accused's perspective, the overall discrepancy seems potentially unfair, and a herald of other imbalances and inequities to come.

Rape Shield

Historically, the justice system has treated women claiming to be rape victims shabbily; their sexual history was put on open display. This was traditionally deemed relevant for two reasons. First, promiscuity on the part of the victim indicated a willingness to sacrifice her chastity or marriage vows, which was viewed as having increased the likelihood of her consenting to sex with the accused. Second, any prior sexual activity (outside the confines of marriage) was deemed a character flaw that undermined her credibility and thus the veracity of her testimony.[19]

In partial response to the concerns raised by the women's liberation movement, most jurisdictions enacted rape-shield laws in the 1970s to remedy this sexist doctrine. As a technical matter, rape-shield provisions function as an exception to an exception within the law of evidence. In general, the rules of evidence exclude character evidence to prove that a person acted in conformity with his or her character on a particular occasion. One exception to this general rule, however, is granted to criminal defendants: they may raise a pertinent character trait of the victim to support a circumstantial defense. For example, the accused in an assault case may present evidence of a victim's violent tendencies to prove circumstantially that the victim threw the first punch. Historically, the accused in a rape case could present evidence that the victim was

---

19. Heather D. Flowe, Ebbe B. Ebbesen & Anila Putcha-Bhagavatula, *Rape Shield Laws and Sexual Behavior Evidence: Effects of Consent Level and Women's Sexual History on Rape Allegations*, 31 LAW & HUM. BEHAV. 159 (2007) ("Many states, for example, once had cautionary instructions to the jury warning of women's propensity to make false charges of rape. Moreover, evidence of promiscuity was routinely admitted at trial to undermine the credibility of a complainant and to demonstrate to the jury that in all likelihood she consented on the occasion in question.").

a floozy, to prove circumstantially that she consented to sex.[20] Rape shields now prohibit the exception in the latter example.[21]

The logic of allowing evidence of the victim's past sexual behavior was tenuous: that a woman has consented to sex with other men reveals little to nothing about whether she consented to sex with the defendant on the occasion. Moreover, facing a public interrogation about one's sex life was an intimidating and humiliating experience. Rape-shield laws were designed to cure these ills and encourage victims to come forward. Shield statutes differ in their approaches, but generally they exclude evidence of the victim's prior sexual behavior or sexual predisposition. They do tend to allow evidence that a person other than the accused was the source of semen or injury, and to allow evidence of a prior relationship between the victim and the accused.

Rape shield is most interesting and controversial in consent cases in which, arguably, the sexual character and history of the complaining woman is most relevant. It is important to note that in the Duke case, the three accused men did not argue consent—that is, that they had sex with the complainant, but she agreed to it—instead, they consistently denied that they had had sex with her at all. If the case had gone to trial, North Carolina's rape-shield rule would have applied. North Carolina Evidence Rule 412 holds that "the sexual behavior of the complainant is irrelevant to any issue in the prosecution."[22] The provision also mandates that a judge hold any rulings on the exceptions in her chambers to protect the victim's privacy.

Because there was uncontroverted evidence that the accused had no prior history with the alleged victim, and because this was not a consent-defense case, some of the exceptions to rape shield would not apply. Two exceptions, however, might have. Rule 412(2) creates an exception for specific instances of sexual behavior with others to show that the defendant did not commit the acts charged; this would have been crucial to the defense in light of the DNA evidence showing the accuser's recent contact with at least four other, unidentified, men. The fact that a specific exception exists for such evidence indicates its importance for the defense and the egregiousness of Nifong's failure to turn it over. A similar exception applied in the Kobe Bryant case, where he could

---

20. Without the protection of a rape shield, such character evidence about the victim could be admissible under Rule 404(a)(2), which permits the accused to raise pertinent character traits about the victim. FED. R. EVID. 404(a)(2).

21. For instance, the federal rape-shield rule generally prohibits: "(1) Evidence offered to prove that any alleged victim engaged in other sexual behavior, [and] (2) [e]vidence offered to prove any alleged victim's sexual predisposition." *Id.* R. 412(a).

22. *Id.* R. 412.

have used evidence of DNA from other men to prove that the victim's injuries were a result of other recent sexual encounters, and not from consensual sex with the accused. Here, because the three accused denied any sexual contact whatsoever, any recent physical evidence of sex—forced or otherwise—that could be attributable to others would be relevant and admissible.

Additionally, the exception in Rule 412(4) permits "evidence of sexual behavior offered as the basis of expert psychological or psychiatric opinion that the complainant fantasized or invented the act or acts charged."[23] This bizarre exception, which invites inquiry into the accuser's mental health, recalls Sigmund Freud's notion that women's charges of sexual abuse are often "hysterical" fabrications emanating from fantasies. Given the defendants' position that they had no sexual contact with the victim, they would have had to portray her as either purposely lying or woefully mistaken. The racist exchange between some men at the party and the two dancers created a potential for portraying the alleged victim as vengeful. More likely, however, had the case gone to trial, the defendants would have attacked the alleged victim as being delusional, either because of her drug use, her mental-health issues, or both. Given the ultimate disposition of the case and the alleged mental-health history of the victim,[24] this may have been a reasonable, even necessary, tactic, but one that nevertheless would have tapped into and reinforced stereotypes about rape victims.

Even with the various exceptions under North Carolina's rape-shield rule, however, the accused could not have raised the alleged victim's general sexual propensities. The fact of her exotic dancing on the evening in question, which was integral to the narrative, probably would have been admissible. But other facts of the victim's sexual history—her regular exotic-dancing gigs, an alleged history of prostitution, and an alleged tendency toward promiscuity—would not. Obviously, in high-profile cases, the internet may release such information to the public and affect local attitudes, even reaching the jury pool. As a technical matter and as a point of principle, however, jurors are supposed to be completely shielded from such information.

Courts generally do not deem prior false rape allegations "sexual behavior."[25] Still, if the victim had made prior allegations and the court determined

---

23. *Id.* R. 412 (b)(4).

24. *See* David Zucchino, *Problems Detailed in Duke Case*, LOS ANGELES TIMES, Apr. 28, 2007, at 9 (describing the victim as a "twenty-eight-year-old single mother with a history of substance abuse and mental health problems.").

25. Joseph A. Colquitt, *Evidence and Ethics: Litigation in the Shadows of the Rules*, FORDHAM L. REV. 1641, 1658–60 (2007) (discussing the false-claim defense). Prior truthful allegations are not admissible; they shed no light on credibility and they undermine the

that the prior rape charges were false (withdrawn allegations are not necessarily false ones), that conduct is relevant to ascertaining the truthfulness of the witness and, with other similar evidence, might fit into an admissible pattern of false allegations.

Finally, as in other types of cases, the accused lacrosse players could have offered relevant evidence to demonstrate that the alleged victim was impaired by alcohol or other substances during the party. This might have been admissible as character evidence under the narrow exception that allows the accused to attack pertinent (other than sexual) traits of the accused. It would also have been admissible to challenge the victim's perceptions, which a foreign substance may have altered or diminished.

Character Evidence about the Accused

In recognition of the reality that rape is often difficult to prove—rarely are there witnesses, and often the focus is on the contested issue of consent—some jurisdictions have recently amended their evidence rules for sex offenses, reversing the general prohibition against the introduction of character evidence pertaining to the accused. For example, Federal Rule of Evidence 413, added in 1995, allows evidence of a defendant's prior sexual misbehavior, whether or not the defendant was actually convicted or even charged. Under this rule, which I have criticized for both its content and application,[26] the accused's prior bad sexual acts are admissible as circumstantial evidence of his general propensity to attack women sexually. Rule 413 may seem particularly appealing in consent cases (in which the trial can degenerate into a "he said-she said" contest and the accused's prior similar behavior might be persuasive as to who was telling the truth), but it applies to all types of sex crimes, not just those involving a consent defense.

Supporters of Rule 413 argue that the probative value of prior wrongful sexual conduct is high because the aggressiveness and proclivities of sex offenders are unique enough to justify a departure from the general rule. Such evidence,

---

rape-shield limitation on sexual history. False allegations could demonstrate intent, knowledge, and lack of credibility generally. Although some evidence existed of a prior rape allegation by the victim in the Duke case, the details remain unknown. *See* Aaron Beard, *Law May Shield Past of Accuser*, THE STAR-LEDGER (Newark, N.J.), Apr. 29, 2006, at 17.

26. Aviva Orenstein, *No Bad Men! A Feminist Analysis of Character Evidence in Rape Trials*, 49 HASTINGS L. REV. 663 (1998) [hereinafter Orenstein, *No Bad Men*]; Aviva Orenstein, *Deviance, Due Process, and the False Promise of Federal Rule 403*, 90 CORNELL L. REV. 1487 (2005).

they argue, will increase conviction rates, thereby protecting women (assuming the right person is convicted). Rule 413 and the handful of state variations that have followed it[27] (some states only allow sexual-propensity evidence in cases of child molestation, but not of adult rape) have been extraordinarily unpopular with evidence scholars, who see the amendment as a radical change in the rules of evidence and an affront to the presumption of innocence.

North Carolina, like most states, did not adopt a version of Rule 413, but it uses other avenues to, at least indirectly, admit evidence of the accused's sexual habits and character. As noted above, evidentiary rules traditionally prohibit the use of character traits or specific incidents that reflect character to prove that the accused acted in conformity with that trait. So, for instance, the fact that the accused possesses the character of a lush or has indulged in past incidents of drunkenness is not admissible to prove the accused's inebriation during the events of a charged case.

North Carolina Rule of Evidence 404(b), however, like its federal analog provides that evidence of other wrongs may be "admissible for other purposes," that is to say, purposes other than the pure propensity argument. Such other purposes include, but are not limited to, "proof of motive, opportunity, intent, preparation, plan, knowledge, identity, or absence of mistake, entrapment, or accident." Therefore, if a prosecutor has a theory other than propensity for introducing the accused's similar bad acts, the prosecutor may do so, subject to a judicial screen for unfairness.

North Carolina jurisprudence is very frank about the fact that "[t]he courts of this State have been markedly liberal in admitting evidence of prior sexual misconduct of a defendant for the purposes cited in Rule 404(b)."[28] This trend is particularly strong in child-molestation cases, in which the accused's prior sexual contact with children is admitted to show motive, intent, or absence of mistake. The liberal approach to 404(b) also applies, however, to those accused of raping adult women.

The prior sexual offenses (whether charged or not) of a man accused of rape in North Carolina are admissible if the prior acts and the charged conduct are "sufficiently similar as to logically establish a common plan or scheme

---

27. *See* Martin A. Schwartz, *Selected Evidence Issues Illustrated—Famous Trials, Movies and Novels*, 769 PRACTICING L. INST./LIT 7 PLI No. 14117, at 32 (Feb. 7, 2008) ("Few states have adopted rules analogous to Rules 413–415."); Edward J. Imwinkelried, *Reshaping the "Grotesque" Doctrine of Character Evidence: The Reform Implications of the Most Recent Psychological Research*, 36 Sw. U. L. REV. 721, 767 (2008) (noting that eleven states have adopted rules similar to Rule 413).

28. State v. Smith, 568 S.E.2d 289, 297 (N.C. Ct. App. 2002).

to commit the offense charged."[29] Such similarities "need not be bizarre or uncanny; they must simply tend to support a *reasonable* inference that the same person committed both the earlier and later acts."[30] North Carolina courts tend to impose a temporal requirement; if the prior sexual offense was too long ago, it may not be admissible. They also require a screen for fairness designed to balance the probative value of the evidence against the prejudice it might cause to the accused. The trial judge is vested with extensive discretion in conducting this balance and deciding whether to admit the defendant's prior sex offenses. Despite the balancing test, the bottom line is that courts have often deemed many prior bad sexual acts admissible. As a practical matter, though Rule 404(b) is more coy than Rule 413, the effect of the liberal application of Rule 404(b) leads to a result similar to that found pursuant to Federal Rule of Evidence 413: the defendant's prior sex offenses will be admitted in sex-offense cases.

No evidence exists about what prior bad sexual acts, if any, Nifong might have tried to introduce at a trial in Durham to prove identity, intent, motive, absence of mistake, common plan, or scheme. Any such evidence, if it existed, would have resulted in tremendous prejudice—causing the jurors to detest the young men and inviting them to make the prohibited propensity argument that the accused were simply the type who attack women sexually.

It would seem especially difficult for jurors to maintain a presumption that the accused is innocent until proven guilty when he is presented as a serial sex offender. As with Rule 413, the prior sexual misconduct need not be the subject of convictions or even arrests; to consider it, the jury must conclude only that its occurrence was more probable than not[31]—a much lower standard of proof than "beyond a reasonable doubt." A woman who had never made a complaint could come forward after reading the newspaper and describe a similar sexual attack by the accused, and under North Carolina's liberal interpretation of Rule 404(b), that evidence would likely be admissible. From the perspective of the accused, it seems particularly unfair that the victim's character and sexual behavior is untouchable because of rape-shield laws, but his own may be dragged through the mud in the public arena and during the trial.

---

29. State v. Summers, 629 S.E.2d 902, 907 (N.C. Ct. App. 2006) (quoting State v. Willis, 526 S.E.2d 191, 193 (N.C. 2000)).

30. *Id.* at 906–07 (quoting State v. Murillo, 509 S.E.2d 752, 764 (N.C. 1998)).

31. *See* Huddleston v. United States, 485 U.S. 681, 689 (1988) ("[S]imilar act evidence is relevant only if the jury can reasonably conclude that the act occurred and that the defendant was the actor."). Despite the word "only," this is a very low standard in a criminal case.

Hearsay Issues

In the course of a criminal trial, the hearsay rule governs the initial admissibility of various out-of-court statements. With some exceptions, out-of-court statements, even those made by someone who will give live testimony at the trial, are not admissible. Therefore, prior statements by victims generally may not supplement the victim's live, in-court testimony.[32] This restriction is of particular concern with regard to child witnesses, whose out-of-court statements are often much more natural and reliable-sounding than their terrified, wooden, overly coached in-court statements. Nevertheless, it is also problematic in the case of adult rape victims whose comments to friends or others may quell concerns that their delay in reporting the rape to the police calls their credibility into question. Reform here should be considered, with the goal of enabling prosecutors to shore up testimony of truthful witnesses whom jurors may otherwise not believe.

Overwhelmingly, special hearsay rules or liberal interpretations of exceptions are designed to protect children who may have cognitive, developmental, or emotional problems that could prevent them from testifying coherently and convincingly. For instance, some states have created "tender years" exceptions that admit prior statements by the children through testimony by various adults, including parents, teachers, police, medical staff, and therapists. Repeating the child's out-of-court statements via competent and confident adult witnesses has the effect of making the child seem more credible, but is arguably unfair to the accused in that the "drumbeat repetition of the victim's original story"[33] will be unduly prejudicial. Additionally, courts sometimes allow children to testify via closed-circuit television.

In addition to newly created hearsay exceptions, courts have tended in recent years to apply traditional exceptions to the hearsay rule, which technically should be subject to the same interpretation across the board, more broadly in cases of sexual assault, although again mostly in child-molestation cases. Specifically, three exceptions to the hearsay rule raise the possibility that courts will treat a rape victim's out-of-court statements differently from those of other declarants. The first is the excited-utterance exception, which pro-

---

32. There is a hearsay exception for rehabilitating a witness who has been charged with recent fabrication or having a motive to lie. Prior statements by that witness indicating that the witness has remained steadfast in her account are admissible, but only if they were made after the alleged motive to fabricate arose. FED. RULE EVID. 801(d)(1)(B); *see* Tome v. United States, 513 U.S. 150 (1988) (imposing the temporal requirement).

33. Modesitt v. State, 578 N.E.2d 649, 653 (Ind. 1991).

vides an exception for statements "relating to a startling event or condition made while the declarant was under the stress of excitement caused by the event or condition."[34] The template of the excited-utterance exception does not currently reflect the way that all women will react to rape and hence may not cover reliable-but-calm statements made by a rape victim after the passage of time. Sometimes the exception is stretched, however, and there are even proposals on the table for making it more relevant in rape cases.[35]

The second expansively used hearsay exception concerns statements made for medical diagnosis or treatment. The exception, which is the same in federal courts and in North Carolina, admits "[s]tatements made for purposes of medical diagnosis or treatment and describing medical history, or past or present symptoms, pain, or sensations, or the inception or general character of the cause or external source thereof insofar as reasonably pertinent to diagnosis or treatment."[36] Interpretative questions arise, especially concerning the applicability of the provision to therapists and the victim's identification of the assailant during medical treatment. Indeed, in the Duke case, Mangum first made her allegations of rape to a nurse in the emergency room. Professor Mosteller has ably demonstrated how courts sometimes stretch this rule in cases of child molestation.[37] This is particularly troubling because children may not understand the importance of accurately communicating with medical professionals, which is the justification for the exception.

---

34. FED. R. EVID. 803(2). The North Carolina rule is identical.

35. I have advocated a special hearsay exception for rape victims. Because no jurisdiction has ever adopted it, I relegate it to a footnote. See Aviva Orenstein, "My God!": A Feminist Critique of the Excited Utterance Exception to the Hearsay Rule, 85 CAL. L. REV. 159 (1997). Professor Collin Miller, documenting a split among the courts, argues persuasively for a more expansive reading of the excited-utterance exception that would include emotional statements made by sexual-assault victims in response to subsequent startling occurrences, even if much time has passed since the original event. See Collin Miller, A Shock to the System: Analyzing the Conflict Among Courts Over Whether and When Excited Utterance May Follow Subsequent Startling Occurrences in Rape and Sexual Assault Cases, 12 WM. & MARY J. WOMEN & L. 49, 51–52 (2005).

36. FED. R. EVID. 803(4).

37. Robert P. Mosteller, The Maturation and Disintegration of the Hearsay Exception for Statements for Medical Examination in Child Sexual Abuse Cases, 65 L. & CONTEMP. PROB. 47 (2002); Robert P. Mosteller, Child Sexual Abuse and Statements for the Purpose of Medical Diagnosis or Treatment, 67 N. CAROLINA L. REV. 257 (1989). Interestingly, North Carolina law tends not to be so flexible, even in the case of children. See State v. Hinnant, 523 S.E.2d 663, 670 (N.C. 2000) ("If the declarant's statements are not pertinent to medical diagnosis, the declarant has no treatment-based motivation to be truthful.").

Additionally, the residual or catch-all hearsay exception has been used to admit child-victim statements.[38] The exception has no precedential value, is applied on a case-by case basis, requires special notice, and demands that "the statement is more probative on the point for which it is offered than any other evidence which the proponent can procure through reasonable efforts."[39] In North Carolina, at least, the only introduction of hearsay statements under the residual clause was in an adult rape case concerning a victim who was mentally handicapped and incompetent to testify—and the appellate court found this to be error, albeit harmless error.[40]

The foregoing analysis has been complicated and in some cases rendered obsolete by the recent reinterpretation of a criminal defendant's right under the Sixth Amendment to confront the witnesses against him. The Confrontation Clause was recently reinterpreted by the U.S. Supreme Court to permit the admission of "testimonial" out-of-court statements against an accused only when (1) the declarant is subject to cross-examination at trial, or (2) the declarant is ruled unavailable and the out-of-court statement in question was subject to prior cross-examination by the accused.[41] The Supreme Court's recent confrontation-clause jurisprudence has called into question the constitutionality of many of the special hearsay exceptions for victims of child molestation, adult rape, and domestic violence.

Since the Court's formulation of its new confrontation jurisprudence, scholars have been scrambling to find ways to preserve the special exceptions for child victims and, to a much lesser degree, for the adult victims of sexual assault and domestic violence.[42] There is still much that is not understood about the new direction the Supreme Court has taken with this clause; scholars debate how much previously admissible hearsay will no longer be constitutional. So long as the victim actually testifies and is subject to cross-examination, however, the issue of whether the prior statements by the victim may be used at trial

---

38. *See* Lynn McLain, *Post-*Crawford: *Time to Liberalize the Substantive Admissibility of a Testifying Witness's Prior Consistent Statements,* 74 UMKC L. Rev. 1, 2–3 (2005) (noting that, pre-*Crawford*, a child-victim's out-of-court statements were admissible via "the excited utterance hearsay exception, the residual 'catch-all' hearsay exception, or the states' "tender years" hearsay exception" (citations omitted)); John E.B. Myers, Ingrid Cordon, Simona Ghetti, Gail S. Goodman, *Hearsay Exceptions: Adjusting the Ratio of Intuition to Psychological Science,* 65 Law & Contemp. Probs. 3, 19–43 (discussing the residual hearsay exception as a commonly used vehicle for admitting children's hearsay).

39. N.C. R. Evid. 803(24).

40. *See* State v. Washington, 506 S.E.2d 283, 288 (N.C. Ct. App. 1998).

41. *See* Crawford v. Washington, 541 U.S. 36, 53–54 (2004).

42. *See, e.g.,* McLain, *supra* note 38.

will remain a question of policy within the purview of various jurisdictions, and subject to their hearsay rule and exceptions.

The bottom line in analyzing this complex, highly technical, and developing area of law is that when rape victims testify (which is more likely than in domestic violence and child molestation cases where victims often recant or refuse to testify), there are no constitutional concerns about admitting the victim's out-of-court statements. The extent to which courts stretch hearsay exceptions or create new ones to admit prior statements by victims reflects issues of public policy. Most of this public-policy concern has surrounded child victims. Had the three young men charged in the Duke case instead been charged with child sexual abuse (rather than rape of an adult woman), the effects on the admissibility of out-of-court statements would have been greater. Although there are subtle hearsay liberalizations for rape cases, the more-marked variations occur in child-molestation cases, a pattern visible in the admissibility of character evidence as well.

Rape Trauma Syndrome and Expert Testimony

Rape Trauma Syndrome (RTS) describes a series of symptoms and reactions common to victims of rape. It was originally developed to treat rape survivors and was not designed as a diagnostic tool.[43] RTS describes a first phase in which the victim is highly agitated or severely withdrawn. Though not technically a form of post-traumatic-stress disorder (PTSD), the later phase of RTS resembles PSTD, and involves a long-term reorganization characterized by sleeplessness, recurring nightmares, phobias, and sexual fears.

Courts struggle with how and to what extent expert testimony on RTS may be used in rape trials. Indeed, some commentators and a minority of jurisdictions do not believe RTS is sufficiently scientific or reliable to be admitted as expert testimony.[44] The majority rule, however, recognizes that expert testimony about RTS can help explain to the jury why, for instance, a subdued victim did not immediately cry out or contact the police. There-

---

43. *See generally* Arthur H. Garrison, *Rape Trauma Syndrome: A Review of a Behavioral Science Theory and Its Admissibility in Criminal Trials,* 23 AM. J. TRIAL ADVOC. 591, 602 (2000) (discussing RTS and asserting that it is "a description of the emotional and psychological reactions that a woman who is raped may have before, during, and after the rape").

44. *See, e.g.,* Mark S. Brodin, *Behavioral Science Evidence in the Age of* Daubert: *Reflections of a Skeptic,* 73 U. CIN. L. REV. 867, 869, 912–15 (2005) (criticizing RTS as derived not from experimentation but observation and for being sufficiently self-contradictory that it does not conform to a diagnosis).

fore, I have advocated using expert testimony not only to counter doubts about the victim's reactions, but also to educate the jury more broadly about the psychological, demographic, and sociological aspects of rape. This has the effect of countering other rape myths (such as only promiscuous women are raped, or men with partners never rape), even if those myths are unspoken.[45]

Appropriate use of expert testimony about RTS helps to dispel myths and stereotypes about rape that might impede a jury from believing the victim but does not use the clinical observations made about RTS to prove the guilt of the accused. Similarly, experts should not provide statistics that point to a witness' credibility, such as testifying that alleged rape victims only lie in 3 percent of cases.[46] North Carolina prohibits the use of experts to bolster the credibility of the defendant,[47] or to prove that a sex crime has occurred.[48] The key case is *State v. Hall*,[49] in which the North Carolina Supreme Court explained:

> the psychiatric procedures used in developing the diagnosis are designed for therapeutic purposes and are not reliable as fact-finding tools to determine whether a rape has in fact occurred.... [T]he potential for prejudice looms large because the jury may accord too much weight to expert opinions stating medical conclusions which were drawn from diagnostic methods having limited merit as fact-finding devices.[50]

Such evidence, however, "may assist in corroborating the victim's story, or it may help to explain delays in reporting the crime."[51] An expert witness in North Carolina may describe RTS and opine that the victim's emotional state was consistent with someone who had been sexually assaulted.[52]

---

45. Orenstein, *No Bad Men*, *supra* note 26, at 704–15.

46. Commonwealth v. Cepull, 568 A.2d 247, 248–49 (Pa. Super. Ct. 1990).

47. *See* State v. Brigman, 632 S.E.2d 498 (N.C. Ct. App. 2006) (criticizing but ultimately finding as harmless error an expert's testimony that the victim was credible on the issue of abuse); State v. Aguallo, 350 S.E.2d 76, 81 (N.C. 1986) (finding reversible error in allowing an expert to testify that a sexual-assault victim was "believable").

48. *See, e.g.*, State v. Isenberg, 557 S.E.2d 568, 572 (N.C. Ct. App. 2001) (holding that an expert is in the best position to determine whether certain behaviors by the victim are consistent with a sexual attack).

49. 412 S.E.2d 883 (N.C. 1992).

50. *Id.* at 889.

51. *Id.* at 891. *See generally* ADRIENNE M. FOX, ADMISSIBILITY OF EVIDENCE IN NORTH CAROLINA §16:23 (4th ed. 2007).

52. State v. O'Hanlan, 570 S.E.2d 751 (N.C. Ct. App. 2002). Some believe that even the explicit mention of RTS may be unfair in consent cases, because an expert's diagnosis in-

There is some concern that expert discussion of RTS, or education of the jury concerning the various ways that a victim may react to a sexual attack, might invite unsought probing of the alleged victim's mental state by the defense. Although legitimate, these concerns seem less relevant in the Duke case because an exception to rape shield in North Carolina would already have permitted intrusive inquiries into the victim's mental health related to her tendency to fantasize. Therefore, it seems that RTS may have been of particular importance for readjusting the jury's expectations of how rape victims might behave.

Expert testimony about RTS presents another important example of the careful balance between allowing the victim to be heard and safeguarding the rights of the accused. Like rape shield, expert testimony about RTS is designed to protect the jury from potential sexist impulses (both perceived and unconscious), and to aid it in focusing on the events of the case in a fair-minded way. RTS is valuable insofar as it educates the jury about the range of possible reactions to a sexual attack and may explain otherwise-anomalous behavior on the part of a victim who did not behave like a "real" rape victim, promptly crying out (as the common law used to demand). True, this special expert testimony will benefit the prosecution and thus influence the trial, but it does not render it unfair. To the extent that rape shield and expert testimony on RTS operate to the disadvantage of the accused, they do so by prohibiting him from capitalizing on prejudicial rape myths or juror ignorance of the range of rape victims' potential reactions.

Postconviction Experiences in Prison and Beyond

The foregoing analysis examined the various ways that evidence rules can shape the jury's and society's determination of guilt in rape cases. The following discussion does not relate to determining guilt, but is nevertheless important in terms of the human story. These postconviction matters do not alter the process of proof, but reinforce the seriousness—and life-altering effects—of a rape conviction.

Rape in Prison

Wrongful conviction and imprisonment is a tragedy of monumental proportions for any innocent person; he is unfairly robbed of his time, freedom,

---

dicates that the victim suffers from a syndrome associated with rape. North Carolina, however, permits an expert to testify that a victim's behavior is consistent with surviving a sexual attack.

dignity, and good name. In addition, it exposes the wrongfully convicted to the possibility of prisoner-on-prisoner rape and violence, which remain serious problems in our penal system. Twenty-two sexual attacks were reported in North Carolina prisons in 2006, though the actual number of attacks is probably much higher.[53] Our society is remarkably blasé about what is clearly cruel, if, unfortunately, not unusual punishment in our prison system. Some cultural evidence even suggests that the acknowledged fact of rape in prison is not only tolerated, but applauded as "just deserts," especially for those who themselves committed sex crimes.[54] Attitudes may be slowly changing, however, as reflected in the recent Prison Rape Elimination Act, which requires the Bureau of Justice Statistics to study sexual violence in prison.[55]

Certain categories of inmates may be at higher risk for being raped, including gays; younger men with slighter builds; white members of the middle class; former law-enforcement personnel; those victimized previously; and inmates in jail for sex crimes, particularly for attacks on children.[56] The scholarship singles out sexual abuse of a minor as the only specific crime associated with a higher risk of rape in prison.[57] In this respect, men accused of adult rape may see only the "normal" level of abuse in prison; other inmates may not perceive adult rape to be as "unmanly," "unnatural," or as deserving of retribution as a sexual attack on a child.

In conducting interviews designed to understand prison culture, one scholar encountered the perception of a decided bias against child molesters, who were placed at the very bottom of the prison pecking order. Interestingly, an interviewed inmate specifically distinguished between child molestation and rape:

> If you a child molester most guys ain't goin' to give you no respect anyway. Cuz, I mean everybody's got kids or their friends or family have

---

53. *See* U.S. Dep't of Justice, Bureau of Justice Statistics, Sexual Violence Reported by Correctional Authorities (2006), http://www.ojp.usdoj.gov/bjs/abstract/svrca06.htm (breaking down prison-rape allegations by state).

54. A *Boston Globe* survey indicated that 50 percent of polled registered voters agreed that society accepts rape in prison as part of the price criminals must pay for their wrongful conduct. *See* Cindy Struckman-Johnson et al., *Sexual Coercion Reported by Men and Women in Prison*, 33 J. Sex. Res. 67, 68 (1996).

55. *See* 45 U.S.C. 15601 *et seq.* (2003); *see generally* National Prison Rape Elimination Comm'n, Home Page, http://www.nprec.us/ (last visited Oct. 29, 2008).

56. Christopher D. Man & John P. Cronan, *Forecasting Sexual Abuse in Prison: The Prison Subculture of Masculinity as a Backdrop for "Deliberate Indifference,"* 92 J. Crim. L. & Criminology 127, 174–75 (2001).

57. *See* Human Rights Watch, No Escape: Male Rape in Prison 10 (2001), http://www.hrw.org/reports/2001/prison/report4.html.

kids. That's something that just hard to accept. You mess with kids. Rapist anymore, it's no big deal.[58]

Looking at the young men accused in the Duke rape case, therefore, the sexual nature of their alleged crimes, in and of itself, would probably not have put them at higher risk for rape or other violence in prison. It appears, however, that they possessed a number of other risk factors: they were young, white, and privileged. Given the charged racial atmosphere surrounding the case, a conviction for raping a black woman might have triggered particular anger and a desire for revenge against these young men had they found themselves wrongly convicted and serving prison terms.[59]

Postconviction Limits on Liberty

It is fair to say that convicted sex offenders are treated as modern-day pariahs, even after they have served their sentences. Some states provide for preventive detention after a penal sentence is complete if the convict is deemed a continuing threat to the safety of others. It is unlikely that the young men accused in the Duke case would have been candidates for such treatment, which is usually reserved for people who purportedly suffer from uncontrollable sexual compulsions or other mental illnesses that make them a danger to society. In any case, North Carolina does not provide for postconviction preventive detention, so this was not a possibility for the Duke lacrosse players, even if they had been wrongly convicted.

Had they been tried and found guilty, however, the Duke players would have been required, under North Carolina law, to register with the local police as sex offenders. The North Carolina Supreme Court explained that "North Carolina, like every other state in the nation, enacted a sex offender registration program to protect the public from the unacceptable risk posed by convicted sex offenders."[60] The North Carolina Sex Offender & Public Protection Registration Program mandates address registration, out-of-county employment notification, residency restrictions, employment restrictions, and a satellite-based monitoring program for selected offenders. Failure to comply with these requirements

---

58. Eric F. Bronson, *Medium Security Prisons and Inmate Subcultures: The "Normal Prison,"* 3 Sw. J. CRIM. JUST. 61, 74 (2006).

59. Man & Cronan, *supra* note 56, at 158–64 (discussing racial tensions in prison); Christopher Hensley, Mary Koscheski & Richard Tewksbury, *Examining the Characteristics of Male Sexual Assault Targets in a Southern Maximum-Security Prison*, 20 J. INTERPERSONAL VIOLENCE 667, 676 (2005).

60. State v. Bryant, 614 S.E.2d 479, 555 (N.C. 2005).

is a felony. These notification laws are deemed public-safety measures that do not impose retroactive "punishment." in violation of the Ex Post Facto Clause.[61]

Had the three young men been convicted, they probably would have been designated "aggravated offenders" under the North Carolina registration system and, for at least ten years after their initial registration, would have been obliged to verify their addresses with the State every ninety days. They would have been prohibited from living within one thousand feet of a school or childcare center, or engaging in childcare. Perhaps even more debilitating than these restrictions on movement, residence, and employment is the public nature of this information, which is available via a few clicks on the internet. The web page warns against using the information for criminal purposes including "threats, intimidation, stalking, [or] harassment." This warning highlights the fact that such sites may have far-reaching effects on the lives of those registered, well beyond the onerous legal requirements, infringing on privacy and physical safety. Both those who have paid their debt to society, and those who were wrongfully accused in the first place, will have the specter of a rape conviction haunting them as they try to reintegrate into society, buy a house, get a job, or join an organization.[62]

Perhaps it is time to reconsider the wisdom and efficacy of the most restrictive of these postconviction requirements, at least for first-time offenders found guilty of the least heinous of sex offenses.[63]

---

61. *Id.* (citing Smith v. Doe, 538 U.S. 84, 90 (2003)).

62. A wide variety of commentators have criticized various aspects of sex-offender registries and restrictions on released-sex-offender movements. *See, e.g., Daniel M. Filler, Silence and the Racial Dimension of Megan's Law*, 89 Iowa L. Rev. 1535 (2004) (discussing the law's disproportionate effect on African-Americans); Rose Corrigan, *Making Meaning of Megan's Law*, 31 Law & Soc. Inquiry 267 (2006) (providing a critical feminist perspective arguing that Megan's Law is radically underinclusive, deflecting attention away from assaults committed by family and friends by not reaching many of the most-common offenders).

In addition, much discussion has centered on the constitutionality and fairness of these laws, *see, e.g.,* Note, *Making Outcasts Out of Outlaws: The Unconstitutionality of Sex Offender Registration and Criminal Alien Detention*, 117 Harv. L. Rev. 2731 (2004), particularly with respect to registration requirements for those convicted due to consensual sex in teenage relationships. *See, e.g.,* Catherine L. Carpenter, *The Constitutionality of Strict Liability in Sex Offender Registration Laws*, 86 B.U. L. Rev. 295 (2006). The appropriate balance between the community's safety and the convicted person's privacy and freedom of movement, even after paying his debt to society, is an important question beyond the scope of this chapter.

63. For example, in some locales, residency restrictions mean that, due to the particular arrangement of schools or childcare facilities, the only place where convicted sex offenders can legally live is on the street or under a bridge—the law has effectively made them

Concluding Observations

Much of the writing about the unique qualities of rape cases has been from the victim's perspective, documenting how she is often humiliated in the public sphere and put on trial herself in the courtroom. I and others have written about the need for special rules, such as rape-shield laws, to protect the alleged victim, although we have acknowledged that formal legal rules cannot entirely overcome entrenched rape myths and societal biases. It is equally valuable, however, and much less common, to examine these questions from the perspective of the accused.

Being unjustly accused of a rape and facing jail, loss of reputation, legal expenses, and emotional upheaval is a harrowing experience. The mere allegation of a crime tends to taint the accused's reputation. Although the most crucial factor in the young men's ordeal was the unethical conduct of the prosecutor, it is nonetheless instructive to examine the various ways—in formal courtroom procedure, society at large, and the postconviction process—that those accused of rape receive quite a different, and arguably worse, deal compared to those accused of other violent crimes. It is important, however, not simply to list these differences and express outrage—an easy and tempting reaction in the context of the three innocent men accused in the Duke lacrosse case. Instead, the differences in the experience of someone accused of a sex crime must be analyzed. How much do they derive from issues over which the state has official control? Of the formal legal differences, are these special liabilities justifiable or are they merely expressions of society's revulsion at sex offenses, unfairly aimed at a person who has not yet been proven guilty?

Not all of the special provisions designed for rape trials are unfair. To distinguish among them, it is useful to return to the narratives with which the chapter began. Evidence that only serves to feed into negative stereotypes and promote the cultural myths of either narrative—the frat boy gone wild or the lying ho—is irrelevant, distracting, and at odds with a fair truth-finding process. Neither the prosecutor nor the defense should win a case by pandering to the jury's belief in demonstrably false and inflammatory negative cultural images of rape victims or perpetrators.

Viewed in this light, properly crafted and implemented shield laws, despite being unique to rape cases, are not unfair to the accused. Rape-shield laws do indeed prevent certain types of arguments by the accused, but the evi-

---

homeless. *See* Sue Carlton, *Deal with Issue of Freed Sex Offenders*, St. Petersburg Times, Apr. 5, 2008, at 1B; Larry Keller, *Residence Limits Keep Sex Offenders on Move*, Palm Beach Post, May 19, 2007, at 1A.

dence shielded is highly prejudicial, deeply personal, and largely irrelevant. Traditionally, information about the sexual behavior and history of the victim was used to embarrass and silence her, not to construct legitimate defense arguments about the accused's innocence. Our nation's history prior to the advent of rape-shield laws indicates that questions about prior sexual history and behavior served only to discourage women from participating in the process. Rape-shield laws operate to limit information that could trigger a juror's belief in and subscription to misogynist and racist stereotypes of the victim. They contain ample exceptions for legitimate information, such as any prior relationship between the alleged victim and the accused. The accused is entitled to a fair trial, but should not be able to capitalize on racist or sexist stereotypes to win an acquittal or humiliate and intimidate a key witness so that there is no trial at all.

By contrast, special rules (either via Rule 413 or via extension of Rule 404(b)) that provide the jury with information concerning prior bad sexual conduct of the accused are simply unfair. They undermine the presumption of innocence and unfairly prejudice the accused in the eyes of the jury. I understand the attraction of admitting prior sexual misconduct to prove lack of consent. It avoids the maddening situation in which a rapist can discredit a series of women individually (claiming each is lying or fantasizing) although he could not discredit them all if their stories were told simultaneously so that a pattern of sexual offenses emerged. Nevertheless, the dangers of such testimony—the demonization of the accused, the distraction of other events, and the tendency of jurors to overvalue past conduct in determining guilt as to the behavior charged—are considerable and outweigh its benefits.

In the Duke case, there was no defense of consent, yet the court could nevertheless have admitted any similar prior sexual misconduct of the accused, thereby prejudicing them and undermining the presumption of innocence. Such evidence, had it existed, would have played into the wild-frat-boy stereotype while distracting the jury from the charges in the case at hand. Furthermore, rules that admit evidence of prior bad acts by the accused feed directly into unfair negative stereotypes about perpetrators. Interestingly, this image contrasts markedly with the very positive image of young men that emerges from the lying-ho narrative—that of female perfidy ruining innocent lives. This is the flip side of the lying-ho rape myth, and is equally unfair.

Additionally, the negative stereotype of frat boys gone wild perpetuates cultural myths about rape, indirectly supporting the belief that only select deviants rape women, and that normal men do not. By demonizing the young men as wild, out-of-control, over-entitled sexual predators, such prior-bad-act evidence undermines our society's recognition that rape presents a persistent, widespread problem and that rapists come from all races, ages, ethnicities, and socioeconomic strata.

As to special hearsay rules, I am more conflicted. The "tender years" exception in child-molestation cases sometimes serves only as an inappropriate conduit for hearsay. Allowing prior statements by rape victims who do testify, however, seems perfectly fair, particularly if the statements counteract the jury's concern about the victim's initial, muted response to the attack. Similarly, expert testimony about RTS is helpful and fair, so long as the expert does not usurp the right of the jury to determine whether a rape occurred. Knowledge about common responses to rape—particularly when those responses are counterintuitive—can truly assist the jury without prejudicing the accused.

The special postconviction treatment of rapists raises issues of fairness, but these are concerns of a different kind, since that treatment does not taint the process of proof. American tolerance of rape and other violence in prison brings shame on us all. To the extent that these horrors occur disproportionately to perpetrators of sex crimes, the solution is not to alter the process of finding guilt but to remedy the conditions of the punishment phase. No one should have to suffer rape—not even a rapist. The irony of a wrongful conviction may add to our sense of outrage, but logically should not alter our response to society's callous treatment of those whom it incarcerates.

Megan's laws and postconviction detention represent other serious consequences of a rape conviction, drastically limiting the convicted person's freedom of movement and ability to reintegrate into society. Public safety, apparently, has been deemed to outweigh the individual's interest in privacy and right to be treated as rehabilitated. When there is a serious chance of danger to the public, perhaps these measures are justified, although they come at a high cost. And query whether, in the end, they encourage the very recidivism that they are designed to protect against.

Two final points emerge from this analysis. First, it is interesting to note how the disabilities attendant on those accused of sex crimes are much more pronounced in the case of child sexual abuse. This difference is particularly apparent in the liberal application of hearsay exceptions and use of experts. The mistreatment of child molesters in jail and postrelease harassment are also more extreme. A separate inquiry should be made into the devastating consequences of child-molestation charges, but we must leave for another day the question whether the rules in this arena have gone too far in favor of conviction and punishment. Special issues concerning children's emotional ability to testify, cognition, memory, and communication skills make this a more complicated calculus. Part of the difference between the treatment of accused rapists and accused child molesters reflects the horror society feels at the violation of children's trust and sexual innocence. One can speculate that it also may reflect a higher tolerance of adult rape in some cases, particularly when the victim is unsympathetic or seemed to be, according to some rape myths, "asking for it." The attitude toward rape victims is complex and not always benign or compassionate. One accepted narrative of the Duke case—the lying ho—emerged in part from a deep hostility to women that has no direct analog in child-molestation cases.

Second, it is interesting to observe the interaction between the legal and social consequences of a rape accusation. Some of what affects both accuser and accused is not directly attributable to formal legal rules, but to social forces outside the law such as the media frenzy and the public's rush to judgment that characterized the Duke case. Many of the rules put in place to protect victims—such as rape-shield laws and prohibitions against naming rape victims—are empty promises in high-profile cases given the ubiquity of the internet and virulence of the blogosphere. Similarly, as Nifong's conduct demonstrated, disseminating information about those accused of rape, thus poisoning the public's opinion of them is easy to do outside the courtroom. For all of the justified sympathy and outrage inspired by the three accused in this case, they do seem fortunate in some ways that others who have been falsely accused are not: they received an apology, their names were fully cleared, and they are suing in civil court. For many others who are falsely accused of crimes, at best the charges are quietly dropped, there is no civil suit, and the taint of scandal remains.

The Duke rape case serves as a sobering reminder that in our efforts to convict the guilty we must constantly bear in mind—and make procedural accommodations for—the possibility that the accused is innocent. In assessing the parade of horribles that can occur to someone unjustifiably accused of rape, we should eliminate those that unfairly prejudice the accused or set him up for unduly harsh treatment. We should not, however, alter those measures designed to allow the victim to tell her story shorn of irrelevant, prejudicial information and unreasonable expectations based on rape myths. Nor should we allow the prosecution to distract and prejudice the jury by piling on information about the accused's prior sexual behavior.

Achieving a fair balance between the needs of the victim, the accused, and the system is particularly difficult when the crime is rape. Such a balance is essential, however, and not merely to assure justice for the individuals involved. Perceptions about the fairness of rape trials shape societal attitudes about rape and about the justice system. Although famous, media-hyped cases such as the Duke rape case are atypical, they serve as a locus for societal conversations about rape and can subtly refashion attitudes about what constitutes the crime and how the legal system should handle it. The conclusions I draw—permitting expert testimony about RTS and some prior statements by the alleged victim, but prohibiting past sexual information about the alleged victim and the alleged rapist—serve to focus that conversation on the relevant facts, screening out sexist and racist stereotypes. My proposal advocates special rules for rape cases; these accommodations are not unfair intrusions upon the presumption of innocence, but rather are designed to keep the trial focused and fair.

Authors' Biographies

MICHÈLE ALEXANDRE, a graduate of Colgate University and Harvard Law School, is currently Associate Professor of Law at the University of Mississippi. Her teaching areas include property, trusts and estates, critical race theory, constitutional law, civil rights, human rights, and feminist legal theory. Professor Alexandre's prior professional experience includes serving as a civil rights attorney with Chestnut Sanders Sanders Pettaway Campbell & Albright L.L.C. in Selma, Alabama; as an associate in the corporate real estate department of Debevoise & Plimpton; and as a law clerk to the Hon. John P. Fullam, Eastern District of Pennsylvania, in Philadelphia. Professor Alexandre has received Fulbright and Watson Fellowships to pursue her research projects. Her work has appeared in such publications as the *Duke Journal of Gender Law and Policy, the UCLA Chicano/a-Latino/a Law Review*, the *Boston College Environmental Affairs Law Review*, and the *Washington and Lee Law Review*. She has articles forthcoming in the *American University Journal of Gender, Social Policy and the Law* and the *William and Mary Journal of Women and the Law*. In addition, she has two chapters forthcoming in LAW, PROPERTY, AND SOCIETY (Robin Paul Malloy ed.) and in TRANSCENDING THE BOUNDARIES OF LAW (Martha Albertson Fineman ed.). She thanks Imani Perry for her comments, and her research assistant, Tannera George.

GEORGE W. DOWDALL is Professor of Sociology at Saint Joseph's University. His publications include THE ECLIPSE OF THE STATE MENTAL HOSPITAL (1996); FINDING OUT WHAT WORKS AND WHY: A GUIDE TO EVALUATING COLLEGE PREVENTION PROGRAMS AND POLICIES (2002); ADVENTURES IN CRIMINAL JUSTICE RESEARCH (2008); and book chapters and journal articles on mental health and substance abuse. His next book is COLLEGE DRINKING: REFRAMING A SOCIAL PROBLEM (Praeger/Greenwood, forthcoming). Dowdall received a Ph.D. in Sociology from Brown University and was an NIMH postdoctoral fellow at the UCLA School of Public Health. He has been a regular faculty member at Indiana University, Buffalo State, and Saint Joseph's, and has held visiting appointments at UCLA, Penn, Brown, and Harvard. He was the American Sociological Association's Congressional Fellow in Senator Joseph Biden's office.

He serves on the Pennsylvania Advisory Council on Drug and Alcohol Abuse, the Board of Directors of Security on Campus, Inc., and SCAN (Stop Child Abuse Now), Inc.

PAUL C. GIANNELLI is the Albert J. Weatherhead III & Richard W. Weatherhead Professor of Law at Case Western Reserve University. He received his J.D. from the University of Virginia, where he served as Articles Editor of the *Virginia Law Review*. His other degrees include an LL.M. from the University of Virginia and an M.S. in Forensic Science from George Washington University. After law school, he served as both a prosecutor and defense counsel in the military. Professor Giannelli has written extensively in the field of evidence and criminal procedure, especially on the topic of scientific evidence. He has authored or co-authored ten books, including SCIENTIFIC EVIDENCE (4th ed. 2007) and has published articles in the Columbia, Virginia, Cornell, Vanderbilt, Fordham, North Carolina, Wisconsin, Ohio State, and Hastings law reviews, as well as in the *Journal of Criminal Law & Criminology*, the *Criminal Law Bulletin*, and the *American Criminal Law Review*. In addition, his work has appeared in interdisciplinary journals, such as the *Journal of Law, Medicine & Ethics, Issues in Science and Technology* (National Academies), *International Journal of Clinical & Experimental Hypnosis*, the *New Biologist*, and the *Journal of Forensic Sciences*. Professor Giannelli's work has been cited in hundreds of court opinions and legal articles, including decisions of the U.S. Supreme Court: *Clark v. Arizona* (2006); *Blakely v. Washington* (2004); *United States v. Scheffer* (1998); *Daubert v. Merrell Dow Pharm., Inc.* (1993); *Hudson v. Palmer* (1984); and *Barefoot v. Estelle* (1983). He served as Reporter for the American Bar Association Criminal Justice Standards on DNA Evidence and co-chair of the ABA's Ad Hoc Committee on Innocence.

LENESE HERBERT is Professor of Law at Albany Law School in Albany, New York, where she teaches Criminal Law, Criminal Procedure, Evidence, and Administrative Law. She has taught as a Visiting Professor at Washington and Lee University School of Law (2007–08) and Howard University School of Law (2008–09). Immediately prior to entering law teaching, Professor Herbert served as an Assistant U.S. Attorney for the District of Columbia (1994–99) in both the civil and criminal divisions. Prior to joining the U.S. Attorney's Office, Professor Herbert served as a trial attorney in the Manipulation and Trade Practice Section of the U.S. Commodity Futures Trading Commission's Division of Enforcement (1991–94), where she investigated and regulated, via administrative-enforcement actions, commodity-futures brokers, supervisors, and firms. Professor Herbert also served as an attorney-advisor in the Chief Counsel's Office of the U.S. Department of Transportation (1990–91). Professor Herbert is the co-author of one criminal-procedure casebook, CONSTITU-

TIONAL CRIMINAL PROCEDURE (3d ed. Foundation Press 2007) and a number of scholarly works in, among other publications, the *University of Illinois Law Review, Howard Law Review, Ohio State Journal of Criminal Procedure*, and the *Michigan Journal of Race & Law*. She has been quoted in several news publications and occasionally serves as a consultant and attorney of counsel in civil and criminal matters.

MICHELLE S. JACOBS is Professor of Law at the University of Florida Levin College of Law. She received her A.B. *cum laude* from Princeton University in 1977 and obtained her *Juris Doctorate* from the Rutgers University School of Law-Newark in 1982. Professor Jacobs began teaching after practicing as a criminal defense lawyer in New York and New Jersey. She currently teaches Criminal Law, International Criminal Law, Critical Race Theory, and a seminar on women defendants in the criminal justice system. Her scholarship explores the issue of access to justice for the poor, particularly in the criminal justice context. Most recently, she has focused specifically on the issues of women who are prosecuted for criminal offenses. Professor Jacobs recently assisted in preparing a section of the U.S. shadow report for the U.N.'s Committee to Eliminate Racial Discrimination.

JANINE YOUNG KIM is Associate Professor of Law at Marquette University Law School, where she teaches courses relating to criminal law and procedure, torts, and race and the law. She received her B.A. and M.A. from Stanford University and her law degree from Yale Law School. Professor Kim is the author of several scholarly works in, among other publications, the *Berkeley Journal of Criminal Law, Tulane Law Review*, and the *Yale Law Journal*. She would like to extend her special thanks to Marvin Vallejo for his valuable research assistance.

ROBERT J. LUCK is an Assistant United States Attorney for the Southern District of Florida. Before that, he served as term law clerk, and then career law clerk, for Judge Ed Carnes of the United States Court of Appeals for the Eleventh Circuit. Between stints with Judge Carnes, Luck was an associate with the Greenberg Traurig law firm in Miami. Luck received his J.D. from the University of Florida Levin College of Law, where he was editor-in-chief of the *Florida Law Review*. This is Luck's first foray into academic legal writing. He thanks his mentor and friend, Mike Seigel, for the privilege and opportunity of working on the book. Robert also thanks his wife, Jennifer, and daughter, Julia, for their love and patience.

ROBERT M. O'NEIL continues to teach a First Amendment Clinic at the University of Virginia School of Law, although he retired from full-time teaching in the summer of 2007. In the spring semester of 2009 he will be teaching Constitutional Law of Church and State at the University of Texas Law School. Formerly President of the University of Wisconsin System (1979–85) and of the

University of Virginia (1985–90), as well as serving in other senior administrative posts at the University of Cincinnati and Indiana University-Bloomington, he has taught Constitutional Law at each institution. He is current
Founding Director of the Thomas Jefferson Center for the Protection of Free
Expression and Director of the Ford Foundation's Difficult Dialogues Initiative. He has held several roles in the American Association of University Professors — twice as general counsel, seven years as chair of Committee A on
Academic Freedom and Tenure, and currently as chair of the Special Committee on Academic Freedom and National Security in Time of Crisis. His
writings include many law-review articles and comments in higher-education
journals; his most recent book is ACADEMIC FREEDOM IN THE WIRED WORLD
(Harvard Press 2008). In 1988 he chaired the Southern Association of Colleges
and Schools Decennial Review Team at Duke University.

AVIVA ORENSTEIN is Professor of Law at Indiana University School of Law-
Bloomington, where she teaches Evidence, Civil Procedure, and Family Law.
She received her A.B. (*summa cum laude* 1981) and J.D. (*magna cum laude*
1986) from Cornell University, and served as an articles editor of the *Cornell
Law Review.* Orenstein clerked for the late Honorable Edward R. Becker, Chief
Judge for the Court of Appeals for the Third Circuit. She is admitted to practice law in New Jersey and Indiana, and has worked on various pro bono projects involving children's rights and family law. She recently testified against
SJR-7, and helped to defeat the marriage amendment to the Indiana Constitution. Orenstein visited at Cornell Law School in 1994 and Cardozo School
of Law from 2001–2003. Her scholarly interests concern the intersection of evidence law and culture, and she has published articles in the *California Law
Review, Cornell Law Review, Fordham Law Review,* and the *Indiana Law Journal,* among others. Orenstein has written on gender and evidence is currently
working on a notorious historical British trial involving domestic violence and
murder-suicide. In her spare time, Orenstein writes a column for her local
newspaper and lectures on Jewish humor. She is married to David Szonyi and
is the proud mother of three grown men, David, 25, Michael, 23, and Benjamin,
19. Professor Orenstein would like to thank Jeannine Bell, Hannah Buxbaum,
Fred Cate, Leandra Lederman, Robert Mosteller, Debra Orenstein, Sylvia Orenstein, Cynthia Reichard, Lauren Robel, David Szonyi, Andrew Taslitz, and
Susan Williams for helpful comments on earlier drafts. She also thanks Martha
Marion and Kevin Dent for excellent research assistance.

SHARON E. RUSH is the Irving Cypen Professor of Law at the University of
Florida Levin College of Law, where she also is cofounder of the Center for
the Study of Race and Race Relations and an associate director of the Center
for Children. She received her B.A. and J.D. *cum laude* from Cornell Univer-

sity. She was a goalie for the Cornell Women's Lacrosse team as an undergraduate. On receiving her law degree, she practiced with the New York firm of Cadwalader, Wickersham and Taft in their D.C. office before starting her teaching career at DePaul University in Chicago. She joined the University of Florida faculty in 1985 and teaches Constitutional Law, Federal Courts, the Constitution and Schools, and the Fourteenth Amendment. Her research focuses on issues of racial equality, particularly for children. She is the author of numerous articles and the book, LOVING ACROSS THE COLOR LINE (2000), which was nominated for an NAACP Image Award. Her most recent book, HUCK'S "HIDDEN" LESSONS: TEACHING AND LEARNING ACROSS THE COLOR LINE, was published in March 2006.

MICHAEL L. SEIGEL is Professor of Law and Alumni Research Scholar at the University of Florida Frederic G. Levin College of Law, where he teaches Criminal Law, Evidence, and White-Collar Crime. He served as Associate Dean for Academic Affairs of the College from 2000–02, and has visited at the University of British Columbia, Stetson University, and the University of San Diego. Professor Seigel has also held many federal prosecutorial posts, including: Special Assistant U.S. Attorney, Eastern District of Pennsylvania (2000–01); First Assistant U.S. Attorney for the Middle District of Florida (1995–99); Assistant U.S. Attorney, Eastern District of Pennsylvania, Organized Crime Strike Force (1990); and Special Attorney, U.S. Department of Justice, Organized Crime and Racketeering Section, Philadelphia Strike Force (1985–89). He is the author of one book, a mystery novel titled IMPROBABLE EVENTS: MURDER AT ELLENTON HALL (2005), and numerous works in such scholarly periodicals as the *American Journal of Criminal Law*, *Boston University Law Review*, *Florida State University Law Review*, *Harvard Law Review*, *Hofstra Law Review*, *Journal of Legal Education*, *Northwestern Law Review*, and the *Wisconsin Law Review*. Professor Seigel is also the author of ten opinion-editorials. His op-ed on the issue of corporate attorney-client privilege waiver, *Corporate America Fights Back*, was published in the *Washington Post* on February 26, 2007.

ANDREW E. TASLITZ is the Welsh S. White Distinguished Visiting Professor of Law at the University of Pittsburgh School of Law for the 2008–09 academic year and is Professor of Law at the Howard University School of Law. He teaches Criminal Law, Criminal Procedure, Evidence, Professional Responsibility, Freedom of Speech, Terrorism and the Law, and advanced courses in those areas. He has also visited at the Duke University Law School and the Villanova University School of Law. A former prosecutor, Professor Taslitz has published over one-hundred works, including scholarly articles in such journals as the *Georgetown Law Journal*, *Boston University Law Review*, Northwestern University's *Journal of Criminal Law and Criminology*, and Duke University's *Law and Con-*

temporary Problems. He has published five books, including RECONSTRUCT-
ING THE FOURTH AMENDMENT: A HISTORY OF SEARCH AND SEIZURE, 1789–1868
(2006); CONSTITUTIONAL CRIMINAL PROCEDURE (3d ed. 2007) (co-authored);
and RAPE AND THE CULTURE OF THE COURTROOM (1999). He is also co-author
of a forthcoming two-volume treatise on criminal procedure. He is the Chair
of the Book Board Committee of the American Bar Association (ABA) Criminal Justice Section, a member and former chair of that section's editorial board,
a former chair of its Committee on Race and Racism, a former codirector of
its Communications Division, and author of the eyewitness-identification
chapter of the report of its Ad Hoc Committee on Innocence and Ensuring
the Integrity of the Criminal Justice System, *Convicting the Guilty, Acquitting
the Innocent.* Additionally, he is a current member of the ABA's Subcommittee on Transactional Surveillance Standards and its Committee on Criminal
Justice Standards. Professor Taslitz has also served as chair of both the Evidence and Criminal Justice Sections of the Association of American Law Schools.
He is the reporter for the National Conference of Commissioners on Uniform
State Law's Drafting Committee on Videotaping Custodial Interrogations, the
former reporter for the National Academy of Sciences Committee on Bomb-
Blast Terrorism, the former reporter for the Constitution Project's Death Penalty
Initiative, and a member of the National Institute of Justice's Advisory Com-
mittee for the Empirical Study of Eyewitness Identification Procedures.

    RODNEY J. UPHOFF is the Elwood L. Thomas Endowed Professor of Law at
the University of Missouri-Columbia and, until recently, served as the school's
Associate Dean of Academic Affairs. He is the Director of the University of
Missouri South African Education Program representing the four Missouri
campuses. Prior to joining the Missouri faculty in 2001, Uphoff taught at the
University of Oklahoma college of Law, where he served as professor and Director of Clinical Legal Education and ran a criminal defense clinic for ten
years. From 1984–1988, Professor Uphoff directed a criminal clinic at the University of Wisconsin Law School. Before law teaching, he was a public defender
in Milwaukee, Wisconsin. Professor Uphoff graduated from the University of
Wisconsin School of Law with honors in 1976 and has a Masters Degree from
the London School of Economics. He has written numerous articles on criminal defense practice, the delivery of indigent defense services, and ethical issues facing those involved in he criminal justice system. In 1995, Uphoff edited
a book for the ABA entitled ETHICAL PROBLEMS FACING THE CRIMINAL DEFENSE
LAWYER. Uphoff was one of four attorneys initially appointed to represent
Terry Nichols in Oklahoma state court. Nichols was convicted of 160 murders
based on the bombing of the Murrah Building in Oklahoma City in April 1995,
but he did not receive the death penalty. Professor Uphoff teaches Trial Prac-

tice, Professional Responsibility, Criminal Procedure, and Criminal Litigation Skills.

GARY L. WELLS is Professor of Psychology at Iowa State University and holds the title of Distinguished Professor. Wells is also Director of Social Science at the Institute of Forensic Science and Public Policy in Greensboro, North Carolina. He is an internationally recognized scholar in scientific psychology and his studies of eyewitness memory are widely known and cited. Wells has authored over 170 articles and chapters and two books. Most of this work has been focused on the reliability of eyewitness identification. His research on eyewitness identification is funded by the National Science Foundation and his findings have been incorporated into standard textbooks in psychology and law. His research-based proposals on lineup procedures, such as the use of double-blind techniques, are being increasingly accepted in law-enforcement practices across the nation. His conclusions about eyewitness identification have received national media attention in such places as *Time* magazine, the *Chicago Tribune*, the *Los Angeles Times*, and the *New York Times*. He has made appearances on CBS's *48 Hours*, the *NBC Nightly News*, Court TV, and NBC's *Today Show*, among others. He was a founding member of the U.S. Department of Justice group that developed the first set of national guidelines for eyewitness evidence and co-chaired the panel that wrote the Justice Department training manual for law enforcement on eyewitness-identification evidence. Wells has worked with prosecutors and police across the nation to reform eyewitness-identification procedures. Wells is a past President of the American Psychology-Law Society and has received Distinguished Contributions awards from the American Psychology-Law Society and the American Psychological Association. In 2008 Wells was awarded an honorary doctorate from John Jay College of Criminal Justice.

KENNETH WILLIAMS received his B.A. from the University of San Francisco in 1983 and his J.D. from the University of Virginia School of Law in 1986. Currently, he is Professor of Law at Southwestern Law School. He has also been a faculty member at Gonzaga University School of Law and at Texas Southern University, Thurgood Marshall School of Law, where he also served as Associate Dean for Academic Affairs. He has been a visiting professor at Michigan State University, University of Hawaii, and University of Oklahoma law schools. Professor Williams has served as habeas counsel for seven Texas death-row inmates. He has been successful before the U.S. Court of Appeals for the Fifth Circuit and the U.S. District Court for the Southern District of Texas in obtaining new trials and hearings for inmates convicted and sentenced to death in violation of their constitutional rights. He is currently representing an Argentine national at the request of the Argentine government. Professor Williams has published articles in law journals throughout the nation in the areas of capital punishment and criminal law and has spoken at conferences and been quoted in newspaper articles on these topics. Professor Williams teaches in the areas of criminal law and procedure, evidence, and capital punishment.

Index

Pages with figures, illustrations and tables are indicated with **bold** font. Pages with appendixes are in **bold** font followed by the letters "**App.**" *Italic* font is used for case names, books and newspapers.

A

AAUP. *See* American Association of University Professors (AAUP)
ABA. *See* American Bar Association
Abram's Show, The, 16
academic freedom, 144n97
  administration's protection of, 51–52
  Arian, Sami al-, 39
  Bollinger, Lee, 43
  Butz, Arthur, 40–41
  Davis, Angela, 40
  and grades, 47–48
  and Group of 88, 38–41
  Harleston, Bernard, 43
  institutional disclaimers, limits of scope, 43–44
  Levin, Michael, 43
  O'Reilly Factor, The, 39
  possible issues, 38–41
academic problems on campuses, 93–94
acquaintance rape, 104
administration. *See also* Brodhead, Richard; faculty; Lange, Peter
  accountability and ethics of, 142–46

Broad, Molly, 52
Burness, John, 19–20
  controlling alcohol use, 80–81
  faculty autonomy and academic freedom, 51–52
  institutional response, 143–46
  Moneta, Larry, 19
  responses from, 17–22, 41–44, 141
  Steel, Bob, 20
  student affairs, in Coleman Report, 82
  Trask, Tallman III, 18, 48–49, 243
  underage drinking by athletes, 113
  Wasiolek, Sue, 17, 113, 241
adult-entertainment industry, 114–19, 147–49
African Americans. *See* racism; women of color
"Ain't I a Woman," 130–31
Ake v. Oklahoma, 257, 344
alcohol abuse, 79–101. *See also* binge drinking; National Institute on Alcohol Abuse and Alcoholism (NIAAA)

alcohol abuse *continued*
  and agency liability, 150
  alcohol policy, 80n5, 83
  alcohol-related problems (1993-
    2001), **92**
  Bogle, Kathleen, 95
  and campus culture, 96–99
  Campus Culture Initiative (CCI),
    86–87
  Coleman Report, 81–83
  consequences of, 91–94
  drinking factors, **91**
  in the incident, 79–81
  intoxicated rape and, 94–96
  by lacrosse team, 34, 81–83
  lessons from incident, 99–101
  and male sexual aggression,
    103–4
  national patterns of, 88–91
  reducing, 98–99
  and social culture, 84–88
  statistics, dependence and, 94
  statistics, drinking trends (1993-
    2001), **89**
  statistics, perception *vs.* reality, 85
  understanding, 90
alleles, 328, 329–31
Allen, Charlotte, 32
Alleva, Joe, 18, 48–49
American Association of University
  Professors (AAUP)
  academic freedom policy, 39–40
  collegiality policy, 45–46
  grading policy, 47–48
  recommendation, 54
  Statement on Academic Freedom
    and Tenure, 38–39
American Bar Association
  Criminal Justice Standards, 274

  Model Grand Jury Act, 294, 296
  Model Rules of Professional Con-
    duct, Rule 3.6, 200–202
  Model Rules of Professional Con-
    duct, Rule 3.8(f), 203
  Standards on DNA Evidence, 343,
    345
  study of death-penalty systems,
    278
American Psychology-Law Society,
  313, 318
  eyewitness procedure *vs.* actual,
    321
American Society of Crime Direc-
  tors/Laboratory Accreditation
  (ASCLD/LAB), 338
Andrews v. State, 323
"announce clause," 205–6
Arian, Sami al-, 39
Ashby, Angela, 332
Ashton-James, Clair, 21, 46
assaults on campuses, 93
athletes. *See also* lacrosse team
  aggressive behavior towards
    women, 104–5
  belief in rape myth and aggressive
    sexual behavior, 107–8
  Coleman Report recommenda-
    tions, 83
  effects of rape accusations, 109
  statistics, rape and alcohol use,
    100
  traditional view of manhood,
    106–7
Athletic Council, 50
athletics department. *See also*
  lacrosse team
  Alleva, Joe, 18, 48–49
  Kennedy, Chris, 17–18, 241

Knight, Bob, 53
Pressler, Mike, 17, 22, 241,
    244–45
autosomal testing. *See* Short Tandem
    Repeats (STR) testing

B

Baartman, Saartjie, **126**–28
    biography, 127n1
Baker, Houston, 20, 35, 194
    and academic freedom, 40
    on *CBS News*, 143–44
    on CNN, 35–36
    Lange's rebuke of, 44
Baker, Lee, 51
Baldwin, Steve, 23, 44–45
Bannon, Brad
    discovery of exculpatory evidence,
        23–24, 251n65, 253–54
    examines Meehan, 338–39
    examines underlying DNA data,
        336–38
    files grievance letter, 245
Barnes, Ernie, 222n50
Bath, Raheem, 85
Beauharnais v. Illinois, 180–81
Benedict, Jeffrey, 105, 108, 115
Best 361 Colleges (2007), The, 84
binge drinking, 85, 87
    alcohol-related problems
        (1993–2001), **92**
    distribution of colleges by per-
        centage of, **90**
    factors predicting, 90
    factors shaping, **91**
    gender reasons for, 110
    gender-specific definition of, 88
    and rape, 100
    statistics, trends (1993-2001), **89**
    successful interventions, 97–98

updated definition of, 98
Bishop, Keith, 13–14
    election results, 17, 226
Black, Freda, 13–14, 212n7
    election results, 17, 226
Black, Larry, 222n50
Black Venus Hottentot, **127**–28
blood typing, 330
"body protest," 152–53
Bogle, Kathleen
    study, campus culture, 95
Bollinger, Lee, 43
Bradley, Ed, 23
Brady v. Maryland, 262, 342
Brandeis, Louis, 180
Brennan, Christine, 16
Broad, Molly, 52
Brodhead, Richard
    apology, 42
    committees to study incident, 22
    explaining condemnation, 195
    letter to Duke community, 22
    meeting with team captains and
        coach, 244–46
    responding, 18–19, 73, 80–81,
        144
    statements by, 19, 20, 41–42
Brodie, H. Keith H., 33
Brown v. Board of Education, 60
Bruschke, John, 189
Bryant, Kobe, 358, 360–61
Bryant, Wanda G., 222n50
buccal samples, 332
Budowle, Bruce, 324
Burness, John, 19–20
Butterfield, G.K., 222n50
Butz, Arthur, 40–41

C

Campbell, William, 299n48

Campus Culture Initiative (CCI)
 Karla Holloway's response, 50
 recommendations about alcohol,
  87
 report, 86–87
campus drinking. *See* alcohol abuse
Cassidy, Michael, 204, 206–7
Castano, Emanuele, 61
CBS Early Show, 15, 16
CBS News, 143, 272
CCI. *See* Campus Culture Initiative
  (CCI)
Center for Public Integrity, 264, 278
Central Park Jogger case, 161,
  168n68
 prosecutorial misconduct, 227–32
Chafe, William, 21, 36
Chapman, Glenn Edward, 276
character, 359–60
 evidence about the accused,
  362–64
 of lacrosse team players, 64–66
Chatman, Charles, 167n67
Cheshire, Joe
 filed grievance letter with state
  bar, 245
 responding to pretrial publicity,
  252
Chicago Tribune
 study of prosecutorial misconduct, 277
child molestation, 303–4
 charges *vs.* rape accusations,
  376–77
 evidence of prior sexual misconduct, 363–64
 and hearsay, 365
 medical treatment exception, 366
 "tender years" exception, 376

Chronicle, The, 36–37
Chronicle of Higher Education, 31
class. *See* social status
classism
 and racism, reflected by commentary, 136–37
 rape myths (frat boys gone wild),
  354
Clayton, Eva, 222n50
Clayton, Richard
 descriptions *vs.* actual characteristics, **320**
 instructions on photo lineup,
  315–16
CNN, 272
Cole, David, 163, 164
Coleman, James E., 23, 81
Coleman, Kevin
 player, DNA match, 334
Coleman Committee, 23
 report, 81–83
Coles, Rom, 50
Coman, James, 25
conduct dignity, 56–57
confessions, coerced, 231n86,
  231n88
confidentiality
 faculty-student privilege, 48–49
confrontation jurisprudence,
  367–68
Connor, Buddy, 247
Cooney, Jim III, 249
 examined Meehan, 339–40
Cooper, Roy, 25, 238n2
 dismissed charges, 255
 wrongful prosecution by, 170n80
Cotter, Bill, 248
Covington, Wes, 18, 241
criminal justice system

defense counsel's role, 259–60
grand jury's role, 261
and prosecutorial discretion, 214
rape shield laws, 359–62
study, misconduct leading to ex-
    onerations, 326
criminal law
alcohol-related problems (1993-
    2001), **92**
black men, incarceration of, 163
black victims, under-enforcement
    of crime, 164
discretion in, 168–72
disparate treatment based on
    race, 160–65
harm to reputation, 176
prosecutorial misconduct,
    169–70
race-specific criminal laws,
    161–62
role of race, 165–66
Crossett, Todd, 105
Cuffee, Angela, 232
"cumulative remedies hypothesis,"
    190
Curtis, Kim, 21, 46–47

D

D. Houston, Inc. v. Love, 149–50
date rape, 94–96, 143n89, 143n90
Davis, Angela, 40, 169n77, 215n20
Davis v. Mississippi, 345
Deadman, Hal, 253, 344
death penalty
DNA evidence exonerations,
    323–26
and rape, 162n41
study of capital cases, 278
deaths on campuses, 93

defamation
and reputation, 180
defense attorneys, 247–80. *See also*
    expert witnesses
Connor, Buddy, 247
Cooney, Jim III, 249, 339–40
Cotter, Bill, 248
defending indigent clients,
    255–60
discovery requests by, 336
dual roles, 199
duty to disclose, 262n5
early stages, 241–44
effective lawyering by, 249–50
Ekstrand, Bob, 243–44, 345
Ekstrand, Samantha, 242,
    243–44
in the grand jury room, 294
Hill, Melissa, 248
Kingsbury, Doug, 248
legal costs, 194, 251
legal strategies of, 247–49
Mack, Julian, 246
Osborn, Kirk, 247
players indicted, 247–48
pretrial motions by, 250–51
and prosecutorial misconduct,
    279–80
providing exculpatory evidence,
    304
relationship with media, 182–85
Smith, Wade, 246, 247–48, 252
special role of, 199–202
studies of capital cases, 278
Thomas, Bill, 242, 246
"defiance narrative," 223
DeKeseredy, Walter, 106
Deni, Theresa Carr, 116n48
Dershowitz, Alan, 120n66

Deutsch, Sally, 21
deviancy, media coverage of, 185–86
dignity, 55–77
    conduct, 56–57
    of Crystal Mangum, 66–68
    definition, 58
    dynamics, 75–77
    hierarchies, Mangum and lacrosse
        team, 69–72
    hierarchy and Nifong, 72–73
    inherent, and race, 62–63
    inherent, definition, 56
    of the players, 63–66
    race and, 69–72
    social, 55–58
    social status of exotic dancers,
        70–71
disaster capitalism, 216–20
    applied by Nifong, 232–34
    applied to DA election, 226
    definition, 216–17
    and Fifth Amendment jurispru-
        dence, 230n85
    requires citizen ignorance,
        230n85
    "Shock Doctrine," 217–19
disbarment, 25–27, 157n12, 196
discovery
    open-file, 280–81
    open-file statute, 291–92, 342
    requests by defense, 336
    of witness statements, 288
Dixon, Marcus, 168n68
DNA evidence, 323–49
    Andrews v. State, 323
    autosomal STR analysis, 346 App
        A
    buccal samples, 332
    databases, 326

defense experts, 344
example, combined suspect, evi-
    dence and victim profiles,
    331
example, suspect vs. evidence,
    330
exclusions and inclusions, 330
exonerations and eyewitness evi-
    dence, 307–8
exonerations from, 168n68,
    231n89, 323–26
facts of police investigation,
    10–11
failure to disclose, 196, 265–66
failure to disclose, by Nifong,
    239–40
forensic evidence, 331–32
forensic lab report results,
    333n43, 334–35
forensic scientists, ethics of, 343
history of, 323
microbiological description of
    DNA, 328
mitochondrial DNA testing,
    329n37
mixtures, 331
Nontestimonial Identification Or-
    ders, 344–45
problems with, 327
processing, 332–33
profiling, 328–31
questionable reporting practices,
    343
rape-kit evidence, 11, 115, 337
Spencer v. Commonwealth,
    323–24
standards for collection, 345
study, mistaken eyewitness identi-
    fications, 325

underlying data provided to defense, 336–38

using experts to understand, 253–55

Y-Chromosome (Y-STR) testing, 331, 334

Y-STR analysis on panties, **348–49**

DNA Identification Act, 326

DNA Security, Inc. (DSI), 333, 334–35

amended report, 335

Dowd, Kyle, 345

grade dispute with Kim Curtis, 46–48

drinking. *See* alcohol abuse

drunk driving, 94

DSI. *See* DNA Security, Inc. (DSI)

Duke, Washington, 58–59

Duke Endowment, 59

Duke University. *See also* administration; faculty

academic standing, 31–32

alcohol abuse, 87, 99–100

alcohol policy, 80n5

athletic achievements, 33

comments by students, 142–46

controlling alcohol use, 80–81

history of, 31–33, 58–59

housing owned by, 133n34

minority faculty and student recruitment, 33

profile, 4

profile, class of 2009, 60n28

racial demographics, 60–61

responding, 17–22, 73, 143–46

social (alcohol) culture, 84–88

stance on alcohol, 83

students' reputation, 64–65

vs. Durham, race and social status, 58–61

Durham. *See also* police

Committee on the Affairs of Black People, 14

profile, 3–4, 56

profile, racial demographics, 60–61

profile, working-class town, 59–60

race relations in, 59

and racial justice, 67

responding to incident, 74

students' reputation in, 65–66

vs. Duke University, race and social status, 58–61

E

Easley, Mike, 13

economics department, 45–46

Ekstrand, Bob, 242, 243–44, 345

Ekstrand, Samantha, 242, 243–44

election

statistics, 226

email. *see* McFadyen, Ryan

empanelment process, grand jury, 287–88

Erikson, Erik, 223–24

erotic-labor force

as independent contractors, 147–49

rationale, players hiring stripper, 139–40

sexual profiling of, 133–37

unsafe working conditions, 146–51

escort agencies. *See* adult-entertainment industry; erotic-labor force

ESPN, 15
ethics. *See also* prosecutorial misconduct
  charges and probable cause, 270–71
  failing to present exculpatory evidence to grand jury, 274–75
  failing to speak to the accuser, 274–75
  false statements to the court, 266–67
  of forensic scientists, 343
  Nifong's failure to disclose, 265–66
  perjury, definition, 267n37
  prejudicing the proceeding and disparaging the accused, 267–69
  professional rules violation by Nifong, 243
  pursuing cases for political gain, 272–73
  restrictions, free speech by attorneys, 200–202
  right to remain silent, 271–72
  Rule 3.8, Rules of Professional Conduct, 263–64
  of using an unconstitutional lineup, 273–74
  violations by Nifong, 340–41
Evans, David, 237, 284
  analysis (autosomal STR) on specimen from, **346 App A**
  analysis (Y-STR) on specimen from, **347**
  charges dismissed, 25
  counseled by coach to hire attorney, 241
  DNA contributor, 333n43, 334
  facts involving, 5–6
  hired defense attorneys, 245
  indictment of, 240
  inherent dignity of, 64
  in photo lineup, 11, 317
  in photo lineup, descriptions *vs.* actual, **320**
  during police search, 332
  positive comments about, 193
Evans, Rae, 220n42, 233n94
evidence. *See also* DNA evidence
  constitutionally inadmissible, 295
  hearsay, 296, 297–98
  materiality, 342n76
  prior sexual misconduct, 363
  "similar act," 364n31
  "tender years" exceptions, 365
evidence, exculpatory, 297
  by defense to grand juries, 304
  failing to present to grand jury, 274–75
  presented to grand juries, 294
  prosecutor's obligation to disclose, 226n66
  release of incomplete evidence by Nifong, 249–50
evidence, false or concealed, 277
evidence law. *See also* Federal Rules of Evidence; North Carolina Rules of Evidence
  narratives in, 353–56
  rape shield laws, 359–62
excited-utterance exception, 365–66
exclusionary rule, 295
exonerations
  Chapman, Glenn Edward, 276
  from DNA evidence, 323–26
  eyewitness evidence *vs.* DNA evidence, 307–8

Gell, Alan, 170n80, 275–76
Hamilton, Jerry Lee, 276
Munsey, Charles, 276
statistics, wrongful convictions,
  259n112
study, misconduct by criminal
  justice system, 326
exotic dancers. *See also* erotic
  dancers; strippers
  "body protest" by, 152–53
  dignity and social status of, 70–71
  as independent contractors,
    147–49
  rape and, 116
  rape myths (lying ho), 354–56
  as rape victims, 117–19
  unsafe working conditions,
    114–19, 146–51
expert witnesses, 254
  Deadman, Hal, 253, 344
  expert testimony about RTS,
    369–70, 376
  and investigators, 253–55
  Loftus, Elizabeth, 254
  surveying prospective jurors, 254
  Wells, Gary, 254
eyewitness-identification procedures,
  307–21. *See also* criminal justice
  system
  actual *vs.* recommended proce-
    dures, **321**
  analyzing procedures used,
    318–19
  descriptions *vs.* actual characteris-
    tics, **320**
  logic and science of, 309–13
  making a relative judgment, 311
  mistaken identification, 308
  pressure and preference, 310–12

primary features of good, 313–14
study, mistaken eyewitness identifications, 325
used with Crystal Mangum,
  314–18

F

facts, 3–27
  administration and faculty re-
    sponses, 17–22
  aftermath, 26–27, 167–68,
    340–41
  background, 155–59, 237–38
  contacting the escort service, 139
  day of incident, 4–9, 79–81
  December 15 hearing, 338–40
  discovery requests by defense, 336
  Durham's profile, 3–4
  evening of incident, 68–69,
    110–11, 137–39
  false rape report, 119–20
  gag order on media coverage, 195
  of the indictment, 11–13
  of the investigation, 9–11
  legal costs of defense, 194
  prosecutorial misconduct,
    175–76
  prosecutor's role, 13–17
  rape-kit evidence collection and
    police search, 332
  truth in court, 22–26
faculty. *See also* Baker, Houston;
    Holloway, Karla
  advertisement, "Group of 88," 22
  Ashton-James, Clair, 21, 46
  autonomy and academic freedom,
    51–52
  Baker, Lee, 51
  Baldwin, Steve, 23, 44–45
  Chafe, William, 21, 36

faculty *continued*
  Coleman, James E., 23, 81
  Curtis, Kim, 21, 46–47
  Deutsch, Sally, 21
  early reactions and responses,
    35–37
  economic department response,
    45–46
  faculty-student privilege, 48–49
  Fox, Faulkner, 19
  governance, 50–53
  grading, 46–48
  Guinn, Chandra Y., 137n57
  Gustafson, Michael, 44–45
  Haagen, Paul, 18
  Huston, Reeve, 21
  Neal, Mark Anthony, 137n57
  opinions *vs.* "fitness for duty,"
    40–41
  Plesser, Ronen, 51
  possible academic-freedom issues,
    38–41
  responses from, 17–22
  Sharpe, Rhonda, 21
  structural relationship, athletics
    and, 33–34, 53–54
  uncollegial, 44–46
  Veraldi, Sam, 21, 45
faculty-student privilege, 48–49
failure to disclose
  disciplining attorneys for, 246n38
  exculpatory evidence, by Nifong,
    225, 340–41
  expert witness reports, 265
  Nifong's ethical misconduct,
    265–66
  pretrial disclosure, 342–43
  prosecutorial legal obligation,
    262–63
  in study by *Chicago Tribune*, 277

  in study of capital cases, 278
Fairstein, Linda
  prosecutorial misconduct,
    229–31
  familial patriarchy, 106
  FBI, 120, 327
  Federal Grand Jury Bill of Rights,
    293–96
  Federal Rules of Evidence
    Rule 413, 362–63
Feinstein, John, 16
Few, Robin, 115
Fifth Amendment
  and disaster capitalism, 230n85
  and Grand Jury clause, 286n7
  nontestimonial order, 344–45
fingerprinting, 345
Finnerty, Collin, 237, 284
  alibi, 254
  charges dismissed, 25
  counseled by coach to hire attor-
    ney, 241
  harmed by pretrial publicity,
    192–93
  indictment of, 240, 289
  inherent dignity of, 64
  in photo lineup, 11, 317, **320**
  positive comments about, 194
Fish, Stanley, 32
Fiske Guide to Colleges 2007, 84
Flannery, Dan, 237
  contacted escort service, 4, 139
  during police search, 332
"Flavor of Love," 131–32
Florida
  preliminary hearing procedure,
    299
Florida Bar v. Went For It, Inc.,
    198–99
Fourth Amendment

search-and-seizure and NTO
    statutes, 345
and Shock Doctrine, 230n85
Fox, Faulkner, 19
fraternity
    culture, alcohol and sexual as-
        sault, 113
    and high-profile sexual assaults,
        111n33
    statistics, sexual assaults by mem-
        bers, 105
    stripper as rape victim by, 118–19
free press
    "announce clause," 205–6
free speech
    about parties *vs.* issues, 207
    prosecutor's "duty to do justice,"
        202–4
    regulation of lawyers' speech,
        200–202
    vs. reputation, 180–81, 197–204
Friedman, Milton
    "Shock Doctrine," 217

G

gag order
    on attorneys, 198–99
    court's justification for, 197–98
    not addressed by Rule 3.8(f), 203
gang rape
    the Central Park Jogger case,
        227–32
    factors contributing to, 106
    factors leading to, 104
    image exploited by Nifong, 226
    by New Orleans Saints, 115
    of prostitute, 108, 116n48
Gary, Willie, 222n50
Gell, Alan, 170n80

exonerated death row prisoner,
    275–76
gender. *See also* women of color
    binge drinking, gender-specific
        definition, 88
    discrimination, 145–46
    sexual profiling and erotic-labor
        force, 133–37
    and sexual stereotypes, 67–68
genotypes, 329
Gentile v. State Bar, 199–202
Gordon, James D., 144n97
gossip
    harming reputation, 180
    as source of pretrial publicity, 187
    via the internet, 182
Gottlieb, Mark, 9–10, 238, 242
    Mangum's descriptions, 314–15
    police misconduct by, 238–39
Grace, Nancy, 16, 35, 194
grading, 46–48
grand jury process, 286–303
    abuse prevention, 292–93
    administrative costs and time,
        298
    basic procedures, 291–93
    citizen participation in, 301
    defense counsel, 294
    defense of, 300
    discovery of witness statements,
        288
    empanelment process, 287–88
    exclusionary rule, 295
    exculpatory evidence, failure to
        present, 274–75
    exculpatory evidence, presenting,
        294
    federal, indictment statistics,
        289n22

grand jury process *continued*
 and governmental overreaching,
  286
 hearsay, 296, 297–98
 historical context, 286–87
 as indictment mill, 301–2
 indictment of lacrosse players,
  240
 instructing jurors on the law, 296
 investigative nature of, 287–88
 judicial discretion in, 292
 in North Carolina, 286–90
 not state requirement, 299
 police role in, 289
 power to nullify, 300
 preliminary hearing and, 285
 preliminary hearing as alternative
  to, 298–301
 presenting constitutionally inadmissible evidence, 295
 and prosecutorial discretion, 214
 providing targets chance to testify,
  295–96
 purpose, 290–91
 reforms, administrative costs of,
  298n47
 reforms applied to incident,
  297–98
 role of, 261
 secrecy of, 301
 select reforms, 293–96
 and sex crime cases, 302–4
 state *vs.* federal, 286–88
 "true bill," 289
Greene, Betty, 137n57
Group of 88, 22, 36–37
 academic freedom and, 38–41
 Coles, Rom, 50
 Holloway, Karla, 50
 Lubiano, Wahneema, 51

O'Reilly Factor, The, 51
 press coverage of, 51
Guinn, Chandra Y., 137n57
Gustafson, Michael, 44–45

H

Haagen, Paul, 18
Hale, Matthew, 357
Hamilton, George Sr., 222n50
Hamilton, Jerry Lee
 exonerated death row prisoner,
  276
Harleston, Bernard
 and academic freedom, 43
harmless error, 278
 and prosecutorial misconduct,
  215n20
 statistics, prosecutorial misconduct *vs.,* 264
Harvard School of Public Health
 College Alcohol Study (HSPH
  CAS), 88–96
Harvard University
 Sexual Misconduct Complaint
  Procedure, 143n89
hate crimes, 158, 269
Hawkins, Yusef, 228n75
Hayes v. Florida, 345
hearsay, 376
 excited-utterance exception,
  365–66
 in grand jury process, 288,
  297–98
 issues in sex crimes, 365–68
 medical treatment exception,
  366–67
 residual or catch-all, 367
"heavy episodic drinking," 88
Hill, Melissa, 248
Himan, Benjamin, 242

descriptions given *vs.* actual char-
      acteristics, **320**
Mangum's descriptions of alleged
      rapists, 314–15
Robert's statement to investigator,
      10
Holloway, Karla, 50, 136n54, 144
      dismantling stereotypes, 145–46
      violence against women and
            sports, 145n100
HSPH CAS. *See* Harvard School of
      Public Health, College Alcohol
      Study (HSPH CAS)
Hunt, Darryl, 170n80
Hurricane Katrina, 218–19
Huston, Reeve, 21
Hyde Amendment, 280

I

I Am Charlotte Simmons, 4
"I Love New York," 131–32
immunity, absolute and qualified,
      281
impartiality, judicial, 205–6
Imus, Don, 135
independent contractors
      entertainers as, 147n109
      legal status of, 148–49
indictments
      basic procedure, 291–93
      failure to indict, 297–98
      grand jury process as indictment
            mills, 289, 301–2
      obligation to secure, 299n49
      vs. informations, 300
inherent dignity, 56
      and race, 62–63
intelligence
      and social status, 61–62

intoxicated rape, 94–96

J

Jackson, Jesse, 160
Jackson, Maynard, 222n50
Jackson, Robert H., 208
Javanovic, Oliver, 232n93
Jeffreys, Alec, 323
Jerry Springer Show, The, 131n23
Johnson, KC, 34, 44, 238n2
      explaining Nifong's behavior, 76
Jones, B.S., 8, 238
Jones, Marion, 64
Jones, Samuel "Mr. Clutch," 222n50
Journal of Forensic Sciences, 343
judicial discretion, 292
judicial review
      of prosecutorial discretion,
            214–15
jury
      defense experts to survey prospec-
            tive jurors, 254
      effects of pretrial publicity on,
            187–90
      scrutiny of acquaintance rape
            charge, 112–13

K

Kanin, Eugene, 120
Kelly, Alex, 354
Kennedy, Chris, 17–18, 241
Kennedy, Randall, 164
Keohane, Nanerl, 33
Kingsbury, Doug, 248
Klein, Naomi, 216, 226
Knight, Bob, 53
Kosse, Susan Hanley, 155n1
Krzyzewski, Mike, 4, 53

L

lacrosse team. *See also* Evans, David; Finnerty, Collin; Flannery, Dan; McFadyen, Ryan; Zash, Matt
aftermath, 123
alcohol abuse by, 34, 81–83
Coleman, Kevin, 334
dignity and status of, 63–66
dignity of, 77
Dowd, Kyle, 46–48, 345
at Duke University, 4
McFadyen, Ryan, 71–72
racial demographics, 60
reputational harm by pretrial publicity, 193–97
Wilson, Matthew, 317
Lamade, Larry
player's father, 242
Lamb, Jeff, 11
Lander, Eric, 324
Lange, Peter, 35
administrative response, 42
explaining Nifong's behavior, 76
refuses to "rush to judgment," 42
responds to Houston Baker, 44, 51–52
Layden, Mary Anne, 117
Lentrecchia, Frank, 32
Levicy, Tara
advised police of rape, 242
rape-kit evidence collection process, 332
sexual-assault nurse trainee, 8, 239
Levin, Michael
professor, academic freedom, 43
Lewis, Jacqueline, 146n107
Leyn, Jennifer, 332
Liebman, James S., 278n106
Limbaugh, Rush, 356

Loftus, Elizabeth
eyewitness-identification researcher, 254
Loges, William E., 189
Lord Hale's Rule, 122n78
Lubiano, Wahneema, 51
lynchings, 162n40, 162n41

M

Mack, Julian, 246
Mangum, Crystal, 151–52
alcohol consumption on the evening, 118
autosomal STR analysis on specimen from, 346 App A
background of, 221–24
descriptions given *vs.* actual characteristics, 320
dignity and social status of, 70–71
eyewitness procedure used by, 314–18
facts of incident involving, 5–9
interviewed by Nifong's office, 24–25
investigated by defense, 253
legal issues, 221–22
photo lineup, 9–10
possible psychological problems, 211n6
reputation after incident, 284
social dignity of, 66–68
as a stripper, 223–24
suggested motives for filing false rape report, 238n2
and unsafe workplace as exotic dancer, 114–19
used by Nifong, 220
written statement by, 11
Manley, Julie, 239

findings of, 332
masculinity, 106–7
Maticka-Tyndale, Eleanor, 146n107
Maury Povich Show, The, 131n23
McClain, Paula, 52
McCray, Antron, 228
McDade Amendment, 280
McFadyen, Ryan
    email from, 71–72, 141, 141n78,
        156–57
    suspended, 73, 141
McMahon, Sarah, 106
McNeill, Kenneth N., 221
media coverage, 14–17, 175–210.
    See also pretrial publicity
    the Central Park Jogger case,
        227–32
    disclosing names, 357–59
    of exonerated prisoners, 167–68
    Group of 88, 51
    harming defendant's reputation,
        182–86
    of high profile cases, 182–91
    interviews by Nifong, 239n8
    justifying gag order, 197–98
    and Model Rule 3.6, 200–202
    Nifong alleging racial motivation,
        269
    Nifong's statements about DNA
        evidence, 333
    offensive, by defense lawyers, 246
    "primacy effect," 188
    prosecutor's use of, 176
    rape myths, 354–56
    relationships with law enforce-
        ment, 183–85
    sensationalizing the case, 158–59
    social and economic dichotomies
        between Durham and Duke,
        157–58

white *vs.* black rape victims,
    161–62
"White woman syndrome,"
    233n97
"wilding," definition, 229n80
medical treatment exception,
    366–67
Meehan, Brian
    at December 15 hearing, 338–39
    incomplete DNA evidence report
        by, 250
    motivations, 342
    Nifong's false statements to the
        court, 266–67
    reports to Nifong, 12–13
    testimony of, 24, 338–40
Megan's laws. *See* sex crimes
Meili, Trisha, 227n73
memory, 308
    double-blind procedure, 321
    memory-source error, 314
    motivation and stress affect wit-
        ness, 310
Michael, Steven D., 275
Miller, Authur, 179
Model Penal Code
    intoxication and rape, 111
molecular biology. *See* DNA evi-
    dence
Moneta, Larry, 19
Mosteller, Robert, 335, 341, 342,
    366
MSNBC, 195
Munsey, Charles
    exonerated death row prisoner,
        276
Murchison, Matthew, 333

N

N-word exchange, 7, 20, 69–70, 138

Nachman, Robert B., 301n58
National Academy of Sciences, 324–25, 343, 344
National Association of Criminal Defense Attorneys, 293
National Institute of Justice, 313, 318
　eyewitness procedure *vs.* actual, **321**
National Institute on Alcohol Abuse and Alcoholism (NIAAA), 93, 96–99
　successful interventions, 97–98
"nature of the business," 149
NBC 17 News, 14
NCCU. *See* North Carolina Central University (NCCU)
Neal, Mark Anthony, 137n57
Nebraska Press Association v. Stuart, 197–98
New Orleans
　overhaul of public school system, 218–19
New York Times
　criticism of lacrosse team in, 16
　Nifong's remarks in, 15
　Nifong's statements to, 271
　statement by Peter Wood in, 20
News & Observer
　negative comments about team in, 194
　Nifong's remarks in, 15
　Paul Haagen's comments in, 18
Newsweek, 16, 193
NIAAA. *See* National Institute on Alcohol Abuse and Alcoholism (NIAAA)
Nichols, Terry, 256

Nifong, Mike. *See also* pretrial publicity; prosecutorial misconduct; prosecutors
　abuse of discretion by, 168–69
　aftermath, 76–77, 167, 235n102, 340–41
　charges, disciplinary, 255
　charges, ethics, 25
　at December 15 hearing, 338–39
　and defense counsel meetings, 244–46
　as disaster capitalist, 220–26
　disbarment, 25–27, 157n12, 196
　discovery requests by defense, 336
　DNA evidence and media coverage, 195
　election, 17, 226
　examining his decisions, 283–85
　exculpatory evidence, failure to disclose, 23–24, 239–40, 265–66
　exculpatory evidence, failure to present to grand jury, 274–75
　exploitation of community shock, 224–25
　facts of incident involving, 11–13
　failure to speak to the accuser, 274–75
　grand jury reforms applied to incident, 297–98
　initial response, 72–73
　manipulating dignity dynamics, 77
　motives, 74–77, 157–58, 224n62, 341–42
　negative pretrial publicity, 193, 194, 267–69, 271–72
　photo lineup, 273–74, 316–18
　politicizing case, 13–17, 272–73
　pretrial remarks by, 14–17

pursuing charges not supported
by probable cause, 270–71
reenactment on MSNBC, 195
as "rogue prosecutor," 235
statements, 225, 333
truth in court, 22–26
under- and over-enforcement by,
164–66
9/11
and disaster capitalism, 219
nonconsensual revelations and reputation, 181–82
nontestimonial order (NTO),
344–45
North Carolina
grand jury process, 286–90
grand jury provision and interpretation, 286–87
Grievance Committee, 340
Innocence Commission, 277,
309, 318, **321**
Nontestimonial Identification
statute, 344–45
preliminary hearing procedures,
299–300
Sex Offender & Public Protection
Registration Program,
372–73
State Bureau of Investigation laboratory, 332
North Carolina Central University
(NCCU)
alumni, 222n50
comments by students, 142–46
history of, 222n47
international student body,
222n49
profile of, 66–67
North Carolina Rules of Evidence
Rule 404(b), 363–64, 375

Rule 412(2), 360
Rule 412(4), 361
Rule 413, 375
North Carolina Rules of Professional
Conduct
as applied to case, 265–66
Rule 3.3, 266–67
Rule 3.6, 263, 269
Rule 3.8, 263–64
Rule 3.8(a), 270–71
Rule 3.8(c), 272
Rule 3.8(d), 265–66
Rule 4.4(a), 273
Rule 8.4, 274
Rule 8.4(d), 273
North Carolina State Bar
ethics charges against Nifong, 25
NTO. *See* nontestimonial order
(NTO)

O

Okrent Daniel, 137n58
O'Reilly Factor, The, 39, 51
Osborn, Kirk, 247
Osgood, Charles, 172n91
Othello, 179–80
overdose
of alcohol, statistics, 86

P

Parker, Kathleen, 235n102
"party problem," 65–66
party rape, 96
patriarchy, 106
PCR. *See* Polymerase Chain Reaction (PCR)
Penrod, Steven, 186–87
People v. Castro, 324–25
perjury. *See* ethics
Perkins, Bill, 231n89

philanthropy, 59
photo lineups. *See also* eyewitness-
    identification procedures
    actual *vs.* recommended proce-
        dures, **321**
    double-blind lineup, 314
    facts, 9–10
    fillers, 312–13, 319, **321**
    flawed, 240
    instructions, Mangum's process,
        315–16
    pressure and preference, 310–12
    primary features of good, 313–14
    removal-without-replacement ef-
        fect, 312
    using unconstitutional lineup,
        11–12, 273–74
Pinochet, Augusto General, 218
Pittsburgh Post-Gazette, 277
plea bargaining, 214, 258
Plesser, Ronen, 51
Plessy v. Ferguson, 60
police. *See also* photo lineups
    actual rape investigation proce-
        dure *vs.* recommended proce-
        dures, **321**
    Ashby, Angela, 332
    black men, closer scrutiny by,
        162–63
    black rape victims and, 160
    black victims, under-enforcement
        by, 164
    case weakness discussed with Ni-
        fong, 270
    Clayton, Richard, 315–16, **320**
    coerced confessions, 231n86,
        231n88
    early reaction, 242–44
    facts of incident involving, 7–8
    failure to follow eyewitness iden-
        tification procedure, 309
    failure to investigate rape allega-
        tions, 121–22
    false rape reporting and, 121
    Gottlieb, Mark, 9–10, 238–39,
        242, 314–15
    in grand jury process, 289
    Himan, Benjamin, 10, 314–15,
        320
    Houston, and DNA-testing defi-
        ciencies, 327
    interrogation, Central Park Jogger
        case, 229n94
    intoxicated woman, scrutiny of
        rape charge, 112
    Jones, B.S., 8, 238
    Lamb, Jeff, 11
    misconduct, modifying
        Mangum's statement, 248
    racially uneven enforcement of
        laws, 171
    rape allegations by prostitutes,
        122
    rape statistics procedure, 122
    relationship with media, 182–85
    report on lacrosse team's behav-
        ior, 82
    Shelton, John C., 7, 238
    St. Louis Police scandal, 121–22
    student involvement with, 94
    students' reputation with, 65–66
    Sutton, Gwendolen, 8
    and "tunnel vision," 258
    using unconstitutional lineup,
        273–74
    "wilding," definition, 229n81
    Wilson, Linwood, 248
political correctness, 172

Polymerase Chain Reaction (PCR), 329

polymorphisms, 328

population genetics. *See* DNA evidence

Post-Traumatic Stress Disorder (PTSD), 368

preliminary hearings
  alternative to grand jury process, 299–301
  as applied to incident, 302–3

Pressler, Mike, 17, 72, 241
  fired, 22
  meeting, Brodhead and team captains, 244–45

pretrial disclosure, 342–43

pretrial publicity, 185–97
  "cumulative remedies hypothesis," 190
  defense attorneys' responses, 252
  of deviancy, 185–86
  effects of time, 189
  effects on juries, 187–90
  ethics violations by Nifong, 341n63
  gossip as source, 187
  negative effects of, 186–89
  negative effects on team by, 193–97
  positive effects of, 189–90
  professional rules violation by Nifong, 243
  and prosecutor's extrajudicial statements, 203
  public harm to reputation, 191–93
  "primacy effect" of pretrial publicity, 188

prior sexual offenses, 363–64, 375

prison rape, 370–72

Prison Rape Elimination Act, 371

privilege, 48–49

probable cause, 270–71, 302
  DNA collection, 345
  grand jury indictment, 296
  to justify an arrest, 290n29
  screening function of grand jury process, 298n47

promiscuity, 359n19

property damage, 94

prosecutorial discretion, 168–72, 213–16
  criticisms of, 215
  definition, 213
  judicial review of, 214–15
  or prosecutorial misconduct, 216
  and regulating prosecutor's speech, 208–9
  and sentencing guidelines, 169n74
  unchecked power and electoral accountability, 215–16

prosecutorial misconduct. *See also* exonerations; Nifong, Mike
  absolute prosecutorial immunity, 281
  abuse of power and grand jury process, 293
  Angela Davis, 169n77
  the Central Park Jogger case, 161, 168n68, 227–32
  Connor, Buddy, 247
  Davis, Angela, 215n20
  exonerated prisoner and, 167n67
  Fairstein, Linda, 229–32, 232n93
  frequency of, 169–70
  and good faith, 284
  harm by unwarranted charges, 290–91
  ill motives, 293

prosecutorial misconduct *continued*
  by Nifong, 249–51
  non-reporting of, 279–80
  or prosecutorial discretion, 216
  political pandering, 170
  proving, 214n18
  reasons for, and how to address,
    279–81
  "rogue prosecutor," 235
  selective prosecution, 273
  and student alcohol abuse, 100
  study by *Chicago Tribune,* 277
  study by *Pittsburgh Post-Gazette,*
    277
  in the U.S., 275–79
prosecutors
  accused's right to remain silent,
    271–72
  duty to disclose, 225n66
  "duty to do justice," 202–4
  early reaction, 242–44
  as elected officers of the court,
    204–9
  electioneering statements by, and
    free speech, 204–7
  ethical and legal obligations,
    262–64
  evidence, constitutional inadmis-
    sible, 295
  exculpatory evidence, failure to
    present, 274–75
  exculpatory evidence, presenting
    to grand jury, 294
  failure to speak to the accuser,
    274–75
  federal, rate of misconduct,
    284n4
  grand juries as indictment aids,
    300–301

instructing jurors, grand jury
    process, 296
  intoxicated woman, scrutiny of
    rape charge, 112
  North Carolina Rules of Profes-
    sional Conduct, 263–64
  power of, and media coverage,
    176–77
  prejudicing the proceeding and
    disparaging the accused,
    267–69
  pursuing cases for political gain,
    272–73
  pursuing charges not supported
    by probable cause, 270–71
  relationships with media, 182–85
  and harm to reputation, 177–78
  role in grand jury process, 288
  Rule 3.8, disclosure to the de-
    fense, 263–64
  and "tunnel vision," 258–59
  under-enforcement of rape laws
    by, 160
  using unconstitutional lineup,
    273–74
prostitution
  Baartman, Saartijie, **126**–28
  in black community, 134n40
  failure to investigate rape allega-
    tions, 122
  Prostitutes' Rights Movement,
    146n107
  and rape, 116
  rape myths (lying ho), 355–56
Proverbs, 179
PTSD. *See* Post-Traumatic Stress
    Disorder (PTSD)
public defenders. *See also* defense at-
    torneys

defending indigent clients, 255–60
incentive efforts of, 184n20
per-case dollar average in Oklahoma, 256n99
relationship with media, 182–85
public health
alcohol use/abuse on campuses, 93–94, 100
publicity. *See* media coverage

R

race
and inherent dignity, 62–63
role in incident, 58–61
racial politics
death penalty, 162n41
and the legislation, 170–71
political correctness, 172
politicizing by Nifong, 170
prison statistics, 163n46
race-specific criminal codes, 161–62
statistics, incarceration of black men, 163
racial profiling, 163, 171
racism
claims by Nifong, 269
and classism reflected by commentary, 136–37
faculty response, 20
N-word exchange, 7, 20, 69–70, 138
NCCU students' response, 67
race reversal, 166, 172
rape myths (lying ho), 354–56
and social status, manipulation by Nifong, 75–77
rape, 351–78. *See also* gang rape

accusations, legal *vs.* social consequences, 377–78
alcohol as risk factor, 109–14
allegations of falsifying statistics, 122
athletes, fraternities and sexual assault, 104–7
and binge drinking, 100
in black community, 130, 134n41
black victims and police, 160
criminal liability for, 111
definition, 111–12
disclosing names, 357–59
DNA Identification Act, 326
exotic dancers and unsafe workplace, 114–19
facts involving, 8–9
failure to investigate, 121–22
false reports of, 119–22
hearsay exceptions, 365–68
indigent defendants, 257–58
institutional and societal norms, 144
intoxicated, 94–96
legal accountability, 144–45
Lord Hale's Rule, 122n78
lying *vs.* genuine error, 308
medical examination of Mangum, 8–9
myths, 107–8, 375–76
penalties for, 109n27, 162n41
prevalence, **95**
prior false rape allegations, 361
prior sexual misbehavior, 362–63
prison, 370–72
and probable cause, 270–71
process fairness, 377–78
prosecution of, 112–13
and prostitution, 116
rape-kit evidence, 332, 337

rape *continued*
  rape shield laws, 359–62, 374–75
  rape-supportive culture, 108
  rape trauma syndrome and expert
    testimony, 368–70
  reporting, 235n102, 351–52
  sexual profiling of women of
    color's bodies, 133–37
  statistics, alcohol use and, 100
  statistics, sexual assault, 105
  stranger rape, 356n11
  of stripper by fraternity members,
    118–19
  underreporting of, 160n26,
    161–62
  "unfounded" rape reports,
    120n66
  victims, historical context,
    159–61
  victims, legal context, 161–64
  vs. child sexual abuse, 376–77
  white *vs.* black victims, media
    coverage of, 161–62
  Williams, Erik, 115
  women of color *vs.* white women,
    media coverage, 151n1
rape myths, 353–54
rape shield laws, 359–62, 374–75
Rape Trauma Syndrome (RTS),
    368–70
  definition, 368
  and expert testimony, 369–70
  expert testimony about, 376
Raw Deal, 119
Rawlins, Earl, 231n89
reasonable suspicion, 345
Republican Party of Minnesota v.
    White, 204–5
reputation
  Arthur Miller, 179

defamation and, 180
free speech and, 180–81
gossip, 182
harm, and redress, 207
harm, and secrecy of grand jury,
    301
harm, from rape allegations,
    290–91, 357–59, 374
harm, undervaluing, 178–82
injuries and consequences to the
    team, 176
legal protections of, 180
media coverage, Central Park Jog-
    ger defendants, 228n76
Model Rules of Professional Con-
    duct, Rule 3.8(f), 203
nonconsensual revelations and,
    181–82
Othello, 179–80
players after incident, 284
and pretrial publicity, 182–86,
    191–93
prosecutors disparaging the ac-
    cused, 268
and prosecutor's extrajudicial
    statements, 203
Proverbs, 179
right to privacy and, 180
vs. free trial, 197–204
Research Triangle, 32
residual hearsay, 367
Restriction Fragment Length Poly-
    morphism (RFLP) analysis, 329
Reyes, Matias, 231
Richardson, Kevin, 228
right to free speech
  vs. right to free trial, 197–204
right to privacy
  as excuse at December 15 hearing,
    338–39

of rape victim, 358–59
and reputation, 180
Roberts, Kim
  alcohol drinking evening of incident, 118
  characterization of allegations, 283
  derogatory exchange, 69, 107, 138
  facts involving, 5–7
  statement to the police, 10
Roberts, Selena, 16
Rolling Stone
  profile, Duke campus culture, 87–88
RTS. *See* Rape Trauma Syndrome (RTS)
Rule 3.6, 200–202
"rush to judgment," 37, 40, 357

S

Salaam, Yusef, 228, 231n86
Sanchez, Lisa E., 116
Santana, Raymond, 228
Scarborough, Joe, 194
Scheck, Barry, 326
Schwartz, Martin, 106
selective prosecution, 273
self-incrimination, 344–45
Seligmann, Reade, 284
  charges dismissed, 25
  DNA evidence, 333n43
  facts involving, 6–7
  impact of media coverage on, 196
  indictment of, 240, 247, 289
  inherent dignity of, 64
  legal costs, 194, 240n11
  in photo lineup, 9–11, 316, 317
  in photo lineup, description *vs.* actual, **320**

positive comments about, 194
on prosecutorial misconduct, 237
sentencing guidelines, 169n74
  crack *vs.* powder cocaine, 171n86
"separate but equal," 60
  and inherent dignity, 62–63, 77
  and NCCU, 66–67
sex crimes. *See also* child molestation; reputation
  grand jury process applied to, 302–4
  notification laws, 373
  post-conviction detention, 376–77
  post-conviction experiences in prison, 370–71
  post-conviction limits on liberty, 372–73
  prior sexual misconduct as evidence, 364
  prison rape, 370–72
sex offenders. *See* sex crimes
sex (unsafe) on campuses, 93
sex workers, 114–19
sexual profiling, 133–37
Shaftesbury, Earl of, 286
Shakespeare, William, 179–80
Sharpe, Rhonda, 21
Shelton, John C., 7, 238
Sheppard v. Maxwell, 198
shield law. *See* faculty-student privilege
"Shock Doctrine," 217–19
  Fourth Amendment jurisprudence, 230n85
Short Tandem Repeats (STR) testing, 329–31
similar act evidence, 364n31
Simons, Travis, 137n57

Sixth Amendment
  right to confront witnesses, 367
60 Minutes, 69
  Kim Roberts' interview, 23, 138
  Richard Brodhead's interview,
    80–81
Smith, Osmund, 250
Smith, Wade
  legal strategy regarding Selig-
    mann's alibi, 247–48
  meeting with Nifong, 246
  responding to pretrial publicity,
    252
social culture
  and campus alcohol abuse, 91–94
  of college drinking, 96–99
  at Duke University, 84–88
  of male athletes, factors influenc-
    ing sexual aggression, 106
  rape-supportive culture and ac-
    ceptance of rape myths, 108
  reducing alcohol problems on
    campuses, 98–99
social dignity, 55–56
  generally, 57–58
social status
  and intelligence, 61–62
  undervaluing harm to reputation,
    178–82
  value and determinants of,
    178–80
societal patriarchy, 106
Southern Association of College and
  Schools, 32
"speaking for the institution," 39
Spencer, Bettina, 61
Spencer v. Commonwealth, 323–24
sports. *See* athletics
St. Louis Police

failure to investigate rape allegations, 121–22
state bars
  role, monitoring prosecutorial
    misconduct, 280
State v. Crummy, 292
State v. Hall, 369–70
State v. Jones, 290
State v. Mann, 159n22
statistics
  academic problems and alcohol
    abuse, 93–94
  acquaintance rapes, 104–5
  alcohol abuse, perceptions *vs.* re-
    ality, 85–86
  alcohol abuse/dependence, 94
  alcohol-related problems (1993-
    2001), **92**
  assaults, 93
  binge drinking, 89, **90**, 91–93
  blood type, 330
  deaths, 93
  drunk driving, 94
  Durham's profile, 3–4, 56
  election, district attorney, 226
  exonerations, wrongful convic-
    tions, 259n112
  false rape reports, 120
  federal grand jury indictments,
    289n22
  legal costs, 194, 251
  minority faculty and student re-
    cruitment, 33
  misconduct by police, prosecu-
    tors, defense counsel, 326
  photo lineup and use of fillers,
    319
  police involvement and alcohol
    use, 94
  prison, black men, 163

prison, by race, 163n46
prison rape, 371
property damage and alcohol use, 94
prosecutorial misconduct, 278
prosecutorial misconduct *vs.* harmless errors, 264
rape and alcohol use, 100
rape on campuses, **95**
sex (unsafe), 93
sexual assault, 105
state grand jury indictments, 289–90
study, mistaken eyewitness identifications, 325
suicide attempts, 94
trends in drinking (1993-2001), **89**
"unfounded" rape reports, 120, 120n66
violence against exotic dancers, 116
Steel, Bob, 20
Stephens, Ronald, 336
stereotypes
    black female promiscuity, 233
    cultural, 354–56
    destructive racial, 166
    negative, 374
    negative, and inherent dignity, 62–63
    racial, 356
    racial/gender, in reality shows, 131–32
    racial/gender, lasting effects of, 136n52
    reactions to facts based on, 129
    sexual, 67–68
    social status, race, and intelligence, 61–62

"White woman syndrome," 233n97
    of women of color's bodies, 130–32
Stewart, Potter, 180
STR. *See* Short Tandem Repeats (STR) testing
strippers. *See also* exotic dancers
    as rape victims, 117, 118–19
Studebaker, Christina, 186–87
suicide attempts on campuses, 94
Sullivan, Thomas P., 301n58
Surette, Ray, 203–4
Sutton, Gwendolen, 8
Sutton, Josiah, 327

T

Talley, Andre Leon, 222n50
Taslitz, Andrew, 356n11
Taylor, Stuart, 34, 44, 238n2
    explaining Nifong's behavior, 76
Tejada, Charles J., 232
"tender years" exceptions, 365, 376
Tennessee
    workers' compensation statutes, 148
testimonial privileges, 48–49
    in grand jury process, 295–96, 303–4
    out-of-court statements, 367
Texas
    liability to independent contractors, 149–50
"the plantation," 4, 59, 157, 160
Thomas, Bill
    Durham defense attorney, 242
    meeting with Nifong, 246
Thompson, Bruce
    father of player, 241
Tigar, Michael, 256

"town-gown." *See* dignity; racism; social status
Trask, Tallman III
criticized team for hiring attorneys, 243
response from, 18
faculty-student privilege, 48–49
Trinity College, 58–59
"true bill," 289
Truth, Sojourner, 130–31
"tunnel vision," 258

U

United States v. Calandra, 295
Until Proven Innocent, 76
USA Today, 15, 16

V

Veraldi, Sam, 21, 45
Vermont
workers' compensation statutes, 149
Vetter, Joe Father, 194
violence against women. *See* rape
Virginia Military Institute (VMI)
and sexual stereotype, 67–68

W

War on Terror
and disaster capitalism, 219–20
Wareham, Roger, 231n89
Warren, Michael, 231n89
Warren, Samuel, 180
Washington, Jr., Earl, 168n68, 327
Wasiolek, Sue, 17
counseled against hiring attorneys, 241
underage drinking, 113
Wechsler, Henry
"secondhand binge effects," 93

surveys, campus drinking, 88
Wells, Gary
eyewitness-identification researcher, 254
Wersal, Gregory, 205
Western Conference of Faculty Representatives, 53
What Colleges Need to Know Now, 98–99
"White woman syndrome," 233n97
"wilding," 229–31
definitions, 229nn80–81
Williams, Butch
meeting with Nifong, 246
Williamson, F. Lane, 341–42
Willimon, William, 84
Wilson, Linwood, 248
Wilson, Matthew
player identified by Mangum, 317
Winn, Rachel, 332
Winstead, Mary, 25
Wise, Kharey, 227n73, 228
witnesses. *See also* expert witnesses; eyewitness-identification procedures
descriptions *vs.* actual characteristics, **320**
in federal grand jury process, 292–93
in grand jury process, 291–92
rehabilitating lying, 365n32
in state grand jury process, 288
using photo lineups, 313–14
women of color, 127–53
as black rape victims and police, 160
devaluing women's bodies, historical context, 127–29
historical perception of, 130–31
as property, 159

rape myths (lying ho), 354–56
as rape victims, historical and
legal context, 159–66
sexual profiling of, 133–37
stereotyped in reality shows,
131–32
vs. white women, media coverage
of rape, 155n1
Wood, Peter, 20, 36
chairman, campus-culture committee, 22
*Workers' Compensation Division v.
Playmate Entertainment, Inc.,*
149
workers' compensation statutes,
148–49
Worrell, Fletcher, 326

Y

Y-Chromosome (Y-STR) testing,
331, 334, 337

analysis on panties, **348–49 App
C–D**
analysis on specimens, **347 App B**
Y-STR. *See* Y-Chromosome (Y-STR)
testing

Z

Zash, Matt, 237
counseled by coach to hire attorney, 241
derogatory exchange with Kim
Roberts, 69, 138
DNA contributor, 333n43
facts involving, 5–6
during police search, 332